Lecture Notes in Artificial Intelli

Edited by J. G. Carbonell and J. Siekmann

Subseries of Lecture Notes in Computer Science

Marie-Pierre Gleizes   Andrea Omicini
Franco Zambonelli (Eds.)

Engineering Societies in the Agents World V

5th International Workshop, ESAW 2004
Toulouse, France, October 20-22, 2004
Revised Selected and Invited Papers

 Springer

Series Editors

Jaime G. Carbonell, Carnegie Mellon University, Pittsburgh, PA, USA
Jörg Siekmann, University of Saarland, Saarbrücken, Germany

Volume Editors

Marie-Pierre Gleizes
Université Paul Sabatier
IRIT, Institut de Recherche en Informatique de Toulouse
118, Route de Narbonne, 31062 Toulouse Cédex, France
E-mail: Marie-Pierre.Gleizes@irit.fr

Andrea Omicini
Università di Bologna a Cesena
DEIS, Dipartimento di Elettronica, Informatica e Sistemistica
Via Venezia 52, 47023 Cesena, Italy
E-mail: andrea.omicini@unibo.it

Franco Zambonelli
Università di Modena e Reggio Emilia
DISMI, Dipartimento di Scienze e Metodi dell'Ingegneria
Via Allegri 13, 42100 Reggio Emilia, Italy
E-mail: franco.zambonelli@unimore.it

Library of Congress Control Number: 2005928542

CR Subject Classification (1998): I.2.11, I.2, C.2.4, D.1.3, D.2.2, D.2.7, D.2.11, I.6

ISSN   0302-9743
ISBN-10   3-540-27330-1 Springer Berlin Heidelberg New York
ISBN-13   978-3-540-27330-1 Springer Berlin Heidelberg New York

Springer is a part of Springer Science+Business Media

springeronline.com

© Springer-Verlag Berlin Heidelberg 2005
Printed in Germany

Typesetting: Camera-ready by author, data conversion by Scientific Publishing Services, Chennai, India
Printed on acid-free paper   SPIN: 11423355   06/3142   5 4 3 2 1 0

Preface

The first workshop "Engineering Societies in the Agents World" (ESAW) was held in August 2000, in conjunction with the 14th European Conference on Artificial Intelligence (ECAI 2000) in Berlin. It was launched by a group of researchers who thought that the design and development of MASs (multi-agent systems) not only needed adequate theoretical foundations but also a call for new techniques, methodologies and infrastructures to develop MASs as artificial societies. The second ESAW was co-located with the European Agent Summer School (ACAI 2001) in Prague, and mostly focused on logics and languages, middleware, infrastructures and applications. In Madrid, the third ESAW concentrated on models and methodologies and took place with the "Cooperative Information Agents" workshop (CIA 2002). The fourth ESAW in London was the first one that ran as a stand-alone event: apart from the usual works on methodologies and models, it also stressed the issues of applications and multidisciplinary models. Based on the success of previous ESAWs, and also given that the difficult challenges in the construction of artificial societies are not yet fully addressed, the fifth ESAW workshop was organized in the same spirit as its predecessors.

In particular, ESAW 2004 took place at the IRIT laboratory of the Université "Paul Sabatier" (Toulouse, France), at the end of October 2004. It was not co-located with any other scientific event, in the same way as ESAW 2003. ESAW 2004 remained committed to the use of the notion of MASs as the seeds for animated, constructive and highly interdisciplinary discussions about technologies, methodologies and tools for the engineering of complex distributed systems. The widespread interest in these topics, as well as the effectiveness of ESAW as a well-established research forum, are witnessed by both the high number of submissions received (46 papers from 20 countries) and by the good participation (46 researchers from 14 countries).

This fifth workshop mainly focused on effective and methodical development of complex software systems in terms of multi-agent societies, as well as on novel approaches to software modelling and engineering to support the successful deployment of software systems made up of massive numbers of autonomous components. While designers should be enabled to control and predict the behavior of their systems, we should also allow emergent global system properties and discovered functionality to become commonplace in the theory and practice of MASs. It is very likely that such innovations will exploit lessons from a variety of different scientific disciplines, such as sociology, economics, organization science, modern thermodynamics, and biology. This is the main reason why the presentations in this workshop covered a number of these domains.

The following different themes were addressed during the three-day meeting:

- *Agent-Oriented Software Engineering.* The presentations of this session concerned methodologies, and discussed requirements analysis, specification, design and deployment phases.
- *Negotiation.* This session covered different mechanisms to enable agents to negotiate and to solve conflicts. The different mechanisms presented were based on biological metaphors, social welfare, and Activity Theory.
- *Large-Scale Multi-agent Systems.* The papers of this session focused on communication in large systems, semantics, and physical accessibility.
- *Roles.* Presentations in this session concentrated on the notion of role in a MAS: in particular, on the notion of role as used in the context of the argumentation process, and during conversation protocols.
- *Organizations.* This is one of the main topics in societies of agents, and was discussed in the context of a normative framework and of virtual knowledge communities.
- *Social Aspects.* This session drew a parallel between human and artificial societies by studying on the one hand the social power theory and on the other hand the role of sanctions in a society.
- *Simulation.* This session elaborated on the issues of simulation by using MASs, focusing on challenges such as the development process and the calibration of parameters in a simulation system.
- *Cooperation.* This session covered one of the most traditional topics in MAS research, that is, cooperation.

Two invited presentations tried to bridge between artificial and natural societies, such as human or animal societies. The first invited talk was given by Vincent Chevrier, who is an assistant professor at the Université Henri Poincaré of Nancy (France) and a researcher at LORIA in the MAIA team. He proposed methodological principles for the design of MASs drawing from the mechanisms observed in natural systems such as stigmergy or resource access.

Pablo Noriega expounded the other invited presentation concerning e-institutions. He is a senior researcher at Anáhuac University, Mexico City (Mexico), as well as a visiting researcher at the Institut d'Investigació en Intelligència Artificial (IIIA) in Barcelona (Spain). He elaborated on how interaction conventions for agents — human or software agents — can be used to engineer complex open systems by using commitments.

Furthermore, discussions during the meeting emphasized the need for tools to design large-scale systems and open systems. From the debate, two main acceptations of the term "openness" clearly emerged: a MAS is open either when agents can be dynamically added or removed, or when the MAS can take into account the perturbations coming from the MAS environment.

The original contributions, the slides of the presentations, as well as more information about the workshop are available online at the ESAW 2004 website (http://www.irit.fr/ESAW04). This postproceedings (ESAW 2004: LNAI 3451) continues the series published by Springer (ESAW 2000: LNAI 1972, ESAW 2001: LNAI 2203, ESAW 2002: LNAI 2577, and ESAW 2003: LNAI 3071).

This volume contains revised, reworked and extended versions of selected papers from ESAW 2004, and also includes the contribution of one of the two invited speakers.

The ESAW 2004 organization would have not been possible without the financial help of:

- Agentlink III
- ARTAL Technologies, Labège, France
- ILOG, Paris, France
- IRIT, Toulouse, France
- Université Paul Sabatier, Toulouse, France
- Whitestein, Switzerland

as well as the scientific support of the Alma Mater Studiorum, Università di Bologna in Cesena, the Università di Modena e Reggio Emilia, and all the members of the Program Committee. Our thanks also go to Alfred Hofmann and all of his Springer crew for their essential role during the realization of the postproceedings. We also want to thank the local organizers who created a studious and convivial ambiance during the workshop.

The next ESAW workshop will take place in Turkey supported by the Ege University of Izmir during the fall of 2005, with Oguz Dikenelli, Marie-Pierre Gleizes and Alessandro Ricci as the chairs and organizers. We expect that the next ESAW workshop will keep up its tradition of innovation and stimulating scientific debate, and also that more applications and demonstrations of running systems will further prove the feasibility and usefulness of the mechanisms and methods recommended by agent researchers.

February 2005   Marie-Pierre Gleizes
                                                        Andrea Omicini
                                                      Franco Zambonelli

Organization

ESAW 2004 Workshop Organizers

Marie-Pierre Gleizes	IRIT, Université Paul Sabatier, Toulouse (France)
Andrea Omicini	DEIS, Alma Mater Studiorum, Università di Bologna a Cesena (Italy)
Franco Zambonelli	Department of Computer Science, Università degli Studi di Modena e Reggio Emilia (Italy)

ESAW 2004 Local Organizing Committee

Marie-Pierre Gleizes	(Local Chair)
Carole Bernon	IRIT,
Valérie Camps	Institut de Recherche en Informatique de Toulouse,
Jean-Pierre Georgé	Université Paul Sabatier,
Davy Capera	Toulouse (France)
Jean-Pierre Mano	

ESAW 2004 Program Committee

Alexander Artikis	Department of Electrical & Electronic Engineering, Imperial College London (UK)
Federico Bergenti	Dipartimento Ingegneria dell'Informazione, Università degli Studi di Parma (Italy)
Carole Bernon	IRIT, Université Paul Sabatier, Toulouse (France)
Olivier Boissier	Ecole Nationale Supérieure des Mines de Saint-Etienne (France)
Monique Calisti	Whitestein Technologies (France/Switzerland)
Jacques Calmet	University of Karlsruhe (Germany)
Cristiano Castelfranchi	Institute of Cognitive Sciences and Technology, CNR (Italy)
Luca Cernuzzi	Universidad Católica de Asuncion (Paraguay)
Paolo Ciancarini	DSI, Alma Mater Studiorum, Università di Bologna (Italy)
Helder Coelho	Department of Informatics of the Faculty of Sciences, University of Lisbon (Portugal)
R. Scott Cost	Department of Computer Science and Electrical Engineering, University of Maryland Baltimore County (USA)
Paul Davidsson	Department of Software Engineering & Computer Science, Blekinge Institute of Technology (Sweden)
Rino Falcone	Institute of Cognitive Sciences and Technology, CNR (Italy)

Stephan Flake	C-LAB, Cooperative Computing & Communication Lab (Germany)
Zahia Guessoum	LIP6, Paris (France)
Andrew Jones	Department of Computer Science, King's College London (UK)
Anthony Karageorgos	University of Thessaly (Greece)
Paul Kearney	Intelligent Agents, BT Exact (UK)
Barbara Dunin-Kęplicz	Institute of Computer Science of the Polish Academy of Sciences, Warsaw (Poland)
Yannis Labrou	Fujitsu Laboratories of America (USA)
Lyndon C. Lee	Intelligent Agents, BT Exact (UK)
Michael Luck	Department of Electronics & Computer Science, University of Southampton (UK)
Peter McBurney	University of Liverpool (UK)
Pablo Noriega	Spanish Scientific Research Council, Campus Universitat Autónoma de Barcelona (Spain)
Eugenio Oliveira	Department of Computer and Electrical Engineering, University of Porto (Portugal)
Sascha Ossowski	Universidad Rey Juan Carlos, Madrid (Spain)
H. Van Dyke Parunak	Altarum Institute, Ann Arbor, MI (USA)
Paolo Petta	Austrian Research Institute for Artificial Intelligence, Vienna (Austria)
Gauthier Picard	IRIT, Université Paul Sabatier, Toulouse (France)
Jeremy Pitt	Department of Electrical & Electronic Engineering, Imperial College London (UK)
Omer Rana	Department of Computer Science, University of Cardiff (UK)
Alessandro Ricci	DEIS, Alma Mater Studiorum, Università di Bologna a Cesena (Italy)
Ken Satoh	National Institute of Informatics, Tokyo (Japan)
Onn Shehory	IBM Haifa Research Laboratories (Israel)
Christophe Sibertin-Blanc	IRIT, Université Paul Sabatier, Toulouse (France)
Munindar Singh	Department of Computer Science, North Carolina State University (USA)
Kostas Stathis	Department of Computer Science, City University, London (UK)
Robert Tolksdorf	Institut für Informatik, Freie Universität Berlin (Germany)
Anand Tripathi	University of Minnesota (USA)
Paola Turci	Università degli Studi di Parma (Italy)
José M. Vidal	Department of Computer Science & Engineering, University of South Carolina (USA)

Table of Contents

Roles, Organizations and Institutions for Agents

Organizations as Socially Constructed Agents in the Agent Oriented
Paradigm
Guido Boella, Leendert van der Torre 1

Virtual Enterprise Normative Framework Within Electronic Institutions
Henrique Lopes Cardoso, Eugénio Oliveira 14

Virtual Knowledge Communities for Corporate Knowledge Issues
Pierre Maret, Mark Hammond, Jacques Calmet 33

Achieving Competence by Argumentation on Rules for Roles
Ioan Alfred Letia, Monica Acalovschi 45

Participation Components for Holding Roles in Multiagent Systems
Protocols
Christophe Sibertin-Blanc, Nabil Hameurlain 60

Semantically Federating Multi-agent Organizations
Riza Cenk Erdur, Oguz Dikenelli, Inanç Seylan, Önder Gürcan 74

Social Issues in Multi-agent Systems

T-Compound Interaction and Overhearing Agents
Eric Platon, Nicolas Sabouret, Shinichi Honiden 90

Managing Conflicts Between Individuals and Societies in Multi-agent
Systems
Rubén Fuentes, Jorge J. Gómez-Sanz, Juan Pavón 106

Motivation-Based Selection of Negotiation Opponents
Steve Munroe, Michael Luck 119

DIAGAL: A Generic ACL for Open Systems
Philippe Pasquier, Mathieu Bergeron, Brahim Chaib-draa 139

Modelling Flexible Social Commitments and Their Enforcement
Philippe Pasquier, Roberto A. Flores, Brahim Chaib-draa 153

Using Social Power to Enable Agents to Reason About Being Part of a
Group
    Cosmin Carabelea, Olivier Boissier, Cristiano Castelfranchi 166

Cooperation and Collective Behaviours in Agent Societies

Strategies for Distributing Goals in a Team of Cooperative Agents
    Laurence Cholvy, Christophe Garion 178

Collectively Cognitive Agents in Cooperative Teams
    Jacek Brzeziński, Piotr Dunin-Kęplicz, Barbara Dunin-Kęplicz 191

Cooperative Agent Model Instantiation to Collective Robotics
    Gauthier Picard 209

From Self-Organized Systems to Collective Problem Solving
    Chevrier Vincent 222

Methodologies and Platforms for Agent-Oriented Engineering

A Sample Application of ADELFE Focusing on Analysis and Design
the Mechanical Synthesis Problem
    Davy Capera, Gauthier Picard, Marie-Pierre Gleizes, Pierre Glize ... 231

SONIA: A Methodology for Natural Agent Development
    Fernando Alonso, Sonia Frutos, Loïc Martínez, César Montes 245

Deployment of Distributed Multi-agent Systems
    *Lars Braubach, Alexander Pokahr, Dirk Bade,
    Karl-Heinz Krempels, Winfried Lamersdorf* 261

Using Stand-In Agents in Partially Accessible Multi-agent Environment
    Martin Rehák, Michal Pěchouček, Jan Tožička, David Šišlák 277

Agent-Oriented Simulation

Controlled Experimentation with Agents — Models and
Implementations
    Mathias Röhl, Adelinde M. Uhrmacher 292

Techniques for Analysis and Calibration of Multi-agent Simulations
    Manuel Fehler, Franziska Klügl, Frank Puppe 305

Models for Multi-agent Systems

Stable Multi-agent Systems
Andrea Bracciali, Paolo Mancarella, Kostas Stathis,
Francesca Toni 322

Welfare Engineering in Practice: On the Variety of Multiagent Resource
Allocation Problems
Yann Chevaleyre, Ulle Endriss, Sylvia Estivie,
Nicolas Maudet 335

Author Index 349

Organizations as Socially Constructed Agents in the Agent Oriented Paradigm

Guido Boella[1] and Leendert van der Torre[2]

Dipartimento di Informatica - Università di Torino - Italy
CWI - Amsterdam and TU Delft The Netherlands

Abstract. In this paper we propose a new role for the agent metaphor in the definition of the organizational structure of multiagent systems. The agent metaphor is extended to consider as agents also social entities like organizations, groups and normative systems, so that mental attitudes can be attributed to them - beliefs, desires and goals - and also an autonomous and proactive behavior. We show how the metaphor can be applied also to structure organizations in functional areas and roles, which are described as agents too. Thus, the agent metaphor can play a role similar to the object oriented metaphor which allows structuring objects in component objects. Finally, we discuss how the agent metaphor addresses the problems of control and communication in such structured organizations.

1 Introduction

The role of software engineering is to provide models and techniques that make it easier to handle the complexity arising from the large number of interactions in a software system [1]. Models and techniques allow expressing knowledge and to support the analysis and reasoning about a system to be developed. As the context and needs of software change, advances are needed to respond to changes. For example, today's systems and their environments are more varied and dynamic, and accommodate more local freedom and initiative [2].

For these reasons, agent orientation emerged as a new paradigm for designing and constructing software systems [1, 2]. The agent oriented approach advocates decomposing problems in terms of autonomous agents that can engage in flexible, high-level interactions. In particular, this is a natural representation for complex systems that are - as many real systems are - invariably distributed [1]. Compared to the still dominant software paradigm, namely object orientation, agent orientation offers a higher level of abstraction for thinking about the characteristics and behaviors of software systems. It can be seen as part of an ongoing trend towards greater interactivity in conceptions of programming and software system design and construction. Much like the concepts of activity and object that have played pivotal roles in earlier modelling paradigms - Yu [2] argues - the agent concept can be instrumental in bringing about a shift to a much richer, socially-oriented ontology that is needed to characterize and analyze today's systems and environments.

M.-P. Gleizes, A. Omicini, and F. Zambonelli (Eds.): ESAW 2004, LNAI 3451, pp. 1–13, 2005.
© Springer-Verlag Berlin Heidelberg 2005

The shift from the object oriented perspective to the agent oriented one is not, however, without losses. Booch [3] identifies three tools which allow coping with complexity: "1) Decomposition: the most basic technique for tackling any large problem is to divide it into smaller, more manageable chunks each of which can then be dealt with in relative isolation. 2) Abstraction: the process of defining a simplified model of the system that emphasises some of the details or properties. 3) Organisation: the process of identifying and managing interrelationships between various problem solving components."

In the agent oriented approach, however, decomposition, abstraction and organization are not yet addressed with the same efficacy as in the object oriented approach, where an object can be composed of other objects, which can be ignored in the analysis at a certain level of abstraction. The agent metaphor is sometimes proposed as a specialization of the object metaphor [4]: agents do not only have - like objects - a behavior which can be invoked by the other agents, but they also autonomously act and react to changes in the environment following their own goals and beliefs. In contrast, the component view of objects in the object metaphor could to be lost. The property of agents, i.e., sociality, closest to the property allowing the aggregation of objects to form more complex objects is not enough to overcome the gap. In particular, multiagent systems offer as aggregation methods the notion of group or of organization. According to Zambonelli *et al.* [5] "a multiagent system can be conceived in terms of an organized society of individuals in which each agent plays specific roles and interacts with other agents". At the same time, they claim that "an organization is more than simply a collection of roles (as most methodologies assume) [...] further organization-oriented abstractions need to be devised and placed in the context of a methodology [...] As soon as the complexity increases, modularity and encapsulation principles suggest dividing the system into different suborganizations". According to Jennings [1], however, most current approaches "possess insufficient mechanisms for dealing with organisational structure". Moreover, what is the semantic principle which allows decomposing organizations into suborganizations must be still made precise.

The research question of this paper, thus, is: how can the agent oriented paradigm be extended with a decomposition structure similar to the one proposed by the object oriented paradigm? How can a multiagent system be designed and constructed as an organization using this structure?

The methodology we use in this paper is a normative multiagent framework we proposed in [6, 7, 8, 9]. The basic idea of this framework is: agents attribute mental attitudes, like beliefs, desires and goals, to the other agents they interact with and also to social entities like groups, normative systems, and organizations. Thus these social entities can be described as agents too, and at the same time, the components of organizations, namely, functional areas and roles, can be described as agents, as in the ontology we present in [7]. We call them *socially constructed agents*.

This paper is organized as follows. In Section 2 we discuss the progress from object orientation to agents and socially constructed agents. In Section 3 we present the formal model and in Section 4 we discuss the issue of control and communication in an multiagent system structured as an organization. A summary closes the paper.

2   From Objects to Socially Constructed Agents

The trend in software and requirements engineering and in programming languages paradigms has been from elements that represent abstract computations towards elements that represent the real world: from procedural to structured programming, from objects to agents. Agent systems have no central control authority, instead each agent is an independent locus of control, and the agent's task drives the control. Delegating control to autonomous components can be considered as an additional dimension of modularity and encapsulation. Intentional concepts such as goals, beliefs, abilities, commitments, *etc.*, provide a higher-level characterization of behavior. One can characterize an agent in terms of its intentional properties without having to know its specific actions in terms of processes and steps. Explicit representation of goals allows motivations and rationales to be expressed. The agent concept provides a local scope, for reconciling and making tradeoffs among competing intentionality, such as conflicting goals and inconsistent beliefs. By adopting intentional modelling, the networks of dependencies among the agents can be modelled and reasoned about at a high level of abstraction. Moreover, cooperation among agents cannot be taken for granted. Because agents are autonomous, the likelihood of successful cooperation is contingent upon many factors. However, an agent that exists within a social network of expectations and obligations has behaviors that are confined by them. The agent can still violate them, but will suffer the consequences. The behavior of a socially situated agent is therefore largely predictable, although not in a precise way.

Given that agents are nowadays conceived as useful abstractions for modelling and engineering large complex systems, the need for a disciplined organizational principle for agent systems emerges clearly in the same way as the formalizatoin of the object decomposition principle does in the case of object oriented systems.

One of the main features of the object perspective is that objects are composed by other objects and that objects can be replaced by other objects with the same properties (e.g., the same interface). This is not entirely true for agents. According to Jennings [1], "the agent oriented approach advocates decomposing problems in terms of autonomous agents", but no further decomposition seems possible. To overcome this flatness limitation, the organization metaphor has been proposed, e.g., by [10, 5]. Organizations are modelled as collections of agents, gathered in groups [10], playing roles [1, 11] or regulated by organizational rules [5]. What is lacking is a notion of organization as a first class abstraction which allows decomposing into subproblems the problem which a system wants to solve, using a recursive mechanism (as the object decomposition is) until autonomous agents composing a multiagent system are reached.

The desired solution is required to model at least simple examples taken from organizational theory in Economics as the following one. Consider a simple enterprise which is composed by a direction area and a production area. The direction area is composed by the CEO and the board. The board is composed by a set of administrators. The production area is composed by two production units; each production unit by a set of workers. The direction area, the board, the production area and the production units are *functional areas*. In particular, the direction area and the production areas belong to the organization, the board to the direction area, *etc.* The CEO, the administrators and the members of the production units are *roles*, each one belonging to a functional area, e.g., the CEO is part of the direction area.

This recursive decomposition terminates with roles: roles, unlike organizations and functional areas, are not composed by further social entities. Rather, roles are played by other agents, real agents (human or software) who have to act as expected by their role.

The object metaphor is not adequate to deal with such a structure, because each entity can be better described in terms of belief, desires and goals, and of its autonomous behavior. We talk, e.g., about the decisions of the CEO, or about the organization's goal to propose a deal, about the belief of the production area that the inventory is finished, *etc.* Hence, at first sight, these entities can be described as autonomous agents. But this is not sufficient, since the agent metaphor does not account for the decomposition structure of an organization relating it with its functional areas and roles. Moreover, organizations, functional areas and roles are entities belonging to social reality: they do not exist in the same sense as (human or software) agents do and do not exist without agents. Thus, if we want to follow this intuition, the agent metaphor must be extended. Inspired by Searle [12]'s analysis of social reality we define organizations, functional areas and roles as *socially constructed agents*. These agents do not exist in the usual sense of the term, but they are abstractions which other agents describe as if they were agents, with their own beliefs, desires and goals, and with their own autonomous behavior. The argument goes as follows:

1. agents can attribute to other (human or software) agents mental attitudes and an autonomous behavior to explain how they work, regardless of the fact that they really have any mental attitudes (the *intentional stance* of Dennett [13]);
2. according to Searle [12], agents create new social entities like institutions - e.g., money and private property - by means of collectively attributing to existing entities - e.g., paper bills - a new functional status - e.g., money - and new qualities.
3. if the new functional status is composed by mental attitudes and autonomous behavior, the new entities are described as agents: *socially constructed agents*.
4. hence, socially constructed agents, *qua* agents, can create new socially constructed agents by attributing mental attitudes to them, in turn.

Agents create organizations by collectively attributing them mental attitudes; organizations, as socially constructed agents, can create new social entities like functional areas and roles which are the components of the organization. Functional areas, as agents, can in turn apply the agent metaphor to create subareas and further roles, and so on. Roles are descriptions of the behavior which is expected by agents who, with their own mental attitudes, play these roles: the role's expected behavior is described in terms of mental attitudes, since roles are considered socially constructed agents. Modelling roles by attributing them mental attitudes allows a more expressive way to describe the expected behavior with respect, e.g., the scripts proposed by Activity Theory [14]. In this manner, we have a way to structure an organization in components with an homogeneous character - since they are all agents - in the same way as the object orientation allows structuring objects by means of objects. An advantage of this way of structuring an organization is that its components can be described as agents with beliefs, desires and goals. Hence, the same decomposition approach advocated by [1] is used for structuring an organization: it is decomposed in a set of autonomous agents: not only real ones, but socially constructed agents like functional areas and roles; socially constructed agents do not exist, but they are only used as abstractions in the design analysis to structure an organization. At the end of the process there are only human or software agents which, to coordinate their behavior, behave as if they all attribute the same beliefs, desires and goals to the organization. This is a subjective approach to coordination [14].

Another reason why organizations, functional areas and roles should be all considered as agents - and not simply groups - is that they have private properties and agents who are employed in them; so a department can possess a building and machines, employ people, *etc.* Moreover they are the addressees of obligations (e.g., to pay the employees), permissions (e.g., a role can use a certain machine) and powers (e.g., the role of CEO can take decisions). This is what is also meant by the law when such social entities are defined as "legal persons": they are considered persons with obligations and rights [15]. Finally, organizations and functional areas, as legal institutions, are normative agents themselves: they are agents who can pose (via agents playing roles in them) obligations on the roles and on the employees, e.g., by giving orders to them, or endow them with permissions and powers.

There is a difference with the decompositional view of the object oriented perspective which must be noticed. The parts of an object exist by themselves and the object itself exists only as long as its (essential) parts exist. In contrast, in an organization the perspective is reversed: the "components" of the organization exist only as long as the organization exists, while the organization itself can exist even without its components. The role of CEO does not have sense if the organization which the role belongs to does not exist anymore. The reason is that an organization as a social entity has no physical realization. The organization exists because of the attribution of mental attitudes by the agents of a society. In turn, functional areas and roles exist only as long as the organization attributes mental attitudes to them. An important consequence of this view is that an organization can restructure itself while continuing to exist.

As [16, 10] claim, a multiagent system should not make any assumption about the implementation of the agents. As Yu [2] notices, the agent perspective does not mean necessary that entities should be implemented with mental attitudes:

> Agent intentionality is externally attributed by the modeller. From a modelling point of view, intentionality may be attributed to some entity if the modeller feels that the intentional characterization offers a useful way for describing and analyzing that entity. For example, some entity that is treated as an agent during modelling may end up being implemented in software that has no explicit representation and manipulation of goals, *etc.*

Socially constructed agents defined in terms of beliefs, desires and goals are only an abstraction for designing the system. Moreover, the behavior of roles is described by mental attitudes, but this does not require that the agents playing roles in the organizations are endowed with beliefs and motivations: it is sufficient that their behavior conforms to that of the role they are playing.

In Figure 1, we summarize the approach: the multiagent system in the oval is composed of three real agents (boxes) who collectively attribute beliefs (B), desires (D) and goals (G) to the organization (parallelogram). The organization, in turn, attributes mental attitudes to two functional areas and functional areas to three roles. The organization and the functional areas are attributed also norms (V), facts (f), institutional facts (i) and decisions (the triangle d).

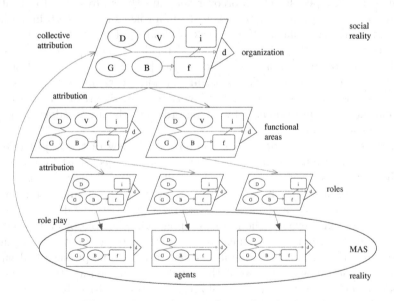

Fig. 1. The attribution of mental attitudes

3   The Conceptual Model

We introduce the conceptual model necessary to cope with socially constructed agents: first the multiagent system with the attribution of mental attitudes to agents, then the normative system.

First of all, the structural concepts and their relations. We describe the different aspects of the world and the relationships among them by introducing a set of propositional variables X and extending it to consider also negative states of affairs: $L(X) = X \cup \{\neg x \mid x \in X\}$. The relations between the propositional variables are given by means of conditional rules written as $R(X) = 2^{L(X)} \times L(X)$: the set of pairs of a set of literals built from X and a literal built from X, written as $l_1 \wedge \ldots \wedge l_n \rightarrow l$ or, when $n = 0$, $\top \rightarrow l$. The rules are used to represent the relations among propositional variables existing in beliefs, desires and goal of the agents.

Then there are the different sorts of agents A we consider. Besides real agents RA (either human or software) we consider as agents in the model also socially constructed agents, i.e., organizations OA, functional areas FA, and roles RO. The different sorts of agents are disjoint and are all subsets of the set of agents A: $RA \cup OA \cup FA \cup RO \subseteq A$. All these agents have mental attitudes; by mental attitudes we mean beliefs B, desires D and goals G.

Mental attitudes are represented by rules, even if they do not coincide with them: $MD : B \cup D \cup G \rightarrow R(X)$. When there is no risk of confusion we abuse the notation by identifying rules and mental states. To resolve conflicts among motivations we introduce a priority relation by means of $\geq$: $A \rightarrow 2^M \times 2^M$ a function from agents to a transitive and reflexive relation on the powerset of the motivations $M = D \cup G$ containing at least the subset relation. We write $\geq_a$ for $\geq (a)$. Moreover, different mental attitudes are attributed to all the different sorts of agents by the agent description relation $AD : A \rightarrow 2^{B \cup D \cup G \cup A}$. We write $B_a = AD(a) \cap B$, $A_a = AD(a) \cap A$ for $a \in A$, etc.

Also agents are in the target of the agent description AD relation for the following reason: organizations, functional areas and roles exist only as profiles attributed by other agents. So they exist only as they are described as agents by other agents, according to the agent description relation. The AD relation specifies that an agent $b \in OA \cup FA \cup RO$ exists only as far as some other agents $\{a \in A \mid b \in A_a\}$ attribute to it mental attitudes. The set $(FA \cup RO) \cap A_o$ represents the immediate "components" of the organization or functional area $o \in OA \cup FA$. The decomposition structure of an organization ends with roles. Roles are described as agents, but they do not create further socially constructed agents; rather, roles are associated with agents playing them, $PL : RO \rightarrow RA$.

We introduce now concepts concerning informational aspects. First of all, the set of variables whose truth value is determined by an agent (decision variables) [17] are distinguished from those P which are not (the parameters). Besides, we need to represent also the so called "institutional facts" I. They are states of affairs which exist only inside normative systems and organizations: as Searle [12] suggests, money, private property, marriages, *etc.* exist only as part of social reality; since we model social reality by means of the attribution of mental attitudes to social entities, institutional facts can be modelled as the beliefs attributed to these agents, as done by [8]. Similarly, we need to represent the fact that social entities like normative systems and organizations are able to change their mental attitudes. The actions determining the changes are called creation actions C. Finally, inspired by Lee [18] we introduce the notion of documents DC: "we use the term 'document' since most information parcels in business practice are mapped on paper documents".

As concerns the relations among these concepts, we have that parameters P are a subset of the propositional variables X. The complement of X and P represents the decision variables controlled by the different agents. Hence we associate with each agent a subset of $X \setminus P$ by extending again the agent description relation $AD : A \rightarrow 2^{B \cup D \cup G \cup A \cup (X \setminus P)}$. We write $X_a = AD(a) \cap X$.

Moreover, the institutional facts I are a subset of the parameters P: $I \subseteq P$. When a belief rule $Y \wedge c \rightarrow p \in B_a$ has an institutional fact $p \in I$ as consequent, we say that $c \in X$ *counts as* p in context Y - using Searle [12]'s terminology - for agent $a \in OA \cup FA \cup RO$.

The creation actions C are a subset of the institutional facts $C \subset I$. Since agents are attributed mental attitudes, we represent their modification by adding new mental attitudes expressed as rules. So the creation action relation $CR :$ $\{b, d, g\} \times A \times R(X) \rightarrow C$ is a mapping from rules (for beliefs, desires and goals) to propositional variables, where $CR(b, a, r)$ stands for the creation of $m \in B_a$, $CR(d, a, r)$ stands for the creation of $m \in D_a$, and $CR(g, a, r)$ stands for the creation of $m \in G_a$, such that the mental attitude m is described by the rule $r \in R(X)$: $r = MD(m)$.

Finally, the document creation relation $CD : DC \rightarrow X$ is a mapping from documents to decision variables representing their creation. We write $CD(d) \in X_a$ for the creation of document $d \in DC$.

We define a multiagent system as $MAS = \langle RA, OA, FA, RO, X, P, B, D, G,$ $AD, MD, PL, \geq, I, C, DC \rangle$.

We introduce obligations posed by organizations and functional areas by means of a normative multiagent system. Let the norms $\{n_1, \ldots, n_m\} = N$ be a set. Let the norm description $V : OA \cup FA \rightarrow (N \times A \rightarrow X)$ be a function from agents to complete functions from the norms and agents to the decision variables: we write V_o for the function $V(o)$ and $V_o(n, a)$ for the decision variable of agent $o \in RA \cup OA \cup FA$ representing that it considers a violation of norm n by agent $a \in A$.

$NMAS = \langle RA, OA, FA, RO, X, P, B, D, G, AD, MD, PL, \geq, I, C, DC, N, V \rangle$ is a normative multiagent system .

Following [6], obligations are defined in terms of goals of the addressee of the norm **a** and of the agent **o**. The definition of obligation contains several clauses. The first one defines obligations of agents as goals of the normative agent, following the 'Your wish is my command' strategy, the remaining ones are instrumental to the respect of the obligation.

Agent $\mathbf{a} \in A$ is *obliged* by normative agent $\mathbf{o} \in OA \cup FA$ to decide to do $x \in L(X_{\mathbf{a}} \cup P)$ with sanction $s \in L(X_{\mathbf{o}} \cup P)$ if $Y \subseteq L(X_{\mathbf{a}} \cup P)$ in $NMAS$, written as $NMAS \models O_{\mathbf{ao}}(x, s|Y)$, if and only if there is a $n \in N$ such that:

1. $Y \to x \in D_{\mathbf{o}} \cap G_{\mathbf{o}}$: if agent $\mathbf{o}$ believes Y then it desires and has as a goal that x.
2. $Y \cup \{\sim x\} \to V_{\mathbf{o}}(n, \mathbf{a}) \in D_{\mathbf{o}} \cap G_{\mathbf{o}}$: if agent $\mathbf{o}$ believes Y and $\sim x$, then it has the goal and the desire $V_{\mathbf{o}}(n, \mathbf{a})$: to recognize it as a violation by agent $\mathbf{a}$.
3. $Y \cup \{V_{\mathbf{o}}(n, \mathbf{a})\} \to s \in D_{\mathbf{o}} \cap G_{\mathbf{o}}$: if agent $\mathbf{o}$ believes Y and decides $V_{\mathbf{o}}(n, \mathbf{a})$, then it desires and has as a goal that it sanctions agent $\mathbf{a}$.
4. $\top \to \sim s \in D_{\mathbf{a}}$: agent $\mathbf{a}$ desires $\sim s$, which expresses that it does not like to be sanctioned.

Since obligations are defined in terms of mental states, they can be created by means of the creation actions C introducing new desires and goals, as shown by [8]. In this paper, we will use the shorthand $CR(\mathbf{o}, O_{\mathbf{ao}}(x, s|Y))$ to represent the set of creation actions necessary to create an obligation $O_{\mathbf{ao}}(x, s|Y)$.

4   Control and Communication in Organizations

Instead of having a single global collection of beliefs and motivations, modelling organizations as socially constructed agents allows allocating different beliefs B_a, desires D_a and goals G_a to separate agents $a \in A_{\mathbf{o}}$ composing the organization $\mathbf{o} \in OA$. Agents can be thought of as a locality for intentionality. In this way it is possible to distribute subgoals of $G_{\mathbf{o}}$ among the different functional areas and roles $a \in A_{\mathbf{o}}$ to decompose problems in a hierarchical way and to avoid to overburden them with too much goals. In particular, the goals G_r attributed to role $r \in RO$ represent the responsibilities which agent $b \in A$ playing that roles $(PL(r) = b)$ has to fulfill.

The beliefs attributed to the organization ($B_{\mathbf{o}}$) and attributed by the organization to its components (B_m and $m \in A_{\mathbf{o}}$) represent their know how and the procedures used to achieve the goals of the organization; these beliefs are represented for example by statutes and manuals of organizations. As in case of goals, different beliefs B_a can be distributed to functional areas and roles $a \in A_{\mathbf{o}}$. In this way the organization can respect the incapsulation principle and preserve security and privacy of information, as requested by [10].

The beliefs, desires and goals of the components of an organization play also another role. They express the institutional relations among the different components: in particular, the control and communication relations among the functional areas and roles. Both issues will be addressed using the notion of *document*. Documents are the way information parcels are represented in organizations and represent also the records of decisions and information flow.

The institutional relations of control and communication among the components of an organization are defined in terms of the "counts as" relation. For Jones and Sergot [19], the "counts as" relation expresses the fact that a state of affairs or an action of an agent "is a sufficient condition to guarantee that the institution creates some (usually normative) state of affairs". As [19] suggest this relation can be considered as "constraints of (operative in) [an] institution". In Section 3 we propose to model "counts as" relations by means of belief rules of the socially constructed agents. They express how an organization, a functional area or a role provide an institutional classification of reality.

In an organization it is fundamental to specify how agents can control other agents by giving orders to them [10, 5]; the control is achieved by the command structure of an organization. In fact, organizations can be seen as burocracies according to [20]. Control has two dimensions: how the organization and its functional areas can pose (via agents playing roles in them) obligations (commands) to roles, and who has the power to create these obligations (since, as organizations and their units are socially constructed agents, they do not act). For example, a production unit can decide to give a production order to its members and the decision of the production unit can be taken by a director of that unit. The basic block of control is the creation of obligations. As described in the conceptual model, an agent can change its own mental attitudes. In particular, an organization $\mathbf{o}$ can change its desires and goals so to create a new obligation $O_{a\mathbf{o}}(x, s \mid Y)$ by means of the creation action $CR(\mathbf{o}, O_{a\mathbf{o}}(x, s \mid Y))$. It is possible to create sanction-based obligations addressed to agent $a \in A$ since the agents involved in organizations are depended on them, for example, for the fact that organizations pay them salaries and decide benefits.

The creation actions C of an organization $\mathbf{o}$ are parameters, hence they are not directly controlled by it: the organization does not act directly, but only by means of the actions of the agents composing it. Creation actions achieve their effect to introduce new obligations if some other action "counts as" a creation action for the organization: this relation is expressed by a belief rule of the organization $\mathbf{o}$, e.g., $c \rightarrow CR(\mathbf{o}, O_{a\mathbf{o}}(x, s \mid Y)) \in B_{\mathbf{o}}$. Since there is no other way for making true the creation action, only the organization itself can specify who create new obligations. In particular, $c \in X_r$ can be an action $CD(d)$ of a role $r \in RO$ of producing a document $d \in DC$: in this way the organization $\mathbf{o}$ specifies that the role r has control over some other role $a \in RO$ such that $a \in A_{\mathbf{o}}$. The document d represents the record of the exercise of the power of agent r. Also functional areas are modelled as agents in an organization: hence, the same mechanism can be used to specify that an agent r has control over role $a \in RO$, where r and a can belong to the same functional area $m \in FA$ ($\{r, a\} \subseteq A_m \cap RO$).

Since the "counts as" relation can be iterated, it is possible to specify how a role $r \in RO$ belonging to a functional area $m \in FA$ ($r \in A_m$) of an organization $\mathbf{o} \in OA$ can create an obligation $O_{a\mathbf{o}}(x, s \mid Y)$ directed to a functional area or role $a \in FA \cup RO$ directly belonging to the organization: $a \in A_{\mathbf{o}}$. This is possible since an action $c \in X_r$ of role r can count as an institutional fact $p \in I$ for the functional area m: $c \rightarrow p \in B_m$. In turn, the institutional fact p can count as the creation of an obligation $O_{a\mathbf{o}}(x, s \mid Y)$ by the organization $\mathbf{o}$: $p \rightarrow CR(b, \mathbf{o}, O_{a\mathbf{o}}(x, s \mid Y) \in B_{\mathbf{o}}$; this obligation is directed towards agent a which belongs to the organization $\mathbf{o}$. These relations are only possible since the beliefs B_m of the functional area m are attributed to agent m by the organization o itself, since $m \in A_o$. For example, a decision of the CEO counts as an obligation of the entire organization since the direction functional area to which the CEO belongs considers the CEO's decision as made by itself and the organization, in turn, considers the decision of the direction as having the obligation as a consequence. In this way, the organization, when it creates its components by attributing mental attitudes to them, at the same time, constructs its control structure.

The second issue is communication among roles. It is often claimed [10] that the organizational structure specifies the communication possibilities of agents. Agents can communicate almost by definition and standard communication languages have been defined for this aim [21]. What the organization can specify is their possibility to communicate to each other in an institutional way by means of documents; as Wooldridge *et al.* [22] claim, organizations specify "systematic institutionalized patterns of interactions".

Communication among socially constructed agents is based on the same principle as control. It relies on the fact that the beliefs of a functional area or of a role are attributed to them by the higher level socially constructed agent which they are attributed mental attitudes by. In this way we can express the fact that a document created by a role $r \in RO$ communicates some belief p to an organization or functional area $m \in OA \cup FA$ it belongs to $r \in A_m$: $CD(d) \rightarrow p \in B_m$, where $CD(d) \in X_r$ is an action creating a document $d \in DC$. This is read as the fact the action of role r "counts as" the official belief p of agent m. The document d represents the record of the communication between r and m.

Analogously, we can specify official communication among roles. A role $r \in RO$ communicates to a role $a \in RO$ that $p \in P$ if there is some action $CD(d) \in X_r$ creating a document $d \in DC$ such that $CD(d) \rightarrow p \in B_a$. Note that B_a are not the beliefs of the agent $b \in RA$ playing role a ($b = PL(a)$). Rather they are the beliefs attributed to the role by the functional area $m \in FA$: since the role a is created by the functional area m, those beliefs are attributed to a by the functional area m. When an agent $b \in RA$ which plays the role $a \in RO$ knows that document d has been created, it has to act as if it had the belief p, while it is not requested to be psychologically convinced that p is true. Otherwise agent b does not stick to its role anymore and it becomes liable to having violated its duties.

5   Summary

In this paper we propose a way to model the organizational structure of multi-agent systems. Organizations are composed by functional areas and roles; functional areas, in turn, are composed by functional areas and roles. Roles are played by agents. Using the methodology of attributing mental attitudes to social entities, we show that organizations and their components can be described as agents: socially constructed agents. Since socially constructed agents are agents, they can construct, in turn, other agents which constitute their components.

This strategy allows creating a decomposition structure as rich as the one in object orientation. Moreover, it allows progressively decomposing an organization in simpler agents described by beliefs and motivations to manage the complexity of a multiagent system. Finally, since agents can be subject to obligations and endowed with permissions and powers, all the social entities composing an organization can be the addressees of norms and powers; at the same time, socially constructed agents can be normative systems imposing obligations on their components, i.e., organizations can be modelled as burocracies [20].

This paper is part of a wider project modelling normative multiagent systems. In [8] we model normative systems by means of the agent metaphor: we attribute them beliefs, desires and goals: beliefs represent the constitutive rules of the organization while regulative rules, like obligations, are modelled in terms of goals of the system. In [6] we extend the model to virtual communities and we use the agent metaphor to describe local and global policies. In [9], constitutive rules are used to define contracts and games among agents are extended to allow an agent to change the obligations enforced by the normative system. Roles have been introduced in [23]. This paper constitutes a step forward in this project in that the agent metaphor is used to explain how organizations can create other social entities like functional areas and roles and, at the same time, specify their behavior. In this way we account for their definitional dependency characteristic of social entities [24]. Our ontology of social reality is presented in [7].

Future work concerns defining the relation between roles described as agents and the agents playing those roles. Moreover, contracts, described in [9] can be introduced to regulate the possibility to create new obligations, new roles and new social entities inside an organization [10].

References

1. Jennings, N.R.: On agent-based software engineering. Artificial Intelligence **117(2)** (2000) 277–296
2. Yu, E.: Agent orientation as a modelling paradigm. Wirtschaftsinformatik **43(2)** (2001) 123–132
3. Booch, G.: Object-Oriented Analysis and Design with Applications. Addison-Wesley, Reading (MA) (1988)
4. Bauer, B., Muller, J., Odell, J.: Agent UML: A formalism for specifying multiagent software systems. Int. Journal of Software Engineering and Knowledge Engineering **11(3)** (2001) 207–230
5. Zambonelli, F., Jennings, N., Wooldridge, M.: Developing multiagent systems: The Gaia methodology. IEEE Transactions of Software Engineering and Methodology **12(3)** (2003) 317–370
6. Boella, G., van der Torre, L.: Local policies for the control of virtual communities. In: Procs. of IEEE/WIC WI'03, IEEE Press (2003) 161–167
7. Boella, G., van der Torre, L.: An agent oriented ontology of social reality. In: Procs. of FOIS'04, Torino (2004)
8. Boella, G., van der Torre, L.: Regulative and constitutive norms in normative multiagent systems. In: Procs. of 9th International Conference on the Principles of Knowledge Representation and Reasoning (KR'04), AAAI Press (2004) 255–265

9. Boella, G., van der Torre, L.: Contracts as legal institutions in organizations of autonomous agents. In: Procs. of AAMAS'04, ACM Press (2004) 948–955
10. Ferber, J., Gutknecht, O., Michel, F.: From agents to organizations: an organizational view of multiagent systems. In: LNCS n. 2935: Procs. of AOSE'03, Springer Verlag (2003) 214–230
11. McCallum, M., Norman, T., Vasconcelos, W.: A formal model of organisations for engineering multi-agent systems. In: Procs. of CEAS Workshop at ECAI'04. (2004)
12. Searle, J.: The Construction of Social Reality. The Free Press, New York (1995)
13. Dennett, D.: The intentional stance. Bradford Books/MIT Press, Cambridge (MA) (1987)
14. Ricci, A., Omicini, A., Denti, E.: Activity theory as a framework for mas coordination. In: Procs. of ESAW'02. (2002) 96–110
15. Pacheco, O., Carmo, J.: A role based model of normative specification of organized collective agency and agents interaction. Autonomous Agents and Multiagent Systems **6** (2003) 145–184
16. Dignum, V., Meyer, J.J., Weigand, H.: Towards an organizational-oriented model for agent societies using contracts. In: Procs. of AAMAS'02, ACM Press (2002) 694–695
17. Lang, J., van der Torre, L., Weydert, E.: Utilitarian desires. Autonomous Agents and Multiagent Systems (2002) 329–363
18. Lee, R.: Documentary Petri nets: A modeling representation for electronic trade procedures. In: Business Process Management, LNCS 1806, Berlin, Springer Verlag (2000) 359–375
19. Jones, A., Sergot, M.: A formal characterisation of institutionalised power. Journal of IGPL **3** (1996) 427–443
20. Ouchi, W.: A conceptual framework for the design of organizational control mechanisms. Management Science **25(9)** (1979) 833–848
21. Finin, T.W., Labrou, Y., Mayfield, J.: KQML as an agent communication language. In Bradshaw, J., ed.: Software Agents. MIT Press, Cambridge (1995)
22. Wooldridge, M., Jennings, N., Kinny, D.: The Gaia methodology for agent-oriented analysis and design. Autonomous Agents and Multi-Agent Systems **3(3)** (2000) 285–312
23. Boella, G., van der Torre, L.: Attributing mental attitudes to roles: The agent metaphor applied to organizational design. In: Procs. of ICEC'04, IEEE Press (2004)
24. Masolo, C., Vieu, L., Bottazzi, E., Catenacci, C., Ferrario, R., Gangemi, A., Guarino, N.: Social roles and their descriptions. In: Procs. of KR'04. (2004)

Virtual Enterprise Normative Framework Within Electronic Institutions

Henrique Lopes Cardoso and Eugénio Oliveira

LIACC, Faculty of Engineering, University of Porto,
R. Dr. Roberto Frias, 4200-465 Porto, Portugal
eco@fe.up.pt
Polytechnic Institute of Bragança,
5301-854 Bragança, Portugal
hlc@ipb.pt

Abstract. Virtual Enterprises are a major trend within the B2B scenario. Technological support towards enabling this cooperation model includes the multi-agent systems paradigm. In this paper we identify requirements of Virtual Enterprise contracts, developing a normative framework for contract validation and enforcement. Furthermore, we enclose this conception within the structure of an Electronic Institution, which governs and supports the interaction of agents in business scenarios, providing specific services such as brokering, reputation, negotiation mediation, and contract related services. We focus on electronic contracting as a means of establishing cooperation agreements, and we describe the institution's role on the e-contracting life-cycle.

1 Introduction

Virtual Enterprises are a major trend in cooperative business. Specialization and flexibility are some of the key aspects of an every day more dynamic and global market. The concept of Virtual Enterprise has been applied to many forms of cooperative business relations, like outsourcing, supply chains, or temporary consortiums. We approach this latter case, since it clearly addresses the demand for flexible and dynamic arrangements between different enterprises. We also find it convenient to relate the constitution of Virtual Enterprises to legislation on consortium contracts [20], which regulates the coordination of efforts between enterprises towards accomplishing some activity, where each participant maintains its own core business, while aligning it with other members' activities.

Technological support to the creation of such relationships is arising in many forms. The most ambitious ones intend to automate (part of) the process of creation and operation of Virtual Enterprises, mainly through multi-agent technology approaches, where each agent can represent each of the different enterprises. In fact, research on multi-agent technology addresses issues that fit the Virtual Enterprise scenario. Agents are autonomous, interact with other agents, and enable approaching inherently distributed problems with negotiation and coordination capabilities.

In this paper we develop on the application of multi-agent systems to the Virtual Enterprise lifecycle, by conceptualizing the more general framework of an Electronic

M.-P. Gleizes, A. Omicini, and F. Zambonelli (Eds.): ESAW 2004, LNAI 3451, pp. 14–32, 2005.

Institution (improving on [23]), which provides assistance to the automated specification of business agreements. The institution represents a normative system that establishes a level of trust enabling the interaction of heterogeneous, independently developed and privately owned agents. We are particularly interested in formalizing business relationships through electronic contracts, and specifically in designing and exploring e-contracts representing Virtual Enterprise configurations.

Therefore, we identify requirements for a contract formalizing the Virtual Enterprise constitution. We then distinguish operational contracts that can be achieved inside this cooperation agreement. Following a normative agent perspective, we suggest the organization of norms in three hierarchical levels of abstraction: (i) institutional norms, used to validate the creation of virtual enterprise contracts; (ii) constitutional norms, expressing the cooperation agreement and used to impose and check the compliance of operational contracts; and (iii) operational norms, which can be monitored and enforced during the Virtual Enterprise activity.

This paper is organized as follows. Section 2 addresses the Virtual Enterprise concept and its lifecycle, bringing to discussion the notion of consortium contracts. In section 3 we develop the Electronic Institution framework, detailing its regulations and services. We then examine, in section 4, the problem of formalizing electronic contracts from a normative perspective, relating contract handling to institutional services; we also identify requirements of a Virtual Enterprise contract. In section 5 we develop a normative framework comprising the institution, the Virtual Enterprise and its operation, and we propose a specification for contracts focusing on the underlying cooperation commitment. We conclude in section 6 describing our current efforts and related work.

2 Virtual Enterprises

The shift, in the last decades, from an industrial economy (based on mass production models) to an information economy associated to the globalization of markets has brought an enormous increase in competitiveness, leading to the need for new organizational models. Enterprise cooperation models have emerged, where different enterprises coordinate the necessary means to accomplish shared activities or reach common goals. This association of strengths enables enterprises to build privileged relationships, based on an increase of advantages through resource and competence sharing, and risk minimization.

Cooperation arrangements are particularly relevant in small and medium enterprises (SME), due to their reduced size and high specialization and flexibility. These kinds of enterprises have been adopting new strategies that enable them to adapt to a constantly changing market, organizing themselves in strategic partnerships. While allowing themselves to maintain their business independence, partners are able to reach otherwise unreachable (physical and customer) markets and to take advantage of economies of scale. Furthermore, many large companies are isolating parts of their businesses, making them autonomous in order to increase the overall flexibility and achieve greater performances. Outsourcing models are also becoming dominant, enabling enterprises to concentrate on their core competencies.

Thus, there is an increasing emphasis in cooperation and coordination of small business units.

The concept of a *Virtual Enterprise (VE)* arose from this trend, and has been defined as "a temporary consortium of autonomous, diverse and possibly geographically dispersed organizations that pool their resources to meet short-term objectives and exploit fast-changing market trends" [6]. We distinguish a VE from a mere tight integration of two business entities in outsourcing (e.g. [15]) or supply chain configurations. In these cases, information technology approaches are focused on managing inter-organizational workflows, providing a fine-grained cooperation between the parties, which in turn tends to the establishment of middle- or long-term relationships. Our conceptualization demands for a greater flexibility, as explicitly stated in the definition presented above.

We associate the creation of a VE to the concept of a *consortium contract*, which is present in the Portuguese legislation [20]. A consortium is a contract according to which two or more entities coordinate their efforts towards accomplishing some activity. This may include the execution of an enterprise (a common example is a civil construction project, like a bridge), the supply of equal or complementary goods produced by the consortium's members to third parties, or the production of goods that can be split amongst the consortium's members. With the creation of a consortium, a new entity can be formed that represents this joint activity to third parties – the consortium is said to be *external*. In other cases, an *internal* consortium can be created, namely when its goal does not include the supply of goods to third parties (although the members' goals might).

The lifecycle of a VE has been studied by some researchers. A simple macro-model that fits our VE conceptualization might include the following stages: *business definition, formation, operation, regulation*, and *dissolution*. Operation and regulation are interleaved phases that go on while the VE exists. The creation of the VE starts with the definition of the business to be developed; this process may initiate because of a client need or because of a market opportunity detected by an enterprise. The formation phase typically includes the definition of goals, the selection of participants through negotiation, and the definition of their roles and respective obligations. The electronic market architecture reported in [21], which this work improves upon, considers a market agent that exists to establish the need (that is, the product or service to be delivered by the VE), and to coordinate the negotiation process in the VE formation phase.

In the operation phase the participants develop the intended business, which may comprise the search for customers (if they are not pre-determined) and the carrying out of activities involved with business enactment. VE adjustments can take place at the regulation phase, when unexpected events occur, making members leave the VE and creating the need for new partners in order to accomplish the established goals. Rules determining how this process is achieved are normally settled at the formation phase. When members verify that the VE has fully accomplished its goals, or decide that it is no longer justified, the VE is dissolved.

There have been lately many research efforts towards infrastructures supporting the VE model. A promising approach is the area of multi-agent systems, which naturally address a number of characteristics in the VE domain, namely their distributed nature, with autonomous enterprises, and the need for coordination and distributed problem solving. Autonomous agents can represent the individual interests of different enterprises and negotiate in order to constitute a VE. They can then cooperate by coordinating their activities in order to fulfill the virtual enterprise's purpose. Approaches to the establishment of VEs through multi-agent negotiation can be found in [21].

3   Electronic Institutions

Interactions between members of a society are regulated by institutions. These institutions define the rules of the game, stating what is forbidden and permitted to the individuals and in what conditions [9]. An *Electronic Institution (EI)* will be the electronic counterpart of such an institution, imposing regulations on electronic members (agents) that adhere to this electronic society. In particular, an EI will rule the interaction between electronic parties engaged in business transactions, providing an environment where regulated agent interactions can take place. One of the main roles of such an environment is to provide the necessary level of trust that enables agents from different sources to safely engage in business interactions.

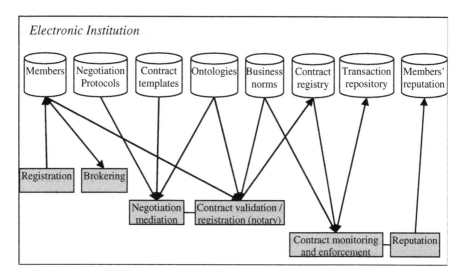

Fig. 1. Regulations and services of an Electronic Institution

First of all, an EI provides a normative system of reference under which agents reach cooperation agreements. When adhering to the institution, an agent abides to a set of imperative norms that regulate and support interactions taking place within the EI. Since the formalization of business relationships (through electronic contracts) are of primary importance, specific regulations on this matter are included as well. The imposed normative system is composed of regulations on the following:

- *Identity of members*: agents must be identified in order to engage in interactions within the EI; also, the signatures of agents when signing contracts must be validated by the institution;
- *Shared ontology specifications*: agents must be able to use the same ontological commitments, so that they can successfully interact, especially in business engagements; the specifications may include both domain-independent business terms and domain-dependent vocabulary;
- *Interaction and negotiation protocols*: the EI may assist the interaction process, imposing a set of well-defined protocols; this is particularly relevant when business relations are created through a process of negotiation, that may require mediation;
- *General business norms*: these are norms applicable to any business engagement, establishing trust by ensuring that certain behaviors are expected and will be enforced;
- *Contract specification*: contracts must be specified according to pre-established directives.

Based on these regulations, the EI also provides support towards facilitating business cooperation between its members. We are particularly interested in mechanisms that enable electronic contract specification and enforcement. In [23] an EI sketch is presented, aiming at supporting the VE lifecycle. Refining that model, we distinguish a set of services that adherent agents can benefit from:

- *Registration*: a service that enables agents to register in the EI, granting them access to the remaining services;
- *Brokering*: yellow-pages support, enabling agents to easily find potential partners;
- *Contract templates*: pre-formatted contracts that boost the formalization of typical business relations, while assuring conformance to contract specification regulations;
- *Negotiation mediation*: using predefined protocols, the EI can act as an intermediary in the negotiation process, taking advantage of template structures and ensuring that resulting contracts are in accordance to business norms;
- *Contract validation*: contracts obtained by two or more parties (and namely not constructed using templates or institutional mediation) can be validated towards the general norms, ensuring that they comply with the overall regulations of the community;
- *Notary*: contract registry services are provided to store consummated (signed) contracts, ensuring their legal existence;
- *Contract monitoring and enforcement*: mechanisms that monitor and enforce the execution of contracts according to their clauses and general institutional norms, registering the fulfillment of transactions and applying predicted non-conformance sanctions;
- *Reputation mechanisms*: these ensure that errant behavior will have a negative impact on an agent's reputation, thus discouraging it.

These regulations and services are depicted in figure 1.

The formation of Virtual Enterprises is an intricate process that typically requires some pre-existing enterprise pool – a *cluster* of enterprises. A cluster has also been referred to as a "breeding" or "nesting" environment [2], where members share some common elements that make cooperation arrangements feasible (be it technologies, business-related resources, etc.). Advances in information and communication technologies make it possible to support cluster formation. In particular, the Electronic Institution concept permits essential elements when establishing VEs, such as mutual trust building, common ontologies and standard business practices.

4 B2B E-Contracts

In B2B electronic commerce, more attention has been given recently to contract formation and fulfillment. In fact, this issue is part of the so-called B2B transaction model, as presented in [14]. Approaches to B2B contract handling (e.g. [13]) identify the need to specify and represent contracts, and further to monitor and enforce them.

Contracts can have different forms, representing business agreements ranging from simple deals used to exchange resources (such as in purchasing a product), to complex business relationships between parties. However, most of the research literature devoted to e-contract automation simplifies contracts to the former type, defining one time relationships between a customer and a seller. Little attention has been given to contracts that result from a Virtual Enterprise formation process (an exception might be [22]). These contracts are more complex in the sense that they need to specify how several involved parties should behave, during a period of time, in order to participate in a cooperation effort towards a common goal.

4.1 E-Contracts and Norms

Contracts are formalizations of the behavior of a group of agents that jointly agree on a specific business activity. Contracts are used as a means of securing transactions between the involved parties, forming a normative structure that explicitly expresses their behaviors' interdependencies. *Electronic contracts* are virtual representations of such contracts. The aim of e-contracting is to improve the efficiency of contracting processes, supporting an increasing automation of both e-contract construction (using automated tools) and execution (integrating with business processes). Within our framework, e-contracts will be obtained by agents representing different enterprises, meeting inside the EI to which they adhered.

The components of a contract include the identification of participants, the specification of products and/or services included and a discrimination of actions to be performed by each participant. These actions are usually accompanied with time and precedence constraints. Typified business relations can recurrently use pre-formatted contracts. In this case, contracts usually have a set of identified *roles* to be fulfilled by the parties involved in the relation.

The core of a contract is composed of contract clauses. These clauses can specify different types of behavior *norms* that will guide the interaction between the parties. Broadly speaking, three types of norms can exist within a contract structure:

- *obligation*: an agent has an obligation towards another agent to bring about a certain state of affairs (by executing some action), before a certain deadline;
- *permission*: an agent is allowed to execute some action, within a given window of opportunity (specified either by a deadline or more generally by a state of affairs);
- *prohibition*: an agent is forbidden to bring about a certain state of affairs (some action is interdicted).

A formal approach to model such norms is *deontic logic* [27] (also known as the logic of normative concepts), a branch of modal logic. The normative concepts obligation, permission and prohibition are analogous to the modal concepts of necessity, possibility and impossibility, respectively.

When representing contracts, another fundamental concept is typically added to the norms above: the *sanction*. Any obligation must be accompanied by at least one sanction, as obligations without sanctions are ineffective [17]. Thus, obligations are not absolute, but relative to their associated sanctions in case of non-performance [24]. Prohibitions can be addressed in an analogous way. A prohibition is sometimes handled as a negated obligation, that is, a duty for not performing some action (see, for instance, [17]).

Approaches to the automation of contractual relationships necessarily include this sanction component. Particularly when that automation is based on the autonomous agent paradigm, norms cannot be taken as constraints on the behavior of each contractual party.[1] Each agent is able to deliberatively reason about its goals and the norms it has committed to (hence the notion, in [3], of *deliberative normative agents*). An agent can violate a norm in order to accomplish a private goal that it considers to be more important. When doing so, the agent is aware of the sanction it will be subject to.

Norms and Electronic Institutions. Contracting is normally subject to contract law. This law is enforced by the court, and can be seen as a normative system that contracts must abide to. Generally speaking, we can thus say that a contractual relationship will have a normative system of reference (enforced by an institution), according to which the contract will be built, detailing the interactions that will take place between the parties. The relation between the contract and the normative system is hierarchical, meaning that the contract can inherit norms from the normative system already established, using it as a ground basis.

Electronic institutions, while regulating the interactions that can take place between agents, can represent normative systems that limit the behavior of participants and describe the penalties incurred when norms are violated. Contractual relations created inside the institution must abide to the imposed norms, specifying the details of a particular business relation.

---

[1] Although most initial research on norms in multi-agent systems has focused on norms as constraints on behavior via social laws. Agents were not allowed to deviate from these laws, which were used to ensure cooperation between interacting autonomous selfish agents.

4.2 E-Contract Handling

Any contractual relationship can be said to evolve through a number of steps. These can be resumed to the following three stages [28]:

- *information discovery*: clients find potential suppliers;
- *contract negotiation*: the parties negotiate the contract terms – the result of this stage is a legally binding contract, reflecting the agreement made;
- *execution*: the contract terms are fulfilled by the parties, namely involving product delivery or service rendering, and the corresponding payments.

The first stage thus comprises the brokering phase of B2B electronic commerce. One can also conceptualize it as a *pre-contractual phase*, involving a definition of the products or services sought/sold by clients/suppliers, and the utilization of yellow-pages services allowing potential partners to contact each other. The second stage is devoted to the negotiation of the terms of an agreement – it is the *contractual phase*, since a contract is being constructed. That agreement will express a number of steps to be performed by the contractual parties. Hence, the parties negotiate not only attributes of products/services but also details of how those products/services will be delivered/rendered and paid. The document that represents the agreement reached is a legally binding contract, signed by those involved. Typically, it will also specify how to handle exception conditions, such as those related with non-fulfillment of duties (e.g. late delivery or non-payment). The third stage is the *post-contractual phase*, that is, after the contract is established it is time to proceed as agreed. It is also referred to as the *fulfillment* phase. In more complex and integrated interactions, the parties involved will eventually engage their business processes, forming an inter-enterprise workflow.

E-contracts are achieved inside controlled environments – Electronic Institutions – that establish certain rules of behavior to be followed by its members, ensuring a level of trust that is crucial to the interaction of heterogeneous, independently developed and privately owned agents. The three stages presented above are supported by the Electronic Institution framework as follows.

Information discovery assistance is a typical function of electronic markets in general, but in the VE case special care can be given to the process of finding potential strategic business partners, with appropriately tailored services. Cooperative business relationships may involve more than the supply of merchandise, requiring a tighter cooperation between the parties involved. Therefore, more attention is needed in the partner selection phase.

The contract negotiation phase is assisted through contract template availability, negotiation mediation services (such as those presented in [21]), and norm conformance checking, allowing only legal and enforceable contracts to be formed. Several researchers acknowledge the need for a starting ground in contracting (see, for instance, [28], [17], and [24]). In fact, starting a negotiation where nothing is fixed represents a too ill-structured problem to consider automating. The importance of a contract template resides on its ability to provide a structure on which negotiation can be based. Furthermore, certain kinds of business relations are formally typified (for instance, sales and purchases). In this sense, instead of beginning from scratch a new contractual relation, two (or more) agents can use an electronic contract template, which is a contract outline containing domain-independent interaction schemata and variable elements (such as price, quantity, deadlines, and so on) to be filled-in with domain-specific data resulting from a negotiation [17]. If all goes well, the result of the negotiation will be an actual contract, instantiated from the template, which will be signed by the parties. Templates thus provide a structure that allows negotiation, as a process of cooperative construction of a business relation, to be focused on those elements that, when instantiated, will distinguish the agreement obtained from other contractual relationships. Meanwhile, the common elements in relations of the same type will be preserved. These common elements might include, for example, outline commitments of the involved parties, which when instantiated through negotiation will detail their concrete objects (eventually including technical properties) and temporal references.

Contract execution is enforced by appropriate monitoring services, which register transactions and deal with non-fulfillment situations. The execution of an e-contract consists on the parties following the norms they committed to when signing the contract. If any deviations from the prescribed behavior should occur, sanctions can be applied as specified in the contract or in its normative system of reference. However, the parties involved will typically not voluntarily submit themselves to such penalties. Therefore, appropriate mechanisms to monitor and enforce norm execution are needed. Only a trusted third party (the EI) can enable the necessary level of confidence between the parties involved in a business relation. The verification of real-world contracts is often dependent on external (physical world) entities, which must interface with the EI to allow the automation of the process.

4.3   Requirements of a Virtual Enterprise Contract

A normative conception of contracts is normally used for contract representation. Hence, general languages for representing norms in contracts have been proposed (e.g. [17], [24], and [8]). However, little research is devoted to the representation of VE contracts.

Normative Statements. Based on the operators of deontic logic, normative statements can be formally represented as [24]:

$$\text{ns: } \varphi \rightarrow \theta_{s,b} \, (\alpha < \psi)$$

where

ns is a label
φ is an activation condition
θ is a deontic operator (obligation, permission, or prohibition)
s is the subject of θ
b is the beneficiary of θ
α is the action to perform or the state of affairs to bring about
ψ is a deadline

In this approach, obligations are not absolute, but relative to their associated sanctions. That is, deviation from prescribed behavior is admitted and properly addressed through sanctions. These are defined just like the other normative statements, but by specifying the non-fulfillment of a given obligation as the activation condition. Sanctions may give rise to other obligations or prohibitions: either the beneficiary of the violated norm is granted a right (the subject has a new obligation towards the beneficiary) or the subject of the violated norm is refused a right (he is forbidden to do something).

This representation of norms allows for the construction of any contract that can be entirely specified using these building blocks. For instance, contracts reflecting simple purchasing operations might be composed of four such norms: (1) a seller's obligation to provide a requested good by a certain deadline; (2) a buyer's obligation to pay by a certain deadline, after receiving the demanded good; (3) a sanction predicting possible non-fulfillment of delivery on the seller's part – e.g. a discount; and (4) a sanction predicting possible late payment on the buyer's side – an interest rate, for example.

Virtual Enterprise Contracts. The contracts we are interested in might also benefit from a group of enhancements that facilitate contract construction. According to our approach, an electronic contract is a formalization of a business agreement that two or more agents, representing different entities, establish as a cooperative business activity.

A VE thus constitutes a complex case of a business agreement, and certain aspects of its nature must be contemplated. Namely, the following list of requirements must be taken into account:

- The contract will represent an ongoing (although limited in duration) relationship between the signatories. This is in contrast to sell/purchase operations, which have a very short-term nature, limited to order-delivery-payment operations (if we disregard possible warranty periods);
- Some interactions between the parties may be continuously repeated. Particularly when the goal of the VE considers the production of goods that are to be supplied to third parties, members exchange resources, production outputs or information in a cyclical manner. The VE (and its formalizing contract) may terminate not by a pre-specified deadline or at the end of a predetermined normative path, but when its members decide to cancel their conjoint operation;
- Support for the exit and entrance of partners has to be given. VE contracts can specify conditions according to which partners may leave or enter the organization. A VE has a flexible structure, allowing for this kind of adjustments to occur, particularly when the involved parties fail to perform their duties. In this case, a member may leave the VE not for its own initiative, but because its behavior imposes an expulsion, possibly with associated indemnities. Nevertheless, the VE's related business can survive with the entrance of new partners;
- When representing a new entity, the VE may establish contracts with third parties, namely customers. The constitution of the VE might regulate the way how these contracts are to be formed;

– An important aspect of the VE operation is how profits are to be exchanged. That is, the transfer of payments can occur depending on the transfer of (partial) products between the members of the VE, or only when goods are sold to the final customers (assuming that the VE's goal is such). In the latter case, a party's return on investment depends on the success of the VE, making risk an explicit factor to consider when entering the joint venture (which typically implies participation both in profits and losses).

A contract representation language that is convenient to formalize VE agreements should therefore take into account these concerns. VE contracts cannot be constructed just with the normative statement represented above. Richer operators are needed to specify such contracts. We also find it convenient to split the VE contractual formalization in two levels of abstraction: constitutional and operational (see section 5).

Practical requirements also arise when one attempts to automate contract monitoring and enforcement. In particular, contracts must provide directions as to how and when to verify their fulfillment. In the next section we distinguish contracts that can be enforced from contracts than can only be verified on creation. A contract will be enforceable if it is possible to verify if the parties' actions conform to the agreement (this verification may eventually require the utilization of external entities' services). Event-based monitoring systems must be exploited in order to check for contract compliance. Many contractual actions are dependent on deadlines, which require a monitoring system to act in response to defined timers [19]. This mixed event and time-based approach allows for checking both if occurring actions are in accordance to the contract and if missing actions are in violation of obligations.

5   Virtual Enterprise Normative Framework

In this section we propose a hierarchical organization of norms, in an environment addressing the establishment and operation of VE contractual relationships.

A VE contract represents a framework within which further interaction between its participants takes place. This will include the establishment of operational settlements (contracts) for the exchange of products/services that implement the desired level of cooperation that led to the formation of the VE in the first place. The VE contract therefore adds a normative layer to the electronic institution's framework. Operational contracts made within the VE constitution must abide to these norms. Figure 2 illustrates the hierarchical relationship between three levels of norms: *institutional*, *constitutional* and *operational*.

According to this model, it is important to distinguish between *verifiability* and *enforceability*. Institutional norms provide a framework against which a VE contract can be validated. Accordingly, this VE cooperation agreement establishes a platform of cooperation within which operational contracts between VE participants can be checked. However, only operational contracts will be enforceable, in the sense that only these contracts specify the concrete interactions that must take place between some of the agents participating in the VE. The verification (validation) of contracts occurs when contracts are created, whereas their monitoring and enforcement takes place at the execution stage. We take a passive perspective on the verification of contracts – the institution will react to the creation of a new contract – and an active one on the enforcement of contracts – the institution will proactively check the fulfillment of contractual norms.

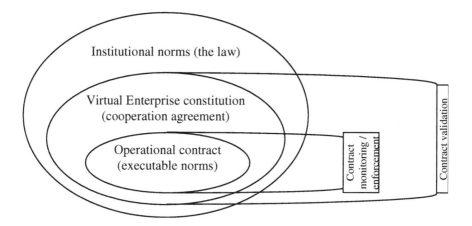

Fig. 2. Normative framework

Besides providing a layer according to which operational contracts are validated, another important role of the VE constitutional contract is to specify the conditions that participants *must* accept when establishing operational contracts. When adhering to the constitution of a given VE, agents impose themselves a level of cooperation that is then reflected in the terms of executable contracts. The non-acceptance of such terms should be sanctioned, ultimately by the expulsion from the VE.

5.1 Institutional Norms

Institutional norms include regulations on general contracting activities and on consortium contracts in particular, as well as default rules to resolve any issues that have not been explicitly addressed by the parties. These two groups of regulations influence the formation of both VE constitutional contracts and operational contracts.

Contract law theory [4] identifies two roles for default rules. On one hand, they can be used to be left in place, that is, they can specify default values that the parties would agree on, with the intent of minimizing contracting effort. On the other hand, certain default rules can intentionally provide unfavorable default values, forcing contractual parties to explicitly deal with specific contract clauses, making sure that every participant is aware of the agreed values. Another use of this latter case is to make contractual parties fill in certain formalities in their contract, without which the contract would not be valid or enforceable.

One possible way to guarantee that parties deal with specific contract details is through the use of institutionally provided *contract templates*. These may contain predefined values as well as un-instantiated (negotiable) parts.

Since different contractual relations can have a lot in common, contracts (and templates) can be underspecified, relying instead on institutional norms to complete the overall picture. These norms include default values for certain contractual issues (e.g. a 5 days deadline for any payment after delivery), and imposed regulations concerning exceptional contract execution situations (though not necessarily contract violations).

Regarding consortium contracts, examples (inspired in [20]) of institutional regulations include general rules about how a consortium contract may be modified, conditions according to which an agent can exonerate himself from the contract, rescind situations towards a non-compliant member, and consortium ending settings. Also, according to the consortium's nature, regulations on the split of externally received payments or profit share policies can be defined.

As figure 2 suggests, we aim at providing a normative background that can be computationally exploited in validating, monitoring and enforcing contracts.

5.2 Virtual Enterprise Constitutional Norms

Depending on the type of VE created (see consortium goals and types in section 2), different kinds of norms can be included in the VE contract. However, some common elements include:

- Duration: specifically, a starting date for the VE operation and ending conditions;
- Membership: rules for the exit of partners and the entrance of new ones;
- Cooperation terms: demanded workload for each partner, agreed prices for each partners' contribution, and workflow process general outline.

In the case of a consortium with the goal of selling the result of the cooperation effort to third parties, the VE contract might also regulate issues on profit exchange and on the creation of contracts that represent such selling activity.

VE Contract Specification. Focusing on the cooperation commitment that parties impose themselves when establishing a VE contract, we consider the following contract structure:

$$VEContract = <H, CoopEff, BP>$$

- *Header (H)*: identifies the contract and its normative system of reference, introduces the organization participants and the resources (products, services, payments, etc.) that are to be exchanged between them, specifies a signing date and includes the parties' digital signatures;

$$H = <Id, NormSys, Partics, Ress, Date, Signs>$$
$$Partics = \{Partic_i\}$$
$$Ress = \{Res_k\}$$
$$Signs = \{Sign_i\}$$

- *Cooperation effort (CoopEff)*: indicates workload acceptance levels and associated prices for each of the participating agents; these are obtained from the negotiation process, as described in [21];

$$CoopEff = \{<Partic_i, Res_k, Wload>\}$$
$$Wload = <MinQt, MaxQt, Freq, UnitPr>$$
$$Freq \in \{per\_day, per\_week, per\_month, per\_year\}$$

- *Business process (BP)*: describes the flow of resources between participants, in the form of *request permits* indicating allowed requests that parties may perform towards their partners; these requests activate *obligation chains* (sequences of obligations where each one is dependent on the fulfillment of the previous one) that implement the business transaction steps composing the required workflow.

$$BP = <\{ReqPerm_m\}, \{OblChain_n\}>$$
$$ReqPerm = <Who, Whom, What>$$
$$Who, Whom \in Partics; \ What \in Ress; \ <Whom, What, \_> \in CoopEff$$
$$OblChain = <OblRule_1, OblRule_2, ..., OblRule_p>$$
$$OblRule = <ActCond, Obl>$$

According to this layout, we regard request permits as permissions (rights) granted to agents for demanding the contribution of the envisaged agent, bounded by the cooperation effort that it committed to. The enactment of such permission activates an obligation chain describing the procedures to carry out. Making these obligations dependent on requests relieves us from pre-specifying the exact dates when all the exchanges should occur, which is difficult to evaluate and subject to contingencies.

The workload acceptance levels (together with their agreed prices) include both a minimum desired production output (under which a partner's participation may not be profitable anymore) and a maximum committed contribution to the organization (over which the partner is not compromised to assure). We intend to exploit these ranges when checking the conformance of agents to their contractual cooperation promises, and when evaluating conditions for contract exoneration.

The VE contract structure should become more complex as we introduce more elements such as sanctions, contract duration, and membership rules. However, these additional elements can just as well be defined as default regulations at the institutional level, keeping the contract contents focused on the essential. The core of a specific cooperation agreement can be captured by the above structure.

5.3 Operational Norms

Contracts representing concrete exchange of products/services will include specific actions to be performed by each of the contractual parties, which must be members of the VE. These contracts implement the VE cooperation agreement, representing the workflow processes outlined in the VE constitutional contract.

Norms present in such contracts consist of obligations related to delivery and payment of such products/services. At this level, contracts may be composed of normative statements as approached in [24] and discussed in section 4.3. The degree of detail of such norms will determine the possibility for monitoring and enforcement of operational contracts.

According to the specification above on VE contracts, operational norms become active when a request is made by an agent concerning the exchange of resources between consortium's participants. The obligation chain indicates actions to be performed by the involved parties, being amenable to institutional monitoring activities based on a business transaction repository.

We can regard the constitutionally predicted obligation chains as templates for operational norms that are instantiated, by the enactment of requests, with specific data depending on the chain scope, such as dates and quantities.

6   Current and Related Work

We are refining our Electronic Institution's model depicted in figure 1, developing a computational framework for facilitating multi-agent contracting in Virtual Enterprise scenarios, and for monitoring contract execution. We develop on [21], where an advanced negotiation protocol is presented, specifically tailored to handle the formation of Virtual Enterprises, and on [23], where a simplified model of an EI is sketched to support the VE lifecycle.

We are applying our efforts on the specification of a representation formalism that allows us to model institutional norms and to represent both constitutional and operational contracts. This representation should allow the validation of contracts (according to the normative framework presented in the previous section), as well as the enforcement of operational contracts and their monitoring. In particular, we are defining an XML schema for specifying VE contracts, according to the structure briefly presented in section 5.2; this will be used to provide contract negotiation support tools. A promising approach towards norm representation and verification is the use of a rule-based inference engine (e.g. JESS, as used in [11]), which allows for a declarative representation and thus facilitates norm updating, both from the creation of new contracts and from institutional norm evolution (see future work below).

Since it is impossible to computationally force an agent to fulfill an obligation, we envisage the effect of triggering sanctions not only as introducing new obligations, but also as disabling certain agent actions while within the institution (prohibitions, in normative jargon). This appears to be the approach taken in [9], with the concept of *normative rules*.

Contract law [4] includes some essential elements that we have adopted. The essence of contract is commitment: the assurance that others will, when the time comes, uphold their end of a bargain. Whereas in some situations reputation mechanisms can provide that assurance, contracting offers an additional recourse when these "non-legal sanctions" are insufficient to constrain opportunism: parties expose themselves to legal sanctions for non-fulfillment of duties. The utilization of default rules, which define the parties' obligations in the absence of any explicit agreement to the contrary, allows resolving issues that have not been explicitly addressed by the parties. Relational contract theory [16] studies continuing relations that are naturally self-enforceable. Instead of a detailed enforceable contract based on a third party, a relational contract is based on repeated interactions and social norms, representing an informal agreement sustained by the value of future relationships. Relational contracts may arise both because of problems in achieving enforceable contracts and due to the costs of legal enforcement. Although formal contracts seem opposite to relational ones, they may coexist. Contracting parties use a mix of legal and extralegal mechanisms. Formal contracts are preferred when establishing relationships between unknown parties. On the other hand, regular partners generally rely on implicit relationships, supported by trust and by the threat of withholding business from anyone who has broken a promise in the past.

Our model of an EI supports these two contractual paradigms, including both reputation facilities and contract enforcement functionalities. We capture contract law elements by exploiting a hierarchical normative framework where the EI has the central role of establishing common business rules.

There is not much work, to the best of our knowledge, devoted to the formalization of VE contractual agreements. In [22], VE contract establishment is addressed, and the authors distinguish between agreements and contracts. Agreements, composed of framework clauses, are seen as mutually accepted rules of engagement between parties, whereas contracts are agreements with a legally binding weight (and sufficiently specific to be legally enforceable).

Within the multi-agent research community, some researchers address the advantages of anticipating sanctions (also called de-commitment penalties) in multi-agent formal contracting, introducing the concept of a *leveled commitment contract* [25], and study reasoning decision processes that consider strategic breaches [25][12].

The execution of contracts is assisted in [24] with a *contract fulfillment protocol*, a collaborative protocol based on the normative statements' lifecycle. Agents communicate about their intentions on fulfilling contractual norms, allowing partners to know what to expect from them and permitting a fluent and prompt execution of contracts, since agents do not have to wait for the fulfillment of their partners' obligations to start executing their own (hence the collaborative nature). In [19] the authors identify, from a monitoring perspective, requirements for a business contract language. They focus on the time-constrained nature of contractual actions and on event-based monitoring of contracts.

The real-world application of agents in automated contract fulfillment is challenged by the presence of complex legal issues and subjective judgments of agent compliance [14]. Some work on these matters has been made, for instance, in [5], where an e-market controller agent (a third party) is suggested to resolve disputes arising from subjective views on contract compliance, thereby playing the role of a judge. This agent holds a representation of the contract, and when a conflict occurs it collects evidence from the involved parties and obtains information from independent advisors, such as certification authorities, regulators, or controllers of other associated markets.

The study of norms in multi-agent systems is relatively recent. Some pertinent references include [1], [18] and [26]. In [1] the authors distinguish between regulative and constitutive norms, which have not a direct correspondence to our institutional and constitutional normative layers. While their approach differentiates norms according to their nature (regulating behavior vs. describing the legal consequences of actions), ours is mainly concerned with norm scope.

A two-level conception of normative agent interactions is also proposed by others. In [7] the authors model a society of agents distinguishing between an institutional level (where social norms and rules are specified) and an operational level (dependent on the goals of each agent). In [24] two classes of sanctions are suggested: *endogenous sanctions*, which are specified in the contract, and *exogenous sanctions*, which are defined within the normative system to which the contract is subject. The latter are applied when clauses without specified endogenous sanctions are violated.

The *electronic institution* concept has been developed by other researchers, although perhaps with different perspectives. One of the most comprehensive works on the design, specification and development of electronic institutions is ISLANDER [10], together with the AMELI infrastructure [11]. This approach considers dialogical institutions, where agent interaction is made by the utterance of illocutions and is fully specified in a performative structure consisting of scenes and transitions among these scenes. Furthermore, norm compliance is assured through the use of mediator agents called *governors*, preventing norm violation. A questionable limitation of this approach is the lack of autonomy agents are confronted with when entering such an institution. Moreover, since the institution is totally based on the definition of interactions among scenes, it becomes a too rigid model, using norms to restrict behavior and avoiding the need for sanctions. Our model intends to be more open, and addresses the wider perspective of an institution providing support for commitment expression through contracts. These can be negotiated inside the institution, but need not be; enforcement mechanisms are to be in place, based on sanction imposition and reputation, thereby guiding agent behavior (as opposed to restricting agent autonomy).

For future work, we intend to develop mechanisms that allow agents to learn the level of detail they should allow their contracts to include, according to their contractual parties' reputations. Also, the EI itself might impose certain specifications in new contracts signed by those who have previously denoted non-fulfillment of duties.

An open topic we intend to investigate is whether new institutional norms can emerge from the continuous operation of the EI. For instance, the EI can observe that a certain kind of business relationship is becoming common, and thus might benefit from specifically tailored regulations, or from appropriate templates facilitating this cooperation structure.

References

1. Boella, G., & van der Torre, L. (2004). Regulative and Constitutive Norms in Normative Multiagent Systems. In *Proceedings of 9th International Conference on the Principles of Knowledge Representation and Reasoning (KR'04)*, Whistler, Canada.
2. Camarinha-Matos, L. M., & Afsarmanesh, H. (2003). Elements of a base VE infrastructure. *Journal of Computers in Industry, 51*(2), pp. 139-163.
3. Castelfranchi, C., Dignum, F., Jonker, C., & Treur, J. (2000). Deliberative Normative Agents: Principles and Architectures. In N. Jennings & Y. Lesperance (eds.), *Intelligent Agents VI: Agent Theories, Architectures, and Languages*, Springer, pp. 364-378.

4. Craswell, R. (2000). Contract Law: General Theories. In B. Bouckaert & G. De Geest (eds.), *Encyclopedia of Law and Economics, Volume III: The Regulation of Contracts*, Cheltenham, Edward Elgar, pp. 1-24.

5. Daskalopulu, A., Dimitrakos, T., & Maibaum, T. (2001). E-Contract Fulfilment and Agents' Attitudes. In *Proceedings of the ERCIM WG E-Commerce Workshop on The Role of Trust in e-Business*, Zurich, Switzerland.

6. Davulcu, H., Kifer, M, Pokorny, L. R., Ramakrishnan, C. R., Ramakrishnan, I. V., & Dawson, S. (1999). Modeling and Analysis of Interactions in Virtual Enterprises. In *Proceedings of the Ninth International Workshop on Research Issues on Data Engineering: Information Technology for Virtual Enterprises (RIDE 1999)*, IEEE Computer Society, pp.12-18.

7. Dignum, V., & Dignum, F. (2001). Modelling agent societies: co-ordination frameworks and institutions. In P. Brazdil & A. Jorge (eds.), *Progress in Artificial Intelligence: Knowledge Extraction, Multi-agent Systems, Logic Programming, and Constraint Solving*, LNAI 2258, Springer, pp. 191-204.

8. Dignum, V., Meyer, J., Dignum, F., & Weigand, H. (2002). Formal Specification of Interaction in Agent Societies. In M. G. Hinchey, J. L. Rash, W. F. Truszkowski, C. Rouff, & D. Gordon-Spears (eds.), *Formal Approaches to Agent-Based Systems*, Springer, pp. 37-52.

9. Esteva, M., Rodríguez-Aguilar, J. A., Sierra, C., Garcia, P., Arcos, J. L. (2001). On the Formal Specification of Electronic Institutions. In Dignum and Sierra (eds.), *Agent-mediated Electronic commerce: The European AgentLink Perspective*, LNAI 1991, Springer, pp. 126-147.

10. Esteva, M., de la Cruz, D., & Sierra, C. (2002). ISLANDER: an electronic institutions editor. In *The First International Joint Conference on Autonomous Agents and Multi-agent Systems (AAMAS 2002)*, ACM Press, pp. 1045-1052.

11. Esteva, M., Rodríguez-Aguilar, J. A., Rosell, B., & Arcos, J. L. (2004). AMELI: An Agent-based Middleware for Electronic Institutions. In N. Jennings, C. Sierra, L. Sonenberg, & M. Tambe (eds.), *The Third International Joint Conference on Autonomous Agents & Multi-agent Systems (AAMAS'04) – Volume 1*, New York: ACM, pp. 236-243.

12. Excelente-Toledo, C. B., Bourne, R. A., & Jennings, N. R. (2001). Reasoning about commitments and penalties for coordination between autonomous agents. In E. André, S. Sen, C. Frasson, & J. P. Müller (eds.), *Proceedings of the Fifth International Conference on Autonomous Agents*, New York: ACM, pp. 131-138.

13. Goodchild, A., Herring, C., & Milosevic, Z. (2000). Business Contracts for B2B. In H. Ludwig, Y. Hoffner, C. Bussler & M. Bichler (eds.), *Proceedings of the CAISE*00 Workshop on Infrastructure for Dynamic Business-to-Business Service Outsourcing (ISDO'00)*, CEUR Workshop Proceedings, pp. 63-74.

14. He, M., Jennings, N. R., & Leung, H. (2003). On agent-mediated electronic commerce. *IEEE Transactions on Knowledge and Data Engineering, 15*(4), 985-1003.

15. Hoffner, Y., Field, S., Grefen, P., & Ludwig, H. (2001). Contract-Driven Creation and Operation of Virtual Enterprises. In *Computer Networks, The International Journal of Computer and Telecommunications Networking*, volume 37, Elsevier North Holland, pp. 111-136.

16. Hviid, M. (2000), Long-Term Contracts and Relational Contracts. In B. Bouckaert and G. De Geest (eds.), *Encyclopedia of Law and Economics, Volume III: The Regulation of Contracts*, Cheltenham, Edward Elgar, pp. 46-72.

17. Kollingbaum, M. J. & Norman, T. J. (2002). Supervised Interaction – Creating a Web of Trust for Contracting Agents in Electronic Environments. In Castelfranchi and Johnson (eds.), In *The First International Joint Conference on Autonomous Agents and Multi-agent Systems (AAMAS 2002)*, ACM Press, pp. 272-279.

18. Lopez y Lopez, F., & Luck, M. (2003). Modelling Norms for Autonomous Agents. In E. Chavez, J. Favela, M. Mejia & A. Oliart (eds.) *Proceedings of the Fourth Mexican International Conference on Computer Science (ENC'03)*, IEEE Computer Society, pp. 238-245.

19. Neal, S., Cole, J., Linington, P. F., Milosevic, Z., Gibson, S., & Kulkarni, S. (2003). Identifying requirements for Business Contract Language: a Monitoring Perspective. In *Proceedings of the 7th International Enterprise Distributed Object Computing Conference (EDOC 2003)*, IEEE Computer Society, pp. 50-61.

20. Neto, A. (2002). Contrato de Consórcio e de Associação em Participação. In *Contratos Comerciais: Legislação, Doutrina e Jurisprudência*, Lisboa: Ediforum, ISBN: 972-8035-56-X, pp. 407-425.

21. Oliveira, E. & Rocha, A. P. (2000) Agents Advanced Features for Negotiation in Electronic Commerce and Virtual Organisations Formation Process. In F. Dignum & C. Sierra (eds.) *Agent Mediated Electronic Commerce: The European AgentLink Perspective*, LNAI 1991, Springer, pp. 78-97.

22. Quirchmayr, G., Milosevic, Z., Tagg, R., Cole, J., & Kulkarni, S. (2002). Establishment of Virtual Enterprise Contracts. In R. Cicchetti, A. Hameurlain, R. Traunmüller (eds.), *Database and Expert Systems Applications: 13th International Conference, DEXA 2002*, Springer, pp. 236-248.

23. Rocha, A. P. & Oliveira, E. (2001) Electronic Institutions as a framework for Agents' Negotiation and mutual Commitment. In P. Brazdil, A. Jorge (eds.), *Progress in Artificial Intelligence: Knowledge Extraction, Multi-agent Systems, Logic Programming, and Constraint Solving*, LNAI 2258, Springer, pp. 232-245.

24. Sallé, M. (2002). Electronic Contract Framework for Contractual Agents. In R. Cohen and B. Spencer (eds.), *Advances in Artificial Intelligence: 15th Conference of the Canadian Society for Computational Studies of Intelligence*, Springer, pp. 349-353.

25. Sandholm, T. W., & Lesser, V. R. (2001). Leveled Commitment Contracts and Strategic Breach. *Games and Economic Behavior, 35*, 212-270.

26. Vázquez-Salceda, J., Aldewereld, H., & Dignum, F. (2004). Implementing norms in multiagent systems. In G. Lindemann, J. Denzinger, I.J. Timm, & R. Unland (eds.) *Multagent System Technologies*, LNAI 3187, Springer, pp. 313-327.

27. von Wright, G. (1951). Deontic logic. *Mind, 60*, 1-15.

28. Weigand, H., Schoop, M., de Moor, A., & Dignum, F. (2003). B2B Negotiation Support: the need for a communication perspective. *Group Decision and Negotiation, 12*(1), 3-29.

Virtual Knowledge Communities for Corporate Knowledge Issues

Pierre Maret[1], Mark Hammond[2,3], and Jacques Calmet[3]

[1] INSA de Lyon, LIRIS (CNRS FRE 2672),
20, avenue Albert Einstein. F-69621 Villeurbanne, France
pierre.maret@insa-lyon.fr
[2] Department of Computing, Imperial College London,
180 Queen's Gate, SW7 2AZ, London, England
mrh00@doc.ic.ac.uk
[3] University of Karlsruhe, IAKS,
Am Fasanengarten 5, D-76131 Karlsruhe, Germany
calmet@ira.uka.de

Abstract. Corporate knowledge consists both of information that is available throughout a company and of information technology frameworks and paradigms. Considering an enterprise as a distributed computational paradigm, multi-agent systems can be proposed to address knowledge management issues within a company. We consider in this paper a new approach for corporate knowledge based on the agent oriented abstraction paradigm. This paradigm provides a high level of abstraction. We investigate here the concept of virtual knowledge communities, which is a convenient concept for addressing dynamical distributed knowledge management. It allows improved simulation and support for knowledge management processes, and therefore to innovate with new methods in this field. Our approach is well-suited for instance to filter the amount of knowledge that is transmitted throughout a company.

1 Introduction

Knowledge management (KM) is a critical issue within knowledge-intensive organizations [1]. Corporate knowledge consists of both information that is available throughout a company and of information technology frameworks and paradigms. Most approaches to knowledge management remain mainly founded on centralization and objectivity. They are generally based on the database paradigm. Examples of such systems are numerous. However centralization and objectivity appear incompatible with the very nature of knowledge. Bonifacio [2] criticizes most current knowledge management systems where "all perspectival aspects of knowledge should be eliminated in favor of an objective and general representation of knowledge". In [2] the authors propose a peer-to-peer architecture which emphasizes distributed knowledge management and knowledge nodes. Kornfeld [3] claimed years ago that diversity and concurrency of (scientific) communities are essential to their progress. We argue that approaches to knowledge

M.-P. Gleizes, A. Omicini, and F. Zambonelli (Eds.): ESAW 2004, LNAI 3451, pp. 33–44, 2005.

management must maintain compliance with the very nature of knowledge that is subjective, distributed and contextual.

Multiagent systems (MAS) have been introduced as a methodology to address distributed computing problems in artificial intelligence. They have evolved as a management methodology and a software engineering design principles leading to object-oriented-like systems. The main software agents developed in the KM area implement functionalities [4] such as extraction of knowledge from document bases [5, 6, 7], user's profile identification [5], and knowledge targeted diffusion [8, 9]. When adequately considering most of these tools, we observe that they solely cover single issues of corporate knowledge and that they do not propose a broad and generic view on corporate knowledge. Indeed, the level of abstraction remains mostly insufficient and the broad scope of available knowledge is not considered appropriately.

Considering an enterprise as a distributed computational paradigm, multi-agent systems can be proposed to address knowledge management issues within a company. Processes within the company tend to make agents produce and exchange knowledge with each other. This constitutes a key issue addressing the domain of agent societies. Examples of such systems are numerous (for instance [10], [11]) Within multi-agent societies, a balanced articulation must be found between organizational control and autonomous social behavior of agents. The works of Lesser concerning organizational design confront the organizational control and emergent organization [12]. Bradshaw proposes a framework to specify, manage and enforce agent behavior using DAML-based policies [13]. Exploring security issues inside open organizations, Omicini [14] calls for a systemic vision of MAS, explicitly accounting for social issues (social intelligence) as opposed to focusing on individual agent's intelligence. Calmet [15] proposed the liberal approach for agent communities, based on the work of Weber in sociology. Weber considers a society as the result of the actions of its actors. This liberal point of view has been taken to describe the Agent Oriented Abstraction [16] where agents are seen as made of two components: the knowledge component and a decision making system. The concept of knowledge management into a society of agents becomes fully meaningful in this context [17].

Among the various approaches to corporate knowledge, the one we adopt considers that corporate knowledge consists of i) the overall knowledge detained by agents and ii) the ability of agents to cooperate with each other for achieving their goals. Corporate knowledge encompasses then any piece of information available in an enterprise from the technology required to design and produce goods to management decision policy through human relations and internal or external communication. The decision mechanism encompasses (but is not limited to) the behavior of agents regarding domains of interests and knowledge exchanges.

In this paper we investigate the concept of virtual knowledge communities, which is a convenient concept for addressing dynamical distributed knowledge management. It is well-suited to filter the amount of knowledge that is transmitted throughout a company. The concept of community (of interest or of practice) is central in the knowledge management area. Examples are [18] and [19]. It seems that this concept has hardly been addressed in the framework of agent societies. We notice however that, like individuals and computer systems (and even internet nodes), agents are autonomous and heterogeneous. Moreover, relative to traditional approaches, agent-based modeling introduces openness and dynamicity, which is highly compatible with knowledge processes. Agent societies therefore constitute the right level of abstraction for modeling and engineering corporate knowledge systems which are complex articulated systems. The Agent Oriented Abstraction provides a high level of abstraction. E-business and enterprise-wide applications could therefore significantly gain from our approach for corporate knowledge. It allows improved simulation and support for knowledge management processes, and therefore allows innovation with new methods in this field.

This paper is organized as follow: section 2 introduces briefly key concepts for the management of knowledge of agents: ontology, knowledge clusters and instances. Then in section 3 we describe the concept of virtual knowledge community. Section 4 concerns the implementation of a Jade-based prototype system. Section 5 consists of a discussion and of some concluding remarks. We illustrate some of the concepts we do use with a purposely almost trivial example. A more significant example taken from corporate knowledge would not fit in the format of the paper.

2   Agents, Ontology and Knowledge

Agents are active objects with the ability to perceive, to reason and to act. In addition, it is assumed that agents have explicitly represented knowledge and communication ability [20]. For our purposes, we discuss hereafter three key notions used in our approach: ontology, knowledge cluster and knowledge instances.

The knowledge of an agent is represented in the vocabulary of an *ontology*. Agents are related to an ontology to talk and reason about things and facts. We consider a high-level ontology for frame-based description of knowledge. Knowledge is described in terms of Predicates, Concepts, Actions. This is compliant with the ACL-FIPA specifications. Attributes related to these terms are such as name, slots, arguments. We call an instance of the ontology a *knowledge cluster*. A knowledge cluster represents some structured knowledge. Basic operators on knowledge clusters can be defined, such as addition, filtering, search, is-sub-part-of, comparison. Knowledge clusters can be defined recursively. A knowledge cluster may be related to the overall knowledge of an agent, a specific task or to a given topic. A simple example of a knowledge cluster related to the domain of software maintenance is given hereafter (with a simplified syntax).

- Concept
  - name: Software
  - slots: Name-Software, Version

- Concept
  - name: Incident
  - slot: Description-Incident
- Concept
  - name: Location
  - slot: Description-Location
- Predicate
  - name: IncidentDecription
  - arguments: Software, Incident, Location

We call *knowledge instances* instances of objects defined into the knowledge clusters. An example of knowledge instances of an agent is given hereafter.

- Software : Jade("3.1")
- IncidentDescription : (Jade("3.1") , "System refuses to...", "While ...")

We assume that agent's knowledge consists of knowledge clusters and instances. Under this assumption, an agent's knowledge varies from agent to agent, which is fully compliant with individuals' knowledge. Moreover, while processing tasks, agents use, produce and acquire knowledge. Thus, knowledge can not be uniquely considered at design time (inherent knowledge). So, we assume that agent's knowledge evolves during the agent's life, thanks to individual activity and exchanges within the agent society. These assumptions are trivial regarding knowledge instances, but they are not trivial regarding knowledge clusters.

3   Virtual Knowledge Communities

We have defined corporate knowledge as the overall knowledge detained by agents within a system and their ability to cooperate with each other in order to achieve their goals. We introduce now the concept of a virtual knowledge community as a means for agents to share knowledge about a topic. The description hereafter aims at equipping agents with a layer through which they have the ability to act as members of knowledge communities. Agents are in charge of tasks within the society and they are provided with knowledge and decision mechanisms (agent oriented abstraction). Membership in a knowledge community does not replace the intrinsic goal of an agent for which it was introduced into the system. The concept of virtual knowledge community aims to increase the efficiency with which information is made available throughout an organization. This leads firstly to a more efficient achievement of the goals assigned to the agents, and secondly, provides a learning or data-mining mechanism. This mechanism can be proactive or reactive depending on the circumstances. Business activities such as e-business or virtual enterprises are usually dynamic processes. Thus, agents ought to be able to create, join, feed, mediate and use knowledge communities dynamically. Also, agents ought to increase their knowledge.

3.1   Modeling Virtual Knowledge Communities

A virtual knowledge community is composed of a topic, members and a space for exchanging messages. We previously described the knowledge of agents in terms of knowledge cluster and instances. Thus, the topic of a knowledge community is described similarly. Agents participating in a community are supposed to send and access messages related to the community topic. We assume that the locations of knowledge exchanges are message buffers where agents' contributions are posted and accessed. The content of messages is composed of a knowledge cluster and a set of knowledge instances.

3.2   Knowledge Community Processes

Agents' actions related to knowledge communities are the following: initiate and terminate a community, join a community and exchange knowledge. Community initiation can be done by any agent which becomes then the community leader. Initiation consists of creating a topic and a message buffer, and of advertising about the community. Advertising is not done through a specific shared feature (for instance the Federation Directory Service in the approch of [10]), which would introduce some centralization. Initiation is done thanks to a broadcast message that each agent of the system is able to send through the system it belongs to. Advertising consists then in broadcasting a community initiation cluster and a buffer reference dedicated to messages' exchanges related to this community. The community initiation cluster is necessary a sub-part of the initiator's cluster. It can also contain instances. An example is given hereafter, continuing the simple previous example:

- Concept
  - name: Software
  - slots: Name-Software, Version

Community termination consists of erasing the community message buffer created during initiation. An agent considers joining communities in receiving and in evaluating the initiation message and more specifically the posted knowledge clusters. An agent may be willing to join a community when the intersection between a community cluster and its own cluster is not empty. It sends then a so-called *join message* to the leader. A negotiation process is initiated with the community leader, which evaluates the candidate and the conflicts that may arise [21]. The role of the leader can be compared to the negotiator introduced in the approach described in [11].

Exchanging knowledge within a community consists of posting and accessing request and inform messages. They are sent to the community buffer and contain a knowledge cluster or instances. An example of an inform message related to the previous community cluster is given hereafter. In this example, the sender agent proposes specializations of the concept Software.

- Concept
  - superconcept: Software
  - name: Proprietary-software
  - slots: Price
- Concept
  - superconcept: Software
  - name : Open-source-software

3.3   Social Behavior as Agent's Knowledge

In an open and moving environment, it can not be assumed that agents use the same terms for the same real world objects. Also, it is not possible to believe that agents will succeed in exchanging knowledge without a *minimum semantic effort*. However this effort and this ability must remain controlled by the agent itself. Agent's autonomy is then preserved. We assume that this ability is itself knowledge. It can take any format in the framework of the knowledge cluster: reference to any accessible "normalized" clusters, implementation of an own matching table or function... Semantic interpretation of the content of any knowledge clusters is then left to the capabilities and features of each agent. It must be outlined that this approach is a design decision for our model. One could select a more generic approach, using for instance KOMET [22] where a mediator system extracts the relevant knowledge from agents in a semantically sound way. The following example illustrates the basic expression of two knowledge matching abilities. The predicate "convert-into" enables the agent to match "SW" with "Software". The action "Convert" expresses the ability for the agent to initiate conversion functions for clusters.

- Predicate
  - name: Convert-into
  - arguments: Software, SW
- Action
  - name: Convert
  - arguments: conversion-function, cluster-in, cluster-out

Regulation of the knowledge community is also a societal issue. Each agent may define policies specifying their behavior regarding knowledge communities: what are the circumstances in which they would choose create, delete, join a community, send and access knowledge. Of course, this policy can be different for every agent and a single agent may implement several policies. For instance, it can range from joining a community if a given cluster or a given instance appears into the community cluster, to joining a community when the intersection with the community cluster reaches a given percentage, etc. The initiator of a community can also perform regulation regarding the use of its community. This may prevent any inappropriate functioning due to (purposely or not) unfair agents. The implemented policy can be very liberal or it can filter or moderate contributions (considering for instance the message sender or the message content). Again, we assume that agent's potential behaviors are part of its knowledge.

The following example sketches behaviors of agents when joining a community. Instances of these behaviors follow. In the example, the agent "knows" three behaviors for deciding to join a community: when the concept "Software" is present into the community cluster, when the instance "Jade(3.1)" is present into the community cluster, or when the community cluster is covered by more than p% of the agent's cluster. One, both or none of the behaviors can be activated.

- Action
  - name: Join-on-cluster
  - arguments: Cluster
- Action
  - name: Join-on-knowledge-instance
  - arguments: Instance
- Action
  - name: Join-on-cluster-intersection-rate
  - arguments: value

- Knowledge instances
  - Join-on-cluster (concept(Software))
  - Join-on-knowledge-instance (Jade("3.1"))
  - Join-on-cluster-intersection-rate (p)

Exchanges in-between agents suppose the existence of communication mechanisms. Again, in an open and generic approach, it can not be considered that agents always use a same and unique communication mechanism. For instance, knowledge exchange within a community can be carried out in a negotiation or in a cooperation mode. Thus, we consider that communication mechanisms belongs to agent's knowledge. Each agent can then possess several communication mechanisms and it selects the appropriate one when creating or joining a community. We are aware that it is easy to argue that many of the implicit societal problems involved in this model could be better discussed. However, we set our approach in a well-defined model of agent society, as previously quoted, and any discussion is more relevant for [15] than for this paper.

4   Implementation of a Prototype System

4.1   Aims of the System

The aim of the prototype is to design and create a working system, in which agents with heterogeneous personal ontologies can create, destroy, leave and join communities in order to share knowledge clusters and instances with each other. Emphasis is on the sharing of knowledge, the creation of mappings between personal concepts and normalized concepts and on establish the mechanisms with which agents can dynamically move between communities and update their personal knowledge.

To summarize what is provided within the prototype we list the inputs to the system, the decisions a decision making system makes on the agents behalf and the results we observe. The prototype allows the creation of multiple agents on different machines, each with a given personal ontology, given personal knowledge instances, a set of given normalized ontologies and a set of mappings for each normalized ontology as inputs. Each one of the sets of mappings details any mappings an agent already has from its personal ontology predicates and concepts to the normalized ones. The agents are allowed to join and leave the system at any given time, in any given order. The agents are not hard-coded with any knowledge about existing communities to join (except for the global 'community of communities') or other agents to communicate with.

In light of the agent-oriented abstraction approach previously cited, agents are provided with a decision making system linked to their knowledge component. The decision making system is involved for instance when an agent creates a new community. Here it specifies which one of the normalized ontologies the agent should use to create this community. The decision making system is also involved whenever the agent encounters a new concept for which it does not already possess a mapping. Here the decision making consists in determining which concept, if any, to map to. Finally, the decision making system is involved when adding goals to an agent (for goal driven agents) or when choosing which part of its knowledge it should share (for altruistic agents). For all of these types of decisions, we implemented a human-based approach. An automated approach could be designed with no conceptual changes.

The results of the prototype system take the form of a user readable interactive output, showing the actions the agent is undertaking while it performs them. Thus, we can analyse the behavior of the agents. This is quite useful since the actions the agents make depend on other agents in the system as well as on themselves. This way, the actions decided by an agent may be non predictable in advance. We observe that agents can update their personal ontology, personal knowledge instances and personal mappings when appropriate.

4.2   System Implementation

JADE (Java Agent Development Framework), a Java based software development framework that fully conforms to FIPA standards for intelligent agents [23], was chosen to implement the prototype system. The most important aspect of JADE that makes it useful for the prototype system is its support for message passing and user defined ontologies. Agents are created by simply extending the `jade.core.Agent` class. This makes the development of different kinds of agents very straightforward.

Classes. The main class of our system is the `CommunityAgent` class. It is an abstract class that all different types of agents must extend. We propose two extensions of the `CommunityAgent`: the `IndividualAgent` and the `SocialAgent`. These two different types of agent have different behaviors. An individualistic agent instigates or joins a community because it needs knowledge from a certain domain, and will leave a community when it has got what it wants from the community or if it is not getting enough from it (e.g. it has been in the commu-

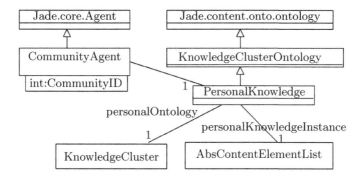

Fig. 1. Simplified class diagram (Unified Modeling Language formalism)

nity too long with no benefit). Its goals are chosen through its decision making mechanism, in the form of concepts that the agent wants to add to its knowledge. An individualistic leader will kill a community once it has completed the knowledge it requires. A *sociable agent* instigates a community purely because it has nothing else to do and for the good of all. The community will only die if everyone leaves the community. Sociable agents join every community that concern them (whose community cluster overlaps his own domain of knowledge) and never leave active communities where they may still be able to offer something. From a security point of view it is difficult to distinguish in this model between social agents and intruding passive agents. However, since JADE is not a secure platform as a forthcoming publication will show, this is not a crucial comment.

Each CommunityAgent has exactly one `PersonalKnowledge` object. The `PersonalKnowledge` class extends the `KnowledgeClusterOntology` class which represents an ontology that describes the classes of objects that make up knowledge clusters, namely concepts and predicates. One might say that the KnowledgeClusterOntology is a meta-ontology that describes knowledge clusters. The personal knowledge consists of both personal ontology (`KnowledgeCluster` class), and personal knowledge instances (`AbsContentElementList` class). The class diagram can be seen in Fig.1 where '1' means 'contains one attribute of class...'.

Agent Communications. Any communication in the system is done through message passing. Messages sent are of type `jade.lang.acl.ACLMessage`, `inform` or `request`. There are three types of *request* messages that can be sent by CommunityAgent's: `joinCommunity`, `readFromBuffer` (request to read from the community buffer) and `KnowledgeCluster` (an agent wishes to increase a cluster with both ontological and instance knowledge). There are four types of *inform* messages: *inform* content message containing a `knowledgeCluster` or `knowledge instances` that are being shared by an agent, `updateRole` (from leaders to members following an update of an agent's role), `leavingCommunity` and `communityDead`.

System run. Let us take the example of two agents (`Mark` and `Jose`), instances of the `IndividualAgent` class. They have different personal names for all the concepts in their ontology (for instance concepts *SW* and *Software*), but they have both a reference to the same normalized ontology. Jose already has the mappings from his personal concepts to the ones in the normalized ontology contained in his mapping file (*Program* stands for *SW*). Mark does not. Moreover, Jose has ontological knowledge that Mark does not have (*OpenSourceSoftware* is a *SW*). Jose has instances of this knowledge also (*JADE* is instance of *Open-SourceSoftware*). While performing the test run, we see that through knowledge communities and agent's goals, knowledge sharing takes place. Mark can gain both ontological knowledge, as well as instances, even though Jose's concepts are not included in the normalized ontology, and Mark and Jose have different names for all the terms they share in common. Agents can then dynamically collaborate, pool their knowledge and gain information, although they did not build it into their initial system.

5   Discussion and Conclusion

Considering an enterprise as a distributed computational paradigm, we proposed in this paper a generalization of corporate knowledge based on the agent paradigm. We used the Agent Oriented Abstraction paradigm, which has been proposed to describe the concept of agents in a fully generic way. It provides a high level of abstraction and considers that agents consist of knowledge and decision mechanisms. This abstraction mechanism leads to practical applications for corporate knowledge.

We described the concept of virtual knowledge community to model instances of corporate knowledge. This concept can be useful in real applications as well as in theoretical researches. The approach extends the field of knowledge management to societies of agents. Virtual knowledge communities constitute a nice framework for addressing and testing various aspects of corporate knowledge, especially knowledge modeling, autonomy of actors and exchange processes. Our work now provides the possibility to simulate and support knowledge management processes more appropriately and therefore to innovate with new methods in this field. Virtual knowledge communities also constitute a non trivial domain for applying and testing agents' key properties such as autonomy, heterogeneity, openness and dynamicity.

The virtual knowledge community concept enables agents to diffuse and to extend their knowledge within a society of agents. Knowledge is not limited to a specific "domain of interest", rather it is considered that knowledge owned by agents also comprises knowledge about communication mechanisms, heterogeneity resolution, and societal behavior. Knowledge exchanges are carried out within a set of agents concerned about a common topic. Exchanging knowledge instances is common and necessitates that the agents possess roughly the same knowledge structure. Thanks to the generalized approach of agent's knowledge, including knowledge matching ability in particular, agents have the ability to share knowledge structures while preserving autonomy. Future works will consider improving the structure and the modeling of agent's knowledge. The concept of knowledge annotations has been introduced in the agent oriented abstraction paradigm to structure the knowledge. However, support for such a paradigm can not be found in traditional agent platforms.

A societal issue is to define well adapted agent policies enabling the emergence of pertinent and fruitful knowledge exchanges. Society's organization may be impacted by the emergent organizations arising from knowledge societies. This is a well known issue in sociology and in human resource management. In this paper, we did not mention the security issue, which is also a societal issue. Since the system is open, it requires security policies to ensure only trustworthy agents can access the communities, and to prevent malicious attacks from untrustworthy agents. Work on this issue is in progress [24].

Practical applications of our approach are numerous. Agents can consist of intelligent knowledge assistants, as described in [25], [26], [23]. The interest of our approach compared to [23] is that we do not consider a unique description of the domain of interest of agents. The approach is also well suited to filter the amount of knowledge that is transmitted throughout a company. Indeed, knowledge broadcast is a high-relevance issue within companies. Another application concerns mobile systems. In this area, agents typically meet others ones that were not designed in coordination. Through knowledge communities, an agent could communicate with others to gain knowledge that is of common interest. In a traditional system, an analyst may need to redesign at least part of the existing system to accommodate this new source of knowledge.

References

1. Fisher, G., Ostwald, J.: Knowledge management: problems, promises, realities and challenges. Intelligent Systems **16** (2001) 60–72
2. Bonifacio, M., Bouquet, P., Mameli, G., Nori, M.: Peer-mediated distributed knowledge management. In: American Association for Artificial Intelligence Spring Symposium Technical Report SS-03-01, 1–8, ISBN 1-57735-078-9. (2003)
3. Kornfeld, W.A., Hewitt, C.: The scientific community metaphor. IEEE Transaction on systems, man and cybernetics **11** (1981) 24–33
4. van Elst, L., Dignum, V., Abecker, A.: Towards agent-mediated knowledge management. In: Agent-Mediated Knowledge Management. Volume 2926 of LNAI., Springer-Verlag (2003)
5. CoMMA: Available electronically at http://www.si.fr.atosorigin.com/sophia/comma/htm/homepage.htm (2004)
6. J.-R. Chen, S.R.W., Wragg, S.D.: A distributed multi-agent system for collaborative information management and sharing. In: Proc. of the 9th ACM International Conference on Information and Knowledge Management. (2000) 382–388
7. FRODO: Home page (2004) Available electronically at http://www.dfki.uni-kl.de/frodo/.
8. Campiello: Home page (2004) Available electronically at http://klee.cootech.disco.unimib.it/~campiello/.
9. Benjamin, V.R.: Skills management in knowledge-intensive organizations. In: Proc. of the EKAW 2002 International Conference. Volume 2473 of LNCS., Springer Verlag (2002) 80–95

10. Cenk-Erdur, R., Dikenelli, O., Seylan, I., Gurcan, O.: Semantically federating multi-agent organizations. In: Engineering Societies in the Agents World (ESAW'04), 20-22 October 2004. (2004)
11. Sibertin-Blanc, C., Hameurlain, N.: Participation components for holding roles in mas protocols. In: Engineering Societies in the Agents World (ESAW'04) 20-22 October 2004, Universit Paul Sabatier, Toulouse, France. (2004)
12. Sims, M., Goldman, C., Lesser, V.: Self-organization through bottom-up coalition formation. In: Proceedings of the second international joint conference on Autonomous agents and multiagent systems, Melbourne, Australia. ACM Press. (2003) 867–874
13. Bradshaw, J.: Representation and reasoning for DAML-based policy and domain services in kaos and nomads. In: Proceedings of the second international joint conference on Autonomous agents and multiagent systems, ACM Press (2003) 835–842
14. Omicini, A., Ricci, A.: Integrating organisation within a mas coordination infrastructure. In: Engineering Societies in the Agents World (ESAW'03), 29-31 October 2003, Imperial College, London, UK. (2003) 165–172
15. Calmet, J., Daemi, A., Endsuleit, R., Mie, T.: A liberal approach to openness in societies of agents. In: Engineering Societies in the Agents World (ESAW'03), London, UK, 29-31 October 2003. Volume 3071 of LNAI., Springer-Verlag (2003) 81–92
16. Calmet, J., Maret, P., Endsuleit, R.: Agent oriented abstraction. Royal Academy of Sciences Journal. Special Issue on Symbolic Computation in Logic and Artificial Intelligence **98** (2004)
17. Maret, P., Calmet, J.: Corporate knowledge in cyberworlds. IEICE Transaction on Information and Systems. Special Issue on Cyberworlds (2005)
18. Bonifacio, M., Bouquet, P., Cuel, R.: Knowledge nodes: the building blocks of a distributed approach to knowledge management. Journal of Universal Computer Science **8** (2002) 652–661
19. Gordon, M., Fan, W., Rafaeli, S., Wu, H., Farag, N.: The architecture of comm-knowledge. combining link structure and user actions to support an online community. Int. J. Electronic Business **1** (2003) 69–82
20. Weiss: Multi-agent Systems. MIT Press (1999)
21. Munroe, S., Luck, M.: Motivation-based selection of negotiation partners. In: Engineering Societies in the Agents World (ESAW'04) 20-22 October 2004, Universit Paul Sabatier, Toulouse, France. (2004)
22. Jacques Calmet, Sebastian Jekutsch, P.K., Schü, J.: KOMET – a system for the integration of heterogeneous information sources. In: International Symposium on Methodologies for Intelligent Systems. Volume 1325 of LNAI., Springer-Verlag (1997) 318–327
23. FIPA: Personal assistant specification (2004) Available electronically at http://www.fipa.org/specs/fipa00083/XC00083B.html.
24. Endsuleit, R., Mie, T.: Secure multi-agents computations. In: Proceedings of International Conference on Security and Management (CSREA) , Las Vegas. (2003)
25. Ford, K.M., Glymour, C., Hayes, P.: Cognitive prostheses. AI Magazine **18** (1997)
26. Hoffman, R.R., Ford, K.M., Hayes, P.J., Bradshaw, J.M.: The Borg hypothesis. Intelligent Systems **18** (2003) 73–75

Achieving Competence by Argumentation on Rules for Roles

Ioan Alfred Letia[1] and Monica Acalovschi[2]

[1] Technical University of Cluj-Napoca,
Department of Computer Science,
Baritiu 28, RO-3400 Cluj-Napoca, Romania
`letia@cs-gw.utcluj.ro`
[2] University of Medicine and Pharmacy Iuliu Hatieganu,
Third Medical Clinic,
RO-3400 Cluj-Napoca, Romania
`monacal@umfcluj.ro`

Abstract. We consider the deep venous thrombosis (DVT) as case study for the specification and implementation of a multi-agent system. The DVT is an application with low clinical accuracy, needing objective tests, some of them satisfactorily accurate in experienced hands and others more definite but invasive. Whether one or more decision makers are involved in this activity is a matter of context, but the main events are decided by a process that has in itself some forms of argumentation. Our approach is an argumentative multi-agent system specified by rules capturing various roles in the diagnosis activity. Although the DVT scenario is a real one, more aspects of health care than the ones presented in this paper can conveniently be accommodated in this framework by extending the set of roles and refining the set of rules.

1 Introduction

There are many situations in the medical setting when conflicts of opinion may appear between different care providers, each judging the situation based on its own knowledge and duty. Consider the case of a patient that has just been diagnosed; there are several possible treatments given the diagnosis and a choice must be made among those treatments. Different care providers may have different opinions about the optimal treatment based on their role and expertise. Still, a decision has to be made based on their possible contrary opinions. Another point of divergence between medical professionals may be the investigations that are more appropriate to perform for establishing a diagnosis. Some investigations are cheaper, while others may be less harmful to the patient.

Although sometimes it is possible to make decisions in diagnosis taking into account just the information available [1], in the cases considered above several roles are involved in the medical decision process, a choice having to be made between the possible conflicting opinions of each role. Additional information may be needed for making that choice, due to the multiple options available.

M.-P. Gleizes, A. Omicini, and F. Zambonelli (Eds.): ESAW 2004, LNAI 3451, pp. 45–59, 2005.

Automated monitoring of medical protocols has been already tackled with a multi-agent system [2], using a negotiation process to mediate between multiple medical protocols, where role refers to a particular service that can be played by a staff person. A multi-agent environment to support training of diagnostic reasoning and modeling of domains with complex and uncertain knowledge [3] uses Bayesian networks to offer physicians probabilistic reasoning.

The framework described in this paper aims to help automate/model the decision making between different roles that are involved in the medical care process by making use of the knowledge base of each role and also by additional knowledge needed to solve conflicts of opinion between roles. Recent work [4, 5] is used to develop a more flexible methodology required by realistic applications in the health providing activity. The particular contributions of this paper are threefold: first, we provide a realistic motivating scenario which is quite pervasive in the health providing world; second, we show how a role specified by rules can be combined with one based on experience; third, we show how experience made public in the Web Ontology Language is used in the argumentation process.

The paper is organized as follows. Next the basic argumentation framework [4, 5] is summarily presented. Then the DVT scenario is explained in terms of rules used by the physicians [6] and results obtained from a controlled trial [7]. Two roles extracted from [6, 7] are then derived as *AIM98Agent* and *NEJM03Agent*, and their interaction by argumentation is portrayed. After a brief description of the implementation and related work some conclusions are drawn.

2   Basic Argumentation Framework

We are using the reasoning in an argumentative manner provided by Gorgias[1] [4, 5], to determine the case in a certain context. Following the example found in the Gorgias package on the agent wanting to find out if its security interest in a certain ship (i) is perfected (c), it currently has possession (p) of the ship, and according to the "Uniform Commercial Code" (u) a security interest in goods may be perfected. According to the federal law "Ship Mortgage Act" (m) a security interest in a ship may only be perfected by filing a financing statement (e). These are the rules used to determine whether the security interest is perfected or not.

$$Rules = \begin{cases} u : c \leftarrow p \\ m : \neg c \leftarrow i, \neg e \end{cases}$$

In this example, other facts are: a statement has not been filed ($\neg e$), the "Uniform Commercial Code" (u) is newer than the "Ship Mortgage Act" (m), with the later a federal act, and the former a state act.

---

[1] http://www.cs.ac.cy/~nkd/gorgias

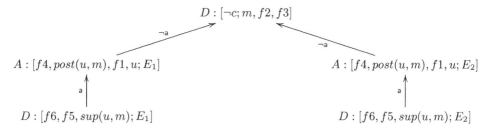

Fig. 1. Defender/attacker argumentation tree

$$Facts = \begin{cases} f1 : p \\ f2 : i \\ f3 : \neg e \\ f4 : n(u,m) \\ f5 : f(m) \\ f6 : s(u) \end{cases}$$

There are two principles expressing contexts: one is the "Lex Posterior", which gives precedence to newer laws (u is newer than m), and the other is the "Lex Superior", which gives precedence to laws supported by the higher authority (m has higher authority since it is a federal law).

$$Contexts = \begin{cases} post(X,Y) : X \prec Y \leftarrow n(X,Y) \\ sup(X,Y) : Y \prec X \leftarrow s(X), f(Y) \\ cpr : sup(X,Y) \prec post(X,Y) \end{cases}$$

The proof tree for $[\neg c]$ is shown in the figure 1, where a node is marked with D for defendant or A for attacker. The two extensions used are $E_1=\{f2, f3, m\}$ and $E_1=\{f2, f3, f5, f6, sup(u,m)\}$.

3   Deep Venous Thrombosis Scenario

Deep venous thrombosis (DVT) could be defined as the presence of an occlusive thrombus (clot) within a deep vein, impairing the normal blood flow. Deep venous thromboses occur most commonly in the lower extremities, and half cause pulmonary emboli (the most severe complication of DVT) in the absence of treatment. A familial or a personal history of prior DVT and the hypercoagulation states: antithrombin III deficiency, antiphospholipidic syndrome, polycytaemia vera, thrombocytemia, . . . are major *predisposing risk factors*. Patients particularly prone to the development of DVT are also those who are seriously ill and have been at bed rest for prolonged periods. Some of the patients who are at highest risk are those who have congestive heart failure, stroke, recent myocardial infarction, malignancies, pelvic /abdominal surgery, especially orthopedic procedures, trauma - particularly with prolonged immobilization. In addition, persons more than 60 years old have an increased incidence of DVT, as do obese persons, patients with varicose veins, users of contraceptives or high-dose estrogen therapy. Pregnancy and the period following childbirth favor DVT. Long journeys, venous compression, venous catheter insertion or injections might favor DVT in the presence of other risk factors.

Episodes of DVT are often *clinically* silent, therefore a high level of suspicion is necessary. Pretest assessment of the probability of DVT is useful (i.e. evaluation of predisposing factors or conditions) when deciding the investigations required to establish diagnosis. History and physical examination are neither sensitive nor specific for diagnosis. The presence of symptoms or signs as pain or edema is not sufficient for diagnosis and implies the need for objective diagnostic testing. The objective testing is crucial, because undiagnosed DVT can cause fatal pulmonary embolism, and because of DVT therapy is effective, but its inappropriate use should be avoided. Clinical suspicion may dictate the speed and type of evaluation.

Among the *objective tests*, the serum level of D-dimers (established by ELISA) has a high sensitivity (>95%), a lower specificity and a high negative predictive value. A positive test makes DVT probable, but requires further evaluation; a negative test excludes with high probability DVT. Venous ultrasonography, combined with Doppler, is satisfactorily accurate in experienced hands, readily available, non-invasive and repeatable. Impedance plethysmography is non-invasive, safe, but useful especially for diagnosing proximal DVT in symptomatic patients. Its performances are increased when associated with other noninvasive tests. Contrast venography is the reference ("gold") standard for the diagnosis of DVT, being the most definitive diagnostic test, but it is an invasive examination, associated with risks for the patient and high technical demands and costs. Therefore, investigation using non-invasive ultrasound techniques in combination with the D-dimer test is often regarded as sufficient in symptomatic patients with suspected DVT.

3.1   Rules for Diagnosis

The findings that are diagnostic of DVT (see [6]) can be expressed by the rules shown in the figure 2 (with a rule of grade A stronger than one of grade B and one of grade B stronger than one of grade C). The first two rules say that

$$diagDVT(grA) \leftarrow ultrasonography(commonFemoral) \lor ultrasonography(popliteal)$$
$$diagDVT(grB) \leftarrow ultrasonography(superficialFemoral)$$
$$\lor ultrasonography(distalPopliteal) \lor ultrasonography(deepCalf)$$
$$diagDVT(grA) \leftarrow plethysmography(abnormal), clinical(high)$$
$$diagDVT(grB) \leftarrow plethysmography(abnormal), (clinical(moderate) \lor clinical(low))$$
$$diagDVT(grA) \leftarrow venography(defect)$$
$$diagDVT(grC) \leftarrow venography(suggestive)$$

Fig. 2. Rules that are diagnostic of DVT

$exclDVT(grA) \leftarrow venography(normal)$
$exclDVT(grA) \leftarrow ultrasonography(normal), clinical(low)$
$exclDVT(grC) \leftarrow ultrasonography(normal), dDimer(normal)$
$exclDVT(grB) \leftarrow plethysmography(normal), dDimer(normal)$

Fig. 3. Rules that exclude DVT

$venography \leftarrow ultrasonography(superficialFemoral)$
$\qquad \vee\ ultrasonography(distalPopliteal) \vee\ ultrasonography(deepCalf)$
$ultrasonography \leftarrow plethysmography(abnormal), (clinical(moderate) \vee clinical(low))$
$venography \leftarrow plethysmography(abnormal), (clinical(moderate) \vee clinical(low))$
$ultrasonography \leftarrow venography(suggestive)$
$plethysmography \leftarrow venography(suggestive)$
$clinical \leftarrow venography(suggestive)$

Fig. 4. Rules recommending examinations

venous ultrasonography shows DVT in the case of non-compressibility of the common femoral vein or popliteal vein (grade A), while non-compressibility that is confined to the superficial femoral vein, the distal portion of the popliteal vein, or the deep veins of the calf is associated with a lower predictive value (grade B). The following two rules express that impedance plethysmography shows DVT in the case of an abnormal result and a high clinical suspicion of deep venous thrombosis (grade A), while an abnormal result of impedance plethysmography combined with a moderate or low clinical suspicion of DVT has lower predictive value (grade B). The last two rules on venography say that an intraluminal filling defect seen in more than one view are diagnostic of DVT (grade A), while onfilling of the deep veins despite repeated injection of contrast, are just highly suggestive of DVT (grade C).

Findings of the group of experts that exclude DVT (see [6]) include the rules shown in the figure 3. The first rule says that a normal result of venography excludes DVT (grade A). A normal ultrasonography and (i) low clinical suspicion of DVT (grade A) or (ii) a normal result on a D-dimer assay (grade C) are shown by the following two rules to exclude DVT. A normal result on impedance plethysmography and a D-dimer assay (grade B) exclude DVT as shown by the last rule.

The recommendations for the diagnosis of DVT (see [6]) also include the rules for investigations shown in the figure 4. Non-compressibility that is confined to the superficial femoral vein, the distal portion of the popliteal vein, or the deep veins of the calf should be evaluated with venography (first rule). An abnormal result of impedance plethysmography combined with a moderate or low clinical suspicion of deep venous thrombosis should be evaluated with venous ultrasonography or venography (second and third rule). Nonfilling of the deep veins despite repeated injection of contrast (highly suggestive of DVT), must be interpreted in the light of clinical presentation and other investigations, such as results of impedance plethysmography or venous ultrasonography (the last three rules).

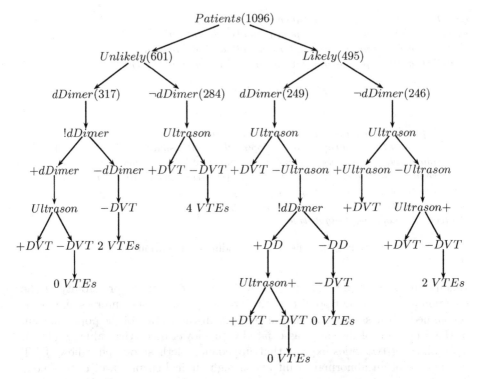

Fig. 5. Patient outcomes in the evaluation trial

3.2   Controlled Trials

An evaluation of D-dimer in the diagnosis of suspected DVT [7] has concluded that DVT can be ruled out in a patient who is judged clinically unlikely to have DVT and who has a negative D-dimer test, and therefore ultrasound testing can be safely omitted in such patients.

The results of this controlled trial are shown in the figure 5 (see [7]). All patients were first evaluated using a clinical model and divided into two groups considered (clinically) unlikely or likely to have DVT. They were then randomly assigned either to undergo ultrasound imaging alone (control group) or to undergo D-dimer testing. Those in the later group then underwent ultrasound imaging (Ultrason) if they had been judged clinically likely to have DVT or if they were judged clinically unlikely but the D-dimer test (!DD) was positive (+DD).

The primary outcome of this evaluation was the development of a venous thrombo-embolic event (VTE) in patients in whom DVT had initially been ruled out. They offer histories for re-evaluating the diagnosis model or, as we consider here, knowledge for an evaluation agent that can also provide cues for argumentation to the diagnosing agent. For example, we can see that there were two patients judged clinically unlikely who, with a negative D-dimer test (–DD), DVT was ruled out (–DVT) but still developed a venous thrombo-embolic event (2 VTE). For the patients judged clinically likely a second ultrasound imaging

(Ultrason+) was performed after one week, which helped to reduce risk in the group with the D-dimer test.

4   Argumentation with Rules for Roles

The diagnosis process takes place on a time line and can be visualized as in the figure 6. In the state s_i the agents know the history H of the diagnosis process

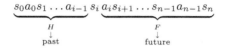

Fig. 6. Course of action

for the patient and have to decide about the future F, the remaining course of actions so that the proper conclusion is reached. That means that the patient will finally be diagnosed either as +DVT and the corresponding treatment will be applied or –DVT and no VTE event should occur in a reasonable period (three months in the controlled trial).

A state of a patient is represented by the results of the investigative actions. For example, $\{-c_0, +d_1, -u_2\}$ shows the state of the patients judged clinically unlikely with a positive D-dimer test and a negative ultrasonography investigation, which should have been ruled out for DVT. The patients with the state $\{+c_0, -u_1, -u_2\}$ have been ruled out for DVT in the evaluation but two of them have developed VTE (see figure 5).

4.1   The AIM98Agent Role [6]

The set of preferences over actions in the DVT scenario, regardless of context, is $\{c \prec v, c \prec u, c \prec p, c \prec d, u \prec v, p \prec v, d \prec v, d \prec u\}$, that is *clinical* examination is preferred to *venography*, . . ., D-dimer is preferred to *ultrasonography*. The preferences on diagnostic rules are:

$$gr_0 : d(A) \prec d(B) \tag{1}$$

$$gr_1 : d(A) \prec d(C) \tag{2}$$

$$gr_2 : d(B) \prec d(C) \tag{3}$$

Our rules that are diagnostic of DVT in the state s_i are transformed from the diagnostic rules of the group of experts discussed previously and shown in the figure 2.

$$d_0 : dvt(A) \leftarrow u(cF) \in s_i \vee u(p) \in s_i \tag{4}$$

$$d_1 : dvt(B) \leftarrow u(sF) \in s_i \vee u(dP) \in s_i \vee u(dC) \in s_i \tag{5}$$

$$d_2 : dvt(A) \leftarrow p(a) \in s_i \wedge c(h) \in s_i \tag{6}$$

$$d_3 : dvt(B) \leftarrow p(a) \in s_i \wedge (c(m) \in s_i \vee c(l) \in s_i) \tag{7}$$

$$d_4 : dvt(A) \leftarrow v(d) \in s_i \tag{8}$$

$$d_5 : dvt(C) \leftarrow v(s) \in s_i \tag{9}$$

while those that exclude DVT are the transformation of the the rules of experts shown in the figure 3.

$$e_0 : \neg dvt(A) \leftarrow v(n) \in s_i \wedge c(l) \in s_i \tag{10}$$

$$e_1 : \neg dvt(C) \leftarrow dd(n) \in s_i \tag{11}$$

$$e_2 : \neg dvt(A) \leftarrow p(n) \in s_i \wedge dd(n) \in s_i \tag{12}$$

The rules recommending an action a_i are in the state s_i include the rules for investigations recommended by experts and shown in the figure 4.

$$a_0 : v(A) \leftarrow u(sF) \in s_i \vee u(dP) \in s_i \vee u(dC) \in s_i \tag{13}$$

$$a_1 : u(B) \leftarrow p(a) \in s_i \wedge (c(m) \in s_i \vee c(l) \in s_i) \tag{14}$$

$$a_2 : v(A) \leftarrow p(a) \in s_i \wedge (c(m) \in s_i \vee c(l) \in s_i) \tag{15}$$

$$a_3 : u(B) \leftarrow v(s) \in s_i \tag{16}$$

$$a_4 : p(A) \leftarrow v(s) \in s_i \tag{17}$$

$$a_5 : c(C) \leftarrow v(s) \in s_i \tag{18}$$

If preferable, we can use rules showing preferences over actions in a given context,

$$c_0 : u \prec v \leftarrow p(a) \in s_i \wedge (c(m) \in s_i \vee c(l) \in s_i) \tag{19}$$

$$c_1 : d \prec u \leftarrow v(s) \in s_i \tag{20}$$

that is ultrasonography is preferred to venography when plethysmography is abnormal and clinical assessment is medium or low, and D-dimer is preferred to ultrasonography when venography is suggestive.

4.2   The NEJM03Agent Role [7]

We use the Web Ontology Language (OWL)[2] to represent ontologies, developed and accessed in the SWI Prolog tool Triple. For instance, an excerpt of the OWL representation of the patient outcomes in the evaluation trial (figure 5) are shown in the figure 7. The rules are also made available to various agents, when public, in OWL with a proper encoding.

An NEJM03Agent has access to the controlled trial histories and is capable to extract a history like

$$\underbrace{\{c(l)_0\}}_{s_0} \underbrace{u_1}_{a_1} \underbrace{\{c(l)_0, u(n)_1\}}_{s_1} \underbrace{\neg dvt}_{a_2} \underbrace{\{c(l)_0, u(n)_1, \neg dvt\}}_{s_2} \underbrace{w}_{a_3} \underbrace{\{c(l)_0, u(n)_1, \neg dvt, VTE\}}_{s_3}$$

---

[2] http://www.w3.org/TR/2004/REC-owl-ref-20040210/

```
<?xml version='1.0' encoding='ISO-8859-1'?>
<!DOCTYPE rdf:RDF [
<!ENTITY owl 'http://www.w3.org/2002/07/owl#'>
<!ENTITY rdf 'http://www.w3.org/1999/02/22-rdf-syntax-ns#'>
<!ENTITY rdfs 'http://www.w3.org/2000/01/rdf-schema#'>
<!ENTITY t20 'http://www.swi-prolog.org/packages/Triple20/'>
<!ENTITY xsd 'http://www.w3.org/2001/XMLSchema#'>
]>
<rdf:RDF
    xmlns:owl="&owl;"
    xmlns:rdf="&rdf;"
    xmlns:rdfs="&rdfs;"
    xmlns:t20="&t20;"
    xmlns:xsd="&xsd;"
>
<owl:DatatypeProperty rdf:about="&t20;nrPatients">
  <rdfs:domain rdf:resource="&t20;Patients"/>
  <rdfs:range rdf:resource="&xsd;positiveInteger"/>
</owl:DatatypeProperty>
<owl:ObjectProperty rdf:about="&t20;testValueDDimer">
 <rdf:type rdf:resource="&owl;FunctionalProperty" />
  <rdfs:domain rdf:resource="&t20;Patients"/>
  <rdfs:range rdf:resource="&t20;DResult"/>
</owl:ObjectProperty>
<owl:ObjectProperty rdf:about="&t20;hasDVT">
 <rdf:type rdf:resource="&owl;FunctionalProperty" />
  <rdfs:domain rdf:resource="&t20;Patients"/>
  <rdfs:range rdf:resource="&t20;DResult"/>
</owl:ObjectProperty>
```

Fig. 7. Excerpt of the evaluation trial in OWL

showing that out of 601 patients found clinically unlikely to have VDT after a normal ultrasonography test on 284 of them the decision (action) has been made that they do not have VDT. But still, after a period of waiting, four of them have developed VTEs.

Another path this agent can extract from the tree of the controlled trial is

$$\underbrace{\{c(h)_0\}}_{s_0} \underbrace{u_1}_{a_1} \underbrace{\{c(h)_0, u(n)_1\}}_{s_1} \underbrace{w(1)_2}_{a_2} \underbrace{\{c(h)_0, u(n)_1, w(1)_2\}}_{s_2} \underbrace{u_3}_{a_3} \underbrace{\{c(h)_0, u(n)_1, w(1)_2, u(n)_3\}}_{s_3}$$

$$\underbrace{\{c(h)_0, u(n)_1, w(1)_2, u(n)_3\}}_{s_3} \underbrace{\neg dvt}_{a_4} \underbrace{\{c(h)_0, u(n)_1, \neg dvt\}}_{s_4} \underbrace{w}_{a_5} \underbrace{\{c(h)_0, u(n)_1, \neg dvt, VTE\}}_{s_5}$$

showing that out of 495 patients found clinically likely to have VDT after two normal ultrasonography consecutive tests on 246 the decision has been made that they do not have VDT. After a period of waiting, two of them have developed

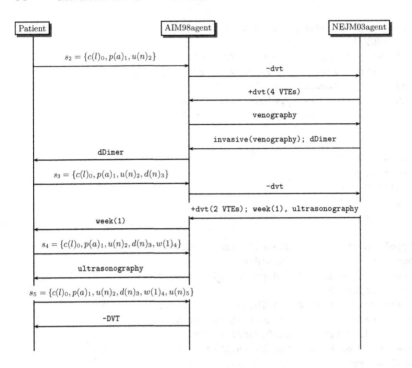

Fig. 8. Sequence diagram illustrating argumentation

VTEs. These histories are exploited by the NEJM03Agent to argue on whether a course of action might be successful or not to attain the goal of either diagnosing the patient as having DVT (to be treated) or not, but without incurring the risk of a VTE.

4.3   Argumentation on DVT Diagnosis

Let us consider the case of a patient judged clinically low to which a plethysmography test revealed abnormality, while the ultrasonography has shown a normal case as shown in the figure 8. The AIM98Agent is tempted to decide no DVT, but to make sure is requesting the NEJM03Agent's opinion about it. The NEJM03Agent retrieves from its OWL controlled trial history four such cases that have later developed VTEs, and therefore cannot accept this decision. The AIM98Agent proposes venography, but then NEJM03Agent replies that it is invasive and proposes instead d-Dimer, to which AIM98Agent agrees. The tree showing this process of argumentation is depicted in the figure 9.

Now in situation s_3, the AIM98Agent decides no DVT, letting NEJM03Agent know about the new proposal. Again, NEJM03 disagrees, this time mentioning two such cases in its historical representation of the controlled trial, and proposing instead ultrasonography after one week. The AIM98Agent agrees and

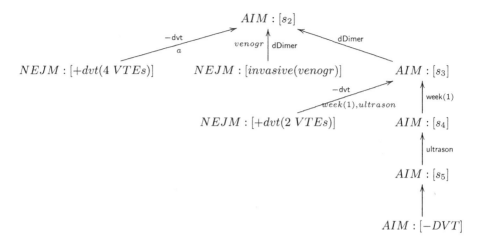

Fig. 9. Sample argumentation tree between the AIM98Agent and the NEJM03Agent

requests the patient to come back after one week and have ultrasonography. On the new state s_5 it decides that the patient does not have DVT.

5   Implementation

The current implementation of the system is in the Open Agent Architecture (OAA)[3]. For each user agent a solvable is defined which is called by the coordinator agent whenever a new reasoning step is performed. The AIM98Agent and the NEJM03Agent are implemented as user agents, defined via solvables through which the coordinator agent can announce them of the opportunity to perform an action or of a decision that has been taken that concerns them.

Other rules are introduced in the system that express the common sense reasoning, which is not expressed in the rules (4 - 18) extracted from the experts in the domain. For instance, rule (21) says that we prefer rule a_2 to rule a_1 when the current course of action is over a certain length k.

$$c_2 : a_2 \prec a_1 \leftarrow i > k \tag{21}$$

The rules for the protocol are similar to the ones in [8], in order to provide more flexibility to the interaction between the agents involved in argumentation.

$$p_0 : tell(Y, X, accept, D) \leftarrow tell(X, Y, propose, D) \wedge \neg counterArg(Y, D) \tag{22}$$
$$p_1 : tell(Y, X, reject, D, D1) \leftarrow tell(X, Y, propose, D) \wedge counterArg(Y, D, D1) \tag{23}$$

Here, p_0 states the accepting alternative, when agent Y has no counterargument to the proposal D of X. The rule p_1 is used by Y when it does not agree with

---

[3] http://www.ai.sri.com/~oaa/

the proposal D of X and shows its counterargument and, eventually, another alternative for action in $D1$.

These rules allow more refinement, particularly important when the agents performing the diagnosis have to face various patients with quite different health history. We also did not consider here the asymptomatic or the recurrent version of DVT [6], which require a more complex dialog between the AIM98 and NEJM03 agents.

6   Related Work

The system for the assistance and supervision of the real-time application of medical protocols presented in [2] is based on the specification by medical protocols of possible sequences of composite, concurrent and repeated actions. In this system the roles specify particular services and medical protocols specify possible interactions between medical services. It is suggested that it can be used to manage both medical guidelines and medical protocols. Our proposal of roles offers more flexibility, in the sense that the behavior of the agents is specified by medical rules and other rules that take into account the context.

The AMPLIA multi-agent intelligent learning environment [3] is designed to support training of diagnostic reasoning and modeling of domains with complex and uncertain knowledge. The system deals with uncertainty using Bayesian networks. Used in the training of medical students, the qualitative and quantitative model built by the learning student is compared with the one provided by a domain expert. The interaction between the domain agent and the learner agent is performed according to an interaction protocol. While our system can be further developed to allow medical students to learn the process of diagnosis, the representation of medical knowledge by rules seems to be more acceptable to human agents and therefore our alternative would provide a significant advantage.

The integration of medical services [11] aims to ease the communication and provide meaningful transformation among distributed and heterogeneous applications. An intelligent broker transforms a client request of a valid high level service into several elementary steps. For each step a specific agent is used to realize the operation configured in the step. The mapping among different vocabularies is done by a semantic component using XML as the interchange format. Our framework has the capability to cover both the contexts that appear in such an application and the communication in OWL which is defined on top of XML may accept a shared ontology or even several ontologies.

The argumentation framework based on the language $\mathcal{E}$ [9] uses a basic ontology of actions, fluents and time-points inspired by the event calculus. We intend to further develop our system to take advantage of the benefits offered by the event calculus.

The PARMA protocol [10] permits argument over proposals for actions, enabling participants to rationally propose, attack, and defend, an action or course of actions. The basic protocol in our system can easily be developed to cover more complex interactions between agents.

A conversation moderator [12] has been devised to guarantee that the shared objectives in the conversation between participants will be observed. The solution of dissociating the *strategic* dimension from the *tactical* dimension in the application of protocol rules has the benefit of defining the role of the conversing agent (concerning strategy) and the role of the moderator (concerning tactics). This line seems to be very convenient to be pursued in the development of our system.

7   Conclusions

Our prototype implementation of argumentation has shown the convenience to extend the scenario of DVT with symptoms caused by different diseases. Thus, given a patient which presents a set of symptoms different specialists with different areas of expertise may draw different conclusions about the disease the patient is suffering of. Controversies may also appear in the medical setting between the medical staff and the administrative personnel. For example, while the main concern of a physician is the healthy state of the patient, the administrative personnel is more concerned with available resources.

Although work on argumentation in negotiation [13] seems to be quite advanced, the roles imposed in some activities in the applications that we envisaged require more cooperation, even if argumentation is a significant instrument in such contexts. In this respect the approach considered in this paper, with application to the health providing service, but also other services, is more in line with the fault-tolerant multi-agent systems by assigning missing roles [14], as the main objective is the quality of the service provided to customers. Viewed as a collective human work activity, a future evaluation of our framework will consider performance through the coordination enabled by the activity theory [15].

Since our main goal is in advising human agents in their decisions on acting in the real world our next step in this line of research will be on how argumentation on the acts could be further refined to better capture their effects on agents' objectives [16]. Ideas of the domino agent model and the PROforma language will be considered for representation in a future development of our argumentation scheme [17]. We are also interested in finding out how electronic institutions [18] can contribute to better model/automate argumentation processes in more realistic applications. To enable comparison with well known and deployed architectures like dMARS we will also develop a specification using the Z notation [19].

Acknowledgments

We are grateful for the comments of reviewers who helped us to improve the paper. Part of this work has been supported by a grant 423-33531 from the National Research Council of the Romanian Ministry for Education and Research. We would also like to acknowledge the contribution of Cristina Feier, Raluca Vartic, Anca Chioran and Robert Baban to the implementation of the current prototype.

References

1. Acalovschi, M., Blendea, D., Feier, C., Letia, I.A., Dumitrascu, D., Veres, A.: Risk factors for symptomatic gallstones in patients with liver cirrhosis: a case control study. American Journal of Gastroenterology **98** (2003) 1856–1860
2. Alsinet, T., Ansotegui, C., Bejar, R., Fernandez, C., Manya, F.: Automated monitoring of medical protocols: a secure and distributed architecture. Artificial Intelligence in Medicine **27** (2003) 367–392
3. Vicari, R.M., Flores, C.D., Silvestre, A.M., Seixas, L.J., Ladeira, M., Coelho, H.: A multi-agent intelligent environment for medical knowledge. Artificial Intelligence in Medicine **27** (2003) 335–366
4. Kakas, A., Moraitis, P.: Argumentation based decision making for autonomous agents. In Rosenchein, J., Wooldridge, M., Sandholm, T., Yokoo, M., eds.: Second International Joint Conference on Autonomous Agents and Multiagent Systems, Melbourne, Australia (2003) 883–890
5. Kakas, A., Moraitis, P.: Argumentative agent deliberation, roles and context. Electronic Notes in Theoretical Computer Science **70** (2002)
6. Kearon, C., Julian, J.A., Newman, T.E., Ginsberg, J.S.: Noninvasive diagnosis of deep venous thrombosis. Annals of Internal Medicine **128** (1998) 663–677
7. Wells, P.S., Anderson, D.A., Rodger, M., Forgie, M., Kearon, C., Dreyer, J., Kovacs, G., Mitchell, M., Lewandowski, B.: Evaluation of D-dimer in the diagnosis of suspected deep-vein thrombosis. The New England Journal of Medicine **349** (2003) 1227–35
8. Endriss, U., Maudet, N., Sadri, F., Toni, F.: Logic-based agent communication protocols. In Dignum, F., ed.: Advances in Agent Communication. LNAI 2922. Springer-Verlag (2004) 91–107
9. Kakas, A., Miller, R., Toni, F.: An argumentation framework for reasoning about actions and change. In Gelfond, M., Leone, N., Pfeifer, G., eds.: International Conference on Logic Programming and Nonmonotonic Reasoning. LNCS 1730, Springer-Verlag (1999) 78–91
10. Atkinson, K., Bench-Capon, T., McBurney, P.: A dialogue game protocol for multi-agent argument over proposal for action. In: 1st International Workshop on Argumentation in Multi-Agent Systems, New York, NY, USA (2004)
11. Xu, Y., Sauquet, D., Degoulet, P., Jaulent, M.C.: Component-based mediaton services for the integration of medical applications. Artificial Intelligence in Medicine **27** (2003) 283–304
12. Sibertin-Blanc, C., Hameurlin, N.: Participation components for holding roles in multiagent systems protocols. In Gleizes, M.P., Omicini, A., Zambonelli, F., eds.: Engineering Societies in the Agents World. Springer-Verlag (2005) This volume.
13. Rahwan, I., Ramchurn, S., Jennings, N., McBurney, P., Parsons, S., Sonenberg, L.: Argumentation-based negotiation. The Knowledge Engineering Review (2004) to appear.
14. Mellouli, S., Mineau, G., Moulin, B.: Laying the foundations for an agent modelling methodology for fault-tolerant multi-agent systems. In Omicini, A., Petta, P., Pitt, J., eds.: Engineering Societies in the Agents World IV, London, UK (2003)
15. Ricci, A., Omicini, A., Denti, E.: Activity theory as a framework of MAS coordination. In Petta, P., Tolksdorf, R., Zambonelli, F., eds.: Engineering Societies in the Agents World III. LNCS 2577. Springer-Verlag (2003) 96–110
16. Greenwood, K., Bench-Capon, T., McBurney, P.: Towards a computational account of persuasion in law. In: International Conference on Artificial Intelligence and Law, Edinburgh, Scotland, ACM Press (2003) 22–31

17. Fox, J., Beveridge, M., Glasspool, D.: Understanding intelligent agents: analysis and synthesis. AI Communications **16** (2003) 139–152
18. Letia, I.A., Vasconcelos, W.W.: Norms and their role in a model of electronic institution. In Lindemann, G., Moldt, D., Paolucci, M., eds.: Regulated Agent-Based Systems. LNAI 2934. Springer-Verlag (2004) 240–258
19. d'Inverno, M., Kinny, D., Luck, M.: The dMARS architecture: a specification of the distributed multi-agent reasoning system. Autonomous Agents and Multi-Agent Systems **9** (2004) 5–53

Participation Components for Holding Roles in Multiagent Systems Protocols

Christophe Sibertin-Blanc[1], Nabil Hameurlain[2]

[1] IRIT, Université Toulouse 1,
Place A. France, F-31042 Toulouse Cedex
sibertin@univ-tlse1.fr
[2] LIUPPA, Université de Pau, Avenue de l'Université,
BP 1155, 64012 Pau Cedex
nabil.hameurlain@univ-pau.fr

Abstract. An autonomous agent in a MAS involves in a protocol – more exactly in a conversation following the rules of a protocol - in order to reach objectives, some ones shared with all other participants, some others specific and private. We assume a MAS architecture where each conversation is monitored by a middleware component - a *conversation moderator* - that guarantees that the shared objectives will be reached. This paper addresses the means an agent requires to be able to exercise its autonomy and reach its own objectives in the course of conversations. The first step is to define these objectives and this leads to distinguish the strategic and tactic levels in agents' behaviours. The strategic level must be handled by the agent itself; the required capabilities are abstract and relevant for larges categories of similar protocols. Once a strategy is set for a conversation, its application at the tactic level can be delegated to a middleware component, called a *participation*, that intervenes in the conversation on the behalf of the agent. This component is specific to the role held by the agent and it is tailored to make the best use of the subtleties of the protocol's rules. This approach brings many engineering benefits.

1   Introduction

Protocols are one of the mechanisms used by the designers of a MAS to ensure coordination between the entities of the system – the agents. A Protocol can be defined as a set of rules that agents respect during *a conversation,* i.e. a process which proceeds according to this protocol. These rules determine who may take part in a conversation, and how each participant can or must contribute to its good processing. The main benefits of coordination by protocol are to ensure the efficiency of interactions among agents and the predictability of the system behaviour.

When an agent engages in a conversation, it is to achieve objectives, some of these objectives being common to all the participants of the conversation and others specific to each agent. For example in an auction, the common objective is to arrive at a transfer of property, while the seller and the bidders have opposite own objectives, to sell at the higher price and to buy at the lower price possible. The bind between the

M.-P. Gleizes, A. Omicini, and F. Zambonelli (Eds.): ESAW 2004, LNAI 3451, pp. 60–73, 2005.
© Springer-Verlag Berlin Heidelberg 2005

participants in a conversation is their agreement mutually recognized on the protocol rules and their engagement to follow them. Thus, the full benefit from coordination by protocols needs on the one hand the protocol rules are respected and also each agent has the insurance that they will be respected by others participants; otherwise, there is no guarantee that the common objectives of the protocol will be achieved. On the other hand, the benefit from coordination by protocols needs each agent is able to act autonomously, in such a way that it uses the protocol's rules in order to reach its own objectives.

Concerning the respect of protocol rules, Hanachi and Sibertin-Blanc proposed to manage each conversation by a specific agent, *the Moderator* of this conversation, charged to enforce the protocol rules [9]. The idea is to dissociate the interventions in the conversation, which are realised by participating agents, and checking whether these interventions obey to the protocol rules, which is entrusted to the conversation's moderator. The participants are thus in physical impossibility to contravene the rules of the protocol [7]. This approach considers protocols as first class components of a system at the design and implementation levels; a conversation is not just the result of interactions between agents but the running of a well defined process. Protocols become resources at the disposal of functional agents, and this gives solution to considerable problems in engineering MASs such as the specification, the verification and the formal validation of protocols, their reuse and adaptive maintenance, the separation of the aspects in the design and implementation of agents, the interoperability between agents, or scaling issues [9].

This paper follows the same approach and studies how to allow agents to fully exercise their autonomy when taking part in conversations. The difficulty is that the proper use of the rules of a protocol in order to achieve a specific objective needs a large amount of knowledge about this protocol. If this knowledge is hard-coded into agents, they will be overloaded and become difficult to maintain when the protocol rules changes; in addition, each agent will be qualified only for a small number of protocols because this knowledge is specific to each protocol. This solution features all the drawbacks of mixing different aspects. Another solution consists in encoding this knowledge in moderators and equipping each agent with an engine allowing it to acquire this knowledge and to deduce how to pursue its own objectives while observing the protocol rules. It is a solution of this kind that is proposed in [2] with a declarative meta-model applicable to all protocols, and in [6] with a language of meta-description of protocols which is pointed as being far from easy to identify. Both solutions are not into line with the moderator approach, because they raise many engineering difficulties about e.g. the size of agents, their maintainability, their interoperability, and the use of a wide variety of protocols as resources.

Another solution is to distinguish and thus to dissociate (so applying the "separation of concern" principle which is the base of the moderator approach), the *strategic* dimension and the *tactical* dimension in the application of protocol rules. Strategic issues are to be managed by agents, because they are closely related to the agents' objectives and to their autonomy. As for tactical issues, that is the operational behaviour that enacts a given strategy, they can be devoted to a new kind of middle agents which we call *Participation*.

In [14] we studied the concepts of strategy and tactic in the context of the participation of agents to conversations. When an agent takes part and holds a role in a conversation, it has its own objectives, which fall into the set of objectives that are compliant with holding that role in a conversation of that protocol. The strategy of the agent with regard to this conversation is merely an operational statement of its objectives, goals or desires. Thus, a strategy is the result of a choice that is to be made by the agent itself. Accordingly, holding a role in conversations of a protocol requires that the agent is equipped with the *strategic kit* associated to this (role, protocol) pair, so that it is able to decide and to state explicitly its own strategy. Let's remark that a strategic kit has a large scope of use since strategic issues are quite abstract; as an example, all the auction protocols have the same strategic kit for the bidder role, and the same holds for the vendor role. Thus agents are not overloaded by the introduction of these strategic kits.

Once an agent has fixed its strategy, the significant choices are made and the tactical details of their application can be delegated to an auxiliary component. This component, which we call a *Participation*, is in charge to take part in one conversation on the behalf of the agent in such a way that it realizes the strategy decided by the agent. Thus it must be aware of the strategic choices of the agent, have a full knowledge of the rules of the protocol followed by the conversation, and relate the both that is: apply the rules in the best way with regard to the strategic instructions. This paper focuses on the design and implementation of Participation components. In the second section, we summarize the principles of specifying and implementing protocols by means of moderators according to [9]. Section three introduces the participation components and the resulting architecture for protocols in MAS. Section four and five address the structure and design of Participations: their strategic part in relation with agents and their tactic part in relation with moderators.

Table 1. Items in the definition of a protocol

• *The variables* that intervene in the definition of the conversation objective or in the characterization of its state with respect to this objective,
• *The roles* that agents can hold in the course of a conversation,
• *The types of intervention* that agents can carry out to take part in a conversation, to make it progress and to influence the variables value,
• *The initial state* of a conversation, i.e. the conditions which must be satisfied so that a conversation can start,
• *The final state* that characterizes the completion of a conversation,
• *Casting constraints* on the attribution of roles that determine the conditions to satisfy so that an agent may take a certain role in a given conversation,
• *The behaviour constraints* that determine the structure of control of the conversations, i.e. in which cases an agent playing a certain role can carry out a given intervention, as well as the effect of this intervention.

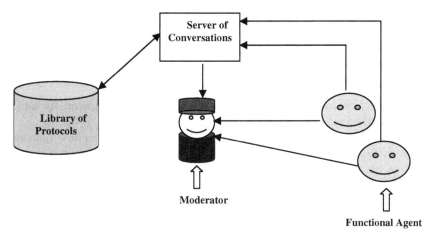

Fig. 1. Architecture for the implementation of protocols with moderators

2 Moderator for the Specification and Implementation of Protocols

Coordination by moderators rests on the architecture shown in Figure 1, of which we introduce the various components.

For a protocol defined by the elements in Table 1, it is possible to conceive an agent type, called a *P_Agent* type. Each instance of this type controls the course of a conversation following this protocol. Such an instance, called a *Moderator,* manages the value of protocol variables and guarantees that the protocol rules are strictly observed. Instantiated at the beginning of a new conversation, a moderator:

– has an attribute for each protocol variable;

– satisfies, at the date of its creation, the conditions of the protocol initial state;

– decides if an agent may become a participant to the conversation. To this end, it receives from agents requests to hold a role in the conversation, and answers positively if (and only if) the request is compatible with the protocol's casting constraints;

– ensures that the course of the conversation fulfils the protocol's behaviour constraints. To this end, any intervention of a participant in the conversation is directed at the moderator; if the current state of the conversation is such that this intervention is coherent with the behaviour rules of the protocol, the moderator accounts for and processes the intervention. The effect of this intervention consists in changing the state of the conversation, modifying the value of the variables, sending an answer to the intervening agent (immediately or differed until the reception of another intervention), or informing other participants of the occurrence of this intervention;

– allows the transparency of this conversation; in compliance with confidentiality rules, it answers the requests about general information (e.g. date of initialisation, number of participants), the state or the value of variables of the conversation; it can also be designed to bring a true help to the agents, for example in announcing the occurrence of meaningful events or in making the rules of the protocol to be known;

–decides the end of the conversation, after having detected either that the final state is reached, or that the conversation is blocked because of the defection of a participant whose contribution is essential to the completion of the conversation.

[9] indicates how to design, validate and implement such moderators by using a formalism based on the Petri nets, the CoOperative Objects [13].

The role of *the Conversation Server* shown in Figure 1 is to allow functional agents to access the protocols and conversations. *The library of protocols* stores information on all protocols, in particular their definition in the form of P_Agents. The Conversation Server manages a database on the conversations in progress or completed, containing information such as the followed protocol, the date of initialisation, the identity of the agent initiator, the identity of the moderator or the date of completion of the conversation. The server of conversation answers questions issued by agents, while taking account of the confidential character of certain conversations. If the system considered extends on a large network, the conversation server can be distributed or duplicated on several sites.

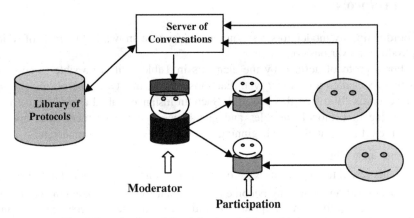

Fig. 2. Introduction of Participations in the architecture

The components of this architecture interact in the following way in the course of a conversation. An agent wishing to launch a new conversation requests the server of conversation; if the conditions of the initial state of the protocol are satisfied, the server creates a new moderator and returns its identity to the agent which becomes entrusted with the role *initiator* of the conversation. To take part in a conversation, an agent must know the identity of the conversation's moderator, obtained from the Conversation Server, the initiator agent, or from any other agent. Then it asks the moderator for the authorization to hold a certain role in this conversation. If the answer is positive, the agent takes part in the conversation by addressing its interventions to the moderator, which takes them into account according to the current state of the conversation and the rules of the protocol; the progress of a conversation is thus completely managed by its moderator. Lastly, when the moderator detects that the conditions of the final state of the conversation are reached, it ends the conversation and finishes its own execution.

3   Participations

A participation is an intermediary component between an agent and the moderator of a conversation, which has the tactical capacity to implement the agent's strategy according to the conversation's rules. As a moderator is an instance of a P_Agent, a participation is an instance of a type, which we call a *R_Agent* type. A R_Agent is defined for a couple (role, protocol), the role being played by the agent in a conversation follwing the protocol.

The life cycle of a participation proceeds as follows. When an agent addresses to a moderator a request to occupy a certain role in a conversation, the latter checks whether this request satisfies the casting constraints on the attribution of roles. If it does, the moderator creates a new participation by instantiating the corresponding *R_Agent* and returns its identity to the agent. This participation will interact with the agent (for the strategic aspects) and with the moderator (for the tactical aspects). At the end of the conversation, the moderator causes the termination of the participation of all agents taking part in the conversation, before finishing itself. If the agent leaves the conversation before its completion, it will be able to cause itself the termination of its participation.

Now the question is: what is the structure and behaviour of a participation, and how to design an R_Agent? The difficulty stems from the fact that a participation component is intended to bridge the gap between an agent's strategy that is abstract and declarative in nature and the moderator's behaviour rules that are much more precise and operational. Thus it must match the requirements of a strategic kit (on the agent side) and of a P_Agent control structure (on the moderator side), and go and come between the two in order to translate strategic objectives into interventions in the conversation, and vice-versa. The resulting architecture of a participation is shown in Figure 3. The two following sections show how the strategy related part is derived from the strategic kit and the behaviour related part is deduced from the protocol's behaviour constraints that apply to this role. As for the tactic engine, it implements the operational semantics of the strategies that can be defined with the strategy kit, so it is to be defined by the designer of the strategy kit.

4   The Strategic Part of an R_Agent

The strategy chosen by an agent allows it to select the conversations in which it intends to take part, either by initiating a new conversation or by holding a role in a running conversation. Once it is engaged in a conversation, this strategy in addition allows the agent to determine how to intervene in this conversation. These interventions are performed by the participation which is the intermediary component between the agent and the moderator of the conversation. The strategy has thus to take the form of instructions given by the agent to the participation.

From there we come naturally to the idea of expressing a strategy as the value taken by a set of parameters. Let us consider for example the strategies that are relevant for a bidder in an auction protocol. From a bidder point of view, the two essential variables of an auction are the object put for sale and the price of the current bid, which last value will be the selling price. On this basis, two opposite strategies can be identified, according to the importance attached to each variable. If the priority is given to the object, the bidder takes part only in auctions where the object corresponds exactly to what it seeks, and it will not hesitate to pay a high price to get this object. If the priority is given to the price, the bidder takes part in auction where the object corresponds roughly to what it seeks, and will abandon as soon as the price rises. In both cases, the price that the bidder is ready to pay is related to both its evaluation of the object value and the amount of its financial resources.

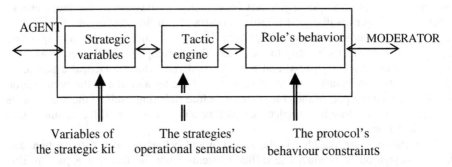

Fig. 3. The structure of an R_Agent

The knowledge needed to determine and express these strategies is given in Table 2. A strategy are characterised by the value of parameters `adequacy_rate` and `financing_rate`. The strategy of priority to the object corresponds to high values for both the `adequacy_rate` and `financing_rate` variables: the agent is ready to overpay the very object it seeks. On the opposite, the strategy of priority to the price corresponds to a low value for each of the two parameters. We have in fact the means of defining a continuum of strategies, including strategies apparently not effective but which may be appropriate in very particular cases: let us name as "thrifty" the strategy with high `adequacy_rate` and low `financing_rate`, and as "bored basket" the one with low `adequacy rate` and high `financing_rate`.

To determine if it will take part in an auction A, an agent use the `matching` function to evaluate the adequacy between the object that it seeks and the object for sale, and then decides according to the criterion: `matching(wanted, A.object)` > `adequacy_rate`. When an agent has decided to participate in an auction, it just has to set the maximum price it is ready to bid, i.e. the value it attributes to the object being sold multiplied by the financial effort it is ready to make, under the bound of its available resources, i.e.:

`Min{value(A.object)*financing_rate,available_amount}.`

Once an agent acts as a bidder in an auction, it just has to pass this maximum price to its participation to makes this participation able to apply the agent's strategy (the participation is a private auxiliary of the agent, and this does not publicly reveal its intention). Then, the participation interacts with the moderator by addressing interventions to take part in the conversation, and by obtaining information either in response to its interventions or by consulting public data.

Table 2. Strategic Kit to define strategies of the bidder role in auction protocols

adequacy_rate: Percentage;	/ the matching between what the agent seeks and the object on sale
financing_rate: Percentage;	/financing effort the agent is ready to make
wanted: Goods;	/object which the agent seeks
available_amount: Currency;	/ financial resources
max_price: Currency;	/the amount it is ready to pay
matching(o1, o2: Goods): Percentage;	/returns the adequacy between o1 and o2
value(o: Goods): Currency;	/ returns an evaluation of the price of o

5   The Behaviour Part of a R_Agent

An R_agent is to be designed in such a way that, once the value of the strategic variables is set by the agent, the interventions issued by the participation towards the conversation's moderator effectively implement the strategy defined by the variables.

For efficiency reasons, it is better to integrate the tactic engine and the behavioural constraints of the role into a single structure, an `event[condition]/action` labelled transition system that describes all the possible behaviours of participations: the effective behaviour of any participation will be a path from the initial state of this *role behaviour transition system* (RBTS for short) to a terminal one. Such transition systems are well-known structures very close to UML State-Transition diagrams [12] or flat StateCharts [10], and we just recall brief indications about their semantics. A *condition* is a guard associated with a transition from a state to another one: the transition can occur only if the condition evaluates to true; the *action* is performed at each occurrence of the transition; as for the *event*, its occurrence enables the occurrence of the transition. The default condition is `True`, the default action is `noop` and the default event is continuously `present`. An example is given in Figure 5. The interactions of the participation with the moderator are mapped to actions and events of the RBTS: a call of the participation towards the moderator is implemented as an action, and a result sent by the moderator to the participation is received as an event. The strategic variables appear in the conditions of the RBTS to select the appropriate transition when several ones are enabled and so determine the effective behaviour of the participation. Conversely, some actions can assign a value to these variables to account for the evolution of the conversation. An RBTS is expected to be deterministic whatever value is given to the strategic variables. The reason for that property is that the behaviour of the participation is controlled by the agent via the strategic variables; thus, undeterministic cases should correspond to situations where there are several equivalent ways to reach a same objective.

The RBTS of a R_Agent is built in two steps. The first step consists in extracting the constraints that apply to the role from the whole set of the protocol's behaviour constraints. It results in an event/action labelled transition system that catches all the behaviours of the role complying with the rules of the protocol; so participations do not overload moderators with irrelevant interventions. It may be a large system, especially if it includes ineffective or inoperative behaviours (This situation occurs if the protocol rules are designed just to protect participants the ones against the others and do not care about the efficiency of agents). According to the formalism used to express the behaviour constraints of the protocol, the generation of this transition system is an automatic step (see table 4). The second step introduces tactic into this transition system to implement the strategies defined by the value of the strategic variables. The aim of this transformation is to reduce the number of paths so that from each state, the only possible action is the one that complies with the objectives stated by the value of the strategic variables. The first kind of transformation is to remove transitions associated with an action inappropriate for whatever strategy, and to remove transitions associated with the related events. The second kind of transformation concerns transitions associated with an action appropriate only within a certain range of value of strategic variables: they have accordingly to be guarded by a condition. Lastly, some actions may be introduced to change the value of strategic variables. All these transformations have to be done by the designer of the Strategic kit. They define the meanings of the strategic variables, according to the places where they appear in conditions and actions, and as a consequence define the operational semantics of the elements in the strategic kit.

Table 3. The fish-market auction protocol

Role and casting constraints: a single fixed *vendor*, any number of *bidders*, the vendor cannot be a bidder.
Initial state: the vendor has a bucket of fish to sell for an initial price.
Final state: the bucket of fish is sold to a bidder (the vendor has given the bucket and the bidder has paid the final price).
Interventions and behavioural constraints: at any moment while the bucket is not yet attributed, a bidder can make a *bid* to signal its interest for the bucket of fish. If no (or more than one) bidder is interested, the vendor *announces* a lower (or higher) price. When one, and only one, bidder is interested, the vendor *attributes* the fish to that bidder. Once the bucket of fish is attributed, the vendor *gives* the fish and receives the payment while the bidder *pays* the price and receives the fish.

An example

To give a flavour of this process, we consider the bidder role (cf. Fig. 5) of the fish market auction protocol as specified in Table 3 [15]. Figure 4 gives an overview of a

```
class FishMarket;
inherits AuctionProtocol;
attributes
 bidders: list of agent*;                        //list of bidder agents
 vendor: agent*;                                 //the creator agent
operations     //the C++ code of operations is not shown
 grant_bidder(a: agent*): bool is <C++Code>      //apply for the bidder role
 current_price(): Currency is <C++Code>          //returns the current price of auction,
 FishMarket(vendor: agent*, p: Currency): FishMarket* is <C++Code>
services
 to_announce(newp: Currency): Status;            //Intervention Services for vendor
 to_attribute(): Status;
 to_give(f: Fish): Currency;
 to_bid(): Status;                               // Intervention Services for bidders
 to_pay(p: Currency): Fish;
 newprice() : Currency;                          //Inquiry services
OBCS
```

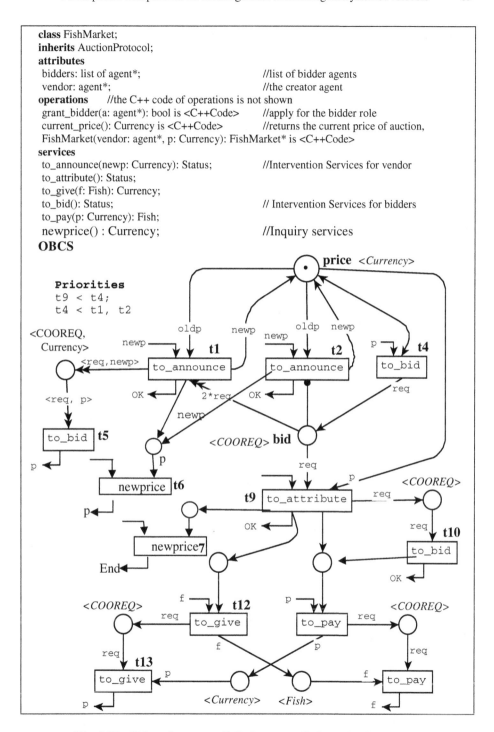

Fig. 4. The Fish market protocol's P_Agent as a CoOperative Object class

CoOperative Object class [13] that is the P_Agent, i.e. the type of the moderators, of this protocol. The behavioural constraints are coded in the high level Petri net, and we explain only the part concerning the bidder role (see [9] for an exhaustive presentation of this P_Agent). As long as the fish is not yet attributed, a bidder participant can send a to_bid() request (transition t4) to intervene in the auction process; it will receive either a R_to_bid(p) answer (transition t5) if there are several bidders, p being the new price announced by the vendor, or a R_to_bid("OK") answer (transition t10) if it is the only one bidder. In this latter case, the vendor attributes the fish to it, it is expected to send a to_pay(p) request and it will receive the fish with the R_to_pay(f) answer. A bidder may also send a newprice() request to the moderator; then it receives either a R_newprice("End") answer (transition t7) if the to_attribute action already occurred, or a R_newprice(p) answer – p being the most recently announced price of the auction (transition t6).

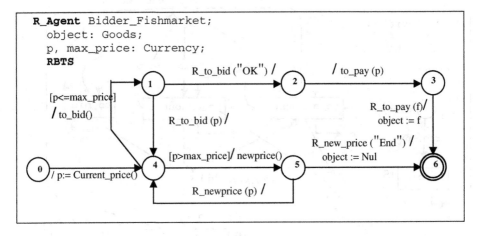

Fig. 5. The R_Agent of the bidder role in the fish market protocol

To select the features concerning the bidder role, this Petri net is abstracted [8] and actions related to other roles are neglected; more precisely, transitions t1, t2, t9, t12 and t13 are labelled with the null action ε. In addition, the net is slightly modified to rule out behaviours that are aberrant while allowed by the protocol's rules: a bidder has never advantage to perform two consecutive bids without receiving the answer to the first one, and it is useless that it performs two consecutive newprice() requests. This transformation adds two places with one initial token each that prevent the repetitive occurrences of transitions t4, t6 and t7. Then the algorithm given in table 4 is applied. It is based on the standard algorithm to compute the marking graph of a Petri net [11] and skips transitions that are ε-labelled. In a call Graphe(($M_1, ..., M_n$), M), ($M_1, ..., M_n$) are markings that are reached by the occurrence of an ε-labelled transition; they will be aggregated with another state by the fusion operation so that they do not appear as individual states in the generated transition system. In the generated transition system, each transition is labelled either by one of the actions to_bid(), to_pay() or newprice(), or by one of the events R_to_bid(p), R_to_bid("OK"), R_to_pay(f), R_newprice("End") or R_newprice(p). This transition system is not shown, it includes 11 states, 5 of them being terminal states.

Table 4. Algorithm for the extraction of the behaviour of a role

```
In : a labelled Petri net N = <P, T, A, λ, M₀> where λ : T → A ∪ {ε}
Out : a labelled transition system  S = <Q, →, q₀ > where → ⊂ Q x A x Q,
      and Language(N) = Language(S)
Begin
   Q:={M₀};  q₀:= M₀;  →:= ∅;
   Graphe((), M₀)
end.
   Graphe((M₁,…,Mₙ), M)
      If (M₁ = M or M∈Q) then
          fusion(M₁,…, Mₙ, M)
          return
      If M is a dead marking then return
      For each t∈T such that M ──ᵗ→M'
          If λ(t) ≠ ε then
              Q:= Q ∪{M'}
              →:= → ∪ {(M, λ(t), M')}
              Graphe((), M')
          Else Graphe((M₁, Mₙ, M), M')
   End;
```

The RBTS shown in figure 5 is obtained by introducing some tactic in this transition system. Some transitions and the corresponding target states have been removed: it is useless to issue a newprice() request while a to_bid() has not yet been answered, since the two requests will provide the same answer - the new price announced. Also it is useless to send a newprice() request once a R_to_bid("OK") has been received. The other transformation consists in adding a condition to the transitions from state 4: according to the level of the auction's current price wrt the agent's max_price either a to_bid() or a newprice() request is to be sent.

6 Conclusion

The idea to define a component realising the behaviour that an agent must follow by adopting a role is not new. However, in proposals such as [1], [3], [4], [16] or [5], role components are embedded into the internal structure of agents. Even if the componential architecture of the agents enables them to adopt and to leave roles without disturbance, the dynamic allocation of the roles is left up to the designer. The autonomy of agents is limited to the management of interactions among their components and they cannot control how the role is held by these components [5].

According to the approach presented in this paper, designing a protocol is to design a P_Agent that implements the protocol's rule and guarantees that these rules are obeyed in the course of conversations. So, no agent can deviate from its task with regard to the whole system. On the other hand, according to the agents' autonomy constitutive principle of MASs, agents require the possibility to define their own objectives and to use protocols' rules in the best way with regard to their resulting strategy. Thus a protocol designer is also concerned by the practical use of protocols by agents, it is required to identify the objectives and strategies compliant with this protocol. The main function of the participation components proposed in this paper precisely is to balance the system and agent requirements and to give the best compromise between the two. The resulting MAS architecture allow to design, to validate and to implement the system's rules and the agents' capabilities as distinct elements. This strengthen the engineering qualities studied in [9], notably the interoperability between agents since no assumption is made about their model or architecture.

References

1. Amiguet, M., Muller, J-P., Baez, J., Adina, N.: The MOCA Platform: Simulating the Dynamics of Social Networks. In MABS'02, AAMAS'02 Workshop, (2002).
2. Bartolini, C., Preist, C., Jennings, N.: Architecting for Reuse; A Software Framework for Automated Negotiation. In Proc. 3rd Int. Workshop on Agent-Oriented Software Engineering, Bologna (It), (2002), 87-98.
3. Becht, M., Gurzki, T., Klarmann, J., Muscholl, M.: ROPE: Role Oriented Programming Environment for Multiagent Systems. In Fourth IFCIS Conference on Cooperative Information Systems, Edinburgh, (1999).
4. Brazier, F. M. T., Dunin Keplicz, B., Jennings, N., Treur, J.: Desire: Modelling Multi-agent Systems in a Compositional Formal Framework. In International Journal of Cooperative Information Systems, 6 (1997), 67-94.
5. Cabri, G., Leonardi, L., Zambonelli, F.: BRAIN: "a Framework for Flexible Role-based Interactions in Multi-agent Systems. In Proceedings of CoopIS 2003, (2003).
6. Carabelea, C., Beaune, P.: Engineering a Protocol Server Using Strategy-Agents". In Proc. CEEMAS 2003, F. Marik & al (Eds), LNAI 2691, (2003). 413-422.
7. Castelfranchi, C.: Engineering Social Order. In Proc. Int. Workshop on Engineering Societies in the Agents World (ESAW 2000), A. Omicini, R. Tolksdorf, F. Zambonelli Eds., LNAI 1972, Berlin, Springer-Verlag, (2000), 1-18.
8. Hameurlain, N.: Formal Semantics for Behavioural Substitutability of Agent Components: Application to Interaction Protocols. In From Theory to Practice in Multi-Agent Systems, LNCS/ LNAI 2296, (2002), 131-140.
9. Hanachi, C., Sibertin-Blanc, C.: Protocol Moderators as Active Middle-Agents in Multi-Agent Systems. In Autonomous Agents and Multi-Agent Systems, Kluwer, 8, 3, (2004), 131-164.
10. Harel, D.: Statecharts: a Visual Formalism for Complex Systems. In Science of Computer Programming, 8 (1987).

11. Murata, T.: Petri Nets: Properties, Analysis and Applications. In Proceedings of the IEEE, 77, 4, (1989), 541-580.
12. OMG Unified Modeling Language Specification UML V1.5, http://www.omg.org/technology/uml/index.htm, (2003).
13. Sibertin-Blanc, C.: CoOperative Objects : Principles, Use and Implementation. In Petri Nets and Object Orientation, G. Agha & F. De Cindio Eds., LNCS Springer-Verlag, (2000), 210-241.
14. Sibertin-Blanc, C., Belhadj, K., Hameurlain, N.: Strategies and tactics for the participation of agents in protocols. Irit report, submitted to publication, (2003).
15. Venkatraman, M., Singh, M. P.: Verifying Compliance with Commitment Protocols: Enabling Open Web-Based Multiagent Systems. In Autonomous Agents and Multi-Agent Systems. vol. 2 (3), (1999), 217-236.
16. Yoo, M-J., Briot, J-P., Ferber, J.: Using Components for Modelling Intelligent and Collaborative Mobile Agents. In Proc. of WETICE'98, IEEE Computer Science, (1998), 276-281.

Semantically Federating
Multi-agent Organizations

Riza Cenk Erdur, Oguz Dikenelli, Inanç Seylan, and Önder Gürcan

Ege University, Department of Computer Engineering,
35100 Bornova, Izmir, Turkey
{erdur, oguzd, seylan, gurcan}@staff.ege.edu.tr

Abstract. We believe that successful co-operation between multi-agent systems providing services in a specific domain can be realized by constructing an infrastructure that supports the semantic interoperability between them. In this paper[1], we introduce a conceptual architecture for the semantic interoperability of multi-agent systems in the large-scale. The most important element of the proposed conceptual architecture is the federation. A federation established for a particular domain specifies the common characteristics of multi-agent systems in that domain. Hence, a special ontology is required at the federation level for defining the common characteristics of each multi-agent system in a particular domain as its own meta-knowledge. This meta-knowledge is then used in the semantic discovery of the multi-agent systems with which to co-operate. Since different multi-agent systems may use different ontologies, an ontology translation service is also defined at the federation level.

1 Introduction

Work on agent development frameworks, tools and methodologies have reached to such a level [1] that it now needs less effort and time to develop a multi-agent system in a specific domain. As a result of this progress, we expect that many commercial or governmental organizations will develop their own multi-agent systems for providing various services on the Internet. We will call each of these organizational multi-agent systems as a "Multi-agent Organization (MO)". For example, we call a multi-agent system that is designed and implemented based on the specific requirements of an organization in tourism domain as a MO in tourism domain. The reason behind introducing the MO concept is the need for defining a basic conceptual element, which will be used as a separate entity at the conceptual level in terms of semantic interoperability.

In an environment where there are a large number of MOs, one of the major challenges will be establishing co-operations between the MOs providing services in the same or similar domains. We believe that successful co-operations

---

[1] This work is supported in part by the Scientific and Technical Research Council of Turkey, Project Number: 102E022.

M.-P. Gleizes, A. Omicini, and F. Zambonelli (Eds.): ESAW 2004, LNAI 3451, pp. 74–89, 2005.

can be established by providing an infrastructure supporting the semantic interoperability of the MOs. To illustrate the need for a semantic interoperability infrastructure, we will give an example from an application in tourism domain. Let us think of a user who is a member of a specific MO in tourism domain and who wants to plan her travel. Typically, she will need to arrange transportation, accommodation and activities during the visit. Now, assume that during the construction of the travel plan, the user only preferred 4-star hotels with a pool and a fitness center. In this case, three possibilities may be considered: The first possibility is that the hotel reservation service is provided in the local MO and the user preferences can be satisfied there. The second possibility is that the local MO already provides hotel reservation service, but at the time of the request user preferences cannot be satisfied. For example, all the 4-star hotels with a pool and a fitness center are all completely booked. In this situation, to construct the best travel plan, co-operations with the related external MOs must be established in order to discover an agent giving a service that is capable of satisfying the user requirements completely. The third possibility is that the local MO does not provide the requested service. In this case, again co-operations with the related external MOs are needed. These examples show that co-operations between MOs are frequently needed and for successful co-operations it is critical to provide the following capabilities in the agent systems:

- Discovery of external MOs: A capability for discovering the most related MOs to co-operate with is needed. To realize this capability, first, a special ontology, which will be used in representing the meta-knowledge belonging to MOs, should be defined. Then, a kind of semantic matching algorithm can be executed over that defined meta-knowledge so that the most semantically related MOs are matched.
- Translating between different ontologies: It cannot be guaranteed that all MOs in a specific domain use the same ontology as the domain ontology. For example, MOs in tourism domain may use different kind of tourism ontologies. In this case, ontology translation service is needed to co-operate with external MOs.

The need for the above capabilities, led us to define a new architectural element above the MO level. We call this new element as "Federation". A federation is established for a specific domain and defines an ontology to represent the meta-knowledge of MOs in that domain. The semantic discovery of external MOs and translating between different ontologies are also realized at the federation level.

In this paper, we propose a conceptual architecture, which forms the basis for the semantic interoperability of MOs and hence large-scale multi-agent integration. Federation is an important concept in the proposed architecture, since the semantic interoperability is realized at federation level. We have instantiated the elements in the proposed conceptual architecture in connection with our FIPA-compliant agent development framework and platform [5]. For example, we have constructed a federation in tourism domain by implementing a federation directory service for discovering external MOs in tourism domain and a federation ontology service for maintaining and translating ontologies. We have then implemented two example MOs in tourism domain and developed a case where the first MO co-operates with the second one using the services provided by the tourism federation.

Finally, we think that to state its difference from the interoperability infrastructures discussed in FIPA's [7] (Foundation for Intelligent Physical Agents) various specifications, will make it more easier to identify where our architecture stands. The first kind of interoperability discussed in FIPA agent message transport service specification [9] is the network protocol level interoperability. In this specification, FIPA proposes IIOP (Internet Inter ORB Protocol) to be used as the underlying protocol for sending and receiving agent communication language messages between different agent platforms. Network level interoperability is of course important, but interoperability at the MO level requires more high-level protocols to be defined. So, we also use IIOP as the underlying network protocol to obey FIPA standards, but our proposed architecture defines the conceptual elements needed for the semantic interoperability of MOs and is therefore independent of the network protocol used in messaging. The other kind of interoperability, which is mentioned in FIPA agent management specification [8], is directory facilitator level interoperability. According to this specification, each directory facilitator in a platform registers with all other directory facilitators in the external platforms. So, when a directory facilitator receives a search request, it may propagate this search to other directory facilitators that are registered with it. We think that this kind of approach, which is based on the cross registration of directory facilitators, is not suitable for open and large-scale multi-agent environments. What we need is an architecture that is specifically designed for integrating MOs in the large scale. In addition, in the directory facilitator FIPA proposes a capability matching based on the parameters and values [8]. Different than FIPA, we benefit from the opportunities provided by the semantic web and use a semantic based capability matching in the directory facilitator in our architecture.

In the rest of the paper, we first define the concepts that we use for defining the architecture for the semantic interoperability of MOs. This will provide a clear understanding of the proposed architecture. Section 3 describes the conceptual architecture for the semantic interoperability of MOs. Section 3 also explains the ontological infrastructure of the given conceptual architecture and gives the agent and service interactions for discovering the requested MOs. In section 4, the semantic matching process, which is used in discovering the most semantically related external MOs, is explained in more detail. Section 5 includes the conclusion and finally references are listed.

2   The Concepts of Semantic Interoperability

To form the basis for the conceptual architecture that is introduced in section 3, we define the basic concepts of semantic interoperability in this section. Three basic concepts, which are the platform, multi-agent organization (MO) and federation, have been defined. The concepts of MO and federation have been partly mentioned in the introduction section so that we could explain our motivation more clear. They will be explained in more detail in this section. The platform and federation concepts have already been used in multi-agent literature, but sometimes in different senses. Hence, another important objective of this section is to define them again from the semantic interoperability perspective.

2.1   Platform

The platform is the physical infrastructure in which the agents are deployed. In literature, there are standards such as FIPA, which defines an agent platform [8]. There are also well known agent platform implementations such as RETSINA [17] and JADE [2]. JADE is a FIPA compliant platform, whereas RETSINA has its own standards. Whether FIPA compliant or not, all these platform implementations define the basic services such as agent management service (AMS), directory service (DS) / directory facilitator (DF) and message transport service (MTS), which are necessary for constructing a multi-agent organization (MO). We use the platform concept in the same sense as previous work and define it generally as the physical infrastructure where agents are deployed and which provides the basic platform services. However, in our case, we made one extension to the standard platform by adding a new element, which has the role of finding out the related external MOs by propagating the search to the federation level. We call this new element as the "External Multi-agent Organization Search Service" (EMOS). This element will be explained in detail in section 3.

2.2   Multi-agent Organization

In our interpretation, a multi-agent organization (MO) is a multi-agent system designed and implemented based on specified requirements in a specific domain. A MO lives on a platform. It may be built using one of the well-known agent oriented software development techniques such as [3, 4, 12, 19]. In the development process, agent behaviors, agent interactions, ontologies used and rules of the organization are defined. Then, each element of the platform is instantiated based on this knowledge. For example, a MO in tourism domain has agents that provide services co-operatively to satisfy their users' requirements, a pre-defined tourism ontology and a directory service ontology. This MO uses the basic services provided by the platform on which it is deployed. Of course, there may be more than one MO deployed on a platform. The important point here is that we try to integrate MOs semantically; hence, in conceptual level each MO on a platform is taken as a separate entity in terms of semantic interoperability. As a conclusion, each MO is the basic conceptual element of semantic interoperability.

2.3   Federation

In agent systems literature, the federation concept has sometimes been used to define an agent organization where agents do not communicate directly with one another. In this kind of organization, which is proposed by Genesereth and Ketchpell [11], agents in a federation communicate with the facilitators of the federation and these facilitators communicate with one another. This federated architecture has been defined as an alternative to direct communication of agents. If this federated architecture is evaluated in terms of FIPA specifications, we can say that the message transport service defined in the FIPA specifications [8] corresponds to the facilitator in the federated architecture and the FIPA agent platform [8] corresponds to the federation concept. Since our architecture aims at providing the interoperability of multi-agent organizations (MOs) deployed on different platforms, we use the term federation in a different meaning. In our architecture, federation is the element that brings together the MOs in a specific domain. For example, a MO in tourism domain subscribes to a federation that is specifically defined for tourism domain.

A federation established for a specific domain defines the common characteristics of the MOs belonging to that domain. A federation also defines federal rules. These common characteristics and rules require an ontology to be defined at the federation level. From this perspective, the most critical part of the federation is the federation directory service (FDS). FDS is used for identifying the specific MOs that provide the required services. Each federation has to define a specific ontology for FDS besides other federal rules such as about pricing policy, certification, etc. The specific ontology of the FDS is maintained by the service, which is called as the federation ontology service (FOS). In our architecture, FDS is the key element in providing the semantic interoperability of MOs, since it is the only element that can be semantically searched to locate the desired external MOs. Both FDS and FOS are explained in detail in section 3.

In reality, different MOs in similar domains may create different federations. In this case, the architecture scales up a level and a "confederation" can be defined so that related federations can be brought together. We believe that

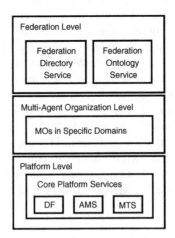

Fig. 1. Concepts and layers of semantic interoperability

the concept of confederation is the next step for creating very large and scalable multi-agent systems. However, before a confederation can be established, there must be a well-defined infrastructure for federation level. In this paper, we focus on defining the infrastructure for the federation level. Hence, the conceptual architecture that is given in the next section defines the elements, ontologies and interactions up to a federation level. The concept of confederation has only been put forward here as an idea for constructing very large multi-agent systems and confederation level of the architecture will not be discussed in this paper.

After defining the concepts of platform, MO and federation, we conclude this section by emphasizing that each of these concepts forms a different layer of the conceptual architecture that is going to be discussed in the following section. The layers of the conceptual architecture and services in each layer are shown in Fig 1. As it can be seen from Fig 1., the platform level includes the directory, agent management, message transport services whereas the federation level includes the federation directory and ontology services as explained before in this section. In the MO level there exists various MOs designed and implemented based on the specific requirements in various domains.

3   Conceptual Architecture for the Semantic Interoperability of Multi-agent Organizations

In this section, first the elements of the conceptual architecture are described. Then, the ontological infrastructure of the given conceptual architecture is discussed. Finally, the interactions that take place during the discovery of remote multi-agent organizations (MOs) are given.

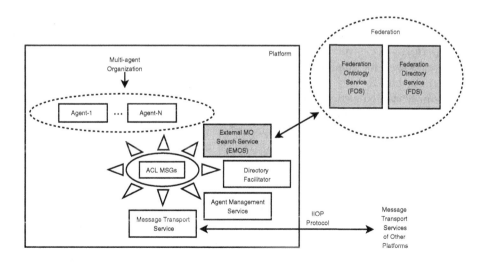

Fig. 2. Elements of the conceptual architecture

3.1   Elements of the Conceptual Architecture

The elements of the conceptual architecture are shown in Fig. 2. Since, the federation is above the MO layer, it is defined as an external service for MOs. The elements of the conceptual architecture are explained in the following paragraphs.

As it is explained in the previous section, the platform consists of elements such as agent management service (AMS), agent directory service / directory facilitator (DF) and message transport service (MTS). In our architecture, these services have been implemented as being compliant to the FIPA standards.

The AMS maintains an index of all the agents that are currently resident on a platform, which includes the names and addresses of agents. At initialization, each agent registers itself with this service. This service is also responsible for managing the operation of the platform, such as maintaining the life cycle of an agent.

The DF provides yellow pages services to other agents in the platform. Agents may register their services with the DF or query it to find out the services offered by other agents.

The MTS, delivers agent communication language messages between agents within a platform and to agents resident on other platforms. To deliver a message to an agent that is resident on an other platform, it is preferred by FIPA that MTS does not directly communicate with the remote agent, instead it communicates with the MTS of the remote platform, which then delivers the message to the requested agent. To provide protocol level interoperability, FIPA specifies that Internet Inter ORB (IIOP) protocol should be used between different MTSs to communicate with each other. The MTS in our implementation has also been developed based on IIOP. However, FIPA does not propose a specific protocol to be used for intra-platform communication. We use a Java Remote Method Invocation (RMI) based infrastructure for intra-platform communication. We preferred Java RMI for intra-platform communication, since it supports pure Java distributed computing and provides a high level interface than sockets. If performance is very important then inter-process communication methods can also be used for communication of agents when the agents are on the same physical machine.

The gray shaded elements in Fig. 2 are the new elements that we have added to support semantic interoperability of the MOs. External MO Search Service (EMOS) is the only platform element, which is responsible for the semantic interoperability. Main functionality of EMOS is to request the federation's directory service to match the semantically related MOs that provide the required goals/services and to get the directory facilitator addresses of the matched MOs. EMOS is designed based on the idea of matchmaking; hence, after querying the remote directory facilitators of the matched MOs and locating the proper agents, it passes the addresses of the remote agents to the user agent. To get the required service from the agents in external MOs, the user agent then using that specific domain's ontology, requests the discovered remote agents to get the required service. However, we cannot expect all the external MOs to use the same domain ontology as the local MO, so an ontology translation service is needed. When this is the case, EMOS gets the request from the user agent and forwards it to the federation ontology service so that the content of the request message is translated into a form, which is represented using the domain ontology of the matched external MO with which to co-operate. The translated message is then sent to the message transport service of the external MO.

The federation has two basic elements, which are the federation directory service (FDS) and the federation ontology service (FOS) as shown in Fig 2. FDS has a semantic matching engine, which matches incoming requests against the stored MO meta-knowledge represented using the federation directory service ontology. The federation directory service ontology together with other ontologies used in the system will be discussed in section 3.2.

MOs may use different domain ontologies locally, but when they have to collaborate, they need to understand each other. For this purpose, we have defined FOS, which is able to translate from one organization's domain ontology to the other. Thus, we can say that FOS is responsible for translating and maintaining domain ontologies. In literature, there are frameworks that are used for mapping between different ontologies. For example, MAFRA framework [15], which is operating within the KAON (Kalsruhe Ontology and Semantic Web Tool) [13] environment, is a well-known ontology-mapping framework. KAON environment of course provides sophisticated support for distributed ontology management and versioning. But, our main purpose is to couple the ontology management service to the multi-agent environment, not to develop a sophisticated semantic web tool suit. Additionally, any agent or service residing on the platform can query the ontology management service at any time using the agent communication language semantics. For these reasons, we have designed our own ontology management service, instead of trying to use an ontology mapping service from the existing work.

3.2   Ontological Infrastructure of the Conceptual Architecture

There are three kinds of ontologies used in the conceptual architecture. The first one is the Directory Service Ontology (DS-Ontology) that is used by the agents in a multi-agent organization (MO) for advertising their capabilities to their local organization's directory services. The DS-Ontology is not related with multi-agent organization interoperability, it is responsible for only locating an agent within a MO. In defining the DS-Ontology, we have followed FIPA specifications and used the directory facilitator agent description template that is defined in the FIPA Agent Management Ontology specification [8]. Although not directly related with the MO interoperability, just to make our local directory service more intelligent than the FIPA's ordinary directory facilitator, we implemented a semantic matching algorithm to match the requests against the agent service descriptions stored in the local directory facilitator.

The second ontology is the Federation Directory Service Ontology (FDS-Ontology). FDS ontology is used in matching remote MOs, so it is important in terms of semantic interoperability of MOs. FDS-Ontology is used by the MOs to advertise their capabilities to the FDS. In our architecture, the user requests are preferred to be satisfied within the organization unless otherwise stated. If the requests cannot be satisfied within the organization, a proper MO is matched based on the FDS-Ontology. In this matching, the aim is to find a structurally identical (e.g. same encoding, protocols, content languages) and semantically similar organization. After a proper MO is matched, the remote agents that are giving the required services are located using the DF-Ontology of the matched MO. After locating the remote agents, the user agent collaborates with those remote agents. This collaboration needs more detailed domain knowledge and can be realized using a domain ontology. As it is implicit in the preceding sentence, the third ontology type used in the architecture is the ontology of the domain at discourse. For example, in a typical tourism application, concepts about the detailed room properties can be specifically used in the collaboration, but they do not need to be used during agent or MO discovery process. This is because, while the DS-Ontology aims at representing services of the agents within an organization and the FDS-Ontology aims at classifying the MOs at a higher level, the domain ontologies contain a lot of domain specific concepts and relations. As mentioned before, the FDS-Ontology, which is specifically defined for the semantic interoperability of MOs, is the most important ontology type in our system and its general structure is shown in Fig. 3.

As shown in Fig. 3, the "Platform Description" concept has slots related with the platform that the MO resides on. For example, message transport service address, supported content languages, ontology languages, protocols and encoding are the slots for this concept. This concept is required for matching a structurally identical organization. The "Provider" concept has slots related with the commercial or governmental organization that developed this MO. The "Service Description" concept is used for expressing the service types provided

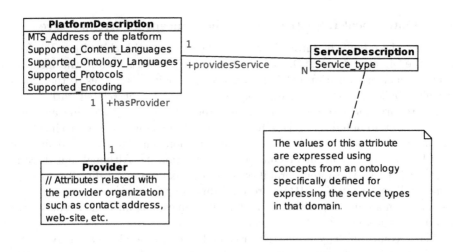

Fig. 3. General structure of the FDS-Ontology describing meta-knowledge about MOs

by that organization. The values for the service type attribute come from an ontology specifically defined for expressing the service types in that domain. Since
each federation is established in a specific domain such as tourism and this is an
implicit knowledge for the federation, we did not need to use a concept about
domain in the FDS-Ontology.

3.3   Agent and Service Interactions for Matching Multi-agent Organizations

The interactions that take place during external multi-agent organization (MO)
and agent discovery are shown as a collaboration diagram in Fig 4.

Each numbered message in the collaboration diagram is explained below:

1. The agent queries the local directory service using the DS-Ontology to find
   out the agents providing the requested service within the MO.
2. In this step, we assume that agents providing the requested services cannot
   be found within the local MO. Hence, the directory service requests the
   EMOS to initiate the external MO discovery.
3. The EMOS prepares a request using the FDS-Ontology and sends it to the
   FDS of that domain's federation. To prepare a FDS request, EMOS gets
   the platform specific knowledge such as supported protocols, encodings and
   content languages from the agent management service of its platform. It then
   adds the requested service type to the FDS request by extracting it from the
   original request.
4. The FDS matches the proper MOs and sends the necessary knowledge (e.g.
   message transport service, directory service addresses of the matched organizations and the degree of semantic match) to the EMOS.
5. The EMOS sends the requests to the directory services of the matched MOs
   beginning from the ones having the highest degree of match (i.e. exact match)

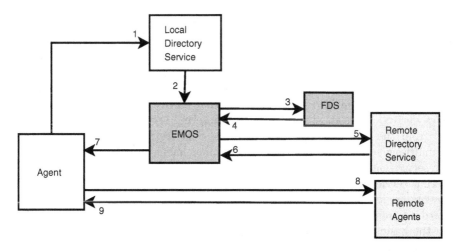

Fig. 4. Collaboration diagram for matching multi-agent organizations

to find out the proper agents in those organizations. We assume in this interaction that the directory service ontologies of the matched platforms are the same (i.e. uses FIPA agent directory service description template). Hence, no ontology translation is needed. However, if they use different directory service ontologies, ontology translation service is needed and this service is provided by the federation ontology service (FOS) as mentioned before.

6. Each matched organization sends EMOS the addresses of the agents that are capable of providing the requested services.
7. EMOS passes the addresses of remote agents to the original requester agent.
8. The agent prepares requests using the ontology it knows for that domain and sends the requests to the matched remote agents. Again, the FOS must be referred in case of any translation need between the different ontologies in that domain.
9. The remote agents send the results to the original requester agent.

4   The Multi-agent Organization Matching Process

We have implemented all services in our architecture based on a generic service definition interface. By this way, we have both defined a common service model and made all the services capable of understanding agent communication language messages. In the following subsections, we first explain the generic service definition interface, since in our environment all services including the federation directory service (FDS) is implemented based on this generic service model. Then, the software architecture of the multi-agent organization (MO) descriptions matching engine that has been integrated into the FDS will be given.

4.1   Generic Service Definition Interface

We preferred each service in a multi-agent environment to be able to handle agent communication language (ACL) messages both to communicate with agents and with each other. Hence, there must be a generic service infrastructure in order to generalize this capability. In our architecture, this is accomplished using an abstract service class. There may be two kinds of services, internal or external. Internal services are inside the platform and by default they communicate using remote method invocation. The internal service logic is implemented in classes derived from an abstract class for internal services, which itself is derived from the basic abstract service class. Services that are to be found in any multi-agent platform such as agent management service, directory facilitator service and message transport service are examples for internal services. External services are services that are outside of any platform boundary and they communicate via Internet Inter ORB protocol (IIOP). The external service structure is realized in an abstract external service class, which is also derived from the basic abstract service class. An example for an external service is the "Federation Directory Service", which is a federation level service as explained in section 3.1.

Extending a service's capabilities should be easy for an agent developer, so command pattern [10] has been used. A message's performative is the main message parameter which differentiates a message from another. Handling of the received message depends on the receiver agent or service. So, the performative of the incoming message and the type of the receiver together form the behavioral difference in the command pattern that is implemented for message handling. The class model for the command interface used is shown in Fig 5 on the next page. The IFIPAMsgCommand is the command interface and each service has its own commands. For example, when the FDS receives an ACL message with the "request" performative, it instantiates the "request" performative specific command for itself, which is shown as the FDSRequestCommand in Fig 5. The other services behave in the same way when an ACL message arrives. This means that they instantiate the specific commands for themselves and pass the execution to these command objects.

The Java code showing how a service creates the specific command based on the ACL message performative and how it passes the control of execution to this command is given in the code fragment below:

```
public void message(FIPATransportMsg msg) {

    ...

        String performative = message.getPerformative();
        // create a command according to performative
        IFIPAMsgCommand command=
        commandFactory.getCommand(performative);
        // execute the command to handle the message
        command.execute(message, this);
    }
```

Within the concrete implementation of the "execute" method, the message content is parsed and the related functionality of the service is called passing the parsed knowledge as parameter. As a conclusion, any platform service is simply connected to the platform by implementing concrete command objects for any type of message that may be sent to the service.

4.2 Software Architecture of the Semantic Matching Engine

We have first defined a generic matcher architecture to facilitate capability matching for any kind of entity such as semantic web services, agents or multi-agent organizations (MOs). Then, different services that need semantic matching capability are implemented based on this generic architecture. For example, the FDS implementation is based on the main interface or classes such as Matcher, AdvertisementDB, Ontolog, MatchResult that are provided by the generic architecture. The algorithm that is used for the semantic matching is derived from the work [14, 16], where semantic matching is used for the autonomous

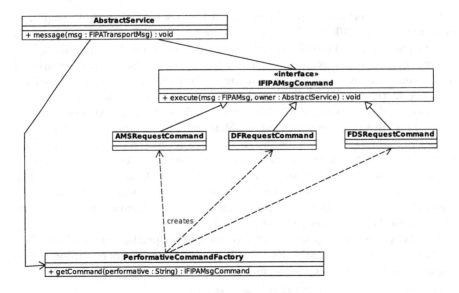

Fig. 5. The command interface for services

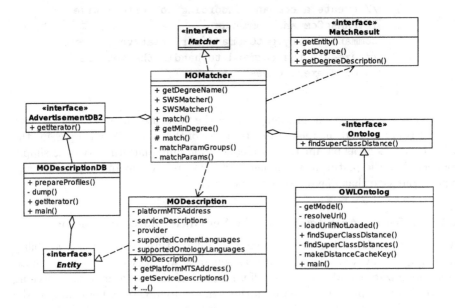

Fig. 6. The software architecture of the MO description matching engine

discovery of semantic web services. The software architecture of the MO description matching engine in the FDS is shown in Fig 6.

We think that a generic capability matching engine should semantically match an Entity against the other entities that are advertised. An entity can be a service profile in a semantic web service domain or it is a MODescription in our case. AdvertisementDB represents the group of the entities, which are semantically processed and compared to a given entity to determine if it supplies the desired capabilities. In FDS implementation, MODescriptionDB class implements the generic AdvertisementDB interface. Ontolog is the generic interface that represents the primitive reasoning module of a matching engine. Implementations of this component will determine ontology class relations and find superclass distances between the ontology classes with specified URIs. Since FDS holds the semantic knowledge (i.e. MO descriptions) in OWL [18] format, a special class named as OwlOntolog that implements the Ontolog interface has been defined.

Any matching engine implementation should implement the Matcher interface. This provides generalization of the different matching implementations and users of those engines will deal with only one service: "match". In the FDS implementation, a MOMatcher class that implements the generic matcher interface has been defined as shown in Fig 6. The result of each semantic match operation is encapsulated in a MatchResult object. The result includes the matched entity and its match degree such as exact, plug-in, subsume, or fail.

When the FDS receives a match request, first of all it has to parse the request. Since the services in our architecture can understand agent communication language messages, the request comes in FIPA ACL as mentioned before. We use FIPA RDF content language to represent the content part of each ACL message. Our choice for the query language is the OWL-QL [6]. The choice of OWL-QL is the natural outcome of storing the directory services' internal knowledge in OWL ontologies. But, OWL-QL is not yet sufficient for being used in semantic matching of agent or service capabilities. For example, a way of passing the requested service's input and output parameters to the semantic matching engine must be found. Hence, we have extended OWL-QL to cope with this problem. The difference of extended OWL-QL is its capability of carrying semantic matching parameters such as exact-match, plug-in-match, subsume-match. In summary, FDS implementation in our system can parse OWL-QL in the FIPA-RDF content in order to extract the concepts to be matched and to understand the required minimum degree of match. Then by satisfying the minimum match degree, the FDS matches the request against the MO meta-knowledge represented in OWL and stored in the FDS.

5   Conclusion

We think that the idea of establishing agent federations will form the basis for constructing open, large and scalable multi-agent systems and will make it possible for different multi-agent systems in specific domains to co-operate. This paper is the first step towards this goal and proposes a conceptual architecture for establishing agent federations by semantically bringing the multi-agent organizations together. The elements defined in the conceptual architecture are instantiated in connection with our FIPA compliant agent development framework and platform [5] and the prototype is tested for example requests in tourism domain.

References

1. AgentLink Web Site.: http://www.agentlink.org
2. Bellifemine, F., Poggi, A., and Rimassa, G.: Developing Multi-agent Systems with a FIPA-Compliant Agent Framework. Software Practice and Experience, 31 (2001) 103-128.
3. Bernon C., Gleizes, M., Peyruqueou, S., and Picard, G.: ADELFE, a methodology for adaptive multi-agent systems. In Petta, P., Tolksdorf, R., Zambonelli, F. (eds). Engineering Societies in the Agents World III (ESAW'02), LNAI 2577, Springer Verlag, (2002) 156-169.
4. Dikenelli, O. and Erdur R.C.: SABPO: A Standards Based and Pattern Oriented Multi-Agent Development Methodology, . In Petta, P., Tolksdorf, R., Zambonelli, F. (eds). Engineering Societies in the Agents World III (ESAW'02), LNAI 2577, Springer Verlag, (2002) 213-226.
5. Erdur, R.C. and Dikenelli, O.: A Standards Based Agent Framework for Instantiating Adaptive Agents. In the proc. of AAMAS'03, Melbourne, Australia, (2003) 984-985.
6. Fikes, R., Hayes, P. and Horrocks, I.: OWL-QL - A Language for Deductive Query Answering on the Semantic Web. Knowledge System Laboratory-Stanford University. (2003), available at http://ksl-web.stanford.edu/KSL-Abstracts/KSL-03-14.html.
7. FIPA(a).: FIPA Web Site: http://www.fipa.org
8. FIPA(b).: Agent Management Specification, Document Number:SC00023K, (2004).
9. FIPA(c).: Agent Message Transport Service Specification, Document Number:SC00067F, (2003).
10. Gamma, E., Helm, R., Johnson, R. and Vlissides, J.: Design Patterns, Addison Wesley, Reading (MA), (1995).
11. Genesereth, M. and Ketchpel, S.: Software Agents. Communications of the ACM. 37(7) (1994) 48-53.
12. Giunchiglia, F, Mylopoulos, J., and Perini, A.: The Tropos Software Development Methodology: Processes, Models and Diagrams. In the proc. of AAMAS'02, Bologna, Italy. (2002) 35-36.
13. Kaon Karlsruhe Ontology and Semantic Web Tool.: available at http://km.aifb.uni-karlsruhe.de/kaon2/server.
14. Li, L. and Horrocks, I.: A Software Framework for Matchmaking Based on Semantic Web Technology. In the proc. of WWW'2003, Budapest, Hungary. (2003) 331-339.
15. Maedche, A., Motik, B., Silva, N. and Volz, R.,; MAFRA: A Mapping Framework for Distributed Ontologies. In the proceedings of Knowledge Engineering and Knowledge Management, Ontologies and the Semantic Web, 13th International Conference, EKAW 2002. Asuncin Gmez-Prez, V. Richard Benjamins (Eds.), Spain, October 1-4, LNCS 2473, Springer Verlag. (2002) 235-250.

16. Paolucci, M., Kawamura, T., Payne, T. R. and Sycara, K.: Semantic Matching of Web Services Capabilities. In the proc. of the First International Semantic Web Conference (ISWC), Sardinia-Italy, June, (2002), available at: http://www.daml.org/services/pub-archive.html.
17. Sycara, K. and Zeng, D.:, Coordination of Multiple Intelligent Software Agents. International Journal of Cooperative Information Systems (IJCIS), 5(2&3) (1996) 181-212.
18. Web Ontology Language (OWL).: http://www.w3.org/TR/PR-owl-features-20031215.
19. Wooldridge, M., Jennings, N.R. and Kinny, D.: The Gaia Methodology for Agent Oriented Analysis and Design. Journal of Autonomous Agents and Multi-Agent Systems, 3(3) (2000) 285-312.

T-Compound Interaction and Overhearing Agents

Eric Platon[1], Nicolas Sabouret[2], and Shinichi Honiden[1]

[1] National Institute of Informatics, 2-1-2 Hitotsubashi,
Chiyoda, 101-8430 Tokyo
[2] Laboratoire d'Informatique de Paris 6, 8,
Rue du Capitaine Scott, 75015 Paris
{platon, honiden}@nii.ac.jp, nicolas.sabouret@lip6.fr

Abstract. Overhearing is an indirect interaction type that enacts agents to listen to direct interactions among other agents without taking explicit part in the exchanges. In this paper, we propose a formal model of overhearing named T-compound and a methodology to describe generalised interaction networks in Multi-Agent Systems. The compound is defined with the π-calculus as an interaction composite. It is handled as an interaction primitive distinct from the traditional point-to-point one, so that our methodology can treat both cases homogeneously.

1 Introduction

Multi-agent systems (MAS) rely on the interactions among their agents, either human, hardware or software. Our work highlights the design of interactions in MAS, and we think relevant to exploit the recent concept of overhearing [1, 2] in addition to traditional direct interactions. This notion refers to one type of indirect interactions that occurs frequently in natural systems, typically when two agents are interacting, say discussing, and a third one is just a passive audience *that could however intervene* if required. This presentation of overhearing presents the positive aspects of the paradigm. The counterpart named 'eavesdropping' in the MAS community implies various concerns including security and reliability. In the frame of this paper, we focus on interaction requirements for *cooperative agents* to leverage overhearing advantages. We let eavesdropping as peculiar issue to be addressed separately.

Present work on overhearing exploited this mechanism in various scenarii such as monitoring agent systems and group formation. These applications show the relevance of the concept and its generality. However, it results from these systems that overhearing relies on an unusual interaction infrastructure, since current technologies only exploit direct links among agents. In this paper, we propose a formal model named the T-compound, based on the π-calculus [3], and a methodology to enable and encapsulate systematic use of overhearing interactions, when required. Exploitation of both direct and indirect interactions leads to new perspectives on systems, and we will show some situations whereby this double usage is even necessary.

M.-P. Gleizes, A. Omicini, and F. Zambonelli (Eds.): ESAW 2004, LNAI 3451, pp. 90–105, 2005.

This paper begins in Section 2 with a presentation of the concept of over-hearing, its interest for MAS, and the relevance of formal modeling with the π–calculus. Then, we propose in Section 3 our model and a methodology to de-scribe the interaction dimension in MAS. In Section 4, we develop an example with the proposed method. Finally, we relate our approach to other activities in modeling overhearing in Section 5, before concluding in Section 6.

2   MAS, Overhearing, and π–Calculus

2.1   MAS and Overhearing

The notion of overhearing was recently introduced in the MAS community as reported by Gutnik *et al.* [4]. It was originally proposed to endow agents with monitoring abilities to reason about the apparent behaviour of other agents, *i.e.* their interactions. This concept endows one agent with the capacity to capture information from the interaction of two or more other agents. Fig.1 depicts such a situation in its simplest case.

MAS presently exploit *direct interactions*, such as the discussion link between agents A and B on Fig.1. Overhearing is an instance of *indirect interaction* that might be relevant in the MAS paradigm. In fact, research in the field of natural sciences show that numerous MAS based on complex societies exploit mean-ingful forms of communication without explicit receiver. For instance, termites build their hills by working together, but they do not exchange any information directly. They rely on the notion of stigmergy whereby they determine their be-haviours according to the current state of the environment. One termite puts a piece of material for the hill, and other termites (including the first one) will then pile on top [5].

Indirect interactions already leveraged relevant results in MAS with stig-mergy and other techniques [6]. Overhearing has now an increasing number of applications. Original work refers to monitoring agent systems [7], large group communication [1], dynamic group formation [2], conversation recognition [4], and some forms of coordinations [8, 9, 10]. In addition, the phenomenon often appears in agent systems that focus on a variety of concerns. Hence, the Helper Agent reacts to *silences* in an instant messaging discussion between humans to suggest common topics and increase the interest of the participants [11]. The M

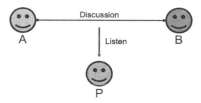

Fig. 1. Overhearing Situation

system surveys the actions of people in a virtual meeting room to optimise their workspaces at run-time [12]. COLLAGEN observes the flight ticket reservation process of the user to propose alternatives when no solution can be found for a given request [13]. In the remainder of this paper, we attempt to make more systematic the usage of overhearing in such systems, and novel applications.

2.2   Interaction and Formal Model

In order to exploit different kinds of interactions, MAS developers need a representation scheme. Formal models consist in proper representations of phenomena and remain mostly neutral regarding implementation details. Also, they can clarify the view of the system and reduce the effects of complexity by using mathematical compact formulae, based for instance on sets or recursivity.

In consequence, we propose in this paper a formal model that relies on the π-calculus from Milner [3] to leverage its interaction- and dynamism-oriented syntax, mechanisms, and expressive power that 'can *in principle* model (...) any computational aspect of agents' [14]. This heritage provides a robust model of traditional interactions and our extension enacts an instance of overhearing.

In addition to the grounds provided with the calculus, Milner developed a set of techniques to study concurrent systems, including equivalence relations. We expect the comparison between interaction structures and between apparent behaviours will enable advanced reasoning capabilities in agents exploiting overhearing. In particular, one agent may hear a conversation and try to match the stream to a known protocol [4]. As it is unlikely to perfectly match an existing models, the notion of equivalence allows more flexibility. In the remainder of this paper, we focus first on the syntax and semantics of the formal model, whereas the exploitation of equivalence belongs to our future work.

2.3   The π-Calculus in This Paper

The model presented in this paper exploits a subset of the π–calculus, originally from R. Milner [3]. This section aims at detailing the elements we retained and their meaning. The π–calculus features much more elements and advanced notions, but the present notations and mechanisms are sufficient in this paper.

The π–calculus is a modern process algebra for concurrent systems. It serves to represent and reason about interactions among concurrent processes and their dynamics such as mobility and changes in the interaction network (reorganisation, life-cycle). *In the frame of this paper*, we call agents the processes of the π–calculus, in the sense of the MAS community [15].

$\mathcal{P}_\pi$ is the set of agent names denoted by capitalised words. The set of Greek letters $\aleph = (\alpha, \beta, ...)$ represents the interaction channels that can link two agents. Other strings and small characters in the set Str label the messages that are sent in the different channels. Finally, I is an interval of integers $[0,1,2,...]$.

Syntax. We now define the well-formed formulae (wff) of our restricted $\pi-$ calculus.

- 0 is the agent termination, in addition to $\mathcal{P}_\pi$
    - → It is usually omitted at the end of definitions, i.e. $P = \alpha.Q$ is written instead of $P = \alpha.Q.0$
- $\langle.\rangle$ and $(.)$ represent the sending and reception operators
    - → They accept the same syntax for any channel α and message x: $\alpha\langle x\rangle$ and $\alpha(x)$. The operator omission denotes any of them is applied.
- '.' (dot) is the successor operator
    - → Given the channels α, β and the agent P, well-formed formulae are $\alpha.P$ and $\alpha.\beta.P$ (it is also generalised to n agents).
- 'new' is the restriction operator
    - → Given the channels α, β and the agent P, well-formed formulae are $\mathrm{new}(\alpha)\mathrm{P}$ and $\mathrm{new}(\alpha)\mathrm{new}(\beta)\mathrm{P}$. In the second case, we also write $\mathrm{new}(\alpha\beta)\mathrm{P}$ to have more compact formulae.
- $+$ represents the choice operator
    - → It allows writting $P + Q$ for any agent P and Q. The generalisation for n of agents is: $\sum_{i=1}^{n} A_i = (A_1 + ... + A_n)$
- $|$ is the concurrent operator
    - → It accepts the formula $P \mid Q$ for any agent P and Q, and the generalisation: $\prod_{i=1}^{n} A_i = (A_1 \mid ... \mid A_n)$

Finally, the well-formed agents verify the following equation. An agent P is either of the items in this formula, and also their compositions with recursive definitions.

$$P ::= \quad 0 \quad \vee \quad \alpha.P_0 \quad \vee \quad new(\alpha)P \quad \vee \quad \sum_{i \in I} P_i \quad \vee \quad \prod_{i \in I} P_i \quad (1)$$

Semantics. First, the agent termination 0 is a constant that means no activity, neither internal nor interactive. It is a final state that represents the termination (end of life) of agents. Along interaction channels, two complementary actions can occur, namely the sending and reception of messages. The formulae $\alpha\langle x\rangle$ and $\beta(y)$ respectively mean that the message x is sent through α and y is received through β. The successor operator '.' defines sequences of channels. The agent $\alpha.P$ means α is used to send or receive messages, and then the behaviour is P. Also, $\alpha.\beta$ denotes a sequence of two channels leading to the termination. The 'new' operator allows controlling the scope of an interaction, in a similar way as local variables in functions of programming languages. $\mathrm{new}(\alpha)\mathrm{P}$ means that α can only be used in the formula of P. Out of the scope of P, the name α refers to *another link*. In particular, the restricted α cannot be used to link P to external agents. The sum of agents relies on the usual choice operator. P can behave as any member of the sum. For instance, $P = \alpha.P_0 + \beta.P_1$ will evolve as P_0 if α is used, and as P_1 if β is triggered. Similarly, the parallel operator '$|$' represents the composed execution of P_0 and P_1. The focus on interactions of the calculus composes agents by communication channels as presented hereafter in the system evolution.

System Evolution. The π-calculus defines how systems evolve. The basic mechanism is the reaction between two composed agents (parallel execution) along a common channel; one sending a message and the other one receiving. Let's illustrate how this is run.

$$P \stackrel{def}{=} (\alpha\langle x\rangle.P_0 + \beta\langle y\rangle.P_1) \quad | \quad \alpha(x).0 \tag{2}$$

According to the reaction rule, $\alpha(x).0$ reacts with the first element $\alpha\langle x\rangle.P_0$ of the sum, so that x is passed through α. The second element of the sum is discarded (choice) and the system becomes (we use the intuitive property that A in parallel with 0 is equivalent to A [3]):

$$(P_0) \quad | \quad 0 \quad = \quad P_0 \tag{3}$$

3   T-Compound Model

3.1   T-Compound Formula

Informally, the T-compound is depicted on Fig.1, page 91; the shape of the interaction justifying the name of the composite. The T-compound is formally a 5-tuple $(A, B, P, \alpha, h_\alpha) \in \mathcal{P}_\pi^3 \times \aleph^2$ that verifies structural properties.

Let us consider 3 different agents $(A, B, P) \in \mathcal{P}_\pi^3$ and 2 distinct channels $(\alpha, h_\alpha) \in \aleph^2$ for the communications (A, B) and (A, P) respectively. This configuration is depicted on Fig.2.

The fundamental case where A sends messages to B and P overhears is formally written as follows:

$$T(A, B, P) \stackrel{def}{=} new(\alpha h_\alpha)(A|B|P) \quad where \quad \begin{cases} A \stackrel{def}{=} \alpha\langle x\rangle.h_\alpha\langle x\rangle.A \\ B \stackrel{def}{=} \alpha(x).B \\ P \stackrel{def}{=} h_\alpha(x).P \end{cases} \tag{4}$$

The definition of the compound means a T is the parallel execution of three agents, each of them playing specific interactions. Agent definitions are recursive to represent the interaction cycle of agents as expected along their lives, that is each agent chooses one of its eligible actions, performs it, and then recovers the capability to choose from its initial action set. The two interaction names used in the T-compound are restricted to these three agents to enforce a proper

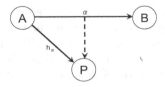

Fig. 2. T-compound Interaction Infrastructure

mechanism of overhearing. Restriction in the π–calculus makes the compound as a coherent interaction entity. It allows the *composition* of T-compounds with other interaction instances as it avoids conflicts among channels (unicity of names and proper scopes).

In the agent formulae, A can first send x through α and *has to* send it through h_α to return to its initial state (otherwise the π-calculus semantics blocks the agent, waiting for triggering h_α). Thus, B receives the message x as a direct interaction through α (the primary intention of A) and P receives a copy of x through h_α representing the overheard event. Fig.2 shows the correspondence with the formula. In the π-calculus, we represent overhearing as a constraint on a direct channel, i.e. the dashed arrow is formally h_α as copy of α.

Note that a channel between two agents does not mean they are actually interacting, since this depends on their intentions or imposed protocols. Instead, *channels represent which interactions are possible* at this level of modeling, *i.e.* the system infrastructure. This is typical for overhearing, where agents may have this ability and use it only in specific situations (possibly ordered by the user).

3.2   Interaction Design Elements

With the T-compound formal model, we now define agent interactions as *two primitives*, and we build a collection of interaction composites relevant in most practical cases. This collection allows constructing a methodology unfolding steps to define generalised MAS interaction infrastructures.

Given $S \subseteq \mathcal{P}_\pi$ an agent set (the system to be modeled), we first define two interaction primitives over the subsets of S, namely $MONO$ and T_0. Then, frequent compositions of these two basic elements allow defining three practical cases named $DUPLEX$, T_1, and T_2. We compiled these interaction elements in Table 1 and detail their syntax and semantics hereafter.

In the following equations, $X \models \phi$ means that the set of agents X satisfies the interaction type ϕ.

$$\forall S_0 \subseteq S: \quad S_0 \models MONO(A, B) \Leftrightarrow \begin{cases} |S_0| = 2, (A, B) \in S_0^2, \ A \neq B, \\ \exists \alpha \in \aleph \ so \ that \\ A = \alpha\langle x\rangle.A \ and \\ B = \alpha(x).B \end{cases} \quad (5)$$

Table 1. Interaction Design Elements

Formal Elements (* primitives)	Meaning
MONO(A,B) *	A sends messages to B.
DUPLEX(A,B)	A and B converse.
T_0(A,B,P) *	A sends messages to B and P hears them.
T_1(A,B,P)	A and B converse and P hears A's talks.
T_2(A,B,P)	A and B converse and P hears both talks.

$$\forall S_0 \subseteq S: \ S_0 \models T_0(A, B, P) \Leftrightarrow \begin{cases} |S_0| = 3, \\ P \in S_0 \ P \neq A, \ P \neq B \\ (A, B, P) \text{ verifies formula (4) for } x \end{cases} \quad (6)$$

$MONO$ represents the fundamental direct interaction, *i.e.* the usual π–calculus channel from one agent to another encapsulated in this interaction compound. T_0 corresponds to the definition (4) and represents the basic case of overhearing.

These two primitives are sufficient to describe MAS interaction infrastructures extended with systematic overhearing. This is due to the fine-grained approach of these interaction compounds. However, MAS interactions shall require coarser-grained elements for practical designs. The simplest and most frequent example is the conversation between two agents, that must be defined with two $MONO$. Therefore, we combine the two primitives into relevant patterns useful for MAS interaction design.

$$\forall S_0 \subseteq S: \quad S_0 \models DUPLEX(A, B) \Leftrightarrow \begin{cases} MONO(A, B) \\ MONO(B, A) \end{cases} \quad (7)$$

$$\forall S_0 \subseteq S: \ S_0 \models T_1(A, B, P) \Leftrightarrow \begin{cases} T_0(A, B, P) \\ MONO(B, A) \end{cases} \quad (8)$$

$$\forall S_0 \subseteq S: \ S_0 \models T_2(A, B, P) \Leftrightarrow \begin{cases} T_0(A, B, P) \\ T_0(B, A, P) \end{cases} \quad (9)$$

$DUPLEX$ describes usual agent conversations. It is built from two symmetrical and complementary $MONO$ that define the utterances from A to B and B to A respectively. T_1 corresponds to situations where agent A and B converse and P can only overhear the messages from A. In practice, this case has been demonstrated relevant to reduce the complexity of conversation recognition [4]. In addition, it allows modeling a case typical to overhearing. Human agents A and P are in the same room and A calls B on the phone (in another room). In this scenario and with normal conditions, P can only listen to A. Finally, T_2 refers to the full case of overhearing where P can hear both A and B. This is the most frequent situation when the three agents share the same 'space'.

3.3   MAS Interactions with Our Model

From this collection of interaction elements, we propose two views of interaction infrastructures, namely the system-level $\mathcal{I}_S$ and agent-centred $\mathcal{I}_A$ interaction sets. These two tools can be of use in the design of MAS interactions, as they provide points of view orthogonal to the traditional interaction protocols. Our sets aim at a comprehensive description of system interactions, while interaction protocols form a library of scenarii played in part or whole of the system. Interaction design can be thought of as a common exploitation of the three views. In the remainder of this section, we describe our methodology to build these two views from static system specifications (that is, the procedure must be re–run if the specifications change).

$\mathcal{I}_{\mathcal{S}}$ represents all system interactions in a single view. It is a set of interaction elements from the collection in Table 1 and thus allows explicitly showing overhearing cases. This feature is important so that designers keep track of this interaction pattern and can better avoid unexpected situations leading to potential eavesdropping breaches. Also, it treats direct interactions and overhearing with equal importance, so that system representations are homogeneous. Formally, $\mathcal{I}_{\mathcal{S}}$ is defined by the following equation, where '*' denotes that the corresponding interaction element can appear zero or several times:

$$\mathcal{I}_{\mathcal{S}} = \{MONO^*, DUPLEX^*, T_0^*, T_1^*, T_2^*\} \tag{10}$$

$\mathcal{I}_{\mathcal{A}}$ is equivalent to $\mathcal{I}_{\mathcal{S}}$, though it represents interactions per agent. Each agent appears together with its set of interactions in the system. This view implies various consequences, such as highlighting overloaded agents that perform too many interactions, defining groups and roles, and aligning the infrastructure with interaction protocols (roles can be assigned to agents in their context). The formal description of $\mathcal{I}_{\mathcal{A}}$ is a π–calculus expression showing the concurrent execution of system agents $(A_i)_{i \leq |S|}$ and their respective interactions $(\sum_{j \leq I_i} \alpha_j)_{i \leq |S|}$.

$$\mathcal{I}_{\mathcal{A}} = \prod_{i \leq |S|} \sum_{j \leq I_i} \alpha_j.A_i \tag{11}$$

Algorithm 1 describes our methodology that takes in input the raw system interaction specifications I and the empty sets $\mathcal{I}_{\mathcal{S}}$ and $\mathcal{I}_{\mathcal{A}}$. Outputs are optimised interaction sets compiled from I, without specification redundancy and improper interaction compounds.

Algorithm 1 Interaction Description Methodology

1: I={raw interaction element list ($MONO$, $DUPLEX$, $etc.$)}, $\mathcal{I}_{\mathcal{S}}$=∅, $\mathcal{I}_{\mathcal{A}}$=∅
2: remove_redundant_elements(I)
3: compose_element_types(I)
4: minimize(I)
5: $\mathcal{I}_{\mathcal{S}}$=I
6: rewrite($\mathcal{I}_{\mathcal{S}}$,$\mathcal{I}_{\mathcal{A}}$)

The method first removes from the specification set I any obvious redundant interaction element with the procedure *remove_redundant_elements* on line 2. This algorithm is not detailed as it merely compares elements and eliminates repeating ones (note that $DUPLEX$ and T_2 feature a 'symmetry', so $T_2(A, B, P)$ and $T_2(B, A, P)$ are redundant). Then, *compose_element_types* on line 3 combines elements according to the properties (7), (8), and (9) (see Appendix). Finally, *minimize* produces $\mathcal{I}_{\mathcal{S}}$ by comparing and removing elements that contain common features. Typically, $MONO(A, B)$ and $T_0(A, B, P)$ can be produced by the specification to outline two different aspects of the interactions between A and B. However, $T_0(A, B, P)$ is enough in terms of interaction infrastructure, while the other element is redundant (see Appendix). Our hypothesis is that if an overhearing case has been explicitly defined, it overrides a matching direct interaction. This hypothesis is appropriate since an overhearing situation must be explicitly decided by the designer and it is a stronger constraint on agent behaviours (T_0 above 'includes' the $MONO$ structural information).

Algorithm 2 rewrite(Input: $\mathcal{I_S}$, Input–Output: $\mathcal{I_A}$)

1: **for all** Interaction element in $\mathcal{I_S}$ **do**
2:     Develop the π-calculus formula
3:     **if** compound agent A in $\mathcal{I_A}$ **then**
4:         Complete the interaction formula of A:
5:             $\mathcal{I_A}=(\mathcal{I_A} \setminus \{\sum_i a_i^{old}.A\}) \cup \{\sum_i a_i^{old}.A + \sum_i a_i^{new}.A\}$
6:     **else**
7:         $\mathcal{I_A}=\mathcal{I_A} \cup \{\sum_i a_i.A\}$
8:     **end if**
9: **end for**

Once $\mathcal{I_S}$ is finished, the procedure builds $\mathcal{I_A}$ by calling *rewrite* on line 6. This sub-procedure shown on Algorithm 2 browses $\mathcal{I_S}$ and develops each encountered interaction element according to its π–calculus formula. Then it extracts the agents contained in the current expression, together with the interactions in which they are involved. If an agent is not part of $\mathcal{I_A}$, it is added with its interactions (line 7). Otherwise, the formula of this agent in $\mathcal{I_A}$ is completed with the new interaction links (line 4–5). The procedure terminates and the two aimed interaction sets are completed. The next section now illustrates an execution of this procedure with an example.

4   Example: The Board of Directors

This example models a meeting among the head of a company and its division directors. In other words, our system targets a user and its software advisor agents. In the following, we first suppose all agents can listen to all discussions, and the user is put aside to receive the final advice from the completed debate. We run the methodology for this simple specification. Then, we suppose that the user agent can also send messages to the assistants (to give new orders, *etc.*). We consequently modify the initial scenario and apply once more the methodology to adapt the interaction sets.

4.1   First Specifications

Given n$\geq$3 agents $(A_i)_{i \leq n}$ and the integers i and j, α_{ij} is the communication channel from A_i to A_j. The agent U represents the user interface that compiles the final report from the board and c_{iu} the corresponding channel from agent i. Consequently, the complete system is $S = \{(A_i)_{i \leq n}, U\}$. Hereafter is the raw

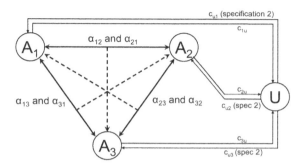

Fig. 3. Board of 3 Directors and the User

interaction set I issued from the specifications for n agents, and we then detail the case $n = 3$ to illustrate the methodology.

$$I = \{(T_2(A_i, A_j, A_k))_{i \neq j \neq k}, (MONO(A_i, U))_{i \leq n}\} \qquad (12)$$

The first term represents the discussions among the advisors and their ability to overhear conversations in the meeting room, even if they are not active participants. The second term is the final report from each agent to the user interface U. Let us now study in more details the case $n = 3$. Fig.3 shows the interactions that must appear according to the scenario specifications.

The application of the methodology based on the specifications yields the following. The input I is processed, and the output is just $\mathcal{I_S}$=I and the corresponding $\mathcal{I_A}$.

1: I=$\{(T_2(A_i, A_j, A_k))_{i \neq j \neq k}, (MONO(A_i, U))_{i \leq 3}\}$, $\mathcal{I_S}$=$\emptyset$, $\mathcal{I_A}$=$\emptyset$
2: remove_redundant_elements(I) does not change I (no redundant element)
3: compose_element_types(I) does not change I (T_2 and $MONO$ do not combine)
4: minimize(I) does not change I (T_2 and $MONO$ involve different agents)
5: $\mathcal{I_S}$=I
6: rewrite($\mathcal{I_S}$,$\mathcal{I_A}$) as described hereafter for the two first iterations.

Rewrite procedure: iteration 1 First element of I:

$T_2(A_1, A_2, A_3) = ($
$\quad P_1 = \alpha_{12}\langle x_{12} \rangle.\alpha_{13}\langle x_{12} \rangle.A_1 + \alpha_{21}(x_{21}).A_1 \mid$
$\quad\quad A_1$ talks to A_2 and allows A_3 to overhear, or A_1 receives from A_2
$\quad P_2 = \alpha_{21}\langle x_{21} \rangle.\alpha_{23}\langle x_{21} \rangle.A_2 + \alpha_{12}(x_{12}).A_2 \mid$
$\quad\quad A_2$ talks to A_1 and allows A_3 to overhear, or A_2 receives from A_1
$\quad P_3 = \alpha_{13}(x_{12}).A_3 + \alpha_{23}(x_{21}).A_3$
$\quad\quad A_3$ receives overheard messages from A_1 or from A_2)
$Consequently : \mathcal{I}_{\mathcal{A}(iteration1)} = (P_1 \mid P_2 \mid P_3)$

$$(13)$$

Rewrite procedure: iteration 2 Idem with the second element of I:

$$T_2(A_2, A_3, A_1) = (\quad Q_1 = \alpha_{23}\langle x_{23}\rangle.\alpha_{21}\langle x_{23}\rangle.A_2 + \alpha_{32}(x_{32}).A_2 \mid$$
$$Q_2 = \alpha_{32}\langle x_{32}\rangle.\alpha_{31}\langle x_{32}\rangle.A_3 + \alpha_{23}\langle x_{23}\rangle.A_3 \mid \qquad (14)$$
$$Q_3 = \alpha_{21}(x_{23}).A_1 + \alpha_{31}(x_{32}).A_1)$$
$$Consequently : \mathcal{I}_{A(iteration2)} = (P_1 + Q_3 \mid P_2 + Q_1 \mid P_3 + Q_2)$$

In the end, $\mathcal{I}_S$ is equal to the raw specifications, and $\mathcal{I}_A$ contains four agents with all their individual interactions.

$$\mathcal{I}_S = \{(T_2(A_i, A_j, A_k)_{i\neq j\neq k}, (MONO(A_i, U))_{i\leq 3}\} \quad \mathcal{I}_A = (\prod_{i=1}^{3} A_i)|cU \qquad (15)$$

where $cU = \sum_{i\leq 3} c_{iu}(r_{iu}).cU$ is the set of interactions for the user agent U. We detail hereafter the formula of A_1 only, as the other formulae are similar.

$$A_1 = (\alpha_{12}\langle x_{12}\rangle.\alpha_{13}\langle x_{12}\rangle.A_1 + \alpha_{13}\langle x_{13}\rangle.\alpha_{12}\langle x_{13}\rangle.A_1+ \quad //A_1 \text{ talks,}$$
$$//\text{others overhear}$$
$$\alpha_{21}(x_{21}).A_1 + \alpha_{31}(x_{31}).A_1+ \qquad //\text{One talk to } A_1$$
$$\alpha_{21}(x_{23}).A_1 + \alpha_{31}(x_{32}).A_1+ \qquad //A_1 \text{ overhears}$$
$$c_{1u}(r_{1u}).A_1) \qquad //A_1 \text{ reports}$$
$$(16)$$

This example shows how $\mathcal{I}_S$ represents all system interactions in a compact syntax, and how $\mathcal{I}_A$ allows handling interactions individually for each agent.

4.2   Second Specifications

In this second case, the specification revision expands the interactions of U (see Fig.3). Our methodology solves the inconsistencies that potentially appear, so that we only need to add the new intended interactions to I. There are two means to extend I and let U be able to engage conversations with assistants. Some designers could add explicit $DUPLEX(U, A_i)$; others would complete the initial reports from assistants to user with symmetrical $MONO(U, A_i)$. Our methodology accepts both cases and computes the same result. We now unfold the procedure twice with the two possible extensions of I, namely J_1 and J_2, and we show it yields the same expected sets.

$$J_1 = I \cup \{(DUPLEX(A_i, U))_{i\leq n}\} \qquad J_2 = I \cup \{(MONO(U, A_i)_{i\leq n}\} \qquad (17)$$

In both cases, the execution of the methodology is similar to the previous section and we will just emphasize the differences.

In the case of J_2, elements are composed on line 3 so that the $MONO$ added by the new specifications are combined as expected with the $MONO$ already representing the reports from assistants to user. Then, the minimization on line 4 does not influence J_2 as there is no compatible item to match. The composition of $MONO$ is performed as follows:

1: $J_X=\{$as defined above$\}$, $\mathcal{I}_S=\emptyset$, $\mathcal{I}_A=\emptyset$
2: remove_redundant_elements(J_X)   /*no change*/
3: compose_element_types(J_X)   /*only modifies J_2*/
4: minimize(J_X)   /*only modifies J_1*/
5: $\mathcal{I}_S=J_X$
6: rewrite($\mathcal{I}_S$,$\mathcal{I}_A$) is given hereafter

compose_element_types(J_2):
$J_2 = J_M \cup J_D \cup J_{T_0} \cup J_{T_1} \cup J_{T_2} = J_M \cup \{\emptyset\} \cup \{\emptyset\} \cup \{\emptyset\} \cup J_{T_2}$ (line 1)
Compose steps: Only one iteration affects the output (line 8):
   compose(J_M, J_M, J_D)
   For $x \in \{1,2,3\}$:
   $MONO(U, A_x)$ matches $MONO(A_x, U)$ (*compose* line 14)
   So $J_M = J_M \backslash \{MONO(U, A_x)\}$ and $J_M = J_M \backslash \{MONO(A_x, U)\}$, and
   $J_D = J_D \cup \{DUPLEX(U, A_x)\}$ (*compose* line 15)
   $\rightarrow J_M$ ends empty and J_D has three new elements
Completion $J_2 = \{\emptyset\} \cup J_D \cup \{\emptyset\} \cup \{\emptyset\} \cup J_{T_2}$ (line 11)
$J_2 = \{(T_2(A_i, A_j, A_k))_{i \neq j \neq k}, (DUPLEX(U, A_i))_{i \leq n}\}$

In the case of J_1, the composition has no effect, and modifications are carried out by the following minimization. As $DUPLEX$ are added to the specifications, the initial $MONO$ representing the reports to the user agent are redundant and will be eliminated.

minimize(J_1):
$J_1 = J_M \cup J_D \cup J_{T_0} \cup J_{T_1} \cup J_{T_2} = J_M \cup J_D \cup \{\emptyset\} \cup \{\emptyset\} \cup J_{T_2}$ (line 1)
Minimize step 1 min(J_M, $J_D \cup J_{T_0} \cup J_{T_1} \cup J_{T_2}$) (line 2)
   For $x \in \{1,2,3\}$:
   $MONO(A_x, U)$ matches $DUPLEX(U, A_x)$ (*min* line 3)
   So $J_M = J_M \backslash \{MONO(U, A_x)\}$ (*min* line 4)
   $\rightarrow J_M$ ends empty
Minimize step 2 min(J_D, $J_{T_0} \cup J_{T_1} \cup J_{T_2}$) has no effect (line 3)
Minimize step 3 min(J_{T_0}, $J_{T_1} \cup J_{T_2}$) has no effect (line 4)
Minimize step 4 min(J_{T_1}, J_{T_2}) has no effect (line 5)
Completion $J_1 = \{\emptyset\} \cup J_D \cup \{\emptyset\} \cup \{\emptyset\} \cup J_{T_2}$ (line 6)
$J_1 = \{(T_2(A_i, A_j, A_k))_{i \neq j \neq k}, (DUPLEX(U, A_i))_{i \leq n}\}$

In the end, both approaches lead to the same interaction set $\mathcal{I}_S=J_1=J_2$, and consequently the same $\mathcal{I}_A$ as follows, with the detail for agent A_1 ($n = 3$).

$$\mathcal{I}_A = (\prod_{i=1}^{n} A_i)|cU \qquad \text{where } cU = \sum_{i \leq n} (c_{iu}(r_{iu}).cU + c_{ui}\langle r_{ui}\rangle.cU) \qquad (18)$$

$$A_1^{specification2} = (A_1^{specification1} + \quad //\text{formula (16)} \\ c_{u1}\langle r_{u1}\rangle.A_1) \quad //A_1 \text{ gets orders} \qquad (19)$$

This example shows the robustness of the methodology to design choices and how incremental design of interactions with $\mathcal{I}_S$ and $\mathcal{I}_A$ could be exploited, especially for open MAS.

5   Work Related to Overhearing Modeling

Gutnik *et al.* proposed the first formal model dedicated to overhearing for conversation recognition [4]. Their representation embodies conversation notions (roles, states, transitions, speech acts, etc.) and the practical exploitation for their issue of identification. Although they propose a 'comprehensive formal model of the general problem' of overhearing, this first attempt is specialised to a peculiar aspect. Our model aims at describing MAS infrastructures with traditional and overhearing interactions, and it is consequently a complementary approach.

Busetta *et al.* proposed an implementation of overhearing [1]. Albeit this work is not a formal model, it stands close to our proposal. It is a multicast communication among agents in a cooperative group. When taking on a channel identified by a discussion theme, all registered listener agents receive the information. This work shows a conceptual difference between our framework and implementation issues. Our approach requires fine-grained details of interactions, whereas the implementation of Busetta is a single broadcast. Thus, implementing efficiently a model is not trivial, especially in the case of *open* MAS. A corollary of this statement is that our formal model do not scale as the implementation.

6   Conclusion

In this paper, we proposed a formal model of interaction in π-calculus that embodies the recent concept of overhearing, represented here as an interaction composite named the T-compound. The aim of this model is to provide a general description of interactions in MAS, orthogonally to other design issues (agents, environment or organisation). This description is performed by a methodology that compiles two views for the study of MAS interactions. The first representation shows all interactions that can occur in a given system. The second one represents an agent-centred description of all these interactions. These two views of the same system can provide MAS designers with relevant information for analysis and design.

Our current model covers static interactions of MAS. Dynamism is not included yet and we intend to introduce this feature necessary in open systems. It will enact considering agents that have new acquaintances, join or quit dynamically the system, or feature mobility. We also pointed out the scalability of our approach is rather low, considering open or large-scale MAS. Hence, we are working on the agent environment so that overhearing would be relayed through it. In fact, Omicini *et al.* and Mamei *et al.* described two infrastructures to support coordination among agents [9, 8] based on the environment. These approaches do not address explicitly the case of overhearing, but they embody related ideas. Our present endeavours are to study the consequences of such environments on our formal definition, methodology, and the pragmatics (computation and management concerns).

References

1. Busetta, P., Donà, A., Nori, M.: Channelled multicast for group communications. In: Autonomous Agents and Multi-Agent Systems. (2002)
2. Legras, F., Tessier, C.: Lotto: Group formation by overhearing in large teams. In: Autonomous Agents and Multi-Agent Systems. (2003)
3. Milner, R.: Communicating and Mobile Systems: the π-calculus. Cambridge Press (1999)
4. Gutnik, G., Kaminka, G.A.: Towards a formal approach to overhearing: Algorithms for conversation identification. In: Autonomous Agents and Multi-Agent Systems. (2004)
5. Resnick, M.: Learning about life. Artificial Life Journal **1** (1994)
6. Keil, D., Goldin, D.: Modelling indirect interaction in open computational systems. In: WETICE. (2003)
7. Kaminka, G.A., Pynadath, D.V., Tambe, M.: Monitoring teams by overhearing: A multi-agent plan-recognition approach. Journal of Artificial Intelligence Research **17** (2002) 83–135
8. Mamei, M., Zambonelli, F.: Motion coordination in the quake 3 arena environment: a field-based approach. In: Workshop on Environment for Multi-Agent Systems. (2004)
9. Omicini, A., Ricci, A., Viroli, M., Castelfranchi, C., Tummolini, L.: Coordination artifacts: Environment-based coordination for intelligent agents. In: Autonomous Agents and Multi-Agent Systems. (2004)
10. Tummolini, L., Castelfranchi, C., Ricci, A., Viroli, M., Omicini, A.: "Exhibitionists" and "Voyeurs" do it better: A shared environment for flexible coordination with tacit messages. In: Workshop on Environment for Multi-Agent Systems. (2004)
11. Isbister, K., Nakanishi, H., Ishida, T., Nass, C.: Helper agent: Designing an assistant for human-human interaction in a virtual meeting space. In: CHI. (2000)
12. Riecken, D.: M: An architecture of integrated agents. In Bradshaw, J., ed.: Software Agents. AAAI Press (2000) 419
13. Rich, C., Sidner, C.: Collagen: When agents collaborate with people. In: First International Conference on Autonomous Agents. (1997)
14. Esterline, A.C., Rorie, T.: Using the π-calculus to model multiagent systems. In: FAABS. Volume 1871 of LNAI., Springer–Verlag (2001) 164–179
15. Ferber, J.: Multi-Agent Systems: An Introduction to Distributed Artificial Intelligence. Addison-Wesley (1999)

A   Algorithm Appendix

Algorithm 3 modifies a set I by combining interaction elements into more complex ones (15 cases) with the sub-procedure *compose* in Algorithm 4.

Algorithm 4 receives three interaction sets I, J, K from the procedure *compose_element_types* in Algorithm 3. Elements of I are matched with elements of J that feature common agents *in reversed order*, and new compounds are produced in K. The procedure applies the composition properties (7), (8), and (9) and solves other to cases such as $T_1(A, B, P)$ and $T_1(B, A, P)$ that, as T_0, breed $T_2(A, B, P)$ in terms of infrastructure (12 more cases).

Algorithm 3 compose_element_types(Input–Output: interaction set I)

1: I=$I_M \cup I_D \cup I_{T_0} \cup I_{T_1} \cup I_{T_2}$
2: **for** $(I_1,I_2) \in \{(I_{T_x},I_{T_x}),(I_M,I_{T_2}),(I_D,I_{T_2}),(I_{T_x},I_{T_{y>x}})\}$, $x \leq 3$ and $y \leq 3$ **do**
3:    compose(I_1, I_2, I_{T_2})   /*This loop handles rule (9) in compose($I_{T_0}, I_{T_0}, I_{T_2}$)*/
4: **end for**
5: **for** $(I_1,I_2) \in \{(I_M,I_{T_{x \leq 1}}),(I_D,I_{T_{x \leq 1}})\}$ **do**
6:    compose(I_1, I_2, I_{T_1})   /*This loop handles rule (8) in compose(I_M, I_{T_0}, I_{T_1})*/
7: **end for**
8: **for** $(I_1,I_2) \in \{(I_X,I_X),(I_M,I_D)\}$, $X \in \{M,D\}$ **do**
9:    compose(I_1, I_2, I_D)   /*This loop handles rule (7) in compose(I_M, I_M, I_D)*/
10: **end for**
11: I=$I_M \cup I_D \cup I_{T_0} \cup I_{T_1} \cup I_{T_2}$

Algorithm 4 compose(Input–Output: interaction sets I,J,K)

1: **for all** $X \in I$ **do**
2:    **for all** $Y \in J$ **do**
3:       **if** $\exists$ agents (A,B,P) so that $X(A, B, P)$ and $Y(B, A, P)$ exist **then**
4:          I=I$\setminus\{X\}$; J=J$\setminus\{Y\}$; K=K$\cup\{T_2(A, B, P)\}$; Break the loop
5:       **end if**
6:       **if** $\exists$ agents (A,B,P) so that $(X(A, B)$ and $Y(B, A, P))$ exist **then**
7:          I=I$\setminus\{X\}$; J=J$\setminus\{Y\}$;
8:          **if** Y is T_2 **then**
9:             K=K$\cup\{T_2(A, B, P)\}$; Break the loop
10:          **else**
11:             K=K$\cup\{T_1(A, B, P)\}$; Break the loop
12:          **end if**
13:       **end if**
14:       **if** $\exists$ agents (A,B) so that $X(A, B)$ and $Y(B, A)$ exist **then**
15:          I=I$\setminus\{X\}$; J=J$\setminus\{Y\}$; K=K$\cup\{DUPLEX(A, B)\}$; Break the loop
16:       **end if**
17:    **end for**
18: **end for**

Algorithm 5 minimize(Input–Output: interaction set I)

1: I=$I_M \cup I_D \cup I_{T_0} \cup I_{T_1} \cup I_{T_2}$
2: min(I_M, $I_D \cup I_{T_0} \cup I_{T_1} \cup I_{T_2}$)   /*Line 2–5 minimize each subset
3: min(I_D, $I_{T_0} \cup I_{T_1} \cup I_{T_2}$)   relative to subsets of
4: min(I_{T_0}, $I_{T_1} \cup I_{T_2}$)   more complex interaction
5: min(I_{T_1}, I_{T_2})   elements*/
6: I=$I_M \cup I_D \cup I_{T_0} \cup I_{T_1} \cup I_{T_2}$

Algorithm 6 min(Input–Output: interaction set I, Input: set list J=$\{(J_i)_{i \leq n}\}$

1: **for all** $X \in I$ **do**
2:    **for all** Y in a set of J **do**
3:       **if** $\exists$ agents (A,B,P) so that $(X(A,B)$ and $Y(A,B))$ or $(X(A,B)$ and $Y(A,B,P))$ or $(X(A,B,P)$ and $Y(A,B,P))$ exist **then**
4:          I=I$\backslash\{X\}$
5:          **if** X is $DUPLEX(A,B)$ and Y is $T_0(A,B,P)$ **then**
6:             J_0=$J_0\backslash\{T_0(A,B,P)\}$ /*corresponds to T_0 interactions in that case*/
7:             J_1=$J_1\cup\{T_1(A,B,P)\}$ /*corresponds to T_1 interactions in that case*/
8:          **end if**
9:          Break the loop
10:       **end if**
11:    **end for**
12: **end for**

Algorithm 5 modifies a set I by matching interaction elements and keeping only the most constraining ones. For example, $MONO(A,B,P)$ matches $DUPLEX(A,B)$, $T_0(A,B,P)$, $T_1(A,B,P)$, and $T_2(A,B,P)$. As it is less constraining, the procedure will eliminate it if one of the others is found. The minimization is performed by the sub-procedure *min* in Algorithm 6.

Algorithm 6 receives from *minimize* in Algorithm 5 a set I and a set list J, ordered by increasing complexity of interaction elements. The aim is to match elements in I with elements in a set of J that feature common agents *in the same order* (line 3). If a match occurs (we counted 15 cases), the element of I is discarded (line 4) as it is redundant and less complete. In the case of $DUPLEX(A,B)$ and $T_0(A,B,P)$ (line 5), there is an exception. The former is a 'conversation' and the second a single overhearing, so the result of the match is a 'conversation overheard on one side', *i.e.* $T_1(A,B,P)$. In such a case, $T_0(A,B,P)$ is also removed (line 6) and $T_1(A,B,P)$ is created (line 7). The procedure ends with a minimized I, relative to J.

Managing Conflicts Between Individuals and Societies in Multi-agent Systems*

Rubén Fuentes, Jorge J. Gómez-Sanz, and Juan Pavón

Universidad Complutense Madrid, Dep. Sistemas Informáticos y Programación
28040 Madrid, Spain
{ruben, jjgomez, jpavon}@sip.ucm.es
http://grasia.fdi.ucm.es

Abstract. The development of multi-agent systems (MAS) implies considering both the social and individual levels of these systems. However, the elements in these levels are not necessarily consistent. Conflicts can arise between the goals of the community and those of individual agents. These contradictions are potentially very complex, given the inherent intentional nature of agents and the interactive features of their societies. Developers can face these problems about contradictions with traditional software engineering verification techniques. Nevertheless, these techniques always depend on the understanding of developers about what properties to check. Abstractions of the agent paradigm offer a new possibility for verification: the use of expert knowledge from social sciences to detect and solve this kind of problems. Social sciences and MAS research share a similar view about their objects of study: societies of intentional actors. With this basis, it is possible to adapt the expertise of social sciences to the study of MAS, providing a new source of knowledge for the verification of MAS focused in their social and intentional features. Based on our previous research, we have developed a method to solve motivational contradictions with one of these social theories, the Activity Theory. This method is explained with a case study about the management of a bookstore.

1 Introduction

In Agent Oriented Software Engineering (AOSE), systems are modelled as organizations of agents that interact to achieve their own goals or those of their designers. When modelling these Multi-Agent Systems (MAS), developers have to consider the objectives that the organization pursues as a whole, but also the goals of its agents. The complete set of goals present in a MAS may be inconsistent. This situation does not always imply analysis mistakes. For example, agents can act on behalf of different customers, the profit of individual agents can be reduced to improve the overall gain of the community, or developers can deal with competing organizations.

* This work has been funded by Spanish Ministry of Science and Technology under grant TIC2002-04516-C03-03.

M.-P. Gleizes, A. Omicini, and F. Zambonelli (Eds.): ESAW 2004, LNAI 3451, pp. 106–118, 2005.

AOSE typically studies this kind of conflictive configurations in a MAS with traditional verification techniques from the software engineering that focus on very concrete social and intentional issues. Examples of these verifications involving specific agents' features are the satisfaction of goals by tasks, e.g. INGENIAS [16], the exchange of the correct information between tasks, e.g. DESIRE [4], or the analysis of the motivation in organizations, e.g. the work in [17]. The disadvantage of this way of working is that it does not consider those features with an overall approach. As it only focuses on some specific aspects, it disregards how other features can have influence over those aspects. These methods conflict the holistic design view that is one of the main concerns in AOSE [19].

Looking for solutions to this problem, our research turned to the use of social sciences. These disciplines study this sort of aspects in human organizations with a systemic approach, i.e. considering both social and individual issues. Besides, the use of social sciences for software engineering has already precedents. They are widely used in Requirements Engineering [15], Computer Supported Cooperative Work (CSCW) [11], or Human-Computer Interaction (HCI) [12]. For AOSE, this interest is increased by the fact that the natural metaphor for most of MAS approaches is that of systems with intentional actors, which is close to human organizations.

In this line, our previous work [7, 8, 9] establishes the suitability of one of these social theories, the Activity Theory, to work with the development of MAS. The Activity Theory (AT) [18] is a framework for the study of human behaviours and actions. It considers activities with both the social and individual levels interleaved in developmental-historical processes. As part of our research with MAS, we provide a design vocabulary for AT that can be translated to different MAS methodologies [7], tools for requirements elicitation in MAS [9], and a process to deal with their contradictions based on AT research [8].

In this paper, we show how these knowledge and techniques can help to deal with motivational conflicts in MAS. Our management of conflicts comprehends the understanding of general *social properties* in MAS. *Social properties* are here considered in the line of [5] as those related with the organizational, cognitive, developmental, evolutionary, and motivational aspects of the system. All of these views have influence over MAS goal problems. That is why the process that verifies and solves this kind of conflicts is built over these *social properties*. As a sketch of the process, we can say that tools for requirements elicitation become the key to expand the specifications in new areas while contradictions allow the study of the goal conflicts in those specifications. The whole approach is illustrated in this paper with a case study of a bookstore in Internet.

The remaining sections are organized as follows. Section 2 gives a brief overview about the vocabulary used to represent the knowledge of the AT and its use inside a MAS software process. The following section focuses on the use of AT techniques to deal with motivational conflicts in MAS. Section 4 presents a case study with these techniques. Finally, there is a discussion about the use of the AT in the example and the benefits and limitations of this approach to study MAS specifications.

2 Activity Theory for MAS

Activity Theory (AT) is based on the psychological and sociological theory of L.S. Vygotsky (1978) and A.N. Leontiev (1989). It focuses on the interaction of human activity and consciousness within its relevant environmental context.

The basic unit of analysis in the AT is the human *activity*. *Activities* are driven by people needs. The basic principles of the AT include *object* orientedness, internalisation/externalisation, mediation, hierarchical structure, and development. In the AT, the human mind emerges, exists, and can only be understood within the context of human interaction with the world and this interaction, i.e., the *activity*, is socially and culturally determined [13].

The principle of mediation plays a central role in the AT. An *activity* always contains various *artefacts* (e.g. instruments, signs, procedures, machines, materials, laws, forms of work, or organisations). These *artefacts* have a mediating role [1]. Relations between elements of an *activity* are not directed, but mediated. *Tools* shape the way human beings interact with their context [14]: the relationship between the *subject* and the *object* of the *activity* is mediated by a *tool*. The *tool* allows the *subject* transforming the *object* into the *product* that satisfies his *objectives*. A *tool* can be anything used in the transformation process, including both material *tools* and *tools* for thinking. The relationship between *subject* and *community* is mediated by *rules* and the relationship between *object* and *community* is mediated by the *division of labour* - how the *activity* is distributed among the members of the *community*, that is, the role each individual in the *community* plays in the *activity*, the power each wields, and the tasks each is held responsible for.

These concepts constitute the common core of the modelling vocabulary for AT as agreed in its research community. This vocabulary has been translated into UML terms using stereotypes [7] to facilitate its use in a software development process. To complete the graphical vocabulary of the AT for MAS, some other entities, e.g. *activity systems* or *roles*, and relationships, e.g. contributions or decompositions, were added to the previous core.

The vocabulary for AT allows developers to represent the knowledge from the AT as diagrams, what we call *structural patterns*. Since our purpose is providing support tools for existing agent-oriented methodologies, these AT patterns have to be translated to agent related terms (according to the corresponding methodology). We have shown in [7] that this translation is feasible for agent-oriented methodologies with an underlying Believe-Desire-Intention (BDI) model [2], by considering the intentional and social features of both theories.

Once the mapping between AT and agent concepts is established, it is possible to apply AT techniques in the MAS development process. Based on this, we have implemented two support tools in the INGENIAS Development Kit (*http://ingenias.sourceforge.net*), the Requirements Elicitation Guide (REG) (formerly known as the Activity Checklist for MAS [9]) and the analysis of contradictions [7].

The REG is based on the Activity Checklist from the AT. The original Activity Checklist [13] is an analytical tool to elicit information about the context of activities in HCI studies. It describes in natural language *areas*, *aspects*, and *questions* that act as reminders for researchers of the elements to analyze. The *areas* are the main topics of introspection about a system according to the AT. These topics include several relevant features for analysis, i.e. the *aspects*. *Questions* describe the relevant information to gather about a given *aspect*. Our work has evolved this checklist adapting it to the particular concerns of MAS requirements. In the new checklist, *questions* have representations with structural patterns in UML that act as frames to collect the information of their answers in a format suitable for software development.

The other key tool obtained from the AT is the analysis of contradictions. Contradictions in the AT [14] represent tensions between the components related in an *activity*. The AT states that these contradictions are the propellers of the system evolution: a system changes trying to solve its inner contradictions. Thus, contradictions are a cardinal topic in AT studies. The expert knowledge of the AT about contradictions and their solutions in humans' organizations has been adapted to MAS [7]. In the same way that the *questions* of the REG, contradictions are described as UML structural patterns with explanations in natural language. These repositories of contradictions contain ready-to-use properties that developers can check in their models thanks to the mappings and a detection process [8].

The combination of these techniques gives developers tools to deal with the social and intentional features of MAS using knowledge from social sciences. They provide guidelines in the development, e.g. "What do I have to introspect?" or "Do my agents have true motives to collaborate?", and language and processes to elicit *social properties*, e.g. those described by the REG, and to solve inconsistencies, e.g. solutions for AT contradictions.

The next section introduces with more detail how to use these tools to manage motivational conflicts.

3   AT to Deal with Conflicts in MAS Design

Most of current approaches to deal with motivational issues in MAS adopt a point of view too constrained [10]. They focus on the goals, the tasks that satisfy them, or the agents that pursue those goals. That way of doing constitutes an extrapolation of traditional verification techniques. It mainly relies on syntactic rules about the elements, e.g. "a *goal* always has a related *task* that is able to satisfy it".

Such approaches to solve motivational issues in MAS have two clear drawbacks. First, they hardly consider the real influence of the environment. That effect is beyond the scope of goals, tasks, or resources involved in MAS workflows; it also encompasses aspects like the structure of the organization, the norms describing power relationships, or the users' interests behind the agents. The second issue is that these approaches heavily depend on developers' knowledge about what useful properties they have to verify or how to solve conflicts. However, these properties are not about common software artefacts and do not belong to the common background in computer science. This makes difficult for developers considering useful situations that are not evident.

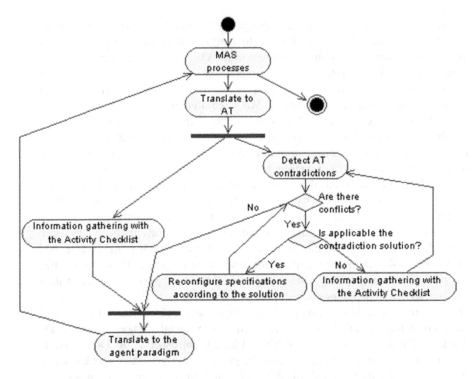

Fig. 1. AT goals conflict management

Our solution for this problem is the use of AT to provide the additional knowledge that developers need to reason about the social and intentional aspects of MAS. The AT tools of the REG [9] and the analysis of contradictions [7] are the required techniques. Their formulation is a join venture between AT and agent experts. These techniques crystallize the conceptual framework and experience of AT research about the analysis of social systems. Consequently, they can provide hints about the aspects that the MAS specifications should consider or the conflicts that can appear and how they can be solved. The process that integrates these tools appears in Fig. 1.

The process in Fig. 1 has as parameter the specifications of a MAS. The first step is to translate the MAS specification into AT terms, what does the corresponding support tool. The result can be represented as a set of views of the MAS in the UML language for AT. This is illustrated later in the case study of section 4. At this point developers can work out two kinds of problems. The first one is whether their specifications cover all the aspects about a given part of the MAS. The second one is that they try to discover whether their MAS has or not motivational conflicts.

The REG is the tool to solve the first problem. As stated before, the REG is structured in *areas*, *aspects*, and *questions*. An example of them appears in Fig. 2. The table includes the *question* used in the case study of section 4 pointed out with a "✓". Developers should read the descriptions of *areas* and *aspects* to determine what are the features of their MAS most probably underspecified. When they make their choice, the guide offers them a set of *questions* representing information that specifications should include about that topic. The results of answering those *questions* are new diagrams for the MAS specifications in the AT language, like that in Fig. 6.

Aspects	Questions
Objectives context	What are the evidences that allow thinking in a given moment that the objective can be achieved? Are there processes that force the actor to respect organization norms? What are the decision mechanisms in the organization? Is it a hierarchy? Is it a committee?
Potential conflicts between objectives	Does the satisfaction of the objectives of the component interfere with the satisfaction of others actor's objectives? ✓ Could society rules force the agent to desist from the objective? Does the agent's objective come from an organization objective?

Fig. 2. Examples of *aspects* and *questions* in the *Means/ends area*

The detection and solution of conflicts relies on the analysis of motivational contradictions. The AT identifies regular patterns, some of which are contradictions, that appear in human organizations, and with them it explains how social systems change or why sometimes they do not behave as expected. Motivational conflicts are among those contradictions. An example of them is the *Need State* contradiction [3], which is illustrated below with the case study. Contradictions are composed by two structural patterns: a match pattern and a solution pattern. The match pattern describes the goal conflict in terms of AT concepts. The detection process traverses the specification looking for groups of elements that correspond with the pattern. An identification of the pattern can point out a motivational conflict (like that in Fig. 7). The solution pattern describes an answer that an organization has adopted for that concrete conflict. It is a hint on how the specifications could be modified. This solution is a rearrangement of the elements in the match pattern, maybe with additional elements. A solution example appears in Fig. 8.

An important remark about the process in Fig. 1 is that it is hard to apply without automated support, as it involves a lot of repetitive work. The process involves repositories of AT properties, which have to be instantiated to concrete MAS specifications thanks to mappings. Besides, the addition of new elements to some given MAS specifications with the REG or carrying out the pattern matching to detect contradictions, require traversing the specifications looking for the correct elements. In this sense, assistants to apply the AT techniques are needed. A partial architecture of one of these assistants appears in [8]. These tools can be integrated through well-defined APIs with existing MAS modelling environments.

4   Case Study: Bookstore in Internet

This example for goals conflict management with the AT in a MAS process is inspired by the *Juul Møller Bokhandel A/S* [6]. Its full specification with the INGENIAS notation can be found at *http://grasia.fdi.ucm.es/ingenias*.

Briefly, *Juul Møller* is a bookstore that works with the Norwegian School of Management. The bookstore has an agreement with the School. Thanks to the agreement, teachers of the School provide to *Juul Møller* the list of books for the next course in advance. In exchange, *Juul Møller* sells the books to students with discounts. This agreement allows *Juul Møller* negotiating with publishers to obtain better prices and increasing sales.

The problems for the bookstore come when students begin to buy books in Internet. They have discovered that sites such as *Amazon.com* (http://amazon.com) or *Blackwell's* (http://www.blackwell.com) are as good providers as *Juul Møller*. They sell books at almost the same prices than *Juul Møller* and their delivery times are even better when teachers change course books at the beginning of the term.

a) Agents

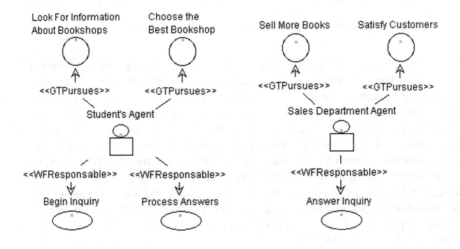

b) Workflow

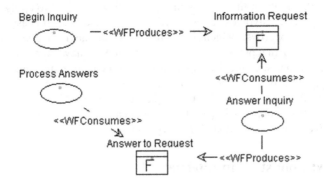

Fig. 3. a) and b) Student's Agent and workflow to buy books with INGENIAS. Circles represent goals, rectangles represent facts, and ellipses represent tasks

Satisfaction relationships

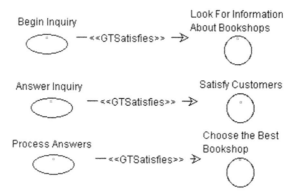

Fig. 4. Satisfaction relationships to buy books with INGENIAS. Circles represent goals and ellipses represent tasks

To avoid losing customers, *Juul Møller* wants to enter in the e-commerce and preserve the agreement. It tries to develop a site that gives to teachers and students appealing new and specialized services. Of course, this new system will be developed with the latest agent technology.

Fig. 3. a) and b) Student's Agent and workflow to buy books with INGENIAS. Circles represent goals, rectangles represent facts, and ellipses represent tasks.

Fig. 4 shows part of the specification of the new system with INGENIAS.

The MAS have agents for students, teachers, different employees of *Juul Møller*, and even to access external bookstores (such as *Amazon.com* or *Blackwell's*) or publishers. Every agent has to carry out tasks on behalf of its user, what can imply that it has to request services. At the same time, it has to offer some services to the overall organization. Fig. 4 focuses in two of these agents, the *Student's Agent* and the *Sales Department Agent*. These agents collaborate when the user needs to find the best place to buy books. The *Student's Agent* compares the prices that the *Sales Department Agents* of different bookstores provide him. The *Sales Department Agent* can represent any bookstore, for instance, that of *Juul Møller*.

As one of the main goals when building the MAS for *Juul Møller* is preserving the current status quo, i.e. the agreement, the MAS has to work in this way. Let see with AT tools if this happens.

The first step is to translate the current MAS specifications to the AT language. This process can be done with an assistant tool that applies the mappings. In this case, the translation uses the mappings for INGENIAS introduced in [8]. The mappings describe how an origin structure with concepts of a given MAS methodology corresponds with another target one that only uses AT concepts. The translation of the specifications encompasses instantiations of all the target structures whose origin structures where identified over the MAS models. Part of the resulting translations for the specifications in Fig. 4 can be seen in Fig. 5.

With the translated information, the development team tries to know if this configuration helps to preserve the agreement between the bookstore and the school.

The agreement is modelled as a set of goals, i.e. AT *objectives*, pursued by actors in the system, i.e. AT *subjects* or *communities*. In this case, the customers who represent *Juul Møller* did not relate the goals that are relevant for the MAS among themselves or with other goals of the context. Therefore, developers need to elicit further information about these relationships.

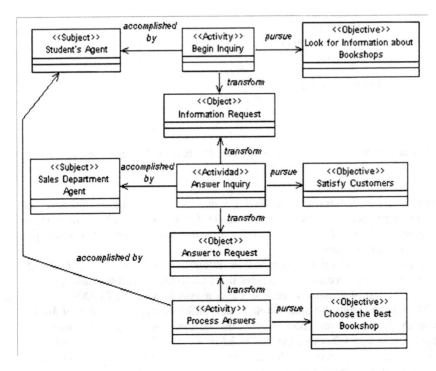

Fig. 5. Partial translation of specifications to AT

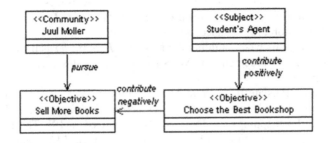

Fig. 6. Answer to a *question* about conflicts between objectives

Developers can use the REG [9] to elicit the new information. The guide includes an *area* called *Means/ends* that has an *aspect* about *Potential Conflicts between Goals*. As an example, its sixth *question* is "Does the satisfaction of the objectives of the component interfere with the satisfaction of others actor's objectives?". Like all the *questions* in the guide, this has a related structural pattern expressed in UML. The pattern acts as a frame of which the customer fills up slots with the information of the answer. This information can be new values or elements already in the specifications. Fig. 6 shows the answer to this *question*. The relationship between the *Student's Agent* and his *objective* comes from his *activities*. The *community Juul Møller* represents the global interests of the bookstore company. This *community* pursues the *objective Sell More Books*. The customer's answer points out to a conflict between goals. When the students choose the best place to buy their books, it could be a different one from *Juul Møller*. In that case, their choice decreases the sales of the bookstore and thus damages the agreement.

The apparent contradiction in Fig. 6 deserves a deeper analysis that determines its real impact over the considered *activities*. If there is a real conflict about this situation, it could raise from different causes and therefore demand different solutions. Developers use the AT contradictions to carry out this analysis. The process presented in [8] admits that developers customize patterns for specific elements. In this case, the elements of interest are those in Fig. 6.

Developers would check (probably with the help of a software assistant) the possible contradictions that can exist in the specifications. In the current problem, a contradiction called the *Need State* [3] appears. An *activity* emerges to satisfy a given need of its *subject* [14]. However, the relation between the *activity* and its needs is not static. The *activity* is characterized by the concrete *object* whose transformation satisfies the needs. As the *object* can change, the *activity* can also be transformed in new *activities*. The *Need State* emerges when the *activity* satisfies no longer the needs of its *subject* because of the changes in its *object*. Fig. shows the *Need State* for *Juul Møller*. All the members of *Juul Møller* and their agents, like the *Sales DepartmentAgent*, share the common goal of *Sell More Books*. Thus, their *activities*

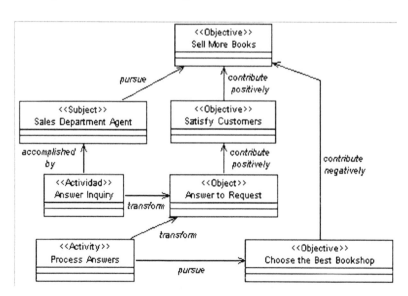

Fig.7. *Need State* contradiction in *Juul Møller*

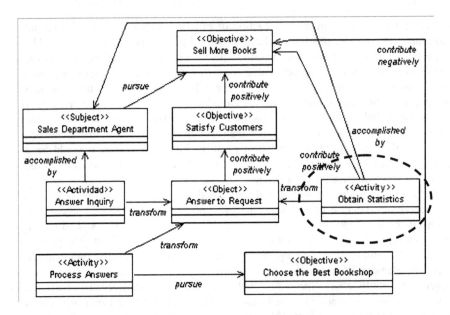

Fig. 8. A possible solution for the *Need State* contradiction in *Juul Møller*

should contribute positively to that goal. However, the *activity Process Answer* that the *Student's Agent* carries out has a negative effect over this goal. In this new situation, the *activity Answer Inquiry* does not guarantee the satisfaction of the *objectives* of the *Sales Department Agent*. A *Need State* contradiction emerges for this agent. Note in Fig. 7. that the information to detect the contradiction was obtained mixing several views in the existing specifications from the INGENIAS methodology.

AT research has studied several possible solutions for a *Need State* contradiction. Fig. 8. presents one of the more common: the addition of a new *activity* that contributes to the satisfaction of the harmed goal. The new *activity* can provide new *objects* or repair existing ones. In the case of *Juul Møller*, developers introduce the new *activity Obtain Statistics*. This *activity* does not interfere with the remaining configuration of the MAS but produces additional *objects* that benefit the *objective* of *Sell More Books*. The statistics about the students' queries can help *Juul Møller* to determine what their habits are. This information helps to improve its service and thus to increase its sales.

The application of these techniques based on the AT is an interactive process with the user. Most of the work in this case study can be automated. Nevertheless, user's decisions are needed about whether the identified contradictions make real sense in the domain or to restrict the search of patterns to certain elements.

5   Conclusions

This paper has shown an approach to the discovering and solving of contradictions about goals in MAS, considering the individual and social level of these systems. This kind of conflicts is common in MAS design because agents may act on behalf of different users and organizations. In this heterogeneous and changing context, developers cannot expect that the considered set of goals is always consistent.

We think that solving this problem is not just a question of traditional verification, where developers have to give a notation and a process to prove properties over specifications in that language. This is also a problem of what the interesting properties are. Here, our research has led us to the use of social sciences, concretely the Activity Theory, to provide this knowledge.

The proposed process allows developers to acquire new information about the MAS and verify its social properties. Main features of this process are:

- Use of the AT as a source of knowledge about *social properties* in human societies. This information can be applied to the elicitation and verification of the same kind of social features in MAS.
- Translation with mappings from the AT language to MAS vocabularies. These correspondences allow the application of AT techniques to agent-oriented methodologies.
- Representation of properties as structural patterns with UML. This representation comes with a textual explanation that facilitates the comprehension of its social meaning. The UML patterns are suitable to represent information in the development process. Besides, they allow approaching the verification process as one of pattern matching.

By having a repository of properties coming from the AT, developers can overcome some of the difficulties with motivational conflicts in MAS. They have ready to use libraries of potentially interesting properties that they could elicit or verify in their MAS. Moreover, they have a method to apply these properties in their development if they provide the mappings for their methodology. Even if they adopt another approach to use the properties, e.g. some formalism, the knowledge about the properties is still reusable for their MAS.

The application of the AT method for MAS can be automated as proved previous research. The resulting tools have interfaces that allow their integration with current modelling environments.

An open issue in this method of conflict management is that developers do not know what the most convenient properties to check in a given situation are. Here, developers need heuristics that help them to decide, and this is a current research topic. These heuristics could be integrated with the support tools in order to guide the developer in this process.

References

1. Bednyi, G. Z., Meister, D.: *The Russian Theory of Activity: Current Application to Design and Learning*. Lawrence Erlbaum Associates. 1997.
2. Bratman, M. E.: *Intentions, Plans, and Practical Reason*. Harvard University Press. 1987.
3. Bratus, B. S., Lishin, O. V.: *Laws of the development of activity and problems in the psychological and pedagogical shaping of the personality*. Soviet Psychology XXI, 38-50. 1983.

4. Brazier, F. M. T., Dunin-Keplicz, B. M., Jennings, N. R., and Treur, J.: *DESIRE:Modelling Multi-Agent Systems in a Compositional Formal Framework.* International Journal of Cooperative Information Systems, special issue on Formal Methods in Cooperative Information Systems: Multi-Agent Systems, 1997.

5. L. L. Constantine: *Constantine on Peopleware.* Englewood Cliffs, NJ: Yourdon Press, 1995.

6. Espen Andersen: *Juul Møller Bokhandel A/S.* Case Study available at http://www.espen.com/. 2001.ï

7. R. Fuentes, J.J. Gómez-Sanz, J. Pavón: *Activity Theory for the Analysis and Design of Multi-Agent Systems.* In Proceedings of the Fourth International Workshop on Agent Oriented Software Engineering (AOSE 2003), Melbourne, Australia, July 2003. Volume 2935 of Lecture Notes in Computer Science, pages 110–122. Springer Verlag. 2003.

8. R. Fuentes, J.J. Gómez-Sanz, J. Pavón: *Social Analysis of Multi-Agent Systems with Activity Theory.* In Proceedings of CAEPIA 2003, San Sebastian, Spain, November 2003. Volume 3040 of Lecture Notes in Artificial Intelligence, pages 526-535. Springer Verlag. 2004.

9. R. Fuentes, J.J. Gómez-Sanz, J. Pavón: *Towards Requirements Elicitation in Multi-Agent Systems.* In Proceedings of the 4th International Symposium From Agent Theory to Agent Implementation, AT2AI 2004, pages 582-587, Vienna, Austria, April 2004.

10. R. Fuentes, J.J. Gómez-Sanz, J. Pavón: *Verification and Validation Techniques for Multi-Agent Systems.* Upgrade, Vol. V, n. 4, August 2004.

11. Hughes, J., King, V., Rodden, T., Andersen, H.: *Moving out from the control room: ethnography in system design.* In Proceedings of the ACM 1994 Conference on Computer Supported Cooperative Work - CSCW'94. ACM Press, pp. 429-439.

12. Hutchins, E., Klausen, T.: *Distributed cognition in an airline cockpit.* In D. Middleton & Y. Engestrom (Eds.), Communication and Cognition at Work. Beverly Hills, CA.: Sage Books. 1992.

13. V. Kaptelinin, B. A. Nardi, C. Macaulay: *The Activity Checklist: A tool for representing the "space" of context.* Interactions, 6 (4), p27-39. 1999.

14. Aleksie Nikolaevich Leontiev: *The problem of activity in the history of Soviet psychology.* In Soviet Psychology, 27(1), 22–39. 1989.

15. Nuseibeh, B.A., Easterbrook, S.M.: *Requirements engineering: A roadmap.* In Proceedings of the 22nd International Conference on Software Engineering (ICSE'00), pp. 35–46. 2000.

16. Pavón, J and Gómez-Sanz, J. J.. *Agent Oriented Software Engineering with INGENIAS.* In: Multi-Agent Systems and Applications III, 3rd International Central and Eastern European Conference on Multi-Agent Systems, CEEMAS 2003. Lecture Notes in Computer Science 2691, Springer Verlag (2003) 394-403.

17. J. Sichman, Y. Demazeau: *On Social Reasoning in Multi-Agent Systems.* Inteligencia Artificial, Revista Iberoamericana de Inteligencia Artificial, Special Issue on Development of Multi-Agent Systems, n°13, pp. 68-84, AEPIA. 2001.

18. L. S. Vygotsky: Mind and Society. Cambridge MA, Harvard University. 1978.

19. Michael J. Wooldridge: *Agent-based software engineering.* IEEE Proceedings on Software Engineering, 144(1):26–37, February 1997.

Motivation-Based Selection of Negotiation Opponents

Steve Munroe and Michael Luck

Electronics and Computer Science,
University of Southampton, Southampton, UK
{sjm01r, mml}@ecs.soton.ac.uk

Abstract. If we are to enable agents to handle increasingly greater levels of complexity, it is necessary to equip them with mechanisms that support greater degrees of autonomy. This is especially the case when it comes to agent-to-agent interaction which, in systems of selfish agents, often follows the format of negotiation. Within this context, a problem which has hitherto received little attention is that of identifying appropriate negotiation opponents. Furthermore, the problem is particularly difficult in dynamic systems where the need to negotiate over issues and the evaluation of resources may change over time. Such dynamics demand high degrees of autonomy from agents so that such factors can be handled at run-time and without the aid of human controllers. To that end, this paper draws inspiration from biological organisms and theories of motivation, and describes a motivation-based architecture comprising a number of motivation-based classification and selection mechanisms used to evaluate and select between negotiation opponents. Opponents are evaluated in terms of the likely issues they will want to negotiate over and the amount of conflict this might entail. Additionally, the expected cost of a negotiation with an opponent is examined in relation to the agent's current motivational evaluation of its resources. The mechanisms allow prioritisation between each method of evaluation dependent upon motivational needs. Some preliminary evaluation of the model is also presented.

1   Introduction

Negotiation is a particularly important form of interaction between agents. It allows agents to reach agreement over shared concerns, and there are many existing frameworks (e.g. [1, 2, 3]). Most frameworks focus on the problems inherent within the negotiation episode, such as which negotiation strategies and tactics offer the best results, and how best to employ them. They provide a host of techniques and methods that allow agents to autonomously navigate through a negotiation episode. However, though the actual steps taken within a negotiation are often left to the agent to decide, the form and focus of the negotiation is still most often handled by some user of the agent. Thus, though an agent may be used to negotiate the conditions of a holiday package for example, the

M.-P. Gleizes, A. Omicini, and F. Zambonelli (Eds.): ESAW 2004, LNAI 3451, pp. 119–138, 2005.

issues negotiated over, the constraints on what are acceptable outcomes, and the opponents negotiated with, are often not decided by the agent, but are presented as given constraints. This may be fine in such purchase negotiation as this but, in persistent, multi-agent systems where agents must go about their tasks away from human direction, this is clearly not adequate. To address this, agents must be given the ability to decide what they need to negotiate about, what constraints impact upon those needs, and which opponents best meet these needs. In fact, there is a growing realisation that the decisions that must be made prior to negotiation represent key problems that must be addressed if agents are to use negotiation more autonomously than they do at present (e.g.[4]).

1.1   Opponent Selection for Negotiation

When the need for negotiation arises, there may be a number of potential negotiation opponents that an agent can choose from. Each opponent may exhibit different service-related characteristics that distinguish it from other opponents. For negotiation to be successful, the preferences of the agent requiring the service must coincide with the service-related characteristics of the opponent. For example, an agent needing to negotiate on the time of delivery of some service, is better served by an opponent who does not have a preference for this issue. In this way, the issue can be settled quickly and at the value most preferred by the agent. In other words, the agent should attempt to avoid those opponents who have strong preferences regarding service delivery times, as this may risk conflict on the issue, potentially leading to a negotiation that is long, difficult and prone to failure. Thus, an agent should have, in order to increase its chances of engaging in successful negotiations, the ability to reason about the compatibility of an opponent's interests with its own in order to avoid negotiations with a high *conflict* potential.

An additional factor that impacts upon opponent choice is the *relative importance* of the negotiation issues chosen. For example, an agent looking to negotiate the purchase of a service, with only limited monetary resources, will place a greater value on that resource and so will be influenced towards those opponents offering cheaper prices. Good performance on price is, therefore, a more influential selection criterion than other issues, and opponent selection should reflect this. At different times, and with different constraints, however, opponent selection may be influenced by different criteria, such as the *quality* of the offered service.

1.2   Autonomy and Motivation

While existing negotiation frameworks allow for autonomous agent behaviour within negotiation, they mostly omit consideration of it before negotiation begins. However, if agents are to make the kinds of decisions that must be made before negotiation begins, they must be able to display autonomy here as well. Our approach to enable such autonomy is to adopt the construct of *motivation*, which is defined in [5] as *"any desire or preference that can lead to the generation and adoption of goals and that affects the outcome of the reasoning or behavioural task intended to satisfy those goals."*

Motivation influences the decision-making of an agent, leading to the adoption of those activities that best serve its motivational interests. This approach is similar to the more commonly used economic approach that uses the notion of *utility* to guide agent activity. Utility-based agents act under the principle of utility-maximisation, in which activities with higher utility are chosen over those with lower utility. However, whereas utility is an economic abstraction of value or benefit that is overlaid on an agent's choices by the agent designer, motivation is an internally derived measure of value determined both by a set of internal state variables (such as hunger or thirst, for example) and the external environment. For example, in the presence of food, an agent may or may not choose to eat depending on the state of its internal environment (specifically its hunger motivation). In this sense, motivation grounds the generation of measures of value (such as utility) in the agent's internal state, and thus is in a sense prior to, and generative of, such notions. By examining options and weighing up their motivational worth, an agent can be guided in choosing motivationally relevant activities, and it is exactly this behaviour that defines for us the essence of *autonomy*. An agent is autonomous if it makes decisions and selects courses of actions that *further its own interests* based upon *its own assessment* of the situation.

In this paper, we describe an approach to the selection of negotiation opponents based upon consideration of the likely amount of conflict that might result form a particular selection, and the extent to which an opponent is expected to meet the constraints that impact upon the agent's ability to settle the issue of price. We describe a *motivated agent architecture* and a number of *motivated decision-making mechanisms* that allow an agent to assess the various needs that it has regarding the issues of the forthcoming negotiation, and evaluate the how a particular opponent meets those needs. While the paper is free of formal description, a formal model of the motivated agent architecture exists and can be obtained from the authors. The paper proceeds as follows. In Section 2 related work is described. Section 3 describes our *motivated agent architecture* and our *negotiation goal model* comprising an attribute classification mechanism, and in Section 5 we discusses the kinds of information needed about opponents for selection to work. Section 6 describes the selection mechanisms that work by either *minimising conflict* or minimising *resource use*, and Section 7 presents some preliminary evaluation of the model. Finally, Section 8 offers some concluding remarks.

2   Related Work

Much work is currently been undertaken that examines opponent selection from the point of view of *trust* and/or *service reputation* (e.g. [6, 7]), where both refer to the fidelity of the opponent's behaviour with regard to the negotiated outcome. Whilst trust and reputation are of great importance for designers of agent systems, especially systems characterised by openness they are, we argue, only part of the story and must be supplemented with the kinds of issues we are investigating in this paper such as information relating to the underlying *interests* and *motivations* of the negotiation participants and how this influences the kinds of negotiation encounter they prefer.

Non trust-based opponent selection has been addressed by a number of researchers too. Work by Tesfatsion [8] examines how agents select opponents based upon the amount by which they exceed a fixed performance-based tolerance threshold. Though this work examines similar problems to those in this paper, it does not address the specific problems of the minimisation of conflict through the smart selection of negotiation opponents, and assumes fixed performance thresholds — whereas we deal with dynamically changing performance requirements. In [9], Banerjee *et al.* examine the formation of coalitions, and agents must choose partners based on the expected payoffs gained over a period of time. Although the work considers partner selection, it focuses on cooperative encounters and does not deal with the problems of negotiation. Another approach to opponent selection, using cognition-based strategies, is described in [10], in which several heuristic decision-functions facilitate the selection of optimal opponents. However, the work does not examine the effects of changing evaluations of resources and how this affects selection of opponents, nor does it deal with considerations of conflict, but instead, focuses on the efficacy of the decision heuristics.

Motivation has long been used in psychology [11] and ethology [12], where it is used to explain the *higher-level desires* of an organism. In computational settings, motivation is increasingly being used as a higher-level control mechanism that directs the goal generation, action-selection and decision-making activities of software agents (e.g. [13, 14]) and robots (e.g. [15, 16]). The importance of motivation as an enabler of autonomy in computational agents was perhaps first identified by d'Inverno and Luck [5], who discuss the importance of motivation in allowing an agent to generate its own goals, as opposed to adopting them from others. Further analysis of this view can be found in [17]. More recent efforts have extended Luck and d'Inverno's ideas to consider cooperation [13], planning [18] and norm-based multi-agent systems [19]. The use of motivation within negotiation is a relatively new approach. An early example is described in [20], where motivation is used to enable cooperative negotiations that aim to increase the utility of all participants. Perhaps the closest work to ours is that of Urbig et al. [4], which looks at the links and interdependencies of issue selection and partner choice, as well as their effect on behaviour during negotiation. However, their approach differs from ours by focusing on a formal specification of the possible interdependencies between the three aspects, rather than the development of an agent architecture and accompanying classification and selection mechanisms to enable the autonomy necessary to address these problems.

3   Motivated Agents and Negotiation Goals

Our previous work [21] has involved the development of a *motivated agent architecture*, which enables autonomous decision-making and action selection for computational agents. In the architecture, the external environment, goals, actions and resources are linked to the motivations of the agent through *motivational cues*, which are essentially beliefs which, when true, impact on the strength of the agent's motivations. The goals pursued, and the actions and resources used to satisfy goals, are all determined by the effects they have upon the agent's motivations via the cues to which they are linked. Thus, for example, a warehouse agent may notice that a box has been left lying in a corridor. If boxes in the wrong location act as cues for the agent, it will affect the intensity of the motivation linked to the cue. This may cause the agent to generate a goal to put the box back into its correct location in the warehouse. Whether this goal is adopted depends upon the size of the effect that satisfying this goal will have on motivational intensity levels. Once a goal is adopted, the agent must then select an appropriate plan, which may call for the use of some resources that enable the plan, and the agent must assess the motivational effects of executing the plans using any associated resources.

Figure 1 shows our motivated agent architecture. The agent forms a view of the environment, which is linked, along with the agent's goals, actions and resources, to cues which, if true, affect the agent's motivational intensity levels. If motivational intensities rise above certain threshold levels, goals are generated and the agent's decision-making module then considers the various actions and resources at its disposal, determines what the effect of their use would be on motivational intensity, and selects those that have the most beneficial effects. These are then passed on to the effectors of the agent to take action. In the rest of this

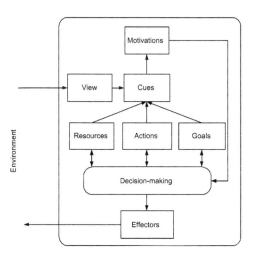

Fig. 1. The motivated agent architecture

Table 1. Possible values for three different negotiation goal attributes

Attribute	Attribute Values				
Price	10	20	30	40	
Delivery	Mon	Tues	Wed	Thurs	Fri
Quality	Low	Med	High		

paper we describe a classification mechanism and two selection mechanisms that lie within the decision-making component of the motivated agent architecture.

3.1   Negotiation Goals

Though the model above provides a general view of motivated agents, we need to refine it to describe how an agent can generate and reason about *negotiation goals*. In our work we have developed a model of negotiation goals that allows agents to autonomously decide what they want to negotiate about, what they do not want to negotiate about and what they do not care about. The components of a goal are its *attributes*, which represent the traditional AI notion of an *atom* composed of a predicate and a sequence of terms. So, for example, an attribute of a goal to place a box in a store room could be represented as: *In(boxA, storeRoom)*.

Our model is unique, however, in that we classify attributes according to their status in a forthcoming negotiation. Those attributes of a negotiation goal that describe what must be achieved are called *fixed attributes*, while those that *may* form the focus of the negotiation are called *potential attributes*. Potential attributes allow us to model negotiation issues such as *price*, *time* or *quality*, and they are composed of a *predicate* and a *set of values* to instantiate the predicate. So, for example, *Price(boxA, X)* must have a range of values that can instantiate the variable, X. Table 1 shows the three potential attributes of *Price*, *Time* and *Quality* along with a set of values for each that can be used for instantiation.

Thus, a negotiation goal initially comprises a set of fixed attributes for describing what must be achieved, and a set of potential attributes that may or may not be negotiated over. Table 2 shows the initial structure of such a goal. The example goal here is the goal to place a box in a particular location. The identity of the box and the name of the location therefore represent fixed attributes of the goal. The potential attributes refer to the price the agent is willing to pay to have this goal satisfied, the time at which the goal is to be satisfied and the quality of the method used to move the box (imagine there are three possible ways to move the box, each with a different chance of damaging the contents of the box). Initially, the goal consists of just these types of attributes (i.e. fixed and potential). The task of the agent upon the generation of this goal is to decide which of the potential attributes are to be made *negotiable*, which should be made *fixed* and therefore, not negotiable, and which are of no importance (called *slack* attributes) and therefore, can be omitted from the negotiation altogether.

Table 2. The initial structure of a negotiation goal

Partial Goal Template		
Attributes	Fixed	Potential
Box id	✓	
Destination	✓	
Price		✓
Time		✓
Quality		✓

The decision about the status of a potential attribute depends on two factors. First, the preferences of the agent towards how the attribute will be instantiated must be considered. Constructing these preferences is achieved by assessing the effects of each instantiation on the agent's current activities. Second, the designer must supply a set of *classification rules* that are applied to the agent's preferences to determine whether the attribute is fixed, negotiable or slack. The form of the classification rules depends on the designer's needs for the domain in question, but we offer some example rules here:

1. An attribute is classified as *fixed* if the preferences of the agent contains *at most* one value that has positive motivational worth and all the rest as having negative motivational worth.
2. An attribute is classified as *negotiable* if the preferences of the agent contains *more than* one value that has positive motivational worth.
3. An attribute is classified as *slack* if *all* the values contained in the agent's preferences have the *same* motivational worth (both positive or negative).

The rationale for these rules is as follows. If only one value of an attribute has positive motivational worth, it is preferable for the agent to demand that this value be met in any forthcoming negotiations as, if any other value is used to instantiate the attribute, the agent will be in a worse state than previously. This means that the agent should include the attribute with the value as a fixed attribute of the negotiation goal. If, however, more than one value is identified that gives the agent positive motivational worth, then the agent can be afford to be flexible with regard to the attribute. Through this flexibility the agent increases its chances of reaching a successful settlement with an opponent, as there is greater room for agreement. Finally, if all the values for a given attribute have the same level of worth, there is no point in negotiating over the attribute, as the agent is indifferent to any instantiation. This allows the agent to prune irrelevant issues, thus making the negotiation more efficient and provides an incentive to opponents to enter into negotiation as, if they know that a preferred issue is irrelevant to the other agent, they can instantiate the attribute using their own preferred value.

In Figure 2, we show our *attribute preference construction and classification mechanism*. The potential attributes from a negotiation goal are passed to the *preference generator* that examines each possible value that can be used to instantiate

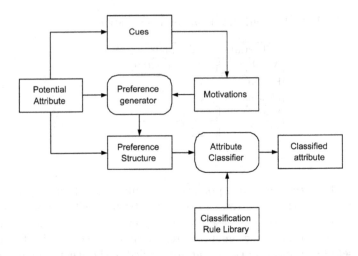

Fig. 2. The attribute preference construction and classification mechanism

Table 3. The final structure of a negotiation goal

Negotiation Goal Template				
Attributes	Fixed	Potential	Negotiable	Slack
Box id	✓			
Destination	✓			
Price			✓	
Time				✓
Quality	✓			

the attribute, and assesses their motivational worth by examining how the use of a value affects motivations via cues linking the attribute to motivations. By doing this for all the values of an attribute, a *preference attribute* is formed, which is simply a potential attribute with an associated preference ordering over its attribute-values. At this point, the preference attribute is passed to the *attribute classifier* that applies the attribute classification rules stored in the *attribute classification rule library*. After the application of the rules, each preference attribute of the negotiation goal is classified as either fixed, negotiable or slack. The final form of a negotiation goal for an agent wanting to engage in negotiation will be like that of Table 3. In the table the *price* attribute has been made negotiable, the *time* attribute has been made slack, and the *quality* attribute has been made fixed, along with the other two previously identified fixed attributes of *box id* and *destination*.

4   Constructing Preferences Over Potential Attributes

Imagine a situation in which an agent is considering a goal regarding the movement of a box from one location to another. The fixed attributes of the goal state

Table 4. Three example plans

Plan name	Description	Quality
planA	Move the box with a trolley	High
planB	Move the box by carrying it manually	Medium
planC	Move the box by dragging it	Low

that a particular box, $boxA$ is to be moved to a particular location, $roomB$, i.e $In(boxA, roomB)$. One of the potential attributes of the goal concern the *quality* of any plans used to satisfy the goal, where there exist three possible plans each with a different *quality* rating $\{high, med, low\}$ (imagine that each plan has a different chance of causing damage to the box, with the plan with the *lowest* chance has the *highest* quality rating). Three example plans are given in Table 4.

Now, in general, higher quality plans are preferred, hence we may have the preference ordering: $planA > planB > planC$ in which case the client agent chooses $planA$. However, there may be times when it is better to use $planB$ or even $planC$. For example, using trolley required for $planA$ might mean that another goal that needs the trolley is affected. However, this information may only be available at runtime, and so it is important for the agent to be able to re-order its preferences to meet the demands of the current situation. In the remainder of this section we show how this can be achieved.

4.1 A Motivated Preference Construction and Classification Mechanism

When considering the different ways in which a potential attribute can be instantiated, it is necessary to determine what effects it has on the agent's current activities. In order to do this we take the current activities of an agent, represented by the agent's *intentions*, each of which comprises a *goal* and a set of *plans* used to satisfy the goal. Plans represent the actions and *subgoals* that must be achieved before the goal can be satisfied and, in order to check whether any given instantiation of a potential attribute hinders or facilitates an intention, we must examine the plans associated with the intention to see what effects the instantiation has.

First we get the subgoals of an intention denoted by the term *subgoals*, which takes an intention and returns the set of subgoals encoded in the plans used to satisfy that intention. Then, we take a specific instantiation and determine those subgoals that are hindered *hindered* and those that are facilitated *facilitated*.

4.2 Scoring the Effect of an Instantiation

Having identified which intentions are hindered and which are facilitated, we next must provide a means to score each instantiation as a function of the *degree* of hinderance and facilitation. Then, we use this score to determine the preference ordering of the various different possible instantiations. The two functions, *hinderscore* and *facilitatescore*, defined below provide this functionality. The functions take an intention, *int*, and obtain its *worth* (derived from the strength of the motivation responsible for the goal's generation), which is then divided by the number of unhindered subgoals in the case of *hinderscore* or the number of facilitated subgoals in the case of *facilitatescore* (+1 is added to the denominator of *hinderedscore* to avoid division by zero).

$$hinderscore = -1 \times \frac{int.worth}{1 + (\#\{int.subgoals\} - \#\{int.hindered\})} \qquad (1)$$

$$facilitatescore = \frac{int.worth}{\#\{int.facilitated\}} \qquad (2)$$

We do this for all of the intentions of the agent and, once this is done, we combine both the hinder and facilitate scores into an overall score.

$$overallscore = \sum_{i=0}^{n} facilitatescore(int_i) + \sum_{i=0}^{j} hinderscore(int_j) \qquad (3)$$

where i is the number of goals that are facilitated, and j is the number of goals that are hindered.

4.3   Potential Attribute Preference Orderings

Once we have calculated the overall score for each of the values associated with a potential attribute we can use this to order the values. This provides us with a *preference ordering* over the values for a potential attribute. Once a preference ordering has been established over the attribute-values associated with a potential attribute we call such an attribute a *preference attribute*. As an example, consider a goal to have a box moved from one room in a warehouse to another. The *time* when the box can be moved is a potential attribute, and the values that can instantiate the attribute are drawn from the set *Days*:

$$Days = \{Mon, Tues, Wed, Thur, Fri, Sat, Sun\}$$

If a preference ordering has been established over this set, then *time* is a preference attribute and its *pref* relation might look like : $\{Wed > Tues > Mon > (Thur, Fri, Sat, Sun)\}$, meaning that Wednesday is preferred over Tuesday, which is preferred over Monday, which is preferred over Thursday, Friday, Saturday and Sunday, all of which are equally preferred.

4.4   Resource Dependent Attributes

In the goal of Table 3, the attribute of price is negotiable. This is the usual situation for such an attribute, as the values that can instantiate the attribute constitute the use of a *resource* and, in general, a preference over the use of different amounts of resource can always be identified. For example, an agent buying a service off another agent always prefers cheaper prices over more expensive ones, and vice versa for an agent selling the service. Such attributes of a negotiation goal are, therefore, classed as *resource dependent*, and the problem here is not one of identifying the structure of the preference, but rather the limits on what values are acceptable.

One way to do this is to simply ensure that the amount that an agent pays [1] must not incur more costs than the benefit the agent gains from the satisfaction of its goal. However, in most negotiation frameworks, the utility to be gained from a goal is fixed, and the amount of acceptable cost is calculated from a position of zero cost. For example, imagine an agent with a goal of utility 10, where utility is measured in dollar units. In determining how much an agent can spend in order to satisfy the goal, it is easy to see that, in order to be efficient, the agent must not spend more that $10. However, we might assume that the agent is only happy to spend this much as long as it has $100 in reserve, but that if this reserve falls to $50 then spending tha that amount might not seem so attractive, and the agent may lower its limit to, say, $8 [2]. By doing so, the agent begins to focus on *optimising* the use of its monetary resources as the resource dwindles, by changing the value placed on the resource in response to changes in the quantity available. Such dynamic evaluation of resources is often overlooked in negotiation frameworks, and we argue that this limits their flexibility to deal with dynamic domains in which access to resources changes over time. Thus, the overall worth of a particular resource cannot be merely represented by its *objective worth*, but must also be supplemented by a *subjective worth* derived by the current *need* an agent has for it. To model this subjective need we use *resource-based motivations* that track the levels of resources available to an agent (via appropriate cues), increasing in intensity when such resources diminish, and decreasing in intensity when they are renewed. The intensity of such motivations is used to identify the *unit value* of a given resource. Only when the unit value of a resource is determined, is it possible to calculate the maximum amount, or the *reservation*, of the resource that can be used to settle an issue. The reservation is thus calculated to be that quantity of resource, the use of which has a cost equal to the benefit gained from the negotiation goal being satisfied.

In order to deal with resource-dependent attributes, we must make some changes to the mechanism shown in Figure 2. Figure 3 shows the amended mechanism, in which the dashed lines indicate the new connections, and there is a decision point where the type of attribute being dealt with is determined. If the attribute is resource dependent, then a *default preference structure* is used that simply describes a, monotonic preference between the different values associated

---

[1] We focus on the perspective of a buyer in the description of the evaluation of resources, though the analysis is similar (albeit reversed) for the seller's perspective

[2] This behaviour is simply that identified by economists when making the point that utility does not equate to monetary worth — in other words, the richer a person, the less utility he gains by increasing his wealth and conversely, as shown above, the less wealthy a person, the more utility is lost by a decrease in wealth.

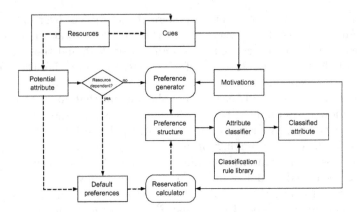

Fig. 3. The attribute preference construction and classification mechanism with resource-dependent attributes

with the attribute. Next, the associated resource is evaluated by the agent's *resource-based motivations* to determine its current unit worth. This is then passed, along with the default preference structure, to the *reservation calculator* that determines the maximum amount of resource that can be used, i.e. that unique quantity of resource whose total worth is equal to the worth of the goal. The amended preference structure is then passed to the attribute classifier as per other, non-resource-dependent attributes, and is classified according to the rules in the classification rule library.

5   Knowledge About Negotiation Opponents

In order for selection to work the agent must have some information about prospective opponents. In this section we describe such information.

5.1   An Opponent's Past Issue Choices for a Negotiation Goal

In previous negotiations, an opponent will have made choices over what potential attributes it wanted to negotiate over. Assuming that a record of these choices has been stored and that there is some regularity to the choices, it it possible to predict the opponent's choice of attributes for a future negotiation over the same goal. If the opponent's choices are variable, then the information about the choice of attributes might be based on a probability distribution over the attributes. To avoid unnecessary complications at this time, we assume that the record of an opponent's attribute choice for a given negotiation goal is of the form of a frequency distribution. Thus, for a given issue, we get the probability of it being chosen by

$$choiceProb = \frac{chosen(a)}{available(a)} \tag{4}$$

Table 5. Table showing the frequency of attribute selection for three negotiation opponents

Opponent	Attributes		
	A	B	C
1	0.5	0.7	0.2
2	0.4	0.4	0.9
3	0.3	0.8	0.4

where $chosen(a)$ returns the number of times the attribute, a, has been chosen by the opponent and $available(a)$ returns the amount of times the attribute a has been available as a potential choice. Thus, for a given negotiation goal with three attributes and three different negotiation opponents we may end up with the information shown in Table 5.

In the table, we can see three potential opponents in the first column labelled 1, 2, and 3. In the second, third and fourth columns, we have probabilities attached to each of the attributes (labelled A, B, C) for each opponent, calculated as the frequency that the attribute has been chosen in past negotiations for the current negotiation goal. A selecting agent then uses these frequency scores in combination with its own set of attribute choices to determine which opponents are likely to select issues that do not conflict with its own choices. We discuss how this can be achieved in Section 6.

5.2   Price Profiles of Negotiation Opponents

We must also provide our agent with information regarding opponent *price ranges* if our agents are to be able to assess the suitability of opponents with regard to current resource levels and their associated value. In negotiation, the participants normally announce *initial ask* prices (which can be considered the prices at which an opponent advertises its services) that then become adjusted through a process of concession-making in order to discover a price that all participants can accept. Initial ask prices tend to exaggerate the reservation price in order to increase the chance that a deal can be struck that is better for the agent than the reservation point.

Now, different agents may have different rules for setting initial ask prices given a reservation price but, for a given agent, the distance between the reservation and initial ask prices will tend to be stable. This means that any observed change in the initial ask price of an agent for a negotiation goal reflects a change in the subjective evaluation of the resource by the agent, where this change gives rise to a new (but private) reservation price and a corresponding publicly observed change in the initial ask price.

The *deal price* of a negotiation is the price at which agreement is found, and it depends upon a number of factors. First, it depends upon the initial ask prices of each participant of the negotiation, second, their reservation prices and third, the sequence of offers and counter offers on price made by each participant, i.e.

Table 6. Ask prices, deal prices and concessionary flexibility for an opponent

Neg	Price Profile For Negotiation Opponent		
Instance	Ask price	Deal price	Concessionary flexibility
1	10	9	0.1
2	9	7	0.2
3	11	8	0.3

their *concession strategy*. Though in general, agents will be able to select from a set of different concession strategies (each of which will affect the deal price), for simplicity we assume the agents only have one concession strategy, and we leave to later work the added complexity that different concession strategies bring to negotiation.

Given a fixed concession strategy for the agents, the distance between the initial ask price and any subsequent deal price will follow a predictable pattern that can be analysed by the other participants in the negotiation to predict what, given a particular initial ask price, the final deal price will be. The information about an opponent's initial ask price and deal price (what we call the *price profile*) must be available if an agent is to make judgements on the quality of an opponent on price.

Thus, over a number of negotiations it becomes possible to predict the deal price that will result in a negotiation for a particular goal with a particular negotiation partner by considering the amount of *concessionary flexibility* an opponent has shown during previous negotiations.

Table 6 shows the the price profile of a seller agent over three separate negotiations for the same negotiation goal. The first column indicates the negotiation instance and the second and third columns represent the initial ask price and the deal prices obtained. The fourth column shows the concessionary flexibility exhibited by the agent, which takes the difference of the initial ask price and the deal price and maps this difference to an interval of $[0,1]$ where 0 means no flexibility and 1 represents maximum flexibility (i.e. the agent has accepted a price of zero. Not a likely situation!). The average concessionary flexibility can then be calculated as

$$ aveCF = \frac{\Sigma_{i=0}^{n} cf_i}{n} \tag{5} $$

where cf_i is the ith concessionary flexibility score and n is the total number of negotiations for which the information is available. So, for any new negotiation over the same goal with this opponent, even with different initial ask prices, we can use the average concessionary flexibility of the opponent to make a prediction about what the deal price will be. The expected deal price can then be compared against the agent's own reservation price to predict whether a negotiation with an opponent advertising an initial ask price is likely to reach a deal on price that is acceptable to the agent.

6   Negotiation Opponent Selection Mechanisms

The process of opponent selection now consists of an analysis of the possible issue selections of the opponent and their expected deal price. To make an optimal selection, the agent must minimise two measures. First, when considering issue selection, the agent should select the opponent that offers a *minimal* amount of *conflict*, and second, when considering price the agent should attempt to *minimise* the use of its *monetary resource*. We describe each of these in detail in the following subsections.

6.1   Selecting To Minimise Conflict

Negotiation issues are those negotiable attributes that have been identified by *more than one* of the participants. Those attributes that have been identified by only one participant are *uncontested*, as none of the other participants in the negotiation have classified the attribute as negotiable and, therefore, do not have a preference for its instantiation. A clear criterion on which selection can therefore be based is the minimisation of the amount of contested attributes in the forthcoming negotiation through the identification of those opponents who contest the *least* number of negotiable attributes.

In Figure 4, two agents have each identified which of a negotiation goal's attributes they want to negotiate over (shown by the two circles covering the attribute set of the negotiation goal). The intersection of these two subsets of attributes are those attributes identified by *both* participants and are therefore contested and thus potentially in conflict. These attributes thus represent the *issues* of the negotiation. When considering different opponents, the agent should

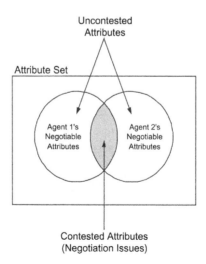

Fig. 4. Identifying Negotiation Issues

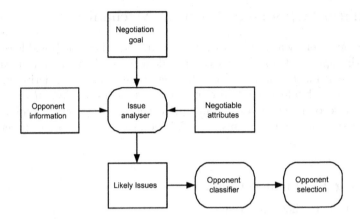

Fig. 5. The conflict minimisation selection mechanism

look for smaller intersections indicating less potential conflict and thus fewer issues to negotiate over. As the number of issues increases, the potential conflict increases and the negotiation becomes more difficult to resolve successfully.

Figure 5 shows the selection mechanism based on minimisation of conflict. The *negotiation goal* and the set of attributes identified as negotiable by the agent is passed, along with information about an opponent, to the *issue analyser*. The issue analyser examines the issues that the opponent is expected to select, and calculates the amount of conflict that can be expected in terms of the number of contested issues identified. This results in a *conflict score* which we calculate as

$$conflictScore = -1 \times \#\{negatt_{agent} \cap negatt_{opponent}\} \tag{6}$$

where $negatt_{agent}$ are the attributes identified as negotiable by the selecting agent and $negatt_{opponent}$ are the expected negotiable attributes of the opponent. The opponent is then rated according to its conflict score and is passed to the *opponent selection* component.

6.2   Price-Based Selection

When considering resources and their use in negotiation, an agent must try to select those opponents that are likely to accept a price that falls within the agent's own current reservation price. Given information about an opponent's concessionary flexibility, the agent takes the opponent's current ask price and estimates what the deal price will be, and then compares this to its own reservation price. If the expected deal price for an opponent exceeds the reservation price, then the opponent is omitted from further analysis, otherwise it is passed to the *opponent selection module*. Figure 6 shows the selection mechanism based on price considerations. Information about the current resource being used (here a monetary resource), the reservation of the resource and information on the current opponent are all passed to the *resource manager*.

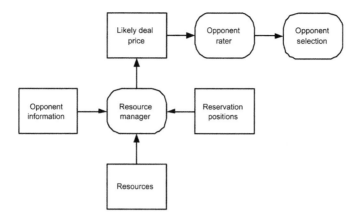

Fig. 6. The price-based selection mechanism

The resource manager calculates the expected deal price, given the initial ask price of the opponent and its concessionary flexibility score, and examines if this is under the reservation price. If this is so, the resource manager sends the information about the opponent to the *opponent rater* which ranks the opponent in relation to the other opponents under consideration. Once all opponents have

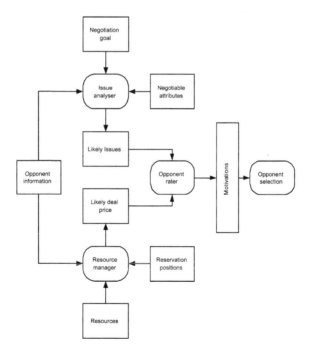

Fig. 7. The opponent selection mechanism

been so ranked, they are sent to the opponent selection module that performs the selection.

6.3   Combining Conflict Minimisation and Price-Based Selection Mechanisms

We now combine both selection processes into one mechanism; the *opponent selection mechanism* shown in Figure 7. In addition to the components in the conflict and resource selection mechanisms, the opponent selection mechanism shows a *motivational component* that can be used to weigh one selection process over another. This allows an agent to change the focus of selection from one criterion to another as required. Thus, for example, at times of extremely low resource levels, the agent can prioritise those opponents who offer extremely cheap services while paying less attention to the number of issues that might need negotiating over. At other times, for example when a negotiation goal has a large amount of value, the agent can prioritise the minimisation of conflict so as to increase the chance of engaging in a successful negotiation while de-emphasising the importance of cost. The mechanism is simply the two selection mechanisms discussed above combined into one, and thus we omit further discussion of the individual components.

7   Evaluating the Model

The work presented in this paper is still in development, but we have performed a limited evaluation to examine if a buyer agent using only the *price-based selection mechanism* is able to select the best negotiation opponent in terms of optimising monetary resources. We tested this in the following way. First we cal-

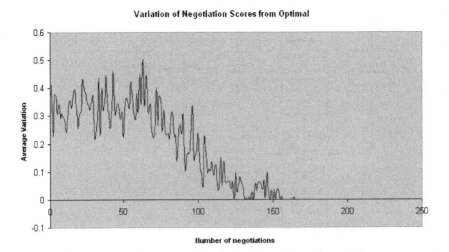

Fig. 8. Performance of price-based opponent selection

culated which opponents, out of a set of available opponents, offered the optimal deal price for the agent given its current resource evaluation, then we allowed the agent itself to choose an opponent and we compared this choice with the previously identified optimal opponents to obtain a measure of variation of the agent's selection choice from optimal. Each run of the experiment lasted for 200 negotiation rounds. In each run there was 1 buyer-agent, a pool of 100 potential opponents, and we performed 20 such runs. The buyer agent had a *conserve money* motivation that determined the current reservation value on the agent's monetary resource. The graph in Figure 8 shows the average variation between the buyer-agent's obtained deal prices resulting from its opponent selection and the optimal deal prices over the 20 experimental runs. The buyer-agent eventually learns to find the best opponents given its current motivational state, shown by the variation line falling to 0 after negotiation number 150. Future work will involve more extensive experimentation on various aspects of the model to ascertain its benefits and limitations.

8   Conclusion

By linking negotiation issues to motivations, agents are able to evaluate prospective negotiation opponents in terms of a) the likelihood that a conflict over issues will exist and b) the expected performance of the opponents on resource-based issues. Such evaluation is important for systems that need agents to act in an autonomous manner. As an agent's circumstances change, the need to negotiate over issues may also change, and this must be considered when making selections over which opponent to negotiate with. In this paper, we have described a motivated agent architecture comprising a classification mechanism and two selection mechanisms that enable an agent to successfully identify those opponents with whom the chances of conducting a negotiation with both minimal conflict and suitable outcomes is possible. In terms of future work, an important factor when investigating negotiation is to consider the impact that protocols and strategies may have on the outcome. Though our work currently ignores these considerations, our aim is to show how an autonomous approach to opponent selection, might be constructed. We expect future work to address the problems involved in opponent selection in more demanding negotiation scenarios such as those that include multiple strategies and protocols.

References

1. David, E., Azoulay-Schwartz, R., Kraus, S.: Protocols and strategies for automated multi-attribute auctions. In: 1st International Conference on Autonomous Agents and MultiAgent Systems (AAMAS 2002), Bologna, Italy, ACM Press (2002) 77–85
2. Sierra, C., Jennings, N.R., Noriega, P., Parsons, S.:   A framework for argumentation-based negotiation. In Singh, M.P., Rao, A.S., Wooldridge, M., eds.: Intelligent Agents IV. Volume 1365 of LNCS. Springer-Verlag (1998) 177–192
3. Faratin, P., Sierra, C., Jennings, N.R.: Negotiation decision functions for autonomous agents. Journal of Robotics and Autonomous Systems **24** (1998) 159–182

4. Urbig, D., Schroter, K.: C-IPS approach to negotiating agents: Specifying dynamic interdependencies between issue, partner, and step. In: 3rd International Joint Conference on Autonomous Agents and Multi Agent Systems (AAMAS 2004). (2004)
5. d'Inverno, M., Luck, M.: Understanding Agent Systems. Springer-Verlag (2001)
6. Sabater, J., Sierra, C.: Social regret, a reputation model based on social relations. SIGecom Exch. **3** (2002) 44–56
7. Ramchurn, S.D., Sierra, C., Godo, L., Jennings, N.R.: Devising a trust model for multi-agent interactions using confidence and reputation. Applied Artificial Intelligence **18** (2004) 833–852
8. Tesfatsion, L.: A trade network game with endogenous partner selection. In: Computational Approaches to Economic Problems. Kluwer (1997) 249–269
9. Banerjee, B., Sen, S.: Selecting partners. In: 4th International Conference on Autonomous Agents (AGENTS 2000), Barcelona, Spain, ACM Press (2000) 261–262
10. Dutta, P.S., Moreau, L., Jennings, N.R.: Finding interaction partners using cognition-based decision strategies. In: IJCAI 2003 Workshop on Cognitive Modeling of Agents and Multi-Agent Interactions. (2003) 46–55
11. Maslow, A.: The farther reaches of human nature. Penguin Books, New York (1971)
12. Tinbergen, N.: The study of instinct. Oxford University Press, Oxford (1989)
13. Griffiths, N.: Motivated Cooperation. PhD thesis, University of Warwick (2000)
14. Coddington, A., Luck, M.: Towards motivation-based plan evaluation. In Russell, I., Haller, S., eds.: 16th International FLAIRS Conference, St. Augustine, FL, USA (2003) 298–302
15. Morignot, P., Hayes-Roth, B.: Adaptable motivational profiles for autonomous agents. Technical report, Knowledge Systems Laboratory, Stanford University (1995)
16. Balkenius, C.: The roots of motivation. In J.A. Mayer, H.L. Roitblat, S.W. Wilson, editors, *From Animals to Animats 2* (Cambridge, MA: MIT Press, 1993)
17. Luck, M., Munroe, S., d'Inverno, M.: Autonomy: Variable and generative. In Hexmoor, H., Castelfranchi, C., Falcone, R., eds.: Agent Autonomy, Kluwer (2003) 9–22
18. Coddington, A.: Self-motivated Planning in Autonomous Agents. PhD thesis, University of London, London (2001)
19. López y López, F., Luck, M., d'Inverno, M.: Constraining autonomy through norms. In: 1st International Conference on Autonomous Agents and MultiAgent Systems (AAMAS 2002), Bologna, Italy, ACM Press (2002) 674–681
20. Zhang, X., Lesser, V., Wagner, T.: A proposed approach to sophisticated negotiation. In AAAI Fall Symposium on Negotiation Methods for Autonomous Cooperative Systems (2001)
21. Munroe, S., Luck, M., d'Inverno, M.: Towards motivation-based decisions for worth goals. In Marik, V., Mueller, J., Pechoucek, M., eds.: 3rd International Central and Eastern European Conference on Multi-Agent Systems (CEEMAS 2003). (2003) 17–28

Modelling Flexible Social Commitments and Their Enforcement

Philippe Pasquier, Roberto A. Flores, and Brahim Chaib-draa

Laval University, Computer Science and Software Engineering Department,
Sainte-Foy, QC, G1K 7P4, Canada
{pasquier, flores, chaib}@iad.ift.ulaval.ca

Abstract. For over a decade, agent research has shown that social commitments support the definition of open multiagent systems by capturing the responsibilities that agents contract toward one another through their communications. These systems, however, rely on the assumption that agents respect the social commitments they adopt. To overcome this limitation, in this paper we investigate the role of sanctions as elements whose enforcement fosters agents' compliance with adopted commitments. In particular, we present a model of flexible social commitments to which sanctions are attached, and where the enforcement of sanctions act as a social control mechanism for the satisfaction of commitments.

1   Introduction

A multi-agent system (MAS) is considered an *open* MAS if the following properties hold [1]:

1. Agents behavior and interactions cannot be predicted in advance;
2. Agents' internal architecture is not publicly known;
3. Agents do not necessarily have common goals, desires or intentions.

The first of those properties implies that the execution of open MAS is *non-deterministic*. Open societies are usually subject to unanticipated outcomes in their interactions. The second property implies that an open MAS can have members with different internal architectures; therefore, they can be *heterogeneous*. The third property implies that the members of an open society may be non-benevolent, non-cooperative or even insincere. In addition, the agents may fail to, or choose not to, conform to some of the normative aspects of the MAS in order to achieve their individual goals. In that context, providing the means and tools for the achievement of a chosen/emergent social order in such system is a challenging issue.

In the MAS literature, the reactive and proactive behavior of deliberative agents has traditionally been modelled using mental states. In systems using these types of agents, social order is naturally achieved on the assumption that agents are cooperative and collaborative, i.e., that they are sincere in following the behavior specified in the system. This raises a particularly acute problem

M.-P. Gleizes, A. Omicini, and F. Zambonelli (Eds.): ESAW 2004, LNAI 3451, pp. 139–151, 2005.

given that mental states are private to agents and cannot be inspected by other agents who wish to verify compliance with the specifications. This same trend has been followed in the specification of the semantics of agent communication languages, whose mentalistic definitions disqualify their use by heterogeneous agents in open systems, which are systems where agents cannot be assumed to be sincere nor to support others inspecting their internal states.

Social commitments are defined as responsibilities contracted by one agent (the debtor) toward another (the creditor), raising the expectation that the debtor will act to satisfy committed responsibilities [2]. This notion of commitment is a social one, and should not be confused with the notion of individual commitment, which emphasizes the persistence of intentions in practical reasoning, nor with the collective commitments of a group of agents. The use of social commitments removes the aforementioned drawbacks of mentalistic approaches, namely: the assumption that agents' internal architectures must conform to a particular mentalistic specification of communication semantics (embedding sincerity) and the assumption that this internal state can be inspected for verification purposes. Accordingly, social commitments can be defined independently of any agent internal architecture and decision making process[1], thus supporting the development of *heterogeneous open systems* [1].

During the 1990s, social commitments were introduced as a way to capture the public aspects of communications [3][2]. From then on, several research efforts have aimed at extending the use of commitments in communications as follows:

- by introducing agent communication languages (e.g., [4, 5, 6]) and models to build interaction protocols (e.g., [7, 8, 9]) using social commitments,
- by extending and complementing these approaches with theoretical [10] and practical [11] advances in the use of commitment-based agent languages.

Social commitments is a second order concept that is difficult to formalize and several social commitment-based formalizations can be found in the agents community. While some are rather restrictive and tend to consider commitments as directed obligations (e.g., using deontic logics [12]), sometimes with the possibility of unilateral de-commitments [11, 13], others are more flexible and allow the dynamic modification of commitments [3].

The notion of social commitment should be more flexible than usual obligations/prohibitions but also more rigid than permissions. More precisely, our contention is that (in the context of agent communications) social commitments are different from other normative propositional attitudes in that operations like modification, cancellation or (eventually unintended) violation should be modelled. This is important since commitments are first-class entities capturing the shared semantics of dialogues, which ground manipulations in the social layer.

---

[1] This doesn't mean that social commitments are independent of usual mental states but rather that this dependency is not part of the social commitment model *per se*.

[2] Although social commitments can be used for system conventions, organizational structures and agent roles, in this paper we restrict our analysis to their use in communications.

Therefore, being able to cancel or modify commitments is a key feature that allows agents to reassess the consequences of past dialogues in the context of dynamic environments. This *semantical flexibility* should not be confused with the commonly considered structural flexibility of dialogues.

This flexibility feature in social commitment models prevents their enforcement through regimentation, as is usually the case in approaches based on deontic logics[3]. However, given this view on flexible commitments in current ACL models, a major question remains unaddressed: what should happen in cases when agents do not respect adopted commitments? Current social commitment-based approaches are valid and useful under the assumption that commitments are generally respected. This is a strong assumption that we should inquire further. Indeed, we should describe the mechanisms supporting this functionality in open, heterogeneous systems.

In our view, the fundamental challenge is how to support the *enforcement of flexible social commitments*. This problem, which has been neglected in the modelling of recent agent communication frameworks, is addressed in this paper by introducing an ontology of social control tools for commitment-based MAS and proposing a model of social commitments compatible with our previous dialogical frameworks [8, 6], which enables the introduction of the previously mentioned social control tools in open MAS.

2   Ontology of Sanctions and Social Control Mechanisms

Introduced in sociology as early as the end of the 19th century, the concept of social control originally denoted the capacity of a group or society to regulate itself and to secure coherency and unity in social life [15]. Social control, in this sense, relates to how social action is coordinated toward a chosen or an emergent social order. Often seen as all-encompassing, practically representing any phenomenon leading to conformity or as a broad representation of regulated mechanisms placed upon society's members, social control can be viewed as the glue holding society together [16].

Modern theories of social control focus on the strategies and techniques that help to regulate agent behavior, and lead to conformity and compliance with the rules of society (at both the macro and the micro levels). In the remainder of this section, we detail the main elements used in the enforcement of social commitments: (1) sanctions, which are considered in their general sense of incentives (the next section presents an ontology of sanctions along their different dimensions), and (2) philosophies of punishment (section 2.2), which result in punishment strategies determining the type of sanction (and its magnitude) to be applied, and explains how sanctions are assigned to social commitments.

---

[3] For example, due to their nature and goals, deontic logics do not even consider the possibility of violation. We refer the reader to [14] for a detailed discussion on the differences between commitments and obligations.

2.1   Sanctions

In this paper, we only consider *individual sanctions* and, for simplicity, leave aside other types of sanctions, such as *collective sanctions* [17] (which may be associated to teams, roles or groups of agents). In the next subsections, we go through the three main dimensions of sanctions: direction, type and style.

Sanction Directions – Sanctions have a specific direction. It is usually useful to consider both:

- *positive sanctions*: positive sanctions are rewards that encourage a continuation of desired behavior. For example, it is common in open systems that agents accept committing to a task only if the associated reward is worth pursuing.
- *negative sanctions*: on the other hand, negative sanctions are used to discourage norm violating behavior. For example, agents that cannot fulfill their commitments are expected to be punished.

In brief, positive sanctions are incentives to pursue a particular behavior while negative sanctions are incentives against its violation. For the sake of simplicity, we will use sanction to denote negative sanction in the rest of the paper, addressing positive sanctions as rewards.

Sanction Types – The first sanction type is *automatic sanctions*, which arises when the violators action carries its own penalty (e.g., because it is not being coordinated with the actions of others). For example, someone who drives on the wrong side of the road has a higher than normal probability of crashing into another car. We will not consider these unintended (since no one decides that they should apply) sanctions in the scope of this paper.

Within the vast literature addressing this topic from various perspectives including economics, criminology, sociology, social psychology, AI and MAS, we encounter three broad types of non-automatic sanctions: (1) material sanctions, (2) social sanctions, and (3) psychological sanctions.

Material sanctions include physical sanctions like violence or repairing actions, as well as financial sanctions like fees. Material sanctions can be applied immediately at the time of occurrence or be delayed through time.

There are *social sanctions* as well. Trust, credibility and reputation are social values that could be affected by social sanctions. As pointed out in [18], social sanctions are usually the effects of some implicit informational disclosure where the violator's action conveys information about himself that he would rather not have others know. For example, that an agent violates a commitment without any explicit reason, unintentionally signals that he does not really care much about respecting the commitment, which is information that other agents could take into account when evaluating his reputation.

Psychological sanction types, which may be more useful in believable agents [19] and which have been used in advanced mono-agent design in mixed communities, can be important as well. Examples of psychological sanctions are guilt (where the violator feels bad about his violation as a result of his knowledge of social norms, quite apart from external consequences), and shame (where the violator feels that his action has lowered himself either in his own eyes or in the eyes of other agents).

The time horizon of sanctions indicates whether the effects of sanctions are long-lasting or short-lived. This concept is important since some sanction types may extend through time (e.g., trust, reputation, credibility) while others may not (e.g., immediate material sanctions). Subtle and complex phenomena, like forgiveness, can require taking into account this time issue.

Sanction Styles – For the specific formal needs of MAS, we distinguish two sanctions styles: implicit and explicit. *Implicit sanctions* are "autonomously" and unilaterally decided by agents. The major difficulty associated with implicit sanctions is that they are not publicly known and agents have to discover whether or not they have been sanctioned (for example, by noticing that others do not communicate with them anymore). On the contrary, *explicit sanctions* are publicly known (at least among the interacting agents).

Another useful distinction can be made between *a priori* decided sanctions and *a posteriori* decided sanctions. In particular, a posteriori decided sanctions should be avoided in MAS, since they do not allow agents to reason about the pros and cons of respecting their commitments. That the punished agent can disagree with the sanction assigned a posteriori may lead to litigation.

In the remainder of the paper, we will consider only a priori defined explicit sanctions. Among a priori known explicit sanctions, we can distinguish *static*, a priori known, explicit, sanction systems provided to all agents at design time, and *dynamically* decided, a priori, explicit sanctions, which are negotiated by the agents through their communications.

2.2   Punishment Policies

Social control mechanisms to enforce social commitments should be designed according to a philosophy of punishment. By punishment, we mean the imposition of sanctions to satisfy open system designers' desire for retribution against wrongdoers. According to social control theorists, there are five different philosophies of punishment from which all *punishment policies* can be derived [20]: deterrence, retribution, incapacitation, rehabilitation and restoration. However, since punishment philosophies like incapacitation, rehabilitation and restoration focus on the choice of sanctions types and styles rather than on the choice of sanctions strength, we will present only the two remaining philosophies, and discuss their adequacy for open MAS:

- *Deterrence*: issued from the classical school of criminology, and supported by philosophers like Beccaria [21] and Bentham [22], deterrence is a utilitarian principle stating that the aim of sanctions is to prevent future violation. For deterrence to be effective, punishment must be swift, certain and severe. Applied to the enforcement of social commitment in MAS, it means that commitments should be associated with heavy and explicit sanctions. This extreme position, i.e. using severe sanctions with a high prohibitive effect, tends to transform social commitments into mere obligations, losing part of the flexibility objective desired for commitments.

– *Retribution*: retribution considers that the violation should be repaired by a penalty as severe as the wrongful act.

Retribution is a practically manageable choice for open MAS. Indeed, the last decades of work in economics and law provide two basic reasons why it is best for sanctions to equal harm[4]. Here, we reformulate these arguments toward retribution punishment policies using MAS terminology.

The first argument concerns the *level of precautions* taken by parties, where the term "precautions" is to be interpreted generally. If sanctions are less than harm, precautions will tend to be inadequate and agents will tend to not respect adopted social commitments when it is to their advantage to do so. Symmetrically, if sanctions exceed harm, precautions will be excessive and may preclude agents committing to wanted commitments (this is the case with the deterrence punishment philosophy). For example, even if sincerely wanting to, an agent will not commit to a course of action if the sanctions attached to violation (which may occur unintentionally) are prohibitive. However, it has been shown that if sanctions equal harm, agents will have socially correct incentives to take precautions [23].

The second reason why it is desirable for sanctions to equal harm involves the agents' *level of activity*, that is, the extent to which agents participate in risky activities. An agent's level of activity affects the magnitude of expected total harm, independently of the precautions taken when engaging in an activity. For example, the more commitments an agent takes (its level of activity), the greater the possible number of accidents (violations) will occur, independently of the safety features of the agent (which affect the expected harm per commitment) [23].

It is worth noticing that concluding that damages should equal harm would require making two assumptions. The first assumption is that agents are *risk neutral*. If injurers are risk averse then the optimal level of sanctions tends to be lower than harm, because it reduces the imposition of risk on injurers and because sanctions do not need to be as high to induce injurers to behave appropriately. The second assumption is that of *strict liability*, which stipulates that injurers are definitely found liable and that no injurer cannot escape the corresponding sanctions.

3   Sanctions in Social Commitment-Based Approaches

In our dialogical frameworks [8, 6], social commitments are mutually established. In these approaches, agent communication is seen as the social process by which

---

[4] Here, harm is the violation of a particular social commitment and is at least equal to the effort that is needed to fulfill the commitment.

the social commitment layer, which captures most of the inter-agent dependencies, is manipulated. The *success conditions* of a dialogue unit (whether in a *protocol for proposal* (*PFP*) in [8], or in a dialogue game instance in [6]) is the social acceptance of the proposed operation on social commitments (i.e., creation, cancellation, modification or discharge) while the *satisfaction conditions* of these dialogue units are linked to the satisfaction conditions of the (eventually) resulting social commitments, which are the conditions under which a social commitment is fulfilled.

So far, we have highlighted three major points in the modelling of social commitments and their enforcement. A model of social commitments should be provided that: (1) support the semantic flexibility described earlier; (2) provide a clear, generic model for the treatment of explicit sanctions, in particular how they are attached to commitments, and the cases in which they apply; and (3) allows for a diversity of punishment policies to be supported. For example, one system could support explicit static sanctions involving only monetary transactions, while another could support agents with the ability to use explicit, dynamically negotiated, repairing actions. The next section introduces our common model of social commitments, which fulfils claims (1), (2) and (3) when explicit sanctions are used.

3.1   A Common Model of Social Commitment and Its Enforcement

In order to introduce sanctions within commitment-based agent communication frameworks, we first present our generic model of social commitments. Given that explicit sanctions are part of the life-cycle of commitments, the model clearly indicates the mechanisms through which sanctions are linked to commitments, and the time when they could apply. At the same time (to support claim (3)), the model is flexible enough to allow designers to control the sanctioning process.

Conceptually, social commitments are directed responsibilities contracted by an agent toward an other. We express commitments as 6-term predicates of the form:

$$C(x, y, \alpha, t, s_x, s_y)$$

where agent x is committed to agent y to satisfy the content α at time t, under sanctions s_x and s_y, which specify the different sanctions that can be applied to x and y according to the states and transitions applicable to this commitment. We leave for a later section the description of the dynamics and mechanisms for associating social commitments with their corresponding sanctions. Figure 1 shows our state/transition model of social commitments, which indicates that a social commitment can be either *accepted* (denoted as $C(x, y, \alpha, t, s_x, s_y)$) or *rejected* (denoted as $\neg C(x, y, \alpha, t, s_x, s_y)$). It is worth noticing that a rejected commitment ($\neg C(x, y, \alpha, \ldots)$) is not equivalent to an accepted commitment with negative content ($C(x, y, \neg\alpha, \ldots)$). In particular, Figure 1 shows that a commitment can be in one of the following states:

- *inactive*: we assume a closed world hypothesis for social commitments. This means that all non-explicitly, socially-accepted commitments are rejected (i.e., they are non-commitments), which means that they are, by default, inactive.

- *active*: a commitment is active if it has been explicitly accepted using a grounding process, and if its conditions of satisfaction (denoted as *CoS* in Figure 1) can be met.
- *violated*: this state arises when an active commitment has been violated, which is the case if it cannot be fulfilled as specified by its content (for example, if its the deadline is past) or if its content is proven to be false (in the case of propositional content). The satisfaction conditions of violated commitments cannot be fulfilled.
- *fulfilled*: a commitment is fulfilled if its content has been achieved or proven to be true (in the case of propositional content). In other words, that the satisfaction conditions of the commitment have been fulfilled[5].
- *cancelled*: this state indicates that the commitment has been socially established as rejected. This state arises in the following circumstances: (1) if an active commitment is explicitly rejected through dialogue, (2) if the sanctions (possibly empty) associated with a violated commitment are applied, meaning that their compensatory effects allow cancelling the commitment, or (3) if the reward (which could also be nil) associated with the commitment is granted. This means that a cancelled commitment does not hold anymore.

Figure 1 also indicates the different transitions that could lead into these states. In order to fulfill the second requirement, we indicate the associated sanction operations for each transition:

1. *creation*: creation does not involve the application of sanctions but rather their attachment to social commitments. In particular, the negotiation of a commitment subsumes the negotiation of its sanctions. This negotiation can be complex (in the case of explicit dynamic sanction systems) or trivial (in the case of explicit static sanction systems shared among agents, where agents simply check whether or not associated sanctions match systems' conventions). This is the only transition in our model that allows the establishment of (a priori) sanctions. In particular, establishing (a posteriori) sanctions in subsequent transitions may lead to phenomena (such as litigation) that lie outside the scope of our analysis.
2. *cancellation*: cancellation deals with the rejection of an accepted active commitment, and opens the possibility of applying the corresponding sanctions. Usually, dialogical frameworks allow the hearer (the non-initiator of a dialogue) of the cancellation to decide whether or not to apply the sanctions for the cancelling agent.
3. *violation*: violation itself is not necessarily achieved through dialogue or any other mutually recognizable event. As such, the occurrence of a transition of

---

[5] It is worth noticing that in practice it may be possible to create an already fulfilled or violated commitment, for example, when referring to the past. However, these types of scenarios are not considered in this analysis.

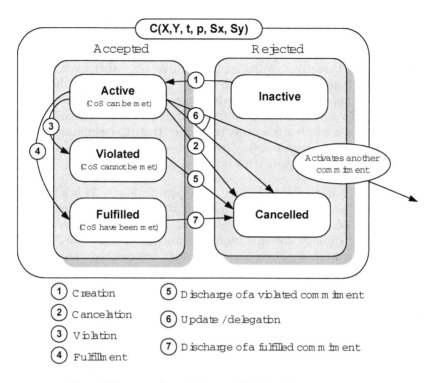

Fig. 1. The state/transition model of social commitments

this type has to be discovered and memorized for a later, socially-grounded, discharge (which is a transition described below).

4. *fulfilment*: analogously to violation, fulfilment is a transition that requires a mutually grounding event. This transition does not bring any reward but entails a socially grounded discharge where these rewards apply.

5. *discharge of a violated commitment*: the discharge of violated commitment leads to dialogues where: (1) it is socially recognized that the commitment has been violated (and that is true forever), and (2) corresponding sanctions are applied. Usually, only the debtor's sanctions (s_x) are applied, given its responsibility to fulfill the commitment. Furthermore, those sanctions could apply independently of the debtor's direct involvement in the violation.

6. *update*[6]: updating a commitment is a double transition (as shown in Figure 1) consisting of cancelling a commitment and creating a new one (and we assume that the new one is different than the one being cancelled). Updates are socially established through dialogue and sanctions can be associated to this transition. However, updating is different from a sequencing of cancellation

---

[6] Some authors [24] consider delegation of debtor or assignment of a new creditor as particular social commitment operations. We do not, and argue that in our dialogical frameworks, delegation is a special case of updating.

and creation with respect to sanctions (which is our main reason for introducing this transition). In practice, the sanctions of updating a commitment may be less severe than those of cancelling, and (in general) it may not be unreasonable that agents could avoid sanctions altogether given satisfactory arguments. Indeed, it will be the hearer of the updating that should decide if sanctions apply or not, and to what extent.

7. *discharge of a fulfilled commitment*: discharging a fulfilled commitment leads to a dialogue in which it is socially recognized that the commitment has been fulfilled (and that is true forever) and whether the eventual reward (indicated as part of the debtor's sanctions (s_x) as a positive sanction) is applied.

Another basic distinction (which does not appear in Figure 1) lies between *established* social commitments and *non-established* social commitments; where non-established states are inactive, violated and fulfilled (which are states that are not reached through socially grounded processes), and established states are active and cancelled (which are states that are reached through socially grounded processes). This means that transitions 1, 2, 5, 6 and 7 occur through dialogue whereas transitions 3 and 4 do not necessarily occur through social processes.

For example, in order to traverse transitions 3 and 4, we programmed our DIAGAL [6] dialogue manager (DM) as follows: each time an action is issued by an agent, the DM of that agent attempts to discover whether this action fulfills or not any of its commitments. If it does, transition 3 is applied, and a discharge dialogue game with the creditor is started to ground this fulfilment and receive potential rewards. In the same manner, all DMs check for violation (usually by observing the expiration of commitments' deadlines) and start a discharge violated commitment game if one is found. This mechanism has the property that both the grounding and the discharge of fulfilled and violated commitments are done at the moment that agents witness the occurrence of such states.

This generic state-transition model defines an operational semantic for our dialogue primitives. In particular, DIAGAL dialogue games, when successful, act as the grounding mechanisms through which transitions are realized. These dialogue games implement the sanction manipulation mechanism described above. In addition, the DIAGAL language is sound and complete with respect to its semantics, which means that all transitions are covered and nothing else[7]. Finally, it is worth noticing that it is possible to avoid the update and cancel transitions by not including the corresponding games in the implementation of a system, which results in a simpler but less flexible model of commitments as the one mentioned in section 1.

3.2   The Enforcement of the Enforcement System

One of the assumptions made in punishment-based social control mechanisms is that harming agents are always sanctioned. This assumption, which we have

---

[7] The same holds true for conversations under the *PFP* [4] approach.

referred to earlier as strict liability, implies that every harm is discovered and that sanctions are always applied as expected. This is a view that has been generally modelled through a regimentation hypothesis, which consists of the strict conformance of system implementations with its corresponding specifications [25]. In the case of social commitments, regimentation was assumed by implying that social commitments were systematically respected by committed agents. By arguing that this is not a realistic scenario, we shifted the focus of regimentation away from commitments and into the domain of sanctions by providing a simple mechanism to ensure efficient harm discovering (through the grounding of every transition of our model including the discharge of fulfilled and violated commitments as described in the previous section).

For the time being, we then suggest the use of software engineering constraints to ensure that the application of sanctions is treated as a strict obligation under regimentation. That is, if sanctions are not respected, they will be somehow discovered and considered as system errors. This could be done by assuming that: (1) the dialogical level rules are obligations (an agent is not allowed to digress from dialogical rules), and (2) the breach of sanctions is considered a system error (the system should be able to coerce agents into respecting the application of sanctions).

On the one hand, explicit material sanctions are easier to consider as firm obligations in a system since they are easier to verify than other sanction types. On the other hand, we assume that it should be the agents' decision whether or not to take psychological and non-material social sanctions into account. And lastly, social sanctions will usually take effect even if the agent does not realize that they exist. As such, the problem of the enforcement of sanctions thus does not have to be considered for these sanctions types.

4   Conclusion

In this paper we have raised the problem of the enforcement of flexible social commitment in open systems. We have introduced tools for treating this problem (section 2), namely sanctions (section 2.1) and punishment philosophies (section 2.2). We have then provided a generic social commitment model (section 3.1) that gives the operational semantic of our previous dialogical frameworks (presented in [8, 6]), supporting the enforcement of social commitments through explicit sanctions (statically specified or dynamically negotiated). Finally, we have presented the conditions under which this solution for the enforcement of social commitment does not lead to the meta-problem of the enforcement of sanctions (section 3.2). The proposed model does not make further assumptions about the agents so that the property of being able to develop open heterogeneous MAS using a flexible social commitment-based model (as introduced in section 1) is safe.

The discharge of commitments, completing their life-cycle, hasn't been fully considered in previous social commitment models. By filling this gap, we think that our model that addresses the problem through agent communication will be helpful for further study of the long term effects of iterated dialogues consequences according to various communication pragmatics and punishment policies. Notice that the design of (domain dependent) punishment policies, linking objective (or subjective) actions values to material sanctions, is an open research issue.

References

1. Hewitt, C.: Open information systems semantics for distributed artificial intelligence. Artificial Intelligence **47** (1991) 76–106
2. Castelfranchi, C.: Commitments: from individual intentions to groups and organizations. In: Proceedings of the First International Conference on Multi-Agent Systems (ICMAS-95), San Francisco, CA (1995) 41–48
3. Singh, M.P.: A social semantics for agent communication languages. In Dignum, F., Greaves, M., eds.: Issues in Agent Communication. Springer-Verlag: Heidelberg, Germany (2000) 31–45
4. Flores, R., Kremer, R.: Bringing coherence to agent conversation. In Wooldridge, M., Ciancarini, P., Weiss, G., eds.: Agent-Oriented Software Engineering II. Volume 2222 of Lecture Notes in Computer Science., Springer-Verlag (2001) 50–67
5. McBurney, P., Parson, S.: Agent ludens : games for agent dialogues. In: Proceedings of the Workshop on Game Theoretic and Decision Theoretic Agents. (2000)
6. Pasquier, P., Bergeron, M., Chaib-draa, B.: DIAGAL : a Generic ACL for Open Systems. In: Proceedings of The Fifth International Workshop Engineering Societies in the Agents World (ESAW). Lecture Notes in Artificial Intelligence (LNAI), Springer-Verlag (2004)
7. Fornara, N., Colombetti, M.: Defining interaction protocols using a commitment-based agent communication langage. In Rosenchein, J.S., Sandholm, T., Wooldridge, M., Yokoo, M., eds.: Proceedings of the second Autonomous Agents and Multi-Agents Systems conference (AAMAS'03), Melbourne, Australie, ACM Press (2003) 520–527
8. Flores, R., Kremer, R.C.: A principled modular approach to construct flexible conversation protocols. In Tawfik, A.Y., Goodwin, S.D., eds.: Proceedings of the 17th Canadian Conference on Artificial Intelligence. Volume 3060 of Lecture Notes in Computer Science (LNCS)., London, Canada, Springer-Verlag (2004)
9. Yolum, P., Singh, M.P.: Flexible protocol specification and execution: Applying event calculus planning using commitments. In Castelfranchi, C., Johnson, W., eds.: Proceedings of the 1st International Joint Conference on Autonomous Agents and MultiAgent Systems (AAMAS), Bologna, Italy (2002) 527–534
10. Pasquier, P., Chaib-draa, B.: The cognitive coherence approach for agent communication pragmatics. In: Proceedings of The Second International Conference on Autonomous Agent and Multi-Agents Sytems (AAMAS'03), ACM Press (2003) 544–552
11. Excelente-Toledo, C.B., Bourne, R.A., Jennings, N.R.: Reasoning about commitments and penalties for coordination between autonomous agents. In Müller, J., Andre, E., Sen, S., Frasson, C., eds.: Proceedings of the Fifth International Conference on Autonomous Agents, Montreal, Canada, ACM Press (2001) 131–138
12. Dignum, F., Kinny, D., Sonenberg, L.: From desires, obligations and norms to goals. Cognitive Science Quarterly **2** (2002) 407–430

13. Sandholm, T.W., Lesser, V.R.: Advantages of a leveled commitment contracting protocol. In: Proceedings of the Thirteenth National Conference on Artificial Intelligence, Portland, OR (1996)
14. Vogel Carey, T.: How to confuse commitment with obligation. The Journal of Philosophy (1975) 276–284
15. Martindale, D.: The theory of social control. In Roucek, J., ed.: Social Control for the 1980s: A Handbook for Order in a Democratic Society. Greenwood Press, Westport, CT (1978) 46–58
16. Hechter, M., Opp, K.D.: Introduction. In Hechter, M., Opp, K.D., eds.: Social Norms, Russell Sage Foundation (2001) xi–xx
17. Levinson, D.J.: Collective sanctions. Public law research paper no. 57, NYU Law School, Ctr for Law and Business Research (2003)
18. Posner, R.A., Rasmusen, E.B.: Creating and enforcing norms, with special reference to sanctions. International Review of Law and Economics **19** (1999) 369–382
19. Bates, J.: The role of emotion in believable agents. Communications of the ACM **37** (1994) 122–125
20. Vold, G.B., Bernard, T.J., Snipes, J.B.: Theoretical Criminology. Fifth edition edn. Oxford University Press (2002)
21. Beccaria, C.: On Crimes and Punishments. New Jersey: Prentice Hall (1963)
22. Bentham, J.: An Introduction to the Principles of Morals and Legislation. The Athlone Press, London (1970)
23. Polinsky, M., Shavel, S.: Punitive damages. In Newman, P., ed.: The New Palgrave Dictionary of Economics and The Law. Volume 3. Macmillan Reference Limited, London (1998) 192–198
24. Singh, M.P.: An ontology for commitments in multiagent systems: Toward a unification of normative concepts. Artificial Intelligence and Law **7** (1999) 97–113
25. Artikis, A.: Executable Specification of Open Norm-Governed Computational Systems. PhD thesis, Department of Electrical and Electronic Engineering, Imperial College London (2003)

DIAGAL: A Generic ACL for Open Systems

Philippe Pasquier, Mathieu Bergeron, and Brahim Chaib-draa

Laval University, Computer Science and Software Engineering Department,
Sainte-Foy, QC, G1K 7P4, Canada
{pasquier, bergeron, chaib}@iad.ift.ulaval.ca

Abstract. In this paper, we present the latest version of our dialogue games based agent communication language (DIAGAL) which allows the agents to manipulate the public layer of social commitments through dialogue. We show that DIAGAL is complete according to the sequential creation, cancellation, update and discharge of social commitments. We also extend and refine notions of success and satisfaction previously associated with speech-acts to this new dialogical setting. Finally, we explain why DIAGAL is a good candidate for open and heterogeneous MAS development.

1 Introduction

Regarding communication, the multi-agent systems (MAS) community has been concentrating for some years on building a standard interactional framework. Main current agent communication languages (ACL), KQML and FIPA-ACL [1], are both based on speech acts theory. In those ACLs, semantics of messages is formulated in terms of mental states, i.e., private aspects of agents [2]. Dialogue is supposed to emerge from the chaining of produced speech acts stemming from agents' intentions by way of recognition and reasoning on others' mental states.

More recently, the use of these approaches for artificial agents communication has been criticized [3, 4]. Among these critics, we can note the semantic verification problem: agents should be able to verify that the others act according to held dialogues[1]. For messages semantics to be verifiable, it would be necessary to have access to agents' private mental states which is generally not possible. A second major problem raised by this formulation is the sincerity assumption. This hypothesis, necessary for the definition of ACL mentalistic semantic, is considered too restrictive by the MAS community since it forbids certain dialogue types in domains where such a hypothesis would not hold, as is the case for negotiation dialogues in electronic business for instance [5].

---

[1] This semantics verification should not be mistaken with the formal semantics checking: agents are implemented in accordance with the ACL mathematical or logical semantics.

M.-P. Gleizes, A. Omicini, and F. Zambonelli (Eds.): ESAW 2004, LNAI 3451, pp. 152–165, 2005.

This is why some authors have proposed social approaches for agent communication introducing a public conventional layer expressed in terms of social commitments [6]. These approaches (1) resolve the semantic verification problem, (2) do away with the sincerity hypothesis and, (3) facilitate the treatment of the social aspects of communication. These new approaches inaugurate a shift of paradigm since *agents do not necessarily have to reason on others intentions anymore but rather they must reason on taken and to be taken social commitments.* These social commitments are those stemming from past dialogues, issued from systems conventions and norms or associated to agents' roles. In that context, dialogue units (which could be speech acts as well as dialogue games) are seen as a means to manipulate the social commitments layer. For example, asking an agent to close the door would be seen as an attempt to commit him to do so (i.e. an attempt to create a new social commitment) instead of an attempt to make him adopt the corresponding (unverifiable) intention. Among these social commitments based approaches, which can be considered as conventional, dialogue games [7, 8, 9, 10] offer a compromise between strictly speech acts based approaches (with either "mentalistic" or "social" semantics) which do not specify anything about dialogue structure (which is supposed to emerge) and protocols which reduce the searching space for possible continuations to its strict minimum, causing the loss of the flexibility and adaptability of conversations.

The next sections will describe (section 2), discuss and exemplify (section 2.6) the main components of our dialogue games agent communication language (DIAGAL). We will then extend and refine the notions of success and satisfaction traditionally associated with speech acts (section 3). Finally, we will discuss DIAGAL for heterogenous agents communication in open systems (section 4) before concluding.

2   A Dialogue Game Agent Language

2.1   Social Commitments

The notion of social commitment should not be confused with the notion of individual commitment used to emphasize individual intention persistence in practical reasoning nor with collective commitments which stand for the internal commitment of a group of agents. Conceptually, commitments are oriented responsibilities contracted towards a partner or a group. Following Walton and Krabbe [11], we distinguish action commitments from propositional commitments. Since [12] discusses our modelling of flexible social commitments and their enforcement through sanctions, we simply re-introduce the basic notations here.

Commitments are expressed as predicates with an arity of 6. Thus, an *accepted* action commitment takes the form:

$$C(x, y, \alpha, t, s_x, s_y)$$

meaning that agent x is committed towards agent y to α at time t, under the sanctions s_x and s_y. An accepted propositional commitment would have propositional content p instead α. *Rejected* commitments, meaning that x is not committed toward y to α, take the form $\neg C(x, y, \alpha, t, s_x, s_y)$. This notation for commitments is inspired from [13], and allows us to compose the actions or propositions involved in the commitments: $\alpha_1 | \alpha_2$ classically stands for the choice, and $\alpha_1 \Rightarrow \alpha_2$ for the conditional statement that α_2 will occur in case of the occurrence of the event α_1. Finally, agents keep track of each commitment in which they are debtor or creditor in their *agendas*, which constitutes a kind of distributed "Commitment Store".

Now, we need to describe the mechanism by which the commitments are discussed and created, updated, cancelled or even discharged through dialogue. This mechanism is precisely modelled within our game structure.

2.2   Game Structure

The main particularity of social commitments is that they must be socially established in order to hold. This means that every change on the social commitment layer (reified in agendas) should be grounded by the conversing agents. We share with others [7, 8, 9] the view of dialogue games as structures regulating the mechanism under which some commitments are discussed through the dialogue. However, unlike previous models [7, 8, 9], we adopt a strict commitment-based approach within game structure and express the dialogue rules in terms of dialogical commitments [6]. To account for the fact that some commitments are established within the contexts of some games and only make sense within this context, we make explicit the fact that those *dialogical commitments* are particular to game g (by indicating g as a subscript). This will typically be the case of the dialogue rules involved in the games, as we will see below. In our approach, games are considered as bilateral structures defined by:

- *entry conditions*, (E): expressed in terms of extra-dialogical commitments, entry conditions are conditions which must be fulfilled to enter the game;
- *dialogue rules*, (R): expressed in terms of dialogical commitments, dialogue rules specify what the conversing agents are "dialogically" committed to do. The fulfilment of those rules will lead to reaching either the success or the failure conditions of the game;
- *success conditions*, (S): success conditions indicate the result, the effect in terms of extra dialogical commitments, of the dialogue game if the modification of the public layer which was the purpose of the game has been socially accepted;
- *failure conditions*, (F): failure conditions indicate the effect in terms of extra dialogical commitments of the dialogue game if the modification of the public layer has been socially rejected.

Move	Operations
$prop.in(x, y, g)$	$create(y, C_g(y, x, acc.in(y, x, g)$
	$\|ref.in(y, x, g)\|prop.in(y, x, g')))$
$prop.out(x, y, g)$	$create(y, C_g(y, x, acc.out(y, x, g)$
	$\|ref.out(y, x, g)))$
$acc.in(x, y, g)$	create dialogical commitments for game g
$acc.out(x, y, g)$	suppress dialogical commitments for game g
$ref.in(x, y, g)$	no effect on the public layer
$ref.out(x, y, g)$	no effect on the public layer

Fig. 1. DIAGAL contextualization game

2.3   Grounding and Composing the Games

The specific question of how games are grounded through the dialogue is certainly one of the most delicate. *Grounding* refers to the process of reaching mutual belief (or common ground) [14]. We model it using presentation and acceptance. Following [15], we assume that agents can use some meta-acts of dialogue to handle the games structuration and thus propose to enter a game, propose to leave a game, and so on. Games can have different status: they can be *open*, *closed*, or simply *proposed*. How this status is discussed in practice is described in a *contextualization* game which regulates this meta-level communication as proposed in [6]. Figure 1 indicates the current contextualization moves and their effects in terms of commitments. For example, when a proposition to enter a game g ($prop.in(x, y, g)$) is played by agent x, agent y is committed to accept ($acc.in$), to refuse ($ref.in$) or to propose entering another game g' ($prop.in(y, x, g')$), which would lead to a presequencing type of dialogue games structuration.

Concerning the possibility of combining the games, the seminal work of [11] and the follow-up formalization of [15] have focused on the classical notions of *embedding* and *sequencing*. Recent works, including ours, extend this to other combinations [16, 9]:

- *Sequencing* noted $g_1; g_2$, which means that g_2 starts immediately after termination of g_1.
- *Choice* noted $g_1|g_2$, which means that participants play either g_1 or g_2 non-deterministically.
- *Pre-sequencing* noted $g_2 \hookrightarrow g_1$, which means that g_2 is opened while g_1 is proposed.
- *Embedding* noted $g_1 < g_2$, which means that g_1 is now opened while g_2 was already opened.

If one wants to make explicit the initiator and partner of each game, compositions can be rewritten as follows: $[x, y]g_1; [y, x]g_2$ or $[x, y]g_1|[y, x]g_2$ or $[x, y]g_2 \hookrightarrow [y, x]g_1$ or $[x, y]g_1 < [y, x]g_2$. In that case, $[x, y]g_1$ means that the initiator of g_1

is x and the partner is y. Notice that the previous contextualization game only considers sequencing, pre-sequencing and embedding.

2.4   Dialog Games

Within our framework, extra-dialogical commitments capture the shared semantics of dialogues seen as the grounded manipulation of the social layer. Being able to cancel or modify commitments is then a key feature that allows the agents to rediscuss the consequences, the common interpretation, of past dialogue as time goes on according to environment changes. This feature is essential in modern MAS deployed in dynamic and complex environments. This *semantical flexibility* should not be confused with the structural flexibility of dialogues.

Our social commitment model (which gives the operational semantics of the dialogue games presented below) is presented in [12] and considers five operations: creation, cancellation, update, discharge of fulfilled commitments and discharge of violated commitments. We have defined basic dialogue games for those operations according to the different types of commitments which can hold between two agents x and y. However, in order to save space and because the games for manipulating propositional commitments are highly similar to those that concern action commitments, we will present only the games that manipulate action commitments. DIAGAL contains 7 dialogue games that allow agents to attempt the aforementioned operations on action commitments:

1. for an attempt to have an action commitment from y toward x accepted, agent x can use a *Request* game (rg);
2. for an attempt to have an action commitment from x toward y accepted, agent x can use an *Offer* game (og);
3. for an attempt to retract an action commitment from x toward y, agent x can use a *Cancel.ActionC* game (cag);
4. for an attempt to retract an action commitment from y toward x, agent x can use a *Release.ActionC* game (rag);
5. for an attempt to update an action commitment , agent x or y can use an *Update.ActionC* game (uag);
6. for an attempt to discharge a violated action commitment, agent x can use a *Discharge.Violated.ActionC* game $(dvag)$;
7. for an attempt to discharge a fulfilled commitment, agent x can use a *Discharge.Fulfilled.ActionC* game $(dfag)$.

Notice that in the assumption that dialogue moves are made sequentially, the set of DIAGAL dialogue games is sound and complete according to our social commitment model (presented in [12]). *Completeness* means that all transitions (creation, cancellation, updating and discharge) of the underlying social-commitment model can be consumed by those games whereas *soundness* indicates that nothing other than those permitted transitions is possible. The latter is ensured through entry conditions that prevent, for example, cancelling a commitment that has not been created,...

Within commitments, time is expressed using a simple instant theory with $<$ as the precedence relation. The next subsections detail these games. Sanctions were omitted in our games specifications for better readability. Notice that the game rules structure provides an elegant turn-taking mechanism by entailing that $t_j < t_k < t_l < t_f$.

Request Game (rg) – This game captures the idea that the initiator x "requests" an action α from the partner y and the latter can "accept" or "refuse". The conditions and rules of the *request* game are as follows:

$$
\begin{array}{l|l}
E_{rg} & \neg C(y,x,\alpha,t_i) \text{ and } \neg C(y,x,\neg\alpha,t_i) \ \ \forall\, t_i,\ t_i < t_j \\
S_{rg} & C(y,x,\alpha,t_f) \\
F_{rg} & \neg C(y,x,\alpha,t_f) \\
R_{rg} & 1)\ C_g(x,y,request_{d_1}(x,y,\alpha),t_j) \\
& 2)\ C_g(y,x,request_{d_1}(x,y,\alpha) \Rightarrow \\
& \quad C_g(y,x,accept_{d_2}(y,x,\alpha)|refuse_{d_3}(y,x,\alpha),t_k),t_j) \\
& 3)\ C_g(y,x,accept_{d_2}(y,x,\alpha) \Rightarrow C(y,x,\alpha,t_f),t_j) \\
& 4)\ C_g(y,x,refuse_{d_3}(y,x,\alpha) \Rightarrow \neg C(y,x,\alpha,t_f),t_j)
\end{array}
$$

Offer Game (og) – An offer is a promise that is conditional upon the partner's acceptance. To make an offer is to put something forward for another's choice (of acceptance or refusal). To offer then, is to perform a conditional commissive. Precisely, to offer α is to perform a commissive under the condition that the partner accepts α. Conditions and rules of the DIAGAL *offer* game are as follows:

$$
\begin{array}{l|l}
E_{og} & \neg C(x,y,\alpha,t_i) \text{ and } \neg C(x,y,\neg\alpha,t_i) \ \ \forall\, t_i,\ t_i < t_j \\
S_{og} & C(x,y,\alpha,t_f) \\
F_{og} & \neg C(x,y,\alpha,t_f) \\
R_{og} & 1)\ C_g(x,y,offer_{d_1}(x,y,\alpha),t_j) \\
& 2)\ C_g(y,x,offer_{d_1}(x,y,\alpha) \Rightarrow \\
& \quad C_g(y,x,accept_{d_2}(y,x,\alpha)|refuse_{d_3}(y,x,\alpha),t_k),t_j) \\
& 3)\ C_g(x,y,accept_{d_2}(y,x,\alpha) \Rightarrow C(x,y,\alpha,t_f),t_j) \\
& 4)\ C_g(x,y,refuse_{d_3}(y,x,\alpha) \Rightarrow \neg C(x,y,\alpha,t_f),t_j)
\end{array}
$$

Cancel.ActionC Game (cag) – This game can be used in order to have an already accepted commitment rejected, i.e. to cancel a commitment. In this game, the debtor (x) of a commitment C_i proposes its cancellation. Then, the creditor can agree or not with the cancellation. If the creditor agrees with the retraction, the debtor will not have to face the sanction attached with the commitment C_i while he will have to do so if he disagrees. According to the creditor's opinion (agree or disagree), the debtor can decide to really cancel the commitment and face the associated sanction or change his mind and keep it (probably to avoid facing the sanctions). The conditions and rules of the *Cancel.Action* game are as follows:

$$E_{cag} \mid \exists\, t_i,\ t_i < t_j : C(x, y, \alpha, t_i)$$
$$S_{cag} \mid \neg C(x, y, \alpha, t_i)$$
$$F_{cag} \mid C(x, y, \alpha, t_i)$$
$$R_{cag} \mid$$
1) $C_g(x, y, cancel_{d_1}(x, y, (\alpha, t_i)), t_j)$
2) $C_g(y, x, cancel_{d_1}(x, y, (\alpha, t_i)) \Rightarrow$
   $\quad C_g(y, x, agree_{d_2}(y, x, cancel_{d_1}(\alpha, t_i))\mid$
   $\qquad disagree_{d_3}(y, x, cancel_{d_1}(\alpha, t_i)), t_k), t_j)$
3) $C_g(x, y, disagree_{d_3}(y, x, cancel_{d_1}(\alpha, t_i)) \Rightarrow$
   $\quad C_g(x, y, confirm_{d_4}(x, y, cancel_{d_1}(\alpha, t_i))\mid$
   $\qquad decline_{d_5}(x, y, cancel_{d_1}(\alpha, t_i)), t_l), t_j)$
4) $C_g(x, y, agree_{d_2}(y, x, cancel_{d_1}(\alpha, t_i)) \Rightarrow \neg C(x, y, \alpha, t_i), t_j)$
5) $C_g(x, y, confirm_{d_4}(x, y, cancel_{d_1}(\alpha, t_i)) \Rightarrow \neg C(x, y, \alpha, t_i), t_j)$
6) $C_g(x, y, decline_{d_5}(x, y, cancel_{d_1}(\alpha, t_i)) \Rightarrow C(x, y, \alpha, t_i), t_j)$

Release.ActionC Game (rag) – Similar to the *Cancel.ActionC* game, the *Release.ActionC* game allows retracting an action commitment and negotiating the sanction applications, but contrary to the former it allows the creditor instead of the debtor to attempt the cancellation. The rules of the *Release.ActionC* game are thus similar to the *Cancel.ActionC* game rules and they are as follows:

$$E_{rag} \mid \exists\, t_i,\ t_i < t_j : C(y, x, \alpha, t_i)$$
$$S_{rag} \mid \neg C(y, x, \alpha, t_i)$$
$$F_{rag} \mid C(y, x, \alpha, t_i)$$
$$R_{rag} \mid$$
1) $C_g(x, y, released_1(x, y, (\alpha, t_i)), t_j)$
2) $C_g(y, x, released_1(x, y, (\alpha, t_i)) \Rightarrow$
   $\quad C_g(y, x, agree_{d_2}(y, x, released_1(\alpha, t_i))\mid$
   $\qquad disagree_{d_3}(y, x, released_1(\alpha, t_i)), t_k), t_j)$
3) $C_g(x, y, disagree_{d_3}(y, x, released_1(\alpha, t_i)) \Rightarrow$
   $\quad C_g(x, y, confirm_{d_4}(x, y, released_1(\alpha, t_i))\mid$
   $\qquad decline_{d_5}(x, y, released_1(\alpha, t_i)), t_l), t_j)$
4) $C_g(x, y, agree_{d_2}(y, x, released_1(\alpha, t_i)) \Rightarrow \neg C(y, x, \alpha, t_i), t_j)$
5) $C_g(x, y, confirm_{d_4}(x, y, released_1(\alpha, t_i)) \Rightarrow \neg C(y, x, \alpha, t_i), t_j)$
6) $C_g(x, y, decline_{d_5}(x, y, released_1(\alpha, t_i)) \Rightarrow C(y, x, \alpha, t_i), t_j)$

Update.ActionC Game (uag) – If an agent wants to modify a commitment (change any attribute(s) of the commitment except the debtor or the creditor), he can try to retract the commitment and create a new one with the new attribute. However, the cancellation may cause some undesirable sanctions to be applied. This is why, we have defined the *Update.ActionC* and *Update.PropC* games that allow attempts to update commitments without having to face sanctions.

In the *Update.ActionC* game, agent x who initiates the game asks agent y if he agrees to cancel the commitment C_i and replace it with the commitment C_j. Then, agent y can agree or not to the modification of the commitment. If the agent y agrees with the modification, the commitment C_i is cancelled and a new commitment C_j is created.

The conditions and rules of the *Update.ActionC* game are indicated here, assuming that: (1) if the initiator x is the creditor then $cre = x$ and $deb = y$ while (2) if the initiator x is the debtor then $cre = y$ and $deb = x$:

$$
\begin{array}{l|l}
E_{uag} & \exists\, t_i,\ t_i < t_j : C(deb, cre, \alpha, t_i) \\
S_{uag} & \neg C(deb, cre, \alpha, t_i) \text{ and } C(deb, cre, \alpha', t_f) \\
F_{uag} & C(deb, cre, \alpha, t_i) \\
R_{uag} & 1)\ C_g(x, y, update_{d_1}(x, y, (\alpha, t_i), \alpha'), t_j) \\
& 2)\ C_g(y, x, update_{d_1}(x, y, (\alpha, t_i), \alpha') \Rightarrow \\
& \quad C_g(y, x, agree_{d_2}(y, x, update_{d_1}((\alpha, t_i), \alpha'))| \\
& \qquad\qquad disagree_{d_3}(y, x, update_{d_1}((\alpha, t_i), \alpha')), t_k), t_j) \\
& 3)\ C_g(x, y, agree_{d_2}(y, x, update_{d_1}((\alpha, t_i), \alpha')) \Rightarrow \\
& \quad C(deb, cre, \alpha', t_f), t_j) \\
& 4)\ C_g(x, y, agree_{d_2}(y, x, update_{d_1}((\alpha, t_i), \alpha')) \Rightarrow \\
& \quad \neg C(deb, cre, \alpha, t_i), t_j) \\
& 5)\ C_g(x, y, disagree_{d_3}(y, x, update_{d_1}((\alpha, t_i), \alpha')) \Rightarrow \\
& \quad C(deb, cre, \alpha, t_i), t_j)
\end{array}
$$

Discharge.Violated.ActionC and Discharge.Fullfilled.ActionC Games.
A socially accepted extra-dialogical commitment can be active (its conditions of satisfaction[2] can be met), violated (its conditions of satisfaction could not be met anymore) or fulfilled (its conditions of satisfaction has been met).

In our model, the violation as well as the fulfilment of an extra-dialogical action commitment must be grounded, and the agents may want the eventual associated sanctions or rewards to apply. The *Discharge.Violated.ActionC (dvg)* is the tool for attempting such a grounding while the *Discharge.Fullfilled.ActionC (dfg)* is used to discharge fulfilled action commitment. The use of those games eventually entail positive (for fulfilment) or negative (for violation) sanctions to apply as discussed in [12]. The conditions and rules of those games are as follows:

$$
\begin{array}{l|l}
E_{dfg} & \exists\, t_i,\ t_i < t_j : C(deb, cre, \alpha, t_i) \\
S_{dfg} & \neg C(deb, cre, \alpha, t_i) \\
F_{dfg} & C(deb, cre, \alpha, t_i) \\
R_{dfg} & 1)\ C_g(x, y, discharge_{d_1}(x, y, C(deb, cre, \alpha, t_i), t_j) \\
& 2)\ C_g(y, x, discharge_{d_1}(x, y, C(deb, cre, \alpha, t_i) \Rightarrow \\
& \quad C_g(y, x, accept_{d_2}|refuse_{d_3}, t_k), t_j) \\
& 3)\ C_g(x, y, accept_{d_2}(y, x, \alpha) \Rightarrow apply(s_x) \text{ and } \neg C(x, y, \alpha, t_i), t_j) \\
& 4)\ C_g(x, y, refuse_{d_3}(y, x, \alpha) \Rightarrow C(x, y, \alpha, t_i), t_j)
\end{array}
$$

---

[2] Which will not be defined here since they depend on the choice of a particular content language, which we leave open for genericness.

$$E_{dvg} \left| \exists\, t_i,\ t_i < t_j : C(deb, cre, \alpha, t_i) \right.$$
$$S_{dvg} \left| \neg C(deb, cre, \alpha, t_i) \right.$$
$$F_{dvg} \left| C(deb, cre, \alpha, t_i) \right.$$
$$R_{dvg} \left| \begin{array}{l} 1)\ C_g(x, y, discharge_{d_1}(x, y, C(deb, cre, \alpha, t_i)), t_j) \\ 2)\ C_g(y, x, discharge_{d_1}(x, y, C(deb, cre, \alpha, t_i)) \Rightarrow \\ \quad C_g(y, x, accept_{d_2} | refuse_{d_3}, t_{j+1}), t_j) \\ 3)\ C_g(x, y, accept_{d_2}(y, x, \alpha) \Rightarrow apply(s_x)\ and\ \neg C(x, y, \alpha, t_i), t_j) \\ 4)\ C_g(x, y, refuse_{d_3}(y, x, \alpha) \Rightarrow C(x, y, \alpha, t_i), t_j) \end{array} \right.$$

2.5   DIAGAL Extra-Features

Intensity Degrees – Notice that in previous games, the embedded speech acts are labelled with an integer d_x indicating the *illocutionary force intensity degree* relative to the default basic illocutionary force degree in Vandervecken [17] classification. For example, in the *request* game the embedded request speech act stands for the directive category for action which is mapped to: *suggest* $= -2$, *direct* $= -1$, *request* $= 0$, *demand* $= 1$, *order* $= 2$, according to the intensity degree factor dynamically chosen by the agent. Allowing agents to use the appropriate illocutionary forces intensity degree for each dialogue/speech act leads to many variations of those basic games. While being crucial in mixed communities, this feature is also important in modern agent communication language since some agent architectures allow the agent to use different meaningful intensity degrees [18].

Deontic Version – In order to use DIAGAL, agents should embed our *dialogue manager* (described in [18]) which (1) loads the contextualization game and the various dialog games and (2) manages the agenda according to dialogues. While doing so reduces the aforementioned semantic flexibility, in certain systems, it is simpler to model commitment as directed obligation that cannot be updated nor cancelled. To do so within DIAGAL, the dialogue managers just have to load the games for creations and discharges only.

Social Context – A great number of agents applications rely on an organizational level that structures the agents acquaintances and facilitates social control. In such systems, it can be the case, for example, that an agent is not allowed to reject requests from a hierarchical superior. In order to take this social context into account, we have supplied our dialogue manager with special features to update the rules of the different dialogue games to take into account three possibilities: (1) the conversing agent is on the same social level as the concerned agent, (2) the conversing agent is superior to the agent, (3) the conversing agent is inferior to the agent. For space reasons, we will just mention those features here.

2.6   Conversation Example

Suppose an agent x wishes that an agent y repair its car. Therefore, agent x proposes to agent y to enter a request game (the only game whose success condition is an action commitment of the wanted form). When the agent y receives the mes-

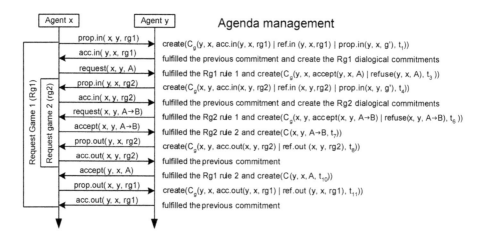

Fig. 2. Conversation example with agendas management

sage *prop.in(x,y,rg)* (issued from the contextualisation game, Figure 1) his dialogue manager adds the commitment $C(y, x, acc.in(y, x, rg)|ref.in(y, x, rg)|prop.in(y, x, g'))$ to his agenda. Agent y thus has three choices to fulfill this commitment: accept to play the game, refuse to play the game or propose another game.

For the sake of our example, we assume that y accepts to play a *Request* game, meaning that he has the resources and the will to enter a dialogue with x. The dialogue managers of x and y then add all the *Request* game rules (indicated in section 2.4) to their respective agendas. The first rule stipulates that x is committed to make a request $C(x, y, request(x, y, \alpha))$. Agent x thus makes his request in order to fulfill this dialogical commitment. The second rule indicates that if x makes a request, y is committed to accept or reject it. On its side, before responding to x's request, y decides to embed another *Request* game as an attempt to commit x to pay him if he accepts the request and repairs the car. The conversation continues according to the different rules sustaining dialogues games and agents' decisions. Finally, at the end of the conversation, two extra-dialogical commitments remain: $C(y, x, A)$ and $C(x, y, A \Rightarrow B)$ where A stands for the action "Repair the car" and B stands for the action "Pay for the car repairs". The complete conversation is presented in Figure 2. The left side of the figure presents the sequence diagram of the conversation between x and y while the right side presents the effects of each message on the contents of their agendas. Notice that the discharge of those commitments will occur once their fulfilment or violation have occurred, which are detected in the way described in [12].

3   Success and Satisfaction in DIAGAL

In standard speech act theory [17], success and satisfaction conditions play a central role. This section indicates how such fundamental notions are extended and refined in DIAGAL.

Success conditions of a speech act are the conditions that must hold in the utterance context in order for the speaker to succeed in its accomplishment. In the case of a promise, for example, the speaker should be ready to commit on the content of his promise and succeed in uttering his promise and he should be heard and understood by the appropriate agents [19].

By providing a dialogical rather than monological approach to language primitives, dialogue games allow extending and redefining success conditions in two different categories: dialogical success and extra-dialogical success. First, each DIAGAL game is played with *dialogical success* (which is close to the monological success conditions previously defined) if and only if all the dialogical commitments attached to it are fulfilled. That means the agents accept to enter the game and play it until the failure or success conditions are reached, with possible interruptions due to dialogue structure. Secondly, through success and failure conditions of the dialogue games, *extra-dialogical success* allows taking into account the hearer and thus introducing a more socially aware notion of success. Since from the hearer's point of view, an assertive succeeds if he agrees to it (independently of the truth of the content which is more related to the satisfaction conditions), a request succeeds if he accepts it.... In this context, there are several reasons why a dialogue game can fail: (1) the hearer can refuse to enter the game for several possible reasons (his attention is kept somewhere else, he doesn't have enough resources to process the communication at this particular time, he doesn't want to communicate with the initiator agent, ...) (2) the initiator embedded speech act success conditions are not fulfilled (meaning that the corresponding dialogical commitments is not fulfilled) (3) the failure conditions are reached, meaning that the hearer refuses the wanted change on the social layer. A dialogue game can thus be played with dialogical success and extra-dialogical failure.

On their side, *Satisfaction* conditions of a speech act gathers the conditions that must be obtained for the perlocutionary effects of this speech act to be obtained. For example, an assertion is satisfied if it's true, a request is satisfied if it is granted, a promise is satisfied if it is kept,... Satisfaction conditions relate speech acts to the world through their coverage of the different directions of fit between world and words. In social commitment based approaches, we need to consider only two of the four basic directions of fit[3]:

1. *The words-to-world direction of fit:* the point of speech acts having this direction of fit is to represent how things were/are/will be in the world. Such speech acts are satisfied when their propositional contents fit the state of affairs existing in the world.
2. *The world-to-words direction of fit:* the point of speech acts having this direction of fit is to have the world transformed by the speaker (commissive) or by the hearer (directive) in order to match the propositional content of

---

[3] The two other directions of fit are not necessary since no operation corresponding to the double direction of fit nor the empty one were defined in those approaches yet. The rationale for that is beyond the scope of this paper.

the utterance. Such a speech act is satisfied when the world is transformed to fit its propositional content.

Within DIAGAL, conditions of satisfaction are captured by the notion fulfilment of social commitments which indicate that the direction of fit between words and world is resolved. In our approach, social commitments keep track of the dialogues from which they are issued between the moment of extra-dialogical success and a hypothetical actual satisfaction time.

Thus, while traditional success and satisfaction conditions have always been problematic to implement and verify in distributed settings (without accessing the agents' mental states), the DIAGAL approach takes a step ahead. Notice that as in speech act theory, success and satisfaction conditions are linked in the sense that one cannot expect satisfaction without previous extra-dialogical success which itself requires dialogical success. Finally, the crucial question of establishing and verifying the fulfilment of social commitments is addressed in [12].

4   DIAGAL for Open Systems

An *open MAS* is characterized by its variable number of agents and the heterogeneity of its agents that are usually independently developed. Since DIAGAL semantics does not relate to any supposition about the decision making mechanisms of the conversing agents, it's an appropriate tool for open and heterogeneous systems communications. In order to use an ACL automatically, agents should be able to process its semantic. With previous mentalistic semantics, a strong assumption was made about the nature of rational agents that should at least have mental states which form and semantics match those used for the ACL semantics. This constraint was known as the semantic alignment problem, described in [5]. DIAGAL does not rely on such a strong assumption about the architecture of agents nor on their decision making mechanism. Since DIAGAL does not involve any references to agents' (hypothetical) mental states, it solves the semantic alignment problem.

Actually, DIAGAL can be used by agents which hold mental states (like the various BDI-like architectures) as well as by agents involving other internal decision process mechanisms. To use DIAGAL, the only assumptions needed are that (1) agents embed our dialogue manager enabling them to use DIAGAL and (2) they shared the model of flexible social commitments and their enforcement described in [12] which gives the operational semantics of the games and (3) the sanction system chosen for the enforcement of commitments should be respected as indicated in [12].

5   Conclusion

We hope to have shown that as an ACL, DIAGAL offers a complete set of tools to manipulate the social commitments layer (reifying in agents agendas) in open or heterogeneous MAS. At the syntactic level, dialogue games appear to be a good alternative between strictly "mentalistic" or "social" approaches and protocols. At the semantic level, the sincerity assumption is avoided and dialogue games are defined in terms of entry conditions, success conditions and failure conditions expressed in terms of verifiable extra-dialogical social commitments. Finally, the conventional part of pragmatics is expressed in terms of conditional dialogical social commitments specifying the rules of the games. Besides, the contextualization game ensures the grounding of dialogue games (taking into account the attentional level of agents) while dialogue games ensure the grounding of each modification in the social commitments layer.

There are at least two ways of using DIAGAL in MAS:

1. DIAGAL can be used to specify protocols as particular compositions of dialogue games. For example, one can express the request for action protocol using DIAGAL games, as in [20].
2. DIAGAL can also be used dynamically as an agent language. For any attempt to get a particular modification on the social commitments layer, an agent just has to choose the DIAGAL game whose success condition unifies with the wanted change. This approach was used to validate our theory of agent communication pragmatics [18].

Finally, a dialogue game simulator (DGS) including many dialogue metrics has been developed to support previous DIAGAL version prototyping. In this framework, contextualization and dialogue games are XML files with their DTD while the standard dialogue manager has been implemented in Java. As future work, we plan to adapt it to the new version presented here and to make this complete yet versatile agent communication framework and test-bed available to the community.

References

1. FIPA: FIPA ACL message structure specification, foundation for intelligent physical agents. http://www.FIPA.org (2002)
2. Labrou, Y., Finin, T.: Semantics for an agent communication language. In Singh, M.P., Rao, A., Wooldridge, M.J., eds.: Intelligent Agents IV: Agent Theories, Architectures, and Languages. Volume 1365 of Lecture Notes in Computer Science. Springer-Verlag, Heidelberg, Germany (1998) 209–214
3. Moulin, B.: The social dimension of interactions in multi-agent systems. In: Agent and Multi-agent Systems. Volume 1441 of Lecture Notes in Artificial Intelligence (LNAI). Springer, Berlin (1997)
4. Singh, M.P.: Agent communication languages: rethinking the principles. IEEE Computer 12 (1998) 40–47
5. Dignum, F., Greaves, M.: Issues in agent communication : An introduction. In Dignum, F., Greaves, M., eds.: Issues in Agent Communication. Number 1916 in LNAI, Springer-Verlag: Heidelberg, Germany (2000) 1–16
6. Maudet, N., Chaib-draa, B.: Commitment-based and dialogue-game based protocols - new trends in agent communication language. Knowledge Engineering 17 (2002) 157–179

7. Dastani, M., Hulstijn, J., der Torre, L.V.: Negotiation protocols and dialogue games. In: Proceedings of the Belgium/Dutch AI Conference (BNAIC'2000), Kaatsheuvel (2000)
8. Flores, R., Kremer, R.: Bringing coherence to agent conversation. In Wooldridge, M., Ciancarini, P., Weiss, G., eds.: Agent-Oriented Software Engineering II. Volume 2222 of Lecture Notes in Computer Science., Springer-Verlag (2001) 50–67
9. McBurney, P. Parsons, S., Wooldridge, M.: Desiderata for agent argumentation protocols. In: Procceedings of the First International Conference on Autonomous Agents and Multi-Agents. (2002)
10. Pasquier, P., Chaib-draa, B.: Engagements, intentions et jeux de dialogue. In Herzig, A., Chaib-draa, B., Mathieu, P., eds.: Modèles formels de l'interaction, Actes des Secondes Journées Francophones, Cépaduès (2003) 289–294 papier court.
11. Walton, D.N., Krabbe, E.: Commitment in Dialogue. Suny Press (1995)
12. Pasquier, P., Flores, R., Chaib-draa, B.: Modelling flexible social commitments and their enforcement. In: Proceedings of the Fifth International Workshop Engineering Societies in the Agents World (ESAW). Lecture Notes in Artificial Intelligence (LNAI), Springer-Verlag (2004)
13. Singh, M.P.: A social semantics for agent communication languages. In Dignum, F., Greaves, M., eds.: Issues in Agent Communication. Springer-Verlag: Heidelberg, Germany (2000) 31–45
14. Clark, H.H.: Using Language. Cambridge University Press (1996)
15. Reed, C.: Dialogue frames in agent communication. In: Proceedings of the Third International Conference on MultiAgent Systems (ICMAS). (1998)
16. Chaib-draa, B., Maudet, N., Labrie, M.A.: DIAGAL, a tool for analyzing and modelling commitment-based dialogues between agents. In: Proceedings of Canadian AI 2003. Number 2671 in Lecture Notes in Artificial Intelligence (2003) 353–369
17. Vanderveken, D.: Meaning and Speech Acts: Principles of Language Use. Cambridge University, Cambridge, UK (1990)
18. Pasquier, P., Andrillon, N., Chaib-draa, B.: An exploration in using cognitive coherence theory to automate BDI agents' communicational behavior. In Dignum, F., ed.: Advances in Agent Communication - International Workshop on Agent Communication Languages, ACL'03. Volume 2922 of Lecture Notes in Artificial Intelligence (LNAI)., Springer-Verlag (2003) 37–58
19. Searle, J.R., Vanderveken, D.: Foundations of Illocutionary Logic. Cambridge University Press, NY (1985)
20. Chaib-draa, B., Maudet, N., Labrie, M.A.: Request for action reconsidered as dialogue games based on commitments. In: Workshop on Agent Communication Language (AAMAS02). (2002)

Using Social Power to Enable Agents to Reason About Being Part of a Group

Cosmin Carabelea[1], Olivier Boissier[1], and Cristiano Castelfranchi[2]

[1] SMA-G2I-ENS Mines de St.Etienne,
158 Cours Fauriel, St.Etienne, F-42030, France
{carabelea, boissier}@emse.fr
[2] ISTC-CNR-Rome, Viale Marx 15, 00137, Rome, Italy
c.castelfranchi@istc.cnr.it

Abstract. One of the main challenges in multi-agent systems is the coordination of autonomous agents. In order to achieve this coordination, the agents are considered to be part of what we call a group (e.g., organization, institution, team, normative society, etc.). Our goal is to enable an agent to reason about the implications of being part of a group: what does it gain or lose, what are the constraints imposed on its behaviour. The theory of social power has been proposed as a paradigm to describe the agent's behaviour. In this paper we use this theory, we formalize it and we extend it to include group-related aspects. We then show how, using this theory, an agent is able to reason about the constraints imposed on its behaviour by the group, for example to decide whether it should enter or not a group.

1 Introduction

One of the main challenges in multi-agent systems is the coordination of autonomous agents. Many mechanisms have been proposed to achieve this coordination. Among them, of interest to our work, we can cite organizational design [17] and norms [1]. In this paper we will use the term *group* to denote a collection of agents coordinated by one or more of these mechanisms. Particular examples of types of groups are institutions [8], teams [16] or normative societies [1]. Generally speaking, a group contains several elements (e.g., agents, roles, norms) and several coordination and control mechanisms. These mechanisms are used, for example, to assign agents to roles [6], or for group's decision-making (e.g., choosing group's goals and distributing them among members) [16], to negotiate or to plan [12], to punish agents that violate norms [1], etc.

Besides designing coordination and control mechanisms for autonomous agents, another difficult problem in open systems is to enable agents to reason about these mechanisms, or, more generally, to reason about what does it mean to be part of a group. For example, when an agent enters a group, how does it understand what it will lose, what it will gain, what new constraints are imposed on its behaviour? *Our aim in this work is to enable an agent to reason about the implications of being part of a group.*

M.-P. Gleizes, A. Omicini, and F. Zambonelli (Eds.): ESAW 2004, LNAI 3451, pp. 166–177, 2005.
© Springer-Verlag Berlin Heidelberg 2005

Several authors have proposed the notion of *social power* as a paradigm that can be used to explain the agents' behaviour (see for example [5] or [11]). One of the uses of this theory of social power is to enable the designer (or an observer) of a multi-agent system to analyze and predict the agents' behaviour in a group. Another interesting use of this theory is to enable the agents to reason about their (and others') powers when being part of the group. Thus, they will be able to understand the implications (i.e., the constraints they face) of being part of a group. However, in order to be used by artificial agents, the theory of social power needs to be formalized.

Based on the work in [4], in this paper we propose formal definitions for several forms of power, ranging from individual and social (Section 2) to group-related ones (Section 3). In Section 4 we describe how an agent can use this power theory to reason about what it means to be part of a group and to decide whether to be part of a group or not. Finally, we draw some concluding remarks and trace directions for future work.

2 Non-institutional Powers

The author of [5] argues that the notion of *power* is not intrinsically social and does not refer only to the theory of society or at least of social action: power can be related to individual. Using as basis the work described in [15], we use the basic notions of action, resource, plan and goal (noted respectively *a, r, pl* and *g*) to describe the behaviour of an agent. These notions will be used to define the *individual powers* of an agent, i.e., the powers it has without considering other agents. We will then use these powers to identify power relationships between agents, to address what we call *social powers*. Although all the following definitions are context dependent, to keep them simple, we will not use in the different formulae an additional parameter representing the context. However, we would like to stress out that an agent can have a power in a context and not have it in another.

Due to space reasons, we will not describe here all the predicates used in our definitions. Most of these predicates have self explanatory names, e.g., *believes*, *can_empower* (an agent can give a permission to another one), *can_commit_to* (an agent can form an intention or commitment to do something), etc. A more detailed description of all the used predicates can be found in [4].

2.1 Individual Powers

An agent can have several types of individual powers: executional powers (*can_do*), deontic powers (*entitled_to*) and full (total) powers (*power*). In what follows we will use as examples only actions and goals. Nevertheless, the notions we introduce can be easily extended for resources or plans.

2.1.1 Executional and Deontic Powers: *Can_do* and *Entitled_to*
We note by *can_do* the executional power an agent has. For example, we say that an agent *can do* an action, if it has all the needed resources, both external and internal (know-how, skills) to execute that action. Or we say that an agent *can do* a goal if it

has a plan (or it can obtain one) to achieve the goal and it *can do* all the subgoals, actions or resources needed by that plan:

$$can\_do(X, r) =^d has(X, r)$$
$$can\_do(X, a) =^d know\_how(X, a) \wedge (\forall r \; needs(a, r) \Rightarrow can\_do(X, r))$$
$$can\_do(X, pl_g) =^d \forall \alpha \in pl_g \; can\_do(X, \alpha), \; \alpha - a \; resource, \; action \; or \; goal \; in \; the \; plan$$
$$can\_do(X, g) =^d \exists \; pl_g \; achieves(pl_g, g) \wedge can\_do(X, pl_g) \tag{1}$$

Besides the executional power, an agent can have a deontic power to execute an action, to achieve a goal, etc. We note this by *entitled_to*. Its meaning is that the agent has all the necessary permissions to execute the action and use the necessary resources. Or, in the case of a goal, the agent is *entitled to* achieve the goal if it has the permissions to pursue the goal and it is entitled to do all the elements of a plan that achieves the goal. The *entitled_to* definitions for resources, actions and goals are similar with the ones above and they are not given here due to space reasons.

Let's take for example an agent A that has the resource *printer*, the only resource needed by the action *print*, and the agent knows how to print documents. We can thus say that *can_do(A, print)*. Even if A knows how to print a document, one must also specify if A is forbidden (or allowed) to use the printer or to print using it. For example, we can say that A has all the rights to print a document using that printer: *entitled_to(A, print)*.

2.1.2 Full Powers: *Power*

If an agent has both the executional (*can_do*) and deontic (*entitled_to*) powers, then we say that it has the *power_of* executing/achieving the action/goal:

$$power\_of(X, a/g) =^d can\_do(X, a/g) \wedge entitled\_to(X, a/g) \tag{2}$$

The above definitions are not sufficient to fully describe a power of an agent. If we consider the agent A from the previous example, it can print and it has the permission for it, so it has the power of doing so: *power_of(A, print)*. A first condition for a cognitive agent to really have a power is to be aware that it has that power (otherwise it cannot use it). Thus, in order to have a full power, an agent must be aware it has that power and it also must be able to form an intention to (or to commit to) use its power. If an agent cannot commit whenever it wants to use its power, it does not really have the full power. This is the reason why we introduce the notion of *having access to a power*, which allows us to define what having a full power (noted *power*) means:

$$access\_to(X, p) =^d believes(X, power\_of(X,p)) \wedge can\_commit\_to(X, p) \tag{3}$$

$$\textbf{power}(X, p) =^d power\_of(X,p) \wedge access\_to(X, p) \tag{4}$$

2.2 Social Powers: Dependence, Power over and Influencing Power

The notions introduced in the previous section are taken from the point of view of an agent and do not take into consideration the other agents in the system. Very often an agent X lacks the *power_of* executing an action or achieving a goal. There are many reasons for this, among them being that it lacks some resources or the knowledge how to do it, or even the permissions to do it. If there is another agent, Y, that can provide X with the thing it lacks, we say that X depends on Y for the execution of the action or the achievement of the goal and we write *depends_on(X, Y, a/g)*. For example, in the case of a goal and a lack of executional power:

$$depends\_on(X, Y, g) =^d \forall pl_g \; achieves(pl_g, g) \Rightarrow \exists \alpha \in pl_g \; \neg can\_do(X, \alpha) \wedge \atop can\_do(Y, \alpha) \tag{5}$$

Or, in the case where the power X lacks is a deontic power:

$$depends\_on(X, Y, g) =^d \neg entitled\_to(X, g) \Rightarrow can\_empower(Y, X, g) \tag{6}$$

In the previous example, the agent A has the power of printing: *power_of(A, print)*. Let's assume there is another agent, B, that has the goal of printing a document D, but it does not know how. If A is the only agent having the power of printing, then B depends on A to achieve its goal: *depends_on(B, A, print document D)*.

Due to space reasons, we will not enter into details here; the dependence relationship is deeply analyzed in [15], together with dependencies towards several agents (OR- and AND-dependence) or the mutual or reciprocal dependences. As seen above, our approach extends the existing theory of dependence by taking into account the deontic aspect: an agent can depend on another due to the lack of deontic power.

We would like to stress out that the dependence relationship is objective, i.e., it exists even if the agents are not aware of it. However, if X believes that it depends on Y for an action/goal, then we say that Y has a *power over* X for that action/goal:

$$power\_over(Y, X, a/g) =^d believes(X, depends\_on(X, Y, a/g)) \tag{7}$$

The last power relationship we introduce here is the *influencing power* an agent has over another one. From the social point of view (i.e., not institutional and not normative), an agent has influencing power over another agent, if the other agent is aware that it depends on the first for one of its goals:

$$infl\_power(Y, X, p) =^d power\_of(X, p) \wedge (\exists g \; goal(X, g) \wedge power\_over(Y, X, g)) \tag{8}$$

In this definition, *p* is a power of X that is not necessarily related to the action or the goal for which X depends on Y. Using the above example, imagine that B also has the power of negotiating objects in e-markets: *power_of(B, negotiate)*. Because B depends on A for its goal to print – *depends_on(B, A, print)* – and both agents are aware of this situation, A acquires the power of influencing B for the power related to negotiation: *infl_power(A, B, power_of(B, negotiate))*.

As we will discuss in Section 3, there are other ways in which an agent can obtain a power of influencing another agent. In the following we will describe how an agent can use its power of influencing over another agent to acquire new powers.

2.3 Putting at the Disposal of

There are many operations the agents can execute in order to modify their powers and/or the powers of another agent, like empowerment, putting at the disposal of, requesting power, etc. (see [5] and [4]). We will focus here on the two operations related to the influencing power: the *putting of a power at the disposal of another agent* and the *request for a putting at the disposal*. But first, we will introduce what we call an indirect power.

The full power of an agent, presented in the previous sections is a *direct* power of an agent. The agent has the power of executing an action (or to satisfy a goal) and it also has *access to* its power. We say that an agent has an *indirect power* if it has access to the power of another agent. The predicate used bellow, *transferred_to* denotes the fact that an agent has transferred the access to its own power to another agent. The indirect power means that an agent cannot use it directly, but if it commits to use it, the other agent will do it:

$$\text{ind\_power } (Y, p) =^d \exists X: \text{power\_of}(X, p) \land \text{transferred\_to}(X, Y, p) \qquad (9)$$

When an agent X that has a full power gives to another agent Y access to its power, we say that X *puts at the disposal of* Y its power. Thus, Y is able to use this power whenever it wants to:

$$\text{power } (X, p) \land \text{puts\_at\_disposal\_of}(X, Y, p) \Rightarrow \text{ind\_power } (Y, p) \qquad (10)$$

We can note that in this definition, X does not offer its power p to Y (e.g., a resource), but the access to the power p (e.g., the access to the resource). In other words, Y has the control over the power of X: it can decide whenever it wants to use (indirectly) the power.

An interesting question is whether X still keeps its direct power of p or it loses it when putting it at the disposal of Y. The nature of the *access_to* predicate makes that X loses its access to its power:

$$\text{power\_of}(X, a/g) \land \text{access\_to}(X, a/g) \land \text{puts\_at\_disposal\_of}(X, Y, a/g) \Rightarrow$$
$$\text{power\_of}(X, a/g) \land \neg\text{access\_to}(X, a/g) \land \text{transferred\_to}(X, Y, a/g) \qquad (11)$$

If an agent has the power of influencing another agent for a power and it wants that power, it requests the second agent to put at its disposal the power:

$$\text{power}(X, p) \land \text{infl\_power}(Y, X, p) \land \text{requests\_power}(Y, X, p) \Rightarrow$$
$$\text{puts\_at\_disposal\_of}(X, Y, p) \qquad (12)$$

Thus, by using the Formula 11, the *request_power* operation has the effect of obtaining an indirect power. Using the previous example, due to a dependence, the agent A has the power of influencing B for B's power of negotiating: *infl_power(A, B, power_of(B, negotiate))*. If A requests B to put at its disposal its power to negotiate, A will obtain an indirect power to negotiate: whenever A decides to, B will negotiate on its behalf – *ind_power (A, negotiate)*. This example illustrates how, by reasoning upon the dependencies existing between them, the agents in a multi-agent system are able to acquire new powers. The next section will show how the fact that they belong to a group enables the agents to obtain even more powers.

While we are aware of the fact that there are autonomous agents that can refuse a *request_power*, in this paper we will not focus on this aspect of the power theory. The interested reader is invited to [4] for more details on how agent autonomy can be defined by using the power theory.

3 Agents' Powers in a Group

The previous section described the various forms of powers an agent have by itself (individual powers) and the power relationships that appear because of dependencies between agents. All the definitions above were given without taking into account institutional aspects, i.e., the fact that the agents belong to a group. In the following we will describe what are the institutional aspects we take into account and we will show how agent's powers are influenced by them.

3.1 What Is a Group Made of ?

There are many approaches on how to coordinate autonomous agents. The top-down ones usually specify an explicit organizational structure that is known to all agents (e.g., the MOISE+ model [9]), while the bottom-up ones try to ensure the coordination without using an organizational structure known by all agents (e.g., GPGP/TAEMS [12]). In this paper we call *group* a collection of agents coordinated by one or more coordination mechanisms. We use this term to denote the common things in the notions of institution [8], organizational structure [3] or [17], team [16], normative society [1], etc. A group contains several elements (e.g., roles, norms) and several coordinations and control mechanisms (e.g., assigning agents to roles [6], punishing agents that violate norms [1], etc.).

In this paper we focus on how the group's elements influence the agents' powers, i.e., what new forms of power appear because the agents belong to a group. Based on the group models proposed in the literature (institutions, normative societies, etc.), we consider a group formed by three types of elements. A group contains a set of *roles*, a set of *authority* relationships between the roles (i.e, a hierarchy of roles) and a set of deontic specifications of the roles' expected behaviour (i.e., *norms*). In the following we will show how this model, although simple, allows us to model the powers that appear in a group. We will then show that the power relationships we introduced can be extended to other coordination elements, such as the *contract* [2] (or its weaker form, the *commitment*) [10].

We would like to point out that in this paper we do not propose formal definitions for the notions we use to define a group (norms, roles, etc.). Defining these notions is a very active research area in the multi-agent community (see for example [1], [6] or [17]). The aim of this paper is not to replace this related work, but to complement it by defining agents' powers using these notions.

3.2 Power Relations in a Group

In Section 2 we introduced the notion of *power over* that describes the power an agent has over another. The source of this power over is the goal (action) dependence of the second agent on the first (Formulae 5 and 6). However, if the agents are part of a group, there are two other sources for the power of an agent over another: the authority relationships and the norms.

3.2.1 Power over Due to *Authority over*

An agent can have power over another because it has authority over that agent. In other words, if there are two roles and there is an authority relation between them, the authority relation will exist between any agents playing the roles and this gives an agent a power over another:

$$power\_over(Y, X, p) =^d \exists\, R_1, R_2: plays(X, R_1) \wedge plays(Y, R_2) \wedge$$
$$authority\_over(R_1, R_2, p) \tag{13}$$

If both agents are aware of the roles they play and of the relations between their roles, then Y has also the power of influencing X (Formula 8). If it requests this power *p* (Formula 12) and X puts it at Y's disposal, then Y acquires the indirect power regarding X's power *p*. Thus, whenever Y wants, X will use its power p.

For example, in the case of a soccer team, there are two roles: *coach* and *player*. Some agents can play only using their right foot, some using their left, and some using both. We model this by saying that an agent has the *power_of(A, play ball with left/right foot)*. We also consider that an agent should be able to play a given move (e.g., pass to another player, run to a given position, receive ball and shoot) – *power_of(A, play move)*. The hierarchical structure in this group specifies that the role coach has authority over the role player for the power of a player to play a move: *authority_over(coach, player, power_of(player, play move))*. If an agent B plays the role coach and an agent A plays the role player, then *power_over(B, A, power_of(A, play move)*. Using the reasoning above, B acquires the indirect power for *power_of(A, play move)* and thus, whenever B (coach) wants, A (player) plays a move.

We would like to point out that the *authority_over* relation (and thus the *power_over* one) depends on the power *p*: a role can have authority over another role for a power, but not have it for another. Using the example above, the authority relation does not say anything about the power of an agent to play the ball with its right/left foot. Thus, the agent playing the role coach cannot decide whenever it wants with what foot a player will play the ball.

3.2.2 Power over Due to *Norms*

Another source for the power over relation is the existence of a norm. If an agent plays a role and there is a norm targeting that role and concerning a power p, then any agent that plays that role has its behaviour regarding p constrained by the norm:

$$power\_over(group, X, p) =^d \exists R\; belongs\_to(R, group) \wedge plays(X, R) \wedge$$
$$has\_norm\_on(group, R, p) \tag{14}$$

The same reasoning concerning the influencing power and the requesting of a power can be done for this form of the power_over. Thus, the group can acquire an indirect power regarding *p*: whenever the group wants, the agent X uses its power p. Using the example above, let's say there is an obligation in the soccer team that all players use the same equipment. This norm targets the role *player* and the power_of a player to wear a given equipment, and thus we have *power_over(soccer team, A, power_of(A, wear equipment))*, where A is an agent playing the role *player*. If the group requests this power from the agent and the agent puts it at the group's disposal, then whenever the group decides that A wears a given equipment, A wears.

It is out of the scope of this paper to talk about agent autonomy, more precisely about norm-autonomy [7]. However, we would like to point out that if an agent refuses the requests_power operation, it does not put at the disposal of the group its power_of. Thus, the decision on what equipment the agent will wear will not be made by the group, but by the agent.

This definition of power_over differs from the others in the sense that it is not another agent which has a power over an agent, but it is the group that has this power. Often, the group *empowers* an agent to act as its representative and thus this agent acquires the power over, but this is just a transfer of power: it is the group that has real power over. A good example of this situation is given in [5]: an agent does not surrender herself to a policeman, but to the institution represented by the policeman.

3.3 Other Sources for the Power over

In this paper we chose to describe a group in terms of roles, authority relations and norms. Other terms have been used as well to define agent institutions or societies. For example, the authors of [2] use the notion of *contract* as a coordination element in a group. We can extend the above definitions by defining the power of an agent over another due to a contract between them:

$$\text{power\_over}(Y, X, p) =^d \exists C: \text{contract}(X, Y, p, C) \tag{15}$$

This is to say that Y has the power over X for p because X signed a contract with Y regarding p. It is obvious that this is just a particular form of the norm-based definition of power_over (Formula 14). Y has this power over because both agents are part of a group in which there is a norm that says that all contracts must be fulfilled. However, in some situations, it can be useful to model this situation directly using the notion of contract and not by passing through the intermediary of norms.

The notion of contract can be weakened to the one of *social commitment* [10][14]. We then say that an agent has power over another because the second is committed towards the first for a power:

$$\text{power\_over}(Y, X, p) =^d \text{committed\_to}(X, Y, p) \tag{16}$$

If an agent X commits to an agent Y for a power p and Y is aware of this, then Y has the power of influencing X for p (Formula 8). It is likely that Y will try to use this influencing power and to request X to put at its disposal the power p (Formula 11). It is still an open question for us whether to use the above definition only when the agents are part of a group or even if there is no group with norms that enforce the fulfillment of commitments. If there is no such norm, there is nothing that ensures that X will fulfill its commitment and thus will put at the disposal of Y its power p.

4   Reasoning About Entering a Group Using the Power Theory

In this paper we are interested in how to enable agents to reason about the existing relationships with other agents and with the society in which they evolve. A similar attempt has been done in [13], where the authors propose a model of normative multi-agent systems and identify the normative constraints imposed to agents. While we generally agree with their approach, we believe their model lacks the capacity of capturing the dynamicity of these constraints, e.g., a norm that is not always active. We believe that the power theory is a suitable tool to model these constraints and that this theory can be tailored to different organization models. In this section we will show how an agent can use the notions introduced in the previous sections to reason about what it means to be part of a group. Such an agent will then be able to decide whether to enter or not a group.

Even if an agent is not part of a group, it still interacts with other agents. It is to be expected that the agent is not self-sufficient, i.e., its powers do not allow it to achieve all its goals. The agent depends on other agents to achieve its goals, so the other agents have power over this agent (see for example the agents A and D in Figure 1). If the others are aware of the existing dependencies, they will have the power of influencing the agent. Thus, there are constraints imposed on the behaviour of the agent because it lacks some of the powers it needs.

When an agent is part of a group, it is also subject of several *power_over* relations. If it plays a role in that group and the group specifies a hierarchy of roles, it is to be expected that some agents playing the appropriate roles will have power over this agent. For example, as Figure 1 shows, agent A belongs to a group G where it plays the role R2. Since the agent B plays the role R1 and there is an *authority_over* relation from R1 to R2, A can compute that B has *power_over* A (cf. Formula 13). For the same reason, A has *power_over* C. Moreover, since the group is a normative one, i.e., the roles' behaviour is regulated by norms (see link *has_norm_on* from group to roles), the group has *power_over* the agents because of the norms (cf. Formula 14). As argued in the previous section, these *power_over* relations are in fact relations of influencing power. Thus, the fact that an agent belongs to a group and plays a role in that group greatly limits the liberty of the agent: other agents (or the group) will have the power of influencing this agent, hence imposing constraints on its behaviour.

In both of situations described above, when an agent does and does not belong to a group, the agent's behaviour is constrained by other agents. However, in the second case, if the agent is not part of the group, the constraints on its behaviour are due to the insufficiency of its powers. When it is part of a group, to these constraints are added those due to the fact that it belongs to a group and thus other agents have the power of influencing it. If those agents request its powers and the agent puts them at their disposal, it will lose access to its powers.

So why should an agent enter a group then, if this means that it loses powers? The answer is that by entering a group, an agent also gains power. The most direct form of power gained is because an agent entering a group usually receives resources (e.g., a payment for playing a role) and *permissions* to use resources of the group (e.g., the permission to use a printer). These powers gained by the agent are represented in

Figure 1 by the *power_of* arrow towards some resources. An agent loses some powers because it plays a role in a hierarchy of roles and thus other agents will have authority over it. But the agent might have authority over other agents, so it will gain access to their powers (e.g., relationship between A and C in Figure 1).

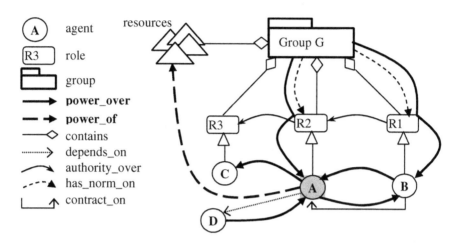

Fig. 1. Several *power_over* relations from the point of view of agent A in a group G

However, the main reason for an agent to enter a group is because of the security the group provides. The agent's behaviour will be constrained by norms, but so will be the behaviour of the other agents too. Even if the agent loses some powers because of the norms, the same powers will be lost by the other agents too. For example, no agent will be able to cheat the others. In Figure 1, this situation is represented by the power that A has over B because of a contract between B and A. Because B's behaviour is regulated by the norms too, B will have to obey the contract it has signed with A (or to disobey and suffer the consequences) since these norms impose such a behaviour.

It is clear for us that an agent facing the decision whether to enter or not a group must be able to do more than just recognize the group's structure or norms. It must be able to understand how the fact that it will be part of the group will hinder or facilitate the achievement of its goals. By using the power theory and reasoning about the power relationships that will appear within the group, the agent will be able to decide whether it is worth or not to enter the group, i.e., whether the power it loses are compensated by the ones it gains or not.

It is worth mentioning that the power theory can be used by the group to reason whether to allow or not an agent to enter a group (or to play a role). If the group has goals and delegates some of them (or subgoals of them) to a role, the agent playing the role should have at least the power of achieving those goals. Thus, reasoning about the powers of an agent, a group computes the utility of that agent for the group.

5   Conclusions

Using the social power theory, a designer (or an observer) of a multi-agent system can analyze and predict the agents' behaviour in a group. Moreover, the same theory can be used by the agents themselves to reason about the constraints imposed to their behaviour when being part of a group. However, in order to enable the agents to use it, one must formalize this theory. In this paper we proposed formal definitions for several forms of power, ranging from individual and social to group-related ones. In order to validate our approach, in the near future we intend to describe a multi-agent application in terms of powers and to enable the agents within the application to reason about their powers. Towards this aim, we started to implement in Prolog a power-based reasoning mechanism. The MOISE+ model [9] allows the specification of organizational structures and it will be used to specify the group-related aspects.

Placing agents together in a group (institution, organization, normative society) does not solve all the problems of coordinating autonomous agents. One must also provide solutions to various problems, such as assigning agents to roles in a group [6], making decisions in a group (e.g., choosing group's goals, assigning subgoals to members) [12][16], punishing norm violation [1], etc. Our power-based model does not try to substitute these solutions, but to provide a complementarity to them. For example, if the group is a normative one (i.e., there are norms constraining the agents' behaviour), norm enforcing mechanisms must be present (e.g., penalties, lowering reputations, etc.). Our model enables agent to be aware of how the norms limit their powers and thus of the constraints imposed on their behaviour by these norms. However, if an autonomous agent decides to disobey a norm, it is the norm enforcing mechanisms that is used to punish it.

As pointed out in [4], there is a direct relationship between autonomy and power. We intend to investigate this relationship and to propose formal definitions for several types of agent autonomy, such as social- or norm-autonomy. Using these definitions, the designer of a multi-agent system will be able to describe the system in terms of power and to detect what degrees of autonomy are necessary for the agents within.

Institutional empowerment is an important operation with power we did not discuss in this paper. As future work, we would like to define this operation and to study the various forms of empowerment that can appear within a group.

Acknowledgements

The authors would like to thank the Rhône-Alpes Region for financing an internship of the first author at ISTC/CNR-Rome, via a EURODOC scholarship. The Ph.D. study of the first author is partially funded by the French Embassy in Romania.

References

1. Boella, G., Lesmo, L.: Norms and Cooperation: Two Sides of Social Rationality. In Hexmoor, H., and Falcone, R., (eds.): Agent Autonomy, Kluwer (2002).
2. Boella, G., van der Torre, L.: Contracts as legal institutions in organizations of autonomous agents. In Proceedings of AAMAS'04, New York (2004).

3. Boella, G., van der Torre, L.: Organizations as socially constructed agents in the agent oriented paradigm. This volume (2005).

4. Carabelea, C., Castelfranchi, C., Boissier, O.: Autonomy and social power. In Proceedings of JFSMA04, Paris (2004), 195-208.

5. Castelfranchi, C.: A micro and macro definition of power. In ProtoSociology – An International Journal of Interdisciplinary Research, 18-19 (2002), 208-268.

6. Dastani, M.M., Dignum, V., Dignum, F.: Role-Assignment in Open Agent Societies. In Proceedings of AAMAS'03, Melbourne, ACM Press (2003).

7. Dignum, F.: Autonomous Agents with Norms. In AI and Law Journal, 7 (1999), 69-79.

8. Esteva, M., Padget, J., Sierra, C.: Formalizing a language for institutions and norms. In Intelligent Agents VIII, LNAI 2333, Springer-Verlag, Berlin (2002), 348-366.

9. Hubner, J., Sichman, J.S., Boissier, O.: A model for the structural, functional, and deontic specification of organizations in multiagent systems. In Proceedings of 16th Brazilian Symposium on Artificial Intelligence, Porto de Galinhas, Brazil (2002), 118-128.

10. Jennings, N.R.: Commitments and Conventions: The Foundation of Coordination in Multi-Agent Systems. The Knowledge Engineering Review, 8 (3), (1993), 223-250.

11. Jones, A.J.J., Sergot, M.: A Formal Characterisation of Institutionalised Power. Journal of IGPL, 3, (1996), 427-443.

12. Lesser, V., et al.: Evolution of the GPGP/TAEMS Domain-Independent Coordination Framework. International Journal of Autonomous Agents and Multi-Agent Systems, 9(1) (2004), 87-143.

13. Lopez y Lopez, F., Luck, M.: A Model of Normative Multi-agent Systems and Dynamic Relationships. In Linderman, G., et al. (eds.): Regulated Agent-Based Social Systems, LNAI 2934, Springer-Verlag, Berlin (2004), 259-280.

14. Pasquier, Ph., Flores, R., Chaib-draa, B.: Modeling flexible social commitments and their enforcement. This volume (2005).

15. Sichman, J., Demazeau, Y., Conte, R., Castelfranchi, C.: A Social Reasoning Mechanism Based on Dependence Networks. In Proceedings of ECAI'94, Amsterdam, (1994).

16. Tambe, M.: Towards Flexible Teamwork. Journal of AI Research, 7 (1997), 83-124.

17. Vazquez-Salceda, J., Dignum, F.: Modelling Electronic Organizations. In Marik, V., et al. (eds.): MAS and applications III, LNAI 2691, Springer-Verlag, Berlin (2003), 584-593.

Strategies for Distributing Goals in a Team of Cooperative Agents

Laurence Cholvy[1] and Christophe Garion[2]

[1] ONERA Toulouse, 2 avenue édouard Belin, 31055 Toulouse, France
cholvy@cert.fr
[2] SUPAERO, 10 avenue édouard Belin, 31055 Toulouse, France
garion@supaero.fr

Abstract. This paper addresses the problem of distributing goals to individual agents inside a team of cooperative agents.

It shows that several parameters determine the goals of particular agents. The first parameter is the set of goals allocated to the team; the second parameter is the description of the real actual world; the third parameter is the description of the agents' ability and commitments. The last parameter is the strategy the team agrees on: for each precise goal, the team may define several strategies which are orders between agents representing, for instance, their relative competence or their relative cost. This paper also shows how to combine strategies. The method used here assumes an order of priority between strategies.

1 Introduction

Reaching a complex goal often needs to consider a group of agents which must cooperate in order to achieve this goal [1]. For instance, nations often group into coalitions in order to maintain peace in a conflicting area, that means sharing information about the situation, providing emergency medical treatment, providing displaced civilian services, providing engineering infrastructure support etc [2].

The goal allocated to the group is some proposition that one desires the group to make true, or equivalently, goals define some desirable worlds the group must reach. But, as Boutilier noted it in [3], goals are not always achievable. It may happen for instance that none of the agents in the team has the ability to make this proposition true. Furthermore, goals may be defeated for reasons other than inability. It is often natural to specify general goals, but list exceptional circumstances that make the goal less desirable than the alternatives. Rather than a categorical distinction between desirable and undesirable situations, it is more general to rank worlds according to their degree of preference. The most preferred worlds correspond to goal states in the classical sense. However, when such states are unreachable, a ranking on alternatives becomes necessary.

In a previous paper [4] we have considered this general case and we have defined a goal distribution process which allocates goals to individual agents

M.-P. Gleizes, A. Omicini, and F. Zambonelli (Eds.): ESAW 2004, LNAI 3451, pp. 178–190, 2005.

of a group, according to the preferences representing the goals allocated to the group, the actual world and the agents' ability and commitments.

The agents we consider are cooperative in the sense that they do not contradict each other in their commitments (for instance, we discard the case when one agent commits himself to make a proposition true whilst another one commits himself to make this proposition false) and their commitments do not contradict a goal of the group. Notice that this process of goals distribution is not based on a negotiation between the agents like in [5, 6, 7]. More precisely, it may be viewed as managed by a central authority which knows how is the real world, what are the agents' abilities and the agents' commitments and which allocates to each agent some goals which correspond to the most preferred situations the group can thus reach.

In this present paper, we refine this work and we show that a fourth parameter can be used for determining the goals of particular agents. This last parameter is the strategies the team agrees on. We will see that a strategy depends on a particular goal and is an order between the agents that are able to achieve it. For instance, given a particular goal, agents may be ordered according to their relative competence for achieving it. Agents may also be ordered according to their relative cost for achieving this goal.

We will also show how to combine strategies. For instance, given a particular goal, we could want to order agents by taking into account their relative competence *and* their relative cost. The method used here for combining strategies assumes a priority order between the strategies.

This paper is organized as follows. In section 2, we summarize the process described in [4]. This process is illustrated on an example in section 3. Section 4 focuses on the notion of strategies and combination of strategies. This point is illustrated in section 5. Finally, section 6 is devoted to a discussion.

2   Distribution of Goals Addressed to a Group of Agents

2.1   Preferences Representation

To represent preferences, we use a logic [3], [8] whose language L_B is based on a set of atomic propositional variables $PROP$ with the usual connectives and two modal operators $\Box$, $\overleftarrow{\Box}$.

Models are of the form $\mathcal{M} = \langle W, \leq val \rangle$. W is a set of possible worlds, $\leq$ is a total *preference* preorder on W (a reflexive and transitive relation on $W \times W$). If w and w' are two worlds of W, then $w \leq w'$ means that w is at least as preferred as w'. Finally, val is a valuation function on W[1]. For any formula φ of W, $val(\varphi)$ is the set of worlds of W which classically satisfy φ.

Let $\mathcal{M} = \langle W, \leq, val \rangle$ be a model. Satisfaction of modal formulas is defined as follows:

---

[1] I.e. $val : PROP \rightarrow 2^W$ and val is such that $val(\neg\varphi) = W - val(\varphi)$ and $val(\varphi_1 \wedge \varphi_2) = val(\varphi_1) \cap val(\varphi_2)$.

- $\mathcal{M} \models_w \Box\varphi$ iff $\forall w' \in W \quad w' \leq w \implies \mathcal{M} \models_{w'} \varphi$.
- $\mathcal{M} \models_w \overline{\Box} \varphi$ iff $\forall w' \in W \quad w' \not\leq w \implies \mathcal{M} \models_{w'} \varphi$.

$\Box\varphi$ is true at a world w if and only if φ is true at all worlds at least as preferred as w (including w). $\overline{\Box} \varphi$ is true at world w if and only if φ is true at all the worlds less preferred than w.

Boutilier then defines two dual modal operators : $\Diamond\varphi \equiv_{def} \neg\Box\neg\varphi$ means that φ is true at some equally or more preferred world and $\overline{\Diamond} \varphi \equiv_{def} \neg \overline{\Box} \neg\varphi$ means that φ is true at some less preferred world.

$\overleftrightarrow{\Box} \varphi \equiv_{def} \Box\varphi \wedge \overline{\Box} \varphi$ and $\overleftrightarrow{\Diamond} \varphi \equiv_{def} \Diamond\varphi \vee \overline{\Diamond} \varphi$ correspond respectively to classical necessity and possibility.

A formula φ is valid in $\mathcal{M}$ (noted $\mathcal{M} \models \varphi$) iff $\forall w \in W \; \mathcal{M} \models_w \varphi$.

Conditional preferences are formulas of the form $I(\beta|\alpha)$ which means that "ideally, if α is true, then β is true". The connective $I(-|-)$ is defined by $I(\beta|\alpha) \equiv_{def} \overleftrightarrow{\Box} \neg\alpha \vee \overleftrightarrow{\Diamond} (\alpha \wedge (\Box\alpha \to \beta))$. $I(\beta|\alpha)$ is valid in $\mathcal{M}$ iff either α is false in every world of W, or there is some world w which satisfies α and such that every world at least as preferred as w satisfies $\alpha \to \beta$.

2.2   Description of the Actual World

Following a centralized approach, we consider that the team of agents is aware of a shared description of the situation. The actual world is thus described by a finite and consistent set of formulas of $PROP$. It is denoted KB[2]. $Cl(KB)$ denotes its closure by classical logical consequence[3].

2.3   Controllability

Let $\mathcal{A} = \{a_1, \dots, a_n\}$ be a finite set of agents. Like Boutilier, for each agent a_i, we partition the literals of $PROP$ into two sets: C_{a_i} (the literals that a_i can control) and $\overline{C_{a_i}}$ (the literals uncontrollable by a_i). We assume that each agent of the group controls at least one literal:

Assumption 1. $\forall a_i \in \mathcal{A} \quad C_{a_i} \neq \phi$

The notion of controllability for a group of agents is then defined by:

Definition 1. *Let $lit(PROP)$ be the set of literals in the propositional language. The set of controllable literals by the group of agents is $C = \bigcup\limits_{a_i \in \mathcal{A}} C_{a_i}$ and the set of uncontrollable literals by the group of agents is $\overline{C} = lit(PROP) - C$.*

Extension to general propositions is given below:

Definition 2. *Let w and w' be two worlds of W. Let us note $w' - w = \{l : w' \models l, w \models \neg l$ and l is a literal\}. A proposition φ is:*

---

[2] Knowledge Base.
[3] In the original work, this closure is defined as a default closure.

- *controllable iff* $\forall w \in W$ $(w \models \neg\varphi$ $\exists w' \in W$ $w' \models \varphi$ *and* $(w' - w) \subseteq C)$;
- *influenceable iff* $\exists w \in W$ $(w \models \neg\varphi$ $\exists w' \in W$ $w' \models \varphi$ *and* $(w' - w) \subseteq C)$. *In this case, we say that* φ *is influenceable in* w.
- *uninfluenceable iff it is not influenceable.*

2.4   Contexts

Definition 3. *A world* $w \in W$ *is a context for some influenceable proposition* φ *iff* φ *is influenceable in* w *or* $w \models \varphi$.

The contexts of an influenceable proposition φ are the worlds in which either φ is false but the agent can change the valuations of some controllable literal to make φ true, or the worlds in which φ is already true.

Definition 4. *The set on non-contextual propositions of KB is defined by:*
$NC(KB) = \{\varphi \in Cl(KB)$: $Cl(KB)$ *is not a context for* $\neg\varphi\}$

$NC(KB)$ represents the propositions whose truth value will not be changed by some agents' actions (because the group of agents has no ability to do that). We suppose here that $NC(KB)$ is complete.

2.5   CK-Goals of the Group

Definition 5. *Let $\mathcal{P}$ be a set of conditional preferences.* φ *is a CK goal[4] for $\mathcal{A}$ iff* $\mathcal{P} \models I(\varphi | NC(KB))$ *and KB is a context for* φ.

2.6   Commitments

Given a literal controllable by an agent, this agent can express that it will do an action that will keep or make this the literal true (we say that the agent commits itself to achieve the literal), or the agent can express that it will not do an action that can make the literal true (we will say that the agent commits itself not to achieve the literal), or finally, the agent can express nothing about the literal (we will say that the agent does not commit itself neither to achieve the literal nor not to achieve the literal).

To represent the commitments of each agent a_i, we will use three subsets of C_{a_i} : Com_{+,a_i}, Com_{-,a_i} and P_{a_i}. defined as follows. If l is a literal, if l is controllable by a_i and $l \in Com_{+,a_i}$, it means that "the agent a_i commits itself to achieve l"; if l is a literal, if l is controllable by a_i and $l \in Com_{-,a_i}$, it means that "the agent a_i commits itself not to achieve l". Finally, $P_{a_i} = C_{a_i} - (Com_{+,a_i} \cup Com_{-,a_i})$ is the set of controllable literals by a_i and for which a_i does not commit itself to anything (i.e. a_i does not commit itself neither to achieve them nor not to achieve them).

We impose two constraints on those sets.

---

[4] For Complete-Knowledge goal as introduced by Boutilier.

Constraint 1. $\forall a_i \in \mathcal{A}$ Com_{+,a_i} is consistent.

Constraint 2. $\forall a_i \in \mathcal{A}$ $Com_{+,a_i} \cap Com_{-,a_i} = \phi$

Those two constraints express a kind of consistency for the agent's commitments. The first constraint expresses the fact that an agent does not commit itself to achieve both l and $\neg l$. The second constraint expresses the fact that an agent cannot commit itself both to achieve l and not to achieve l.

Definition 6. $Com_{+,\mathcal{A}}$ is the set of positive commitments of the agents:
$$Com_{+,\mathcal{A}} = \bigcup_{a_i \in \mathcal{A}} Com_{+,a_i}$$

$Com_{-,\mathcal{A}}$ is the set of "negative" commitments of the agents:
$Com_{-,\mathcal{A}} = \{l \in KB \ : \ \forall a_i \in \mathcal{A} \ \neg l \ controllable \ by \ a_i \Rightarrow \neg l \in Com_{-,a_i}\}.$

The meaning of $Com_{-,\mathcal{A}}$ is the following: if all the agents that control a literal l commit themselves not to achieve l and $\neg l \in KB$, we will consider that $\neg l$ will remain true. We suppose that there is no external intervention.

An assumption that we do on the agents' commitments is: *every CK goal of $\mathcal{A}$ is consistent with the union of $Com_{+,\mathcal{A}}$ and of $Com_{-,\mathcal{A}}$.*

Assumption 2. For every formula φ such that $\mathcal{P} \models I(\varphi|NC(KB))$ and KB is a context for φ, then $Com_{-,\mathcal{A}} \cup Com_{+,\mathcal{A}} \cup \{\varphi\}$ is consistent.

This restriction allows to eliminate some problematic cases like the case where an agent which controls l commits itself to achieve l and another one which controls $\neg l$ commits itself to achieve $\neg l$ (i.e. $Com_{+,\mathcal{A}}$ not consistent). It also eliminates the case where a literal, which is not consistent with the group's CK goals, is true in KB and will remain true because the agents of the group which could make it false do not commit themselves to it, or finally, the case where the positive and negative commitments of the group are not consistent with some CK goal of the group. If this assumption is not verified, the agents must review their commitments.

2.7   Effective Goals

If the assumption 2 is verified, then the agents' commitments are consistent with the group's CK goals. The goals of each agent do not only depend on $NC(KB)$, but also on the commitments of the other agents.

Definition 7. We define:

$$D(KB) = NC(KB) \cup Com_{+,\mathcal{A}} \cup Com_{-,\mathcal{A}}$$

$D(KB)$ contains the propositions of KB for which KB is not a context, i.e. $NC(KB)$, plus the set of positive commitments of the agents, i.e. $Com_{+,\mathcal{A}}$ and the set of "negative" commitments of the agents, i.e. $Com_{-,\mathcal{A}}$. We have proved that $D(KB)$ is consistent. This set will be used in the *conditional* part of $I(-|-)$ to deduce the effective goals of each agent as follows:

Definition 8. *Let $\mathcal{P}$ be a set of preferences addressed to the group $\mathcal{A}$. φ is an effective goal for a_i, denoted by $EGoal_{a_i}(\varphi)$, iff $\mathcal{P} \models I(\varphi|D(KB))$ and KB is a context for φ for a_i.*

As we use the $I(-|-)$ operator, we are sure that an agent cannot have contradictory goals.

Effective atomic goals are defined by :

Definition 9. *Let $\mathcal{P}$ be a set of conditional preferences. A set of atomic goals is a set of controllable literals $\mathcal{L} = \{l_1, \ldots, l_n\}$ such that:*

- $\forall i \in \{1, \ldots, n\}$ $Cl(KB)$ is a context for l_i.
- *for all CK goal φ given $\mathcal{P}$, $\mathcal{P} \models NC(KB) \wedge \mathcal{L} \to \varphi$.*

In the following, $Ag(\varphi)$ will denote the set of agents who have φ as effective goal:

Definition 10. $Ag(\varphi) = \{a_i \in \mathcal{A} : \Sigma \models I(\varphi|D(KB))$ *et KB is a context for φ for $a_i\}$.*

3   Example

Let us consider a group of two agents a_1 and a_2 and assume that the preferences imposed to the group $\{a_1, a_2\}$ are the following: if the door is sanded, then it should be lacquered and not covered with paper and if the door is not sanded, then it should be covered with paper and not lacquered.

The representation of this scenario is the following: $\mathcal{P} = \{I(l \wedge \neg p|s), I(p \wedge \neg l|\neg s)\}$. For each model of $\mathcal{P}$, $I(l \wedge \neg p|s)$ means that there is a world which satisfies s and such that all preferred worlds satisfy $s \to l \wedge \neg p$. $I(p \wedge \neg l|\neg s)$ means that there is a world which satisfies $\neg s$ and such that all preferred worlds satisfy $\neg s \to \neg l \wedge p$.

1. Suppose that $KB = \{s, \neg l, \neg p\}$ i.e. the door is sanded but not lacquered nor covered with paper. We have $Cl(KB) = KB$.

   Suppose that $\neg s$ is uncontrollable by the agents (i.e. the agents have no "means" to unsand the door). Furthermore, suppose that $C_{a_1} = \{l\}$ and that $C_{a_2} = \{p, \neg p\}$ (i.e. a_1 can lacquer the door, a_2 can cover it with paper or remove the paper if necessary). In this case, $NC(KB) = \{s\}$, because KB is a context for l and for p. $l \wedge \neg p$ is a CK goal of the group[5].

   If the agents do not commit themselves to anything, $D(KB) = \{s\}$, and then $EGoal_{a_1}(l)$ and $EGoal_{a_2}(\neg p)$ hold. a_1 has for atomic goal set $\{l\}$ (i.e. its only goal is to lacquer the door) and a_2 has $\{\neg p\}$ for atomic goals set (i.e. its only goal is not to cover the door with paper). This implies $Ag(l) = a_1$, $Ag(\neg p) = a_2$ and $Ag(\neg l) = Ag(s) = Ag(\neg s) = Ag(p) = \emptyset$.

---

[5] In fact, it is theonly one that is interesting. We can also deduce for instance that $(l \wedge \neg p) \vee p$ is a CK goal of the group.

2. Suppose now that $KB = \{\neg s, \neg l, \neg p\}$, $C_{a_1} = \{l, \neg l\}$ and $C_{a_2} = \{s, p, \neg p\}$. In this case, $NC(KB) = \phi$ and $(l \wedge \neg p) \vee (\neg l \wedge p)$ is a CK goal of the group.

   If $D(KB) = \phi$ (i.e. the agents do not commit themselves to anything), no effective goal can be derived, because a_2 controls s and could make s true.

   But if a_2 commits itself not to achieve s (i.e. it commits itself not to sand the door), then $Com_-(\{a_1, a_2\}) = \{\neg s\}$ and $EGoal_{a_2}(p)$ and $EGoal_{a_1}(\neg l)$ can be deduced: a_2 has for effective goal to cover the door with paper and a_1 has for effective goal to keep the door unlacquered. I.e $Ag(p) = a_2$, $Ag(\neg l) = a_1$ and $Ag(l) = Ag(\neg p) = Ag(s) = Ag(\neg s) = \emptyset$.

4   Strategies

The process described in the previous sections allocates goals to agents by taking into account their ability and their commitments. Here, we show how to extend this process in order to take into account more characteristics of the agents (like for instance, their competence, their cost or the required duration for achieving a goal). But, in order to be as general as possible, these characteristics are represented by preference order among the agents and are associated with each goal. These preference orders are called strategies.

4.1   Mathematical Preliminaries and Notations

Definition 11. *Let E be a set. $\leq_E$ is an order on E iff $\leq_E$ is a reflexive, anti-symmetrical and transitive relation on E.*

Definition 12. *Let E be a set and $\leq_E$ an order on E. Then $\min_{\leq_E}(E) = \{e_i \in E : \forall e_j \in E \ e_j \leq_E e_i \Rightarrow e_j = e_i\}$.*

We define also the minimum of a set for a family of orders.

Definition 13. *Let E be a set and $\leq_E = \{\leq_E^i : i \in \{1, \ldots, n\}\}$ a set of orders on E. Then $\min_{\leq_E}(E) = \bigcap_{i \in \{1, \ldots, n\}} \min_{\leq_E^i} E$.*

4.2   Notion of Strategy

Definition 14. *A strategy is a function $S : lit(PROP) \to \mathcal{A} \times \mathcal{A}$ such that for any literal l, $S(l)$ is an order $\leq_{S(l)}$ on $Ag(l)$.*

Being a function, a strategy associates a literal with at most one order which will be used to select one or several agents. For instance, let us consider a group of three agents $\{a_1, a_2, a_3\}$ achieving a task l. We know that a_1 and a_2 are more competent than a_3 to do l. We can define a strategy S reflecting this relative level of competence by imposing that $a_1 \leq_{S(l)} a_3$ and $a_2 \leq_{S(l)} a_3$ hold.

4.3   Effective Goals

The notion of effective goals can then be refined by taking into account the notion of strategy as follows:

Definition 15. $\mathcal{A}' \subseteq \mathcal{A}$ *is optimal for l according to the strategy $\mathcal{S}$ iff $\mathcal{A}' = \min_{\leq_{S(\varphi)}} Ag(l)$*

This is denoted by $OGoal^{\mathcal{S}}_{\mathcal{A}'}(l)$. This means intuitively that $\mathcal{A}'$ is the subgroup of agents preferred according to $\mathcal{S}$ in order to achieve l.

Let us notice some basic properties:

– As $\mathcal{A}' \subseteq Ag(l)$, every agent in $\mathcal{A}'$ is such that l is an effective goal for it;
– Consider a literal l such that l is an effective goal for only one agent. In this case, according to the previous definition, this agent will be optimal for l whatever the strategy we consider (if we assimilate the agent and the subgroup constituted by this single agent).
– Let l be a literal which is not an effective goal. In this case, $Ag(l) = \emptyset$. Thus, for any strategy $\mathcal{S}$, $\min_{\leq_{S(l)}} Ag(l) = \emptyset$. So $OGoal^{\mathcal{S}}_{\emptyset}(l)$ holds and no agent is optimal for l.

4.4   Families of Strategies

We present in the following two main classifications of strategies.

Selective and Non-selective Strategies. Selective strategies are strategies which select a single agent among the agents for which l is an effective goal.

Definition 16. *A strategy $\mathcal{S}$ is a selective strategy for l iff $|\min_{\leq_{S(\varphi)}} Ag(\varphi)| = 1$.*

Example 1. Let us resume the example provided in section 3. Suppose that $KB = \{\neg p, \neg l, \neg r\}$, $C_{a_1} = \{p, l\}$ and $C_{a_2} = \{l, r, \neg r\}$. If a_1 commits itself to do p and a_2 commits itself to do l, then $D(KB) = \{p, l\}$. Thus $OGoal_{a_1}(p \wedge l)$ and $OGoal_{a_2}(l \wedge \neg r)$. Both a_1 and a_2 have l for effective goal.

First, notice that as $Ag(p) = \{a_1\}$ and $Ag(\neg r) = \{a_2\}$, for every strategy $(\mathcal{S})$, $OGoal^{\mathcal{S}}_{\{a_1\}}(p)$ and $OGoal^{\mathcal{S}}_{\{a_2\}}(\neg r)$ hold.

Consider here a selective strategy $\mathcal{S}$. Suppose that $\min_{\leq_{S(l)}} Ag(l) = \{a_1\}$, then $OGoal^{\mathcal{S}}_{\{a_1\}}(p)$, $OGoal^{\mathcal{S}}_{\{a_2\}}(\neg r)$ and $OGoal^{\mathcal{S}}_{\{a_1\}}(l)$ hold.

Non-selective strategies are strategies which allocate a goal to several agents.

Definition 17. *A strategy $\mathcal{S}$ is a non-selective strategy for l iff $|\min_{\leq_{S(\varphi)}} Ag(\varphi)| > 1$.*

Example 2. In the previous example, suppose now that $\mathcal{S}$ is a non-selective strategy for l, then $|\min_{\leq_{S(\varphi)}} Ag(\varphi)| > 1$. But $Ag(\varphi) = \{a_1, a_2\}$, thus $\min_{\leq_{S(\varphi)}} Ag(\varphi) = \{a_1, a_2\}$. In this case, we cannot deduce that $OGoal^{\mathcal{S}}_{\{a_1\}}(l)$ nor $OGoal^{\mathcal{S}}_{\{a_2\}}(l)$ holds. But $OGoal^{\mathcal{S}}_{\{a_1, a_2\}}(l)$ holds.

Voluntary and Non-voluntary Strategies. Voluntary strategies assign a task to the agents which committed themselves to achieve it. The formal definition is the following:

Definition 18. *Let l be a literal and S a strategy. S is a voluntary strategyφ iff $\forall a_i \in Ag(l)\ \forall a_j \in Ag(l)\ a_i \leq_{S(l)} a_j$ iff $Eng_+(a_i) \models l$ and $Eng_+(a_j) \not\models l$.*

By using such an order, all the agents in $\min_{\leq_{S(\varphi)}} Ag(l)$ commit themselves to achieve l. Non-voluntary strategies do not assign a goal to the agents which commit themselves not to achieve it. These strategies are less restrictive than the previous ones: an agent which did not commit itself to do l nor to not do l can be selected.

Definition 19. *Let l be a literal and S a strategy. S is a non-voluntary strategy for l iff $\forall a_i \in Ag(l)\ \forall a_j \in Ag(l)\ a_i \leq_{S(l)} a_j$ iff $Eng_-(a_i) \not\models l$ and $Eng_-(a_j) \models l$.*

4.5 Combining Strategies

We can wonder on what we will define strategies. The first possibility is to use "primitive" strategies, i.e. strategies which are defined on only one criteria. This criteria can be for instance the relative competence of the agents, the cost of each agent in term of resources or the time an agent will take in order to achieve the task.

There are of course lots of other primitive criteria on which a strategy can be based. Most important is the fact that "in real life", such decisions are not taken considering only one primitive factor, but several criteria which are combined in order to determine the "best" agents to select. To take this into account, we have to combine strategies.

For doing so, we suggest to use a *priority relation* between strategies. This comes to associate levels of importance to criteria. For instance, we could want to choose the agents which are, for a given task, the most competent to achieve it and the less costly, assuming that the competence is a criteria which is more important than the cost.

In the following, we present a mathematical framework for combining strategies.

Our objective is the following: we consider two orders $\leq_1$ and $\leq_2$ on the same set E and we want to obtain one or several orders $\leq_{1 \circ 2}$, called *orders combined considering $\leq_1$ having priority on $\leq_2$*, which verify first the order $\leq_1$ and then are "completed" by a part of $\leq_2$. We suggest to use the technique developed in belief bases priority merging [9] by representing the order relation by a binary predicate of a first order logic.

Definition 20. *Let $E = \{e_1, \ldots, e_n\}$ be a finite set. Let $\leq_E = \{\leq_i\ :\ i \in \mathbb{N}\}$ the set of possible orders on E. E and $\leq_E$ are represented by the first-order language $\mathcal{L}_E$ and the theory $\mathcal{T}_E$ defined as in the following:*

1. *the language $\mathcal{L}_E$ is constituted by classical logical symbols (an enumerable set of variables, connectives, quantifiers), a set of constants symbols defined*

by $\{e_1, \ldots, e_n\}$, a set of predicate symbols $\{\preceq_i \quad : \quad \leq_i \in \leq_E\} \cup \{=\}$ where each $\preceq_i$ and $=$ are binary predicate symbols.

2. $\mathcal{T}_E = \{\neg(e_i = e_j) \ : \ (i, j) \in \{1 \ldots n\}^2 \ i \neq j\} \cup \bigcup_{\leq_i \in \leq_E} RAT(\preceq_i)$

where $RAT(\preceq_i) = \{\forall x \quad \preceq_i (x, x), \ \forall x \forall y \quad \preceq_i (x, y) \wedge \preceq_i (y, x) \rightarrow x = y, \ \forall x \forall y \forall z \quad \preceq_i (x, y) \wedge \preceq_i (y, z) \rightarrow \preceq_i (x, z)\}$.

The theory $\mathcal{T}_E$ lists the Unique Name Axioms and the mathematical properties of orders. For the sake of simplicity, we will denote $\preceq_i (x, y)$ by $x \preceq_i y$ in the following.

When someone wants to represent an order on a set, he/she does not describe the order by extension. On the contrary, he/she gives the relations which are verified by the elements of the set, the remaining relations are deduced by using the mathematical properties of orders. Thus, we will consider a set of *explicit* literals which will allow to generate the whole order (by using transitivity, antisymmetry and reflexivity).

For instance, if we consider a set $E_1 = \{a_1, a_2, a_3\}$, then the explicit set $\{a_1 \leq_{E_1} a_2, a_2 \leq_{E_1} a_3\}$ allows to build the order $\leq_{E_1}$ on $\{a_1, a_2, a_3\}$ such that $a_1 \leq_{E_1} a_2$, $a_1 \leq_{E_1} a_3$, $a_2 \leq_{E_1} a_3$, $a_1 \leq_{E_1} a_1$, $a_2 \leq_{E_1} a_2$, $a_3 \leq_{E_1} a_3$, $a_2 \not\leq_{E_1} a_1$, $a_3 \not\leq_{E_1} a_2$ and $a_3 \not\leq_{E_1} a_1$.

We will characterize orders by generating them from explicit sets associated to a theory.

Definition 21. *Let E be a set, $\mathcal{L}_E$ and $\mathcal{T}_E$ as previously defined. $\mathcal{E}_i$, set of formulas of the kind $e_i \preceq_i e_j$ with $e_i \in E$ and $e_j \in E$ is an explicit set iff $Cl(\mathcal{T}_E \cup \mathcal{E}_i)$ is consistent.*

The order $\leq_i$ on E called order generated by $\mathcal{E}_i$ is defined by: $\forall e_i \in E \ \forall e_j \in e \ \ e_i \leq_E e_j$ iff $Cl(\mathcal{T}_E \cup \mathcal{E}_i) \vdash e_i \preceq_i e_j$

It is easy to prove that we obtain an order by using the axioms in $\mathcal{T}_E$.

For instance, in the previous example, we can see that $\{a_1 \preceq_{E_1} a_2, a_2 \preceq_{E_1} a_3\}$ is an explicit set generating $\leq_{E_1}$.

We now define how to combine two orders, one having priority on the other. We use the explicit sets defining the orders for building maximal consistent sets of first-order formulas. Notice that we can obtain several explicit sets.

Definition 22. *Let E be a set and $\mathcal{L}_E$ the first-order language associated with E. Let $\mathcal{E}_1 \ \mathcal{E}_2$ two explicit sets generating respectively the orders $\leq_1$ and $\leq_2$ on E. We note $\mathcal{E}_{1 \to 1 \circ 2} = \{e_i \preceq_{1 \circ 2} e_j \ : \ e_i \preceq_1 e_j \in \mathcal{E}_1\}$ and $\mathcal{E}_{2 \to 1 \circ 2} = \{e_i \preceq_{1 \circ 2} e_j \ : \ e_i \preceq_2 e_j \in \mathcal{E}_2\}$.*

The explicit set $\mathcal{E}^i_{1 \circ 2}$ is defined by $\mathcal{E}^i_{1 \circ 2} = \{e_j \preceq^i_{1 \circ 2} e_k \ : \ (e_j \preceq_{1 \circ 2} e_k) \in (\mathcal{E}_{1 \to 1 \circ 2} \cup \mathcal{E}^i_{2 \to 1 \circ 2})\}$ where $\mathcal{E}^i_{2 \to 1 \circ 2}$ is a maximal subset of $\mathcal{E}_{2 \to 1 \circ 2}$ such that $\mathcal{E}_{1 \to 1 \circ 2} \cup \mathcal{E}^i_{2 \to 1 \circ 2} \cup \mathcal{T}_E$ is consistent.

We note $\leq^i_{1 \circ 2}$ the order on E generated by $\mathcal{E}^i_{1 \circ 2}$ and we denote by $n_{1 \circ 2}$ the number of different orders we can obtain from $\leq_1$ and $\leq_2$ by giving priority to $\leq_1$.

If the different orders can be reduced to a single order, we will note $\leq_{1\circ2}$ this order.

Definition 23. *If $\exists i \in \{1,\dots,n_{1\circ2}\}$ such that $\forall j \in \{1,\dots,n_{1\circ2}\}$ $\mathcal{E}_{1\circ2}^j \subseteq \mathcal{E}_{1\circ2}^i$, then we note $\mathcal{E}_{1\circ2} = \mathcal{E}_{1\circ2}^i$.*

Example 3. Let us consider $E = \{e_1, e_2, e_3\}$ and examine some examples:

Suppose that $\leq_1$ is generated by $\{e_3 \preceq_1 e_2\}$ and $\leq_2$ is generated by $\{e_2 \preceq_2 e_3, e_1 \preceq_2 e_2\}$. Then $\mathcal{E}_{1\rightarrow1\circ2} = \{e_3 \preceq_{1\circ2} e_2\}$ and $\mathcal{E}_{2\rightarrow1\circ2} = \{e_2 \preceq_{1\circ2} e_3, e_1 \preceq_{1\circ2} e_2\}$. The only subset of $\mathcal{E}_{2\rightarrow1\circ2}$ consistent with $\mathcal{E}_{1\rightarrow1\circ2} \cup T_E$ is $\{e_1 \preceq_{1\circ2} e_2\}$ (because $\mathcal{E}_{1\rightarrow1\circ2} \cup T_E \vdash \neg e_2 \preceq_{1\circ2} e_3$), thus we obtain an order $\leq_{1\circ2}$ generated by $\{e_3 \preceq_{1\circ2} e_2, e_1 \preceq_{1\circ2} e_2\}$. In this case $\min_{\leq_{1\circ2}} E = \{e_1, e_3\}$.

Suppose now that $\leq_1$ is generated by $\{e_3 \preceq_1 e_2\}$ and $\leq_2$ is generated by $\{e_1 \preceq_2 e_3, e_2 \preceq_2 e_1\}$. Then $\mathcal{E}_{1\rightarrow1\circ2} = \{e_3 \preceq_{1\circ2} e_2\}$ et $\mathcal{E}_{2\rightarrow1\circ2} = \{e_1 \preceq_{1\circ2} e_3, e_2 \preceq_{1\circ2} e_1\}$. There are two maximal consistent subset of $\mathcal{E}_{2\rightarrow1\circ2}$ consistent with $\mathcal{E}_{1\rightarrow1\circ2} \cup T_E$. Thus we obtain two orders: $\leq_{1\circ2}^1$, generated by $\{e_3 \leq_{1\circ2}^1 e_2, e_1 \leq_{1\circ2}^1 e_3\}$ and $\leq_{1\circ2}^2$, generated by $\{e_3 \leq_{1\circ2}^2 e_2, e_2 \leq_{1\circ2}^2 e_1\}$. In this case, $\min_{\leq_{1\circ2}} E = \emptyset$.

5   Example

Let us resume the example in section 3 and consider a group of three agents $\{a_1, a_2, a_3\}$. Let us suppose that $KB = \{\neg s, \neg l, \neg p\}$, that $C_{a_1} = \{s, l\}$, that $C_{a_2} = \{l, p, \neg p\}$ and that $C_{a_3} = \{l\}$. if a_1 commits itself to do s, that a_2 and a_3 commit themselves to do l, then $D(KB) = \{s, l\}$. Thus $OGoal_{a_1}(s \wedge l)$, $OGoal_{a_2}(l \wedge \neg p)$ and $OGoal_{a_3}(l)$ hold. The three agents have to lacquer the door.

Let us suppose that we do not want that several agents have the same task for efficiency reason. We have to find a selective strategy to select only one agent.

A voluntary strategy $\mathcal{S}_V$ for l gives the following order: $a_2 \leq_{\mathcal{S}_V(l)} a_1$ and $a_3 \leq_{\mathcal{S}_V(l)} a_1$. This strategy is not sufficient to select a single agent because it cannot choose between a_2 and a_3.

Let us suppose that there is a strategy $\mathcal{S}_E$ for l which reflects the relative efficiency of the agents to achieve l: $a_1 \leq_{\mathcal{S}_E(l)} a_2$ and $a_2 \leq_{\mathcal{S}_E(l)} a_3$. In this case, there are two solutions: either $\leq_{\mathcal{S}_E(l)\circ\mathcal{S}_V(l)}$ is chosen (the efficiency of the agent is privileged) and thus a_1 is optimal for l, either $\leq_{\mathcal{S}_V(l)\circ\mathcal{S}_C(l)}$ is chosen (the voluntary agents are privileged) and in this case a_2 is optimal for l.

6   Discussion

This work focused on determining the individual goals of agents from goals addressed to a team of agents, a representation of agents and strategies. In order to do that, we have relied on the support of some previous work and Boutilier's work on qualitative decision theory. We have defined the notion of strategy for allocating tasks to a sub-team of agents and we have shown how to combine strategies in order to refine the allocation process. We are aware that, as for the strategies combination method, we could have used another one like, for instance an arbitration method [10]. It would have come to select the "less worst" agent given all the primitive criteria (this can be viewed as a maximin selection). This present work does not contribute in combination techniques. Its originality concerns the use of the Qualitative Decision Logic to the case of a team of several agents and the extension of the model of agents since we consider their ability, their commitments and, through the notion of strategy, any other characteristics we want.

However, this work is rather preliminary and it could be extended in several ways.

First, instead of having an unique set KB which represents a common point of view about the real world, we could consider that the agents do not share the same beliefs about the real world. In the worst cases, these beliefs may happen to be contradictory and belief bases merging techniques (cf. [10, 11]) could be used in order to solve the conflicts. We could also consider that there is no central entity and that the agents communicate in order to inform the others about their commitments.

We also intend to work on the notion of strategy in order to obtain general properties on strategies and define global strategies. Moreover, the present strategies are defined for literals only and we could envisage to define them to propositions. However, in this case, relations between for instance $\mathcal{S}(l)$, $\mathcal{S}(l')$ and $\mathcal{S}(l \wedge l')$ should be defined.

References

1. Kraus, S., Shehory, O.: Methods for task allocation via agent coalition formation. Artificial Intelligence **101** (1998) 165–200
2. Barès, M.: Formal approach of the interoperability of C4IRS operating within a coalition. In: Proceedings of the 5th International Command and Control Research and Technology Syposium. (2000)
3. Boutilier, C.: Toward a logic for qualitative decision theory. In Doyle, J., Sandewall, E., Torasso, P., eds.: Principles of Knowledge Representation and Reasoning (KR'94), Morgan Kaufmann (1994) 75–86
4. Cholvy, L., Garion, C.: Distribution of goals addressed to a group of agents. In Rosenschein, J.S., Sandholm, T., Wooldridge, M., Yokoo, M., eds.: Proceedings of the Second International Joint Conference on Autonomous Agents and Multiagent Systems, ACM Press (2003) 765–772
5. Kraus, S.: Negociation and cooperation in multi-agent environments. Artificial Intelligence Journal - Special Issue on Economic Principles of Multi-Agent Systems **94** (1997) 79–98
6. Grosz, B., Hunsberger, L., Kraus, S.: Planning and acting together. AI Magazine **20** (1999) 23–34
7. Soh, L., Tsatsoulis, C.: Allocation algorithms in dynamic negotiation-based coalition formation. In: Workshop on Teamwork and Coalition Formation (affiliate workshop of 1st International Conference On Autonomous Agents and MultiAgent Systems). (2002)

8. Boutilier, C.: Conditional logics of normality : a modal approach. Artificial Intelligence **68** (1994) 87–154
9. Cholvy, L.: Reasoning about merged information. In Gabay, D., Smets, P., eds.: Handbook of Defeasible Reasoning and Uncertainty Management Systems. Volume 3. Kluwer Academic Publishers (1998) 233–263
10. Konieczny, S., Pino-Pérez, R.: Merging information under constraints: a qualitative framework. Journal of Logic and Computation **12** (2002) 773–808
11. Cholvy, L., Garion, C.: Answering queries addressed to several databases according to a majority approach. Journal of Intelligent Information Systems **22** (2004) 175–201

Collectively Cognitive Agents in Cooperative Teams

Jacek Brzeziński[1], Piotr Dunin-Kęplicz[1], and Barbara Dunin-Kęplicz[1,2]

[1] Institute of Computer Science, Polish Academy of Sciences,
Ordona 21, 01-237 Warsaw, Poland
[2] Institute of Informatics, Warsaw University
Banacha 2, 02-097 Warsaw, Poland

Abstract. This research continues a line of recent investigation resulting already in Dunin-Kęplicz and Verbrugge theory of collective motivational attitudes as well as a formal theory of teamwork.

In this paper we aim to describe our work over a theory of collective commitments in cooperative teams basing on a software test–bed for conducting trust–based agent experiments. First, short introductions to the theories of collective commitments and trust are given. Next, the most important properties of the system are presented together with a scenario of interplay. Finally several tests are described that compare different versions of a commitment applied in various situations.

1 Introduction

A lion's share of a novelty of MAS, in particular in BDI systems, pertains to the concept of motivational attitudes in Cooperative Problem Solving (CPS). What characterizes intentions and commitments, especially the collective ones, is the interplay between environmental and social aspects, which may become rather complex nowadays due to the increasing complexity of MAS. For example, when asking what it means for a group of agents to be *collectively committed* to do something, both circumstances in which the group is acting and properties of the organization it is part of, have to be taken into account. This shows the importance of differentiating the scope and the strength of the notion of collective commitment. The resulting characteristics may differ significantly, and even become logically incomparable.

To formally model different aspects of collective commitments, including different scopes and degrees of awareness of cooperating agents, the idea of a dial used to tune the nature of the commitment to the particular purpose seems to be both technically interesting and intuitively appealing. In [3] a sort of *tuning mechanism* is provided. This logical device enables the system developer to *calibrate* a type of collective commitment fitting the circumstances, analogously to adjusting dials on a sound system. The appropriate dials, characterized in the sequel, belong to the device representing a general schema of collective commitment. The resulting notion of (group) commitment, described in multi-modal

M.-P. Gleizes, A. Omicini, and F. Zambonelli (Eds.): ESAW 2004, LNAI 3451, pp. 191–208, 2005.

logics, may then be naturally implemented in a created multi–agent system. This way the tuning mechanism may be viewed as a bridge between theory and practice.

This paper presents a simulation framework to investigate some properties of BDI systems in which different definitions of collective commitments will be used. These properties include overall condition of the system, agents behaviour, level of interaction between agents and their willingness to cooperate. This simulator that allows one to conduct his own experiments bases on the Dunin-Kęplicz and Verbrugge theory ([3, 7]), uses the Castelfranchi and Falcone theory of trust ([1, 8]) to distinguish different levels of agents' collective awareness and uses the ideas developed in the social agents framework ([9, 10]) as a basis for the implementation.

Two factors seem the most interesting. First of all different levels of social awareness require different amount of data to be sent to each of the participating agents. Therefore agents use different equations which take into account only information they receive to estimate chances of succeeding the plan. We would like to find out which level is sufficient for productive cooperation. Also, agents may tend to avoid projects that are likely to fail. When the group consist of many agents with low rate of ability to do atomic actions leading to the realization of the overall goal it might be better to use one of the weaker cases of commitment to tempt them to take part in the cooperation.

The type of collective commitment used in the MAS is not simply a matter of communication limitations or system developer's assumptions. The amount of information that is known to the group can be limited by the legal aspects of the system. Some information about the contract has to be hidden from the contractors so e.g. the robust collective commitment model cannot be used. Our aim is to check how trust information can be collected and used in the commitment models with limited knowledge.

The paper is structured in the following way. In section 2, different notions of collective commitments are briefly treated, while section 3 presents basic notions of the theory of trust. In section 4 essential building blocks of the presented simulator are sketched. The central section 5 presents a scenario of agents interaction as well as discussion on different cases of collective commitments. Next, in the section 6 some details about the experimental results are presented. Finally, section 7 discusses possible extensions of the simulator and conclusions.

2   Collective Commitments in CPS

Dynamic aspects of social and collective commitments in teams of agents involved in Cooperative Problem Solving (CPS) have been extensively described in [7]. Ever changing motivational attitudes as well as different levels of social awareness affect the way agents interact with each other in a multi–agent system are formally expressed in a *tuning machine* for collective commitments. In order to formally illustrate the expressive power of such a logical device, five definitions of commitments corresponding to different teamwork types occurring in practice are presented. Apparently, the entire spectrum of possibilities is much wider, due to the number of possibly independent choices to be made.

Collective intentions of doing a complex action lead to building collective commitment among a team of agents. The four–stage model of agents' interaction ([13]) is adopted here to model an example of CPS. The consecutive stages are:

1. **potential recognition**, when the leading agent recognizes the potential for cooperative action in order to reach its complex goal,
2. **team formation**, at which stage the leading agent attempts to establish a group of agents that can collectively fulfill the goal by means of building a collective intention in this group,
3. **plan generation**, when the social plan of fulfilling the goal is built and the collective commitment is formed,
4. **team action**, when the agents involved in the group do their tasks as described in the social plan and eventually achieve the main goal.

In our example this model is slightly modified — the team formation level outputs with a ready social plan. Also, at any level agents can fail to do some actions or can be presented with new opportunities. Such changes lead to *the reconfiguration problem* when the group has to react to alterations in their environment while still being able to fulfill the overall goal. However we will not deal with reconfiguration here while it is on a list of the future enhancements to the system. Failure at the stage of the team formation will result in repeating this stage with a different group of agents. If the social plan fails to succeed (one of the atomic actions fails) the leading agent will not pay for any part of the job, whether succeeded or not.

Let us present the most important formulas used in this paper, which are formally defined in [3]:

BEL(i, φ) agent i believes proposition φ.
C-BEL$_G(i, \varphi)$ group G collectively believes proposition φ, that is: every agent
 believes in φ, every agent believes that every agents believe in φ and so forth.
COMM(i, j, φ) agent i commits to agent j to make φ true.
COMM(i, j, α) agent i commits to agent j to perform action α.
GOAL(i, φ) agent i has a goal that φ be true.
INT(i, φ) agent i has an intention to make φ true.
E-INT$_G(\varphi)$ every agent in group G has an individual intention to make φ true.
C-INT$_G(\varphi)$ group G has a collective intention to make φ true.
constitute(φ, P) the social plan P is correct with respect to the overall goal
 φ, meaning that after the successful realization of plan P, φ holds.

Following Dunin-Kęplicz and Verbrugge ([3]) we will present different notions of collective commitments. Even though they express solely basic ingredients constituting such structures, they are applicable in different situations manifesting various strengths of the commitment.

Robust Collective Commitment (RCC)[1]. In the case of *the robust collective commitment*, for every action α that occur in a social plan P there should be one agent in the group who is socially committed to at least one (mostly other) agent in the group to fulfill the action. Moreover the team as a whole is aware of every single social commitment that has been established about particular action from the social plan. This way everybody's responsibility is in public:

$$\text{R-COMM}_{G,P}(\alpha) \leftrightarrow$$
$$\text{C-INT}_G(\alpha) \wedge \text{constitute}(\varphi, P) \wedge \text{C-BEL}_G(\text{constitute}(\varphi, P)) \wedge$$
$$(\forall_{\alpha \in P} \exists_{i,j \in G} \text{COMM}(i, j, \alpha)) \wedge (\forall_{\alpha \in P} \exists_{i,j \in G} \text{C-BEL}_G(\text{COMM}(i, j, \alpha))).$$

Strong Collective Commitment (SCC). In the case of *the strong collective commitment* there is no public awareness about particular social commitments, but the group as a whole believes that every part of the plan is within someone's responsibility:

$$\text{S-COMM}_{G,P}(\alpha) \leftrightarrow$$
$$\text{C-INT}_G(\alpha) \wedge \text{constitute}(\varphi, P) \wedge \text{C-BEL}_G(\text{constitute}(\varphi, P)) \wedge$$
$$(\forall_{\alpha \in P} \exists_{i,j \in G} \text{COMM}(i, j, \alpha)) \wedge \text{C-BEL}_G(\forall_{\alpha \in P} \exists_{i,j \in G} \text{COMM}(i, j, \alpha)).$$

Weak Collective Commitment (WCC). In case of *the weak collective commitment* there is no awareness in the team that the plan leads to proper realization of the goal, however agents are still aware about their share in the overall goal and the fact, that all actions are taken on by committed members:

$$\text{W-COMM}_{G,P}(\alpha) \leftrightarrow$$
$$\text{C-INT}_G(\alpha) \wedge \text{constitute}(\varphi, P) \wedge (\forall_{\alpha \in P} \exists_{i,j \in G} \text{COMM}(i, j, \alpha)) \wedge$$
$$\text{C-BEL}_G(\forall_{\alpha \in P} \exists_{i,j \in G} \text{COMM}(i, j, \alpha)).$$

Team Commitment (TC). The following definition of *the team commitment* represents another step in weakening the notion of collective commitments. There is no collective belief that all actions have been adopted by committed members, but a team as a whole still exists:

$$\text{T-COMM}_{G,P}(\alpha) \leftrightarrow$$
$$\text{C-INT}_G(\alpha) \wedge \text{constitute}(\varphi, P) \wedge (\forall_{\alpha \in P} \exists_{i,j \in G} \text{COMM}(i, j, \alpha)).$$

Distributed Commitment (DC). The case of *the distributed commitment* deals with situation, when agents remain aware solely about their piece of work. They

---

[1] We will use acronyms like RCC, SCC, WCC, TC and DC when describing different notions of a collective commitment.

do not know neither the overall goal nor other members of the team. They become a loosely coupled group of agents that work in a distributed manner sharing some undefined goal:

$$\text{D-COMM}_{G,P}(\alpha) \leftrightarrow \text{constitute}(\varphi, P) \wedge (\forall_{\alpha \in P} \exists_{i,j \in G} \text{COMM}(i, j, \alpha)).$$

3   Theory of Trust

Basic Properties. The interaction between agents in this framework is closely related to the socio-cognitive theories, as in [1, 8]. Several properties of an agent are considered:

- **trustworthiness** of an agent a — an objective probability that a will successfully execute a delegated task g in a world of state W:
  trustworthiness(a, g, W)=F(DoA(a, g, W), DoW(a, g, W)).
  DoA describes agent a's degree of ability to do task g and DoW describes agent's willingness to do task g,
- **trust** — a degree in which agent a trusts agent b about g in W: subjective probability, a function of a's belief about the willingness and ability of b executing task g in W:
  DoT(a, b, g, W)=F'(SDoA(a, b, g, W), SDoW(a, b, g, W)).
  The functions SDoA and SDoW take into account direct experience of agent b (described by function SExpA and SExpW) and testimonies (reputation assertions) regarding b made by its peers (described by SRepA and SRepW).

Direct Experience. The degree of trust between agents changes dynamically as described in the following trust modifier equations ([12]):
  SExpW$(a, b, g) := $ SExpW$(a, b, g) + (\alpha * (1 - $ SExpW$(a, b, g))$
  SExpW$(a, b, g) := $ SExpW$(a, b, g) + \beta * $ SExpW(a, b, g).
  The α and β are rewarding and punishing parameters, that is: rates in which good (bad) experience increases (decreases) trust. Similar equations can be used to modify SExpA.
  In our framework agent's use only the trust values, not taking into account the testimonies of other agents, that constitute a reputation of an agent.

Reputation. The reputation is based on testimonies that other agents give about specific agent. The following function takes into account strength and number of assertions as well as creditability of the sources:
  SRepW$(a, b, g) = \frac{1}{n} \sum_{i=1..n}($RecW$(r_i, b, g)*DoT(a, r_i, REC))$, where RecW is r_i's recommendation about b and DoT here describes the degree of a's trust in r_i's ability of making such recommendations.
  In our framework this value is calculated to obtain a difference between reputation and agents' objective probability, which is then used to graphically present the weighted difference between subjective and objective abilities of agents.

Our trust model is extremely simple, but it is good enough to present all the needed traits of the system. In future work we plan to address this issue, because with more detailed and complex trust model, the system should perform better in sense of terms of learning and the number of successful contracts.

4   Architecture of the Simulation Framework

We are now going to present the main components of the system: the agents, values of trust and protocols used in the communication.

4.1   Agents

Our multi-agent system consists of BDI agents with the following properties:

- **Beliefs:** *believes(A, f)* — means that f is a belief of the agent A.
- **Intentions:** *intends(A, a)* — means that the agent A intends to perform the action a
- **Abilities:** *able(A, a, x)* — means that the agent A is able to perform the action a, and a probability of the success of a is x. We assume that each agent knows his own abilities, so the following formula is true: believes(A, able(A, a, x)) for each action a. We also use the following notation for specific agents: DoA(A, a)=x.
- **Trust:** *trusts(A, B, a, x)* — means that the degree of trust of the agent A to the agent B about the action a is x. We also use the following notation: DoT(A, B, a)=x.

Agents act in the world which allows a set of elementary environmental actions to be performed:

- Actions = $\{a_1..a_n\}$.

There are three routines that can be executed by the agents:

- sendMessage(m) — sending a message m (always succeeds),
- broadcastMessage(G, m) — broadcasting a message m to a group of agents G (always succeeds),
- performAction(o) — execution of elementary action o.

Two roles of agents are considered:

- Managers — agents that execute tropisms to generate tasks. Task is a complex action, represented as a set of elementary actions to be performed for specific amount of money. Managers are not allowed to execute elementary environmental actions, but they are able to delegate specific actions (or sets of actions) to other agents (Workers),
- Workers — agents able to perform elementary environmental actions. Workers cannot delegate actions.

4.2   Trust

All agents store the following trust values: trust to Workers about executing specific actions and trust to Managers.

In our example trust describes abilities of agents only. We assume that all the agents are always 100% willing to perform all the actions, so we do not need willingness factor for a time being.

Agents' reputation is calculated only to represent an average difference between reputation and objective abilities.

4.3   Protocols

In the process of interaction we use the following communication protocols:

Introduction: when the agents perform a kind of handshake before establishing cooperation.

Contract Net: launched by the Manager to establish collective commitment in a group of selected agents and then perform a compound task.

Information: sending a single piece of information.

5   Scenario of Agents Interaction

Let us now present interaction scenario scheme, other interesting properties of the system and eventually how the different notions of collective commitments affect the agents.

5.1   Generic Scheme

1. Agent M (Manager) has got a task to perform in a form of (O - set of elementary actions, s - budget).
2. **Potential recognition phase:**
   (a) agent M sends "call for proposals" to all the Worker agents in the system (content = (O - set of actions)):
   (b) agents respond returning a set of pairs: {(action, price), ...}
   (c) agent M generates the first element from a sequence of possible groups that can perform the task collectively using the group quality function. This function takes into account:
      i. trust of M to other agents in the group,
      ii. prices proposed by the agents (and their relation to the task budget),
      iii. a risk factor describing preferences of M (M can prefer cheaper but less trustworthy groups, or more expensive but more trustworthy ones),
   (d) the collective commitment is built (we assume that workers' decisions mean that bilateral commitments between workers and Manager are set, which implies that collective commitment is in place).

Group G . Group consists of agents that are collectively able to perform task $O = \{o_1, ..., o_n\}$. Each of the agents in the group can be expected to perform one or more elementary actions. So we can divide task O into the disjoint subsets of O, representing subtasks delegated to other agents. A set of those subsets we call S. Allocation of actions L is a set of pairs (A, s), where A is an agent, and s is a subset of O representing actions to be realized by agent A.

3. **Team formation phase:**

   (a) Agent M selects a group G from a sequence of groups.

   (b) Agent M broadcasts specific information to all the agents of G. This set of information depends on the model of collective commitments. We assume that the following information are broadcasted using *broadcastMessage()* so we assume that they are 100% trustworthy and all the agents in the group are aware of that. The components are:

       i. An offer to form a group G *[RCC, SCC, WCC, TC]*[2]

       ii. An offer to participate in task $O = \{o_1..o_n\}$ *[RCC, SCC, WCC, TC]*

       iii. An allocation of elementary actions L *[RCC]*

       iv. Division of task O into subtasks S *[SCC, WCC]*

       v. An offer to perform specific action (or actions) for price x *[RCC, SCC, WCC, TC, DC]*

   (c) Agents decide whether they want to join the group G or not taking into account the estimation of success chance of the task. Agents can estimate the probability of such success taking into account the information they have received in the previous step. So, the formula for a function estimating task success chance depends on the mental state of the agent (level of the agent's knowledge about the task) which depends on the model of collective commitments. The task success estimation function is a subjective conditional probability value that consists of some of the following factors:

       i. Trust to the Manager M *[RCC, SCC, WCC, TC, DC]*

       ii. Trust to other members of the group G *[RCC, SCC, WCC, TC]*

       iii. Ability to perform a delegated set of actions S_A *[RCC, SCC, WCC, TC, DC]*

   Agent decides to join the group if the value of the task result estimation function is above a predetermined threshold.

   (d) If all the agents decide to enter the group G, the collective commitment is constructed. If not, agent M withdraws the current task and attempts to start another.

4. **Plan generation phase** is not applicable here because the plan has a very simple form and is already constructed.

5. **Team action phase:**

   (a) Agents perform their actions and inform M about the results.

   (b) If all the agents' actions have succeeded, the task also succeeds and all the agents collect their payments.

---

[2] Applicable commitment models are specified in square brackets.

(c) On the other hand, if one or more actions failed, no agent collects his payment and all the group members receive information about failure.

(d) Agents modify their trust value based on direct experience to other group members depending on information about action results they receive from the Manager. This information is also dependent on the model of collective commitment.

5.2   Properties of the System

Let us now present some important properties of the system.

Trust. Each agent stores a degree of trust to other agents and the information about their abilities to perform atomic actions. The initial value of DoT(A, B, a) is set to DoA(A, a). The assumption that other agents in the group have similar abilities seems reasonable and practical — similarly to the real world case, at first agents have no other premises to believe that it is not true. The degree of trust to the Manager will be set to a constant value chosen in an experimental way.

While the system is working the value of DoT evolves. Depending on the model of the commitment agents receive different information when the task fails. In the stronger model agents are informed precisely about the cause of the failure and can punish (in terms of adjusting trust) only those agents that have not fulfilled their parts of the plan. In the weaker cases the failure affects trust values to all the agents in the group. In case of the success all the agents in the group are awarded for completing the task.

Task Result Estimation Function. The task result estimation function is a product of factors which depend on publicly known properties of the plan. The stronger the model of the commitment is, the more precise is the estimation of chances of success of performing the task.

The choice of the task result estimation function as well as changing the values of trust to other agents is crucial for the system. Our goal is to modify these functions if appropriate, so that eventually the values of DoT of particular agents strive for the real abilities of the others. The weaker the commitment is, the harder it may be to fulfill this condition — in these cases the degree of trust to the Manager is one of the most important factor in the task result estimation function.

The commitment structure in our system is fairly simple — the Manager is a part of every bilateral commitment of the plan. This can be later enhanced so that the responsibility for failed tasks is more diffused in the system, as set forth in section 7.

Bidding. Manager decides to hire Workers if he can find appropriate group among Workers that sent bids. Manager chooses group, and sends award messages to all the members along with some data regarding group and its members dependent on the collective commitment model. In the next step all the members have to decide if they really want to participate in the task. They can base this decision on the estimation of probability of success of the task, which can be calculated from current trust values and received data (see above). This estimation of probability is compared to quotient of investment and gain (investment is a sum of costs of all the actions that agent has to perform in order to complete his part of the task; gain is the money that he will receive when the task succeeds). If estimation of probability is greater than investment to gain ratio, agent decides to participate.

Agent bids only if two conditions hold: its abilities concerning actions in the task are greater than ability threshold. The agent also has to have enough money to perform all the actions that he bids for.

Budget. We assume that Manager has some budget that he can spend on the payoffs. In the tests we use budget-per-action factor, so overall budget is calculated as product of this factor and number of actions. Manager selects a group of Workers by choosing the best Workers that he can afford to hire (sum of their proposed prices is less or equal to the budget). Budget is an important factor in the tests — when it is high, the Manager can afford to hire more expensive agents with higher abilities. If budget is low, Manager is only able to hire Workers with low abilities, so the probability of failure increases.

Payment that the Worker expects is calculated using the following formula: *payment* = *at* * *atp* + *a* * *ap*, where *at* is the ability threshold, *atp* is the ability-threshold-to-price factor, *a* is the agent ability and *ap* is ability-to-price factor.

5.3   Analysis of Robust Collective Commitment

Properties. Collective intention is in place, all the agents know the properties of the plan, all the agents know the action allocation and commitment allocation.

Comment. Goal, plan details, contract details, group structure, commitment structure and responsibility in the group are public. Since all the information is public all agents have the perfect information about the planned activity of the group, so the task result estimation function should be very accurate (given valid trust data).

Information Sent to Workers. An offer to create a group G with intention to realize task O (C-BEL), an offer to participate in task $O = \{o_1..o_n\}$ (C-BEL), an allocation of sets of elementary actions $L = \{(I, S_I): I \in G \setminus \{M\}, S_I \subseteq O\}$ (C-BEL), an offer to perform a set of actions S_A for a price of x.

Task Result Estimation Function. Factors: trust to the Manager, agent's abilities to execute its actions, trust to the other members of group G about their allocated actions. Formally:

$$\text{DoT}(A, M, \text{"team-selection"}) * \prod_{a \in S_A} \text{DoA}(A, a) *$$
$$T\prod_{I \in G \setminus \{A,M\}} \prod_{a \in S_I} \text{DoT}(A, I, a).$$

Direct Experience Modification. All the information about successes and failures of the group members is broadcasted. The agents can use very accurate data to modify their trust values.

5.4   Analysis of Strong Collective Commitment

Properties. Collective intention is in place, all the agents know the properties of the plan.

Comment. Goal, plan details, contract details and group participation are public. Commitment structure is not public, so part of responsibility is on side of the Manager. Agents do not know the allocation of actions so they can use some average value of degree of trust concerning all actions performed by the group in the task result estimation function.

Information Sent to Workers. An offer to create a group G with intention to realize task O (C-BEL), an offer to participate in task $O = \{o_1, ..., o_n\}$ (C-BEL), number of elementary actions allocated to specific agents $N = \{(I, N_I): I \in G \setminus \{M, A\}, N_I \in \mathbb{N}\}$ (C-BEL), an offer to perform a set of actions S_A for a price of x.

Task Result Estimation Function. Factors: trust to the Manager, agent's abilities to execute its actions, trust to the other agents of the group G, calculated as an average trust about executing remaining actions. Formally:

$$\text{DoT}(A, M, \text{"team-selection"}) * \prod_{a \in S_A} \text{DoA}(A, a) *$$
$$\prod_{I \setminus \{A, M\}} \left(\frac{1}{|O| - |S_A|} \sum_{a \in O \setminus S_A} \text{DoT}(A, I, a) \right)^{N_I}.$$

Direct Experience Modification. Only failure information is broadcasted. The message contains the following: agent, failed action.

5.5   Analysis of Weak Collective Commitment

Properties. Collective intention is in place, agents do not know the properties of the plan.

Comment. Goal, plan details, group structure are public. Commitment structure is not public, so part of responsibility is on side of the Manager. Contract details are not public neither, so group members do not know if contract is valid. Group has to trust the Manager about validity of the contract and "team-selection".

Information Sent to Workers. An offer to create a group G with intention to realize task O (C-BEL), an offer to participate in task $O = \{o_1, ..., o_n\}$ (C-BEL), agent's abilities to execute its actions, an offer to perform a set of actions S_A for a price of x.

Task Result Estimation Function. Factors: trust to Manager, agent's abilities to execute its actions, trust to other agents of the group G, calculated as an average of trust values to those agents on all the actions from O. Formally:

$\mathrm{DoT}(A, M, \text{"team-selection"}) * \prod_{a \in S_A} \mathrm{DoA}(A, a) *$
$\prod_{a \in O \setminus S_A} (\frac{1}{|G|-2} \sum_{I \setminus \{A, M\}} \mathrm{DoT}(A, I, a)).$

Direct Experience Modification. Only failure information is broadcasted. The message contains the following: agent, failed action.

5.6   Analysis of Team Commitment

Properties. Collective intention is in place; agents know only about their own part in the task.

Comment. Agent receive no information about the causes of the failure (so it is only informed that some anonymous agent in the group has failed).

Information Sent to Workers. An offer to create a group G with intention to realize task O (C-BEL), an offer to participate in task $O = \{o_1, ..., o_n\}$ (C-BEL), an offer to perform a set of actions S_A for a price of x.

Task Result Estimation Function. Factors: trust to Manager, agent's abilities to execute its actions, trust to other agents of the group G, calculated as an average of trust values about remaining actions. Formally:

$\mathrm{DoT}(A, M, \text{"team-selection"}) * \prod_{a \in S_A} \mathrm{DoA}(A, a) *$
$\prod_{a \in O \setminus S_A} (\frac{1}{|G|-2} \sum_{I \setminus \{A, M\}} \mathrm{DoT}(A, I, a)).$

Direct Experience Modification. Only the team action result is broadcasted.

5.7   Analysis of Distributed Commitment

Properties. There is no real group G. Agents know only about their own tasks.

Comment. No information is public. Agent has no information about other team members so he has no trust values to other team members. Trust to the Manager is the most important component of the task result estimation function.

Information Sent to Workers. An offer to perform a set of actions S_A for a price of x.

Task Result Estimation Function. Factors: agent's abilities to execute its actions, trust to the Manager. Formally:

$\mathrm{DoT}(A, M, \text{"team-selection"}) * \prod_{a \in S_A} \mathrm{DoA}(A, a).$

Direct Experience Modification. No information is broadcasted. The only trust values that is modified as a result of the team action is the trust to the Manager.

6   Test Results

6.1   Implementation

This framework has been developed in C++. There are several configuration parameters, for example: `alpha_reward`, `beta_punish` (real) – rewarding and punishing values for modification of direct experience. `default_trust_value` (real) is the initial value of a subjective degree of trust. If not set, the agent will use its own ability values. Another parameter, `random_default_trust` (real) can be used to slightly randomize the default trust value.

6.2   Test Configuration

Series of tests were conducted to compare agents' behaviour when using different notions of collective commitments. These tests share similar properties: there are 16 Workers controlled by 1 Manager. Tests run up to 100000 contracts (which translates to approximately 300000 ticks of the internal clock).

A task size is one of the important configuration parameters. The bigger the task is the more rules of a particular type of a commitment affect the results. With one action there is only one Worker that decides whether he wants to execute the task. With bigger tasks, agents decide if they want to cooperate with other ones and this is where the rules of a collective commitment affect their decisions. However, if a task is too big it may be hard to execute it successfully — therefore we have chosen experimentally a value of 4 actions in every task.

While there are several properties that can be tested at a time, the following are the most important:

- **successes**, i.e. number of successful contracts,
- **failures**, i.e. number of failed contracts,
- **efficiency**, i.e. ratio of successful contracts to total number of contracts. This value is taken from the contracts within the last 10000 ticks, because otherwise the history of older contracts would strongly affect it,
- **reputation_diff**, i.e. an average difference between agents' reputation and their real abilities.

One should expect that the stronger the notion of a commitment is, the higher the efficiency value should be at en expense of smaller number of contracts in total. With weaker models this ratio should be significantly lower but with higher number of total completed tasks.

The results of the simulation should not be dependent on the agents' abilities. In fact with higher abilities it is only easier for the system to find a group of agents that is able to fulfill the task. Therefore we set these abilities randomly between 0.5 and 1. Action cost was set to 0.5 which means that the expected investment/gain ratio (calculated by the Workers in order to decide whether to participate or not) is 50%.

6.3   Discussion

At first, in order to check a behaviour of the system we set the `alpha_reward` and `beta_punish` parameters to 0. Together with setting `random_default_trust` to a low value it makes the system behave ideally — when trust is equal to abilities. This is the state the system with real settings should be led to.

When choosing a default trust value we can do one of the following things: either use actual ability slightly affected by the `random_default_trust` parameter (effectively we can observe the simulation in a state that is in fact very close to what we expect) or set `default_trust_value` to 1. It would give us a clearer view of the evolution of the system — this value is incorrect but forces the agents to be more interactive and to accept more contracts when the simulation starts.

Efficiency. (Fig. 1 and 2.) Using RCC gives us the best efficiency at a level up to 72%. There are many successful contracts generated (above 2600) and quickly the system reaches an ideal state — generating only contracts which are very likely to succeed. SCC gives a lower efficiency (maximum of 58%), thus it takes more time to reach a good state. However there is a significantly bigger number of successful contracts. It is worth noting that the value of the efficiency is still higher than the expected value of investment/gain ratio (50%) which means that the system earns more comparing to the investments made by the agents. Both WCC and TC have an average efficiency rate at a similar level comparing to the stronger models, but with less contracts (around 2000 and 500 respectively). The TC behaviour is unstable — at times which it can generate 90% of successful contracts, but after a while its efficiency falls dramatically (due to a low number of tasks accepted by the agents). DC has a very low but stable ratio of successful contracts (37%) — close to expected, with an average ability to successfully perform an action of 0.75 and 4 actions in a task the probability of positive effects of a contract is $0.75^4 = 0.32$.

Learning. Comparing the efficiency and reputation_diff curves (fig. 2) show the differences in the learning time when using different notions of collective commitments. It is clear that the stronger the collective commitment used is, the faster the agents learn. The reputation_diff factor is stable and low with RCC, SCC and WCC, which means that there is not much difference between agents' beliefs about abilities of the others. With TC this value is even lower but the agents are very conservative when deciding about joining a group. With DC agents are in fact unable to learn so they bid in every contract and fail often.

Other Conclusions. Some of the properties of the presented example of a simulation arise from the fact that the Manager chooses a random group of the agents from the bids it has received. Should the Manager choose Workers basing of its trust it would most likely make the number of successful contracts higher but on the other hand it would obscure the view of the interactions we wanted to show in the simulation.

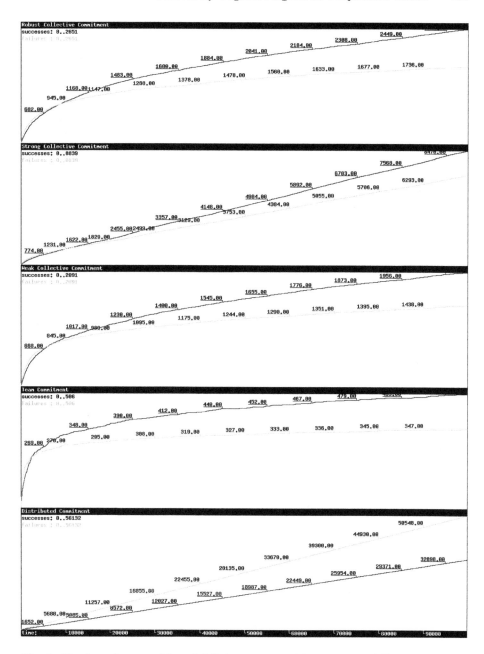

Fig. 1. Number of successful and failed contracts with respect to different models of collective commitment

It is clear that using the strong notions of a collective commitment allows agents to learn quickly and therefore to carefully (but not too carefully) decide about a cooperation with the others. With plenty of information they receive

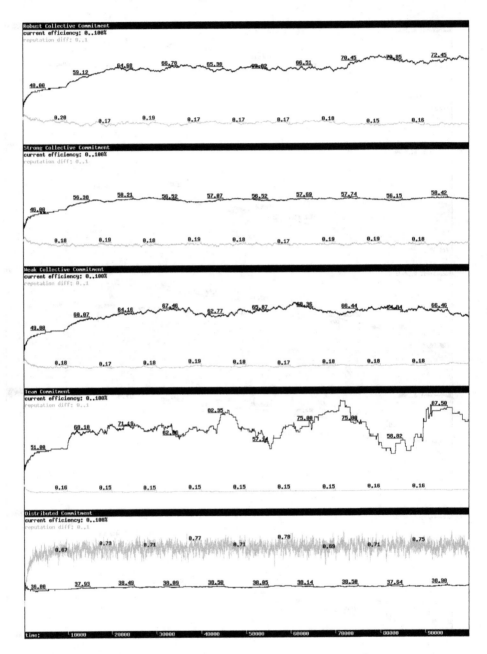

Fig. 2. Evolving efficiency and reputation_diff values

they can pretty well estimate chances of success and act accordingly. Comparing the strongest notions, RCC and SCC, it is clear that in a longer period of time SCC gives the best results — with many successful contracts and pretty high efficiency.

7   Conclusions and Possible Extensions

We have created a small but useful application that can be used to investigate dependencies between the model of a collective commitment applied to a team-work and the evolution of trust in a group. Designed to be simple and efficient, it allows conducting large and long-term experiments. New theories of collective commitments and trust have been applied — agents interact with each other in a way of a simplified contract-net protocol and form teams that can be described by different notions of a commitment. The decision process whether to join or leave the group is done basing on ever evolving trust values. Since with different models of the group structure agents receive different amount of information one can observe how these various properties of a commitment applied in a team can affect the way the agents learn how to choose their collaborators to help them complete their tasks.

It should be noted that the proposed models of building a collective commit-ment within a group are not the only ones that can be built using the tuning machine proposed in [3]. They reflect some typical organizational structures that can be observed in the real world but other ones could be developed in this frame-work as well. We also assume that the commitment model is given and all the agents in the system commit to perform actions only if their mental state is relevant to that model. But we can also assume that Manager agent can try dif-ferent models of commitment structure (even complex commitment structure — consisting of different types of commitments in different subgroups) to realize the task.

There are some extensions considered. Firstly, expanding the hierarchy of the agents allows us to use more complex and more realistic commitment sce-narios. Also we can introduce a realistic situation when while the compound task succeeds the Manager fails to pay out for the work. This would allow us to differ-entiate between the trust values for "team–selection" and "team–management" thus leading to slightly different formulas of the task result estimation functions. Secondly, we can introduce institutional restrictions, i.e. permissions for agents to perform specific actions (agent is able to perform an action, but it is not allowed to, however it can occasionally perform the action, i.e. to increase its profit). We can test different trust modifications models based on agents' moral attitude etc. Thirdly, we can introduce the reconfiguration algorithm as in [2], allowing dynamic evolution of the group and commitment structure. It would allow us to examine role of trust in a dynamic evolution of the group.

Acknowledgements

This work is supported by the Polish KBN Grant 7T11C 006 20 and by the Polish KBN grant supporting EU-funded ALFEBIITE Project (IST-1999-10298).

References

1. Castelfranchi C., Falcone, R.: Socio-cognitive theory of trust. Technical Report. In: ALFEBIITE Deliverable report D1 (2001)
2. Dunin-Kęplicz, B., Verbrugge, R.: A Reconfiguration Algorithm for Distributed Problem Solving. In: Engineering Simulation **18** (2001) 227-246
3. Dunin-Kęplicz, B., Verbrugge, R.: A tuning machine for collective commitments. In: Procs. of The First International Workshop on Formal Approaches to Multi-Agent Systems, FAMAS'03, Warsaw (2003) 99-116
4. Dunin-Kęplicz, B., Verbrugge, R.: Tuning machine for Cooperative Problem Solving. In: Fundamenta Informaticae **63(2-3)** (2004) 283-307
5. Dunin-Kęplicz, B., Verbrugge, R.: Calibrating collective commitments. In Marik, V., Mueller, J., Pechoucek, M, eds.: Procs. of The 3rd International Central and Eastern European Conference on Multi-Agent Systems (CEEMAS 2003), LNAI 2691 (2003) 73-83
6. Dunin-Kęplicz, B., Verbrugge, R.: Collective intentions. In: Fundamenta Informaticae **51(3)** (2002) 271-295
7. Dunin-Kęplicz, B., Verbrugge, R.: Evolution of collective commitments during teamwork. In: Fundamenta Informaticae **56(4)** (2003) 329-371
8. Falcone, R., Castelfranchi, C.: The socio-cognitive dynamics of trust. Does trust create trust? In Falcone, R., Singh, M., Tan, Y., eds.: Trust in Cyber-Societies: Integrating the Human and Artificial Perspectives, LNAI 2246 (2001)
9. Kamara, L., Artikis, A., Neville, B., Pitt, J.: Simulating Computational Societies. In Petta, P., Tolksdorf, R., Zambonelli, F., eds.: Engineering Societies in the Agents World III, 3rd International Workshop, ESAW 2002, Madrid, Spain, September 16-17, 2002, Revised Papers, LNCS 2577 (2003) 53-67
10. Neville, B., Pitt, J.: A Computational Framework for Social Agents in Agent Mediated E-commerce. In Omicini, A, Petta, P., Pitt, J., eds.: Engineering Societies in the Agents World IV, 4th International Workshop, ESAW 2003, London, UK, October 29-31, 2003, Revised Selected and Invited Papers, LNCS 3071 (2004) 376-391
11. Smith, R. G., Davis, R.: Distributed Problem Solving: The Contract-Net Approach. In: Proceedings of 2nd Conference of Canadian Society for Computational Studies of Intelligence (1978)
12. Witkowski, M., Artikis, A., Pitt, J.: Experiments in building experimental trust in a society of objective-trust based agents.In Falcone, R., Singh, M., Tan, Y., eds.: Trust in Cyber-Societies: Integrating the Human and Artificial Perspectives, LNAI 2246 (2001)
13. Wooldridge, M., Jennings, N.: Towards a theory of collective problem solving. In Perram, J. Mueller, J., eds.: Distributed Software Agents and Applications, LNAI 1069 (1996) 40-53

Cooperative Agent Model Instantiation to Collective Robotics

Gauthier Picard

IRIT, Université Paul Sabatier,
F-31062 Toulouse Cedex, France
picard@irit.fr
http://www.irit.fr/SMAC

Abstract. The general aim of our work is to provide tools, methods and models to adaptive multi-agent systems designers. These systems consist in several interacting agents and have to optimize problem solving in a dynamic environment. In this context, the ADELFE method, which is based on a self-organizing adaptive multi-agent system model, was developed. Cooperation is used as a local criterion to self-organize the collective in order to reach functional adequacy with the environment. One key stage during the design process is to instantiate a cooperative agent model that is an extension to classical reactive models in which cooperation subsumes any other nominal behavior. A sample implementation of the agent model in the collective robotics domain – resource transportation – will illustrate a discussion on the model.

1 Introduction

Self-organization in artificial systems promises to be an appropriate solution to overcome openness, flexibility and adaptiveness requirements in dynamical environments. Adaptive Multi-Agent Systems (or *AMAS*) paradigm proposes to use cooperation notion as the engine of self-organization mechanisms in order to make the system reach functional adequacy [1]. Therefore, designers of such agent societies must focus on the parts rather than the whole global system; i.e. *a priori* equipping parts with organization capabilities rather than organizing them. Implementations of such systems have already successfully solved complex problems such as flood forecasting with STAFF in which data, originated from sensors, self-organize to reach the right prevision function [2].

In this context, ADELFE method establishes an AMAS design process [3] which aims at guiding non-specialist engineers to develop MAS from A to Z. Besides notations (UML and A-UML) and tools (OpenTool[1]), ADELFE provides a cooperative agent model which has already been described in the previous ESAW edition [4]. Figure 1 describes this model. Unlike some other multi-agent engineering approaches which try to fit agent design with nature-inspired models,

---

[1] OpenTool is released by TNI-Valiosys (www.tni-valiosys.com).

M.-P. Gleizes, A. Omicini, and F. Zambonelli (Eds.): ESAW 2004, LNAI 3451, pp. 209–221, 2005.

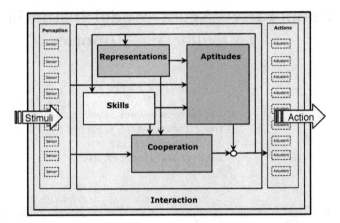

Fig. 1. The different modules of a cooperative agent and their dependencies. Aptitudes and Cooperation modules process in parallel during the decision phase to make the agent act. Cooperative behavior subsumes nominal behavior

such as ant behaviors, ADELFE lies on a theoretical notion which comes near to the social notion of *cooperation*. The challenge resides in specifying local cooperation rules that will lead agents to organizational changes and therefore to change the global function of the system.

Cooperative behavior will be defined in a proscriptive approach: "An agent is cooperative if it avoids non cooperative situations (or NCS)". The AMAS theory identifies several types of NCS, resulting from the analysis of the cooperation definition: an agent is cooperative if: (c_1) all perceived signals are understood without ambiguity *and* (c_2) the received information is useful for the agent's reasoning *and* (c_3) reasoning leads to useful actions toward other agents. Therefore, a NCS occurs when $\neg c_1 \vee \neg c_2 \vee \neg c_3$. We identify seven NCS subtypes that express these conditions: *incomprehension* (an input has no interpretation), *ambiguity* (an input has two or more interpretations), *incompetence* (the agent has no rule to process input), *unproductiveness* (the agent's reasoning do not lead to any conclusion), *concurrency* (two agents execute actions that lead to same conclusions), *conflict* (the agent's action put another agent out) and *uselessness* (the agent's action has no impact in its environment). The cooperative attitude of an agent must avoid all these NCS. Cooperative agent design focuses on NCS specification – like a kind of exception-oriented programming in which designers focus on exceptions.

This article aims at detailing the agent design in ADELFE and showing the optimization of a problem solving concerning resources transportation, described in section 2 realized by an cooperative agents society in which the global behavior presents emergent properties. For more information about the ADELFE process usage, see [3] or the paper in the same workshop about the Mechanical Synthesis Problem [5]. In section 3, the cooperative agent model is instantiated to solve the resource transportation problem. Section 4 studies different possible cooperative behaviors that can be assigned to agents. Some experiments have been done to compare these different solutions in section 5, which leads to a discussion in section 6. Finally, section 7 concludes on perspectives.

2   Resource Transportation Problem

The resource transportation problem is a classical task in Collective Robotics [6], and was proposed as a relevant benchmark for robotic systems by [7]. Robots must transport resources (boxes) as fast a possible from a zone A to a zone B, separated by a constrained environment. In our example, these zones are linked by two corridors too narrow for robots to cross one another side by side (cf. figure 2). This environment leads to a spatial interference problem, e.g. robots must share common resources: the corridors. Once engaged in a corridor, what must a robot do when facing another robot moving in the opposite sense? Spatial interference has been tackled by [8] in the case of robots circulating in corridors and having to cross narrow passages (doors). Their solution is to solve conflicts by aggressive competition (with explicit hierarchy), similarly to eco-resolution by [9]. [10] propose to solve such problems thanks to attraction-repulsion mechanisms based on altruistic behaviors triggering – a reverse vision of the eco-resolution. In our case, we expound a viewpoint halfway between the two firsts, in which robots are neither altruistic nor individualist and cannot directly communicate any information or intention. Moreover, no planifier system will anticipate trajectories because the use of planification in multi-robot domain remains inefficient, considering the high dynamics of a robot's environment.

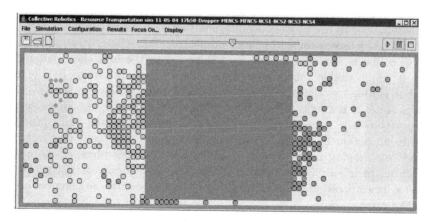

Fig. 2. The environment of the resource transportation problem is composed of: a claim room (at left), a laying room (at right) and two narrow corridors (at top and bottom). Robots pick boxes against the left wall of the claim room (claim zone) and drop them against the right wall of the laying room (laying zone)

3   Cooperative Model Instantiation

This section shows the instantiation – i.e. fulfilling each module – of the cooperative agent model in order to design robots able to realize the transportation task. This work appears in the ADELFE process in the *Design Work Definition*, and more precisely in the *Design Agents Activity* [3]. ADELFE process is an extension to the *Rational Unified Process* (RUP) and consists in four work definitions – specifically extended to agent oriented engineering – : preliminary requirements, final requirements, analysis and design. Requirements defines the environmental context of the system. Analysis identifies the agents within other object classes.

3.1   Modules Fulfilling

The *Perceptions Module* represents inputs for agents. Concerning robots, they can know positions of the two zones (claim and laying). Indeed, this paper only focuses on adaptation to a circulation problem rather than a foraging one, i.e. robots' task is not to find boxes but to transport them from a room to another. Here is a possible list of perceptions for transporter robots: position of the claim zone, position of the laying zone, a perception cone in which objects are differentiable (robot, box or wall), proximity sensors (forward, backward, left and right), a compass and the absolute spatial position. The environment is discretized as a grid whose cells represent atomic parts on which a robot, a box or a wall can be situated. The Perceptions Module also defined limit values of perceptions (e.g. 5 cells).

The *Actions Module* represents outputs of agents on their environment. Possible actions for transporter robots are: *rest, pick, drop, forward, backward, left* and *right*. Robots cannot drop boxes anywhere in the environment but only in the laying zone. They cannot communicate directly or drop land marks on the environment. In the case of social agents that are able to communicate, communication acts are specified in this module.

The *Skills Module* contains knowledge about the task the agent must perform. Skills enable robots to achieve their transportation goals. Therefore, a robot is able to calculate which objective it must achieve in terms of its current state: if it carries a box then it must go to the laying zone else it must reach the claim zone. As a function of its current goal, the Skills Module provides an action to process to achieve it. Robot's goals are: *reach claim zone* and *reach laying zone*. Moreover, robots have intrinsic physical characteristics such as their speed, the number of transportable boxes or the preference to move forward rather than backward – as ants have. Such preferences are called *reflex values*.

The *Representations Module* contains knowledge about the environment (physical or social). Representation a robot has on its environment is very limited. From its perceptions, it cannot identify a robot from another, but can know if it is carrying a box or not. It also can memorize its past absolute position, direction, goal and action.

The *Aptitudes Module* enables an agent to choose an action in terms of its perceptions, skills and representations. Concerning transporter robots, a design choice must be taken at this stage. In terms of the current goal, the Skills Module provides preferences on each action the robot may do. The Aptitudes Module chooses among these actions what will be the next action to reach the goal. Many decision functions can be considered; e.g. an arbitrary policy (the action having the highest preference is chosen) or a Monte Carlo method-based policy that is chosen for our example. Therefore, the Aptitudes Modules can be summed up in a Monte Carlo decision function on the preference vector (the list of action preferences for an agent) provided by the Skills Module. In the same manner, the *Cooperation Module* provides preference vectors in order to solve NCS described in section 4.

3.2   Action Choosing

At each time t, a robot has to choose between different actions that are proposed by the two decision modules (skills and cooperation). At time t, each action act_j of the robot r_i is evaluated. For each action, this value is calculated in terms of perceptions, representations and reflexes in the case of a nominal behavior:

$$V_{r_i}^{nomi}(act_j, t) = wp_{r_i}(act_j, t) + wm_{r_i}(act_j, t) + wr_{r_i}(act_j)$$

with:

- $V_{r_i}^{nomi}(act_j, t)$ represents the value for the action act_j at time t for the robot r_i,
- $wp_{r_i}(act_j, t)$ represents the calculated value in terms of perceptions,
- $wm_{r_i}(act_j, t)$ represents the calculated value in terms of memory,
- $wr_{r_i}(act_j, t)$ represents the calculated value in terms of reflexes.

As for aptitudes, an action preference vector is generated by the Cooperation Module: $V_{r_i}^{coop}(act_j, t)$. Once these values calculated by the two modules for each action of a robot, the vector on which the Monte Carlo drawing will process is a combination of the two vectors in which the cooperation vector subsumes the nominal vector:

$$V_{r_i}(t) = V_{r_i}^{nomi}(t) \prec V_{r_i}^{coop}(t)$$

3.3   Nominal Behavior

The nominal behavior is described with rules that modify the values in the V^{nomi} preference vector. This vector is obtained by adding values[2] from perceptions $(wp_{r_i}(act_j, t))$ and values from reflexes $(wr_{r_i}(act_j, t))$. The table 1 shows values to increase in the $wp_{r_i}(act_j, t)$ to achieve to two disjoint goals : *reach claim zone* ($\neg car$) and *reach laying zone* (car).

---

[2] Memory is not necessary to process a nominal behavior.

Table 1. Specification of the nominal behavior in terms of perceptions

Perceptions	Effects
$\neg car \wedge cBox$	$\nearrow wp_{r_i}(pick, t)$
$\neg car \wedge \neg cBox \wedge sBox$	$\nearrow wp_{r_i}(forward, t)$
$\neg car \wedge \neg cBox \wedge \neg sBox \wedge \neg inCZ$	$\nearrow wp_{r_i}(< CZdir >, t)$
$\neg car \wedge \neg cBox \wedge \neg sBox \wedge inCZ$	$\nearrow wp_{r_i}(backward, t)$
	$\nearrow wp_{r_i}(forward, t)$
	$\nearrow wp_{r_i}(left, t)$
	$\nearrow wp_{r_i}(right, t)$
$car \wedge cLZ$	$\nearrow wp_{r_i}(drop, t)$
$car \wedge \neg cLZ$	$\nearrow wp_{r_i}(< LZdir >, t)$

- car: r_i is carrying a box;
- $cBox$: r_i is close a box;
- $sBox$: r_i is seeing a box;
- $inCZ$: r_i is in the claim zone;
- cLZ: r_i is close to laying zone;
- cLZ: r_i is close to laying zone;
- $< CZdir >$: the move to do to go to claim zone;
- $< LZdir >$: the move to do to go to laying zone;
- $\nearrow$: increasing.

Reflex values are static and also depend on perceptions – but only on the direction of the robot. As for ants, robots may prefer moving forward then backward [11]. For example, values for $wr_{r_i}(act_j, t)$ can be :

- $wr_{r_i}(forward, t) = 50$;
- $wr_{r_i}(left, t) = 10$;
- $wr_{r_i}(right, t) = 10$;
- $wr_{r_i}(backward, t) = 0$;

Thus, even if a goal leads a robot to a wall, the robot can move by side, as ants do to forage and to avoid dead end. Nevertheless, this mechanism is not sufficient to avoid deadlocks in long narrow corridors in which robots cannot cross. The goal is more influent than reflexes. As a consequence, we need to define cooperation rules to enable all robots to achieve their tasks without deadlock.

Finally, robots do not process their nominal next action from a memory. Therefore, $\forall j, wm_{r_i}(act_j, t) = 0$.

4   Cooperative Behaviors Study

In the previous section, the different modules of a robot and its components have been detailed, except the Cooperation Module. This section aims at discussing cooperation rules to establish in order to enable the multi-robot system to be in functional adequacy with its environment.

4.1   Cooperative Unblocking

Beyond two robots acting to transport boxes in a same environment, the nominal behavior cannot be adequate. Indeed, a robot owns skills to achieve its tasks, but not to work with other robots. In this very constrained environment, spatial interference zones appear. If two robots, a first one carrying a box and moving to the laying zone and a second one moving to the claim zone to pick a box, meet in a corridor, the circulation is blocked – because they cannot drop boxes outside the laying zone. Then, it is necessary to provide cooperative behaviors to robots. Two main NCS (non cooperative situations) can be reactively solved:

A robot is blocked. A robot r_1 cannot move forward because it is in front of a wall or another robot r_2 moving in the opposite sense[3]. In this case, if it is possible, r_1 must move to its sides (left or right). This corresponds to increasing values of the cooperative action vector related to side movements: $V_{r_1}^{coop}(t, right)$ and $V_{r_1}^{coop}(t, left)$. If r_1 cannot laterally move, two other solutions are openned. If r_2 has an antagonist goal, the robot which is the most distant from its goal will move backward (increasing $V_{r_i}^{coop}(t, backward)$) to free the way for the robot which is the closest to its goal (increasing $V_{r_i}^{coop}(t, forward)$ even if it may wait). If r_2 has the same goal than r_1, except if r_1 is followed by an antagonist robot or if r_1 moves away from its goal (visibly it moves to a risky[4] region), r_1 moves backward; else r_1 moves forward and r_2 moves backward.

A robot is returning. A robot r_1 is returning[5] as a consequence of a traffic blockage. If it is possible, r_1 moves to its sides (an is no more returning). Else, r_1 moves forward until it cannot continue or if encounters another robot r_2 which is returning and is closer to its goal than r_1. Table 2 sums up the behavior in this situation. If there is a line of robot, the first returning robot is seen by the second one that will return too. Therefore, the third one will return too and so on until there is no more obstacle.

These rules correspond to resource *conflict* (corridors) or *uselessness* when a robot must move backward and away from its goal. In the case of robots, situations will not be specified as incomprehension because robots are unable to communicate directly. These rules, which are simple to express, ensure that robots cannot block each other in corridors. But, this cooperation attitude only solves problem instantly, creating returning movement and then implies time loss to transport boxes.

4.2   Cooperative Anticipation

By taking into account the previous remark, it seems possible to specify cooperation rules to anticipate blockage situations in order to make the collective

---

[3] If r_2 moves in another direction than the opposite direction of r_1, it is not considered as blocking because it will not block the traffic anymore.

[4] It is risky in the sense it may occur a lot of non cooperative situations such as conflicts.

[5] A robot is considered as returning until it has no choice of side movements.

Table 2. Example of specification of the *"a robot is returning"* uselessness NCS

Condition	Action
$ret \wedge freeR$	$\nearrow V_{r_i}^{coop}(t, right)$
$ret \wedge freeL$	$\nearrow V_{r_i}^{coop}(t, left)$
$ret \wedge \neg(freeL \vee freeR) \wedge ant \wedge toGoal \wedge cGoal$	$\nearrow V_{r_i}^{coop}(t, backward)$
$ret \wedge \neg(freeL \vee freeR) \wedge ant \wedge toGoal \wedge \neg cGoal$	$\nearrow V_{r_i}^{coop}(t, forward)$
$ret \wedge \neg(freeL \vee freeR) \wedge ant \wedge \neg toGoal$	$\nearrow V_{r_i}^{coop}(t, backward)$
$ret \wedge \neg(freeL \vee freeR) \wedge \neg ant$	$\nearrow V_{r_i}^{coop}(t, forward)$

With:
- ret: r_i is returning;
- $freeR$: right cell is free;
- $freeL$: left cell is free;
- ant: in front of an antinomic robot;
- $toGoal$: r_i is moving to goal;
- $cGoal$: r_i is closer to its goal than its opposite one;
- $\nearrow$: increasing.

more efficient. We call this *optimisation* cooperation rules. Previous rules enable robots to extract from blockage. A robot is in such a situation because it was crossing a zone frequented by antinomic robots. So as to prevent this situation, robots must be able to avoid such risky zones: zones from which antinomic robots come. Then, an anticipation rule can be specified:

A robot sees an antinomic robot. If a robot r_1 perceives a robot r_2 having an antinomic goal, if r_1 can move to its sides it does it else it moves forward.

Nevertheless, this reactive anticipation presents a major problem: once a robot has avoided the risky zone, no mechanism ensures that it will not go in it again, led by its goal. In order to tackle this difficulty, robots can be equipped with a memory of the risky zones (in the Representations Module). Each time t a robot r_i experiments an anticipation situation facing a robot r_j, it adds to its memory a tuple (or virtual marker) $\langle posX(r_j, t), posY(r_j, t), goal(r_i, t), w \rangle$ in which $posX(r_i, t)$ and $posY(r_i, t)$ represent the coordinates of r_j at the moment t. $goal(r_i, t)$ represents the goal r_i was achieving at time t. w represents a repulsion value. The higher the value is, the more the robot will try to avoid the zone described by the marker when it is achieving another goal than $goal(r_i, t)$. Therefore, the robot inspects all its personal markers[6] whose distance is inferior to the perception limit (to fulfill the locality principle). A marker with a weight w and situated in the direction dir at a distance d induces that $V_{r_i}^{coop}(t, dir_{opp})$ will be increased of w (dir_{opp} is the opposite direction to dir).

As the memory is limited, tuples that are added must disappear during simulation run-time. For example, the weight w can decrease of a given value δ_w (called *forgetting factor*) at each step. Once $w = 0$, the tuple is removed from the memory. This method corresponds to the use of *virtual* and *personal* pheromones. Finally, as ants do, robots can reinforce their markers: a robot

---

[6] Robots cannot share their memory as they cannot communicate.

moving to a position corresponding to one of its marker with another goal, re-initializes the marker. In fact, if the robot is at this position, it might be a risky zone when it tries to achieve another goal.

5   Experiments

In order to validate this approach and to compare cooperative behaviors of transporter robots, the expounded model has been implemented and simulated.

5.1   Experimental Setup

The simulation environment corresponds to two rooms (25 x 30 cells) separated by two long and narrow corridors (30 x 1 cells). 300 robots are randomly placed in the claim room. These robots can perceive at 5 cells, and can make a move of one cell at each step. If they can anticipate conflicts, their memory can contain 1500 tuples with $w = 400$ and $\delta_w = 1$.

5.2   Reaction Versus Anticipation

The figure 3 shows a comparison between the results of the previously presented cooperative behaviors. The unblocking behavior-equipped robots obtain a linear efficiency with no blockage, unlike nominal behavior-equipped individualist robots. By adding blockage anticipation, the collective becomes more efficient (at least 30% more boxes are transported). This corresponds to an optimisation of the unblocking behavior. According to the AMAS paradigm, we can experimentally observe that the local resorption of NCS leads to the collective functional

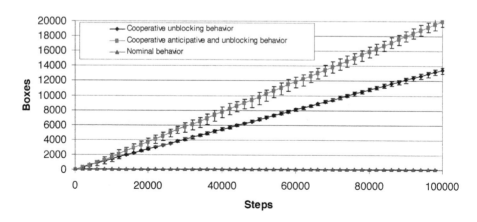

Fig. 3. Number of transported boxes for 15 simulations (300 robots, 2 corridors, 5-ranged perception), corresponding to the nominal behavior (individualist) and the two cooperative ones: the cooperative unblocking behavior (see section 4.1) and the cooperative anticipation behavior (see section 4.2)

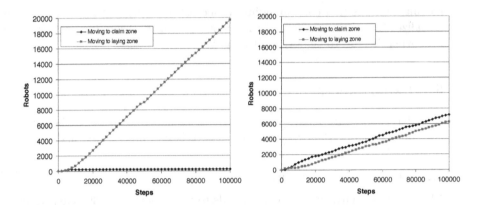

Fig. 4. Number of incoming robots for a corridor and for the two cooperative behaviors: unblocking behavior (right) and anticipation unblocking behavior (left)

adequacy. Finally, the more the NCS are taken into account, the higher the performances are.

5.3   Emergence of Corridor Dedication

The figure 4 presents the corridor-going for the two cooperative behaviors. In the case of anticipation behavior, we can observe the emergence of a sense of traffic. Robots dedicate corridors to particular goals. We can assign the emergent property to this phenomenon because robots do not have any notion of corridor – unlike some previous work [12]. Thus, just thanks to local data, robots established a coherent traffic behavior that leads to an optimization of the output.

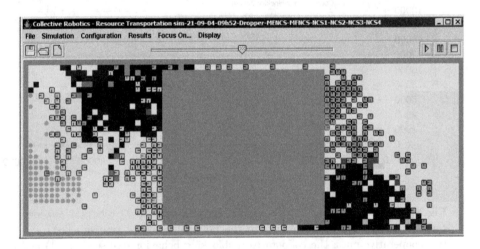

Fig. 5. Global markers positioning (sum of all individual memories)

Moreover, the sense of traffic varies from a simulation to another with only little initial variations of some robots.

In fact, markers are positioned only at one corridor entry for one direction as figure 5 shows. This figure shows the sum of all the markers for all the robots. This data is not known from robots. It is only calculated for monitoring purpose.

According to the distinction made by [13], the functionality of system is *weakly* emergent because robots do not have any global knowledge about the number of boxes they have transported and it does not motivate them to transport more boxes.

5.4   Adaptation and Robustness

Some simulations has been launched in dynamic environments with random corridor closures. These simulations show the collective always sets another corridor dedication unless the corridor closure frequency is to high in comparison with the forgetting factor (δ_w).

6   Discussion

By regarding the previous results, instantiating the agent model proposed by ADELFE has several advantages. Firstly, unlike ant-inspired algorithms [7], robots do not mark their environment with pheromones but memorize virtual and personal markers. Secondly, contrary to competition-based [8] or altruistic [10] approaches, robots do not need direct communication to alarm, inform close robots or exchange requests and intentions. Thirdly, cooperative behavior encoding is insensitive to the number of robots, to the topography and to the dimensions of the environment. Fourthly, no global feedback is needed to lead the system to functional adequacy, which prevents the system to reach local extrema. Finally, the incremental method proposed by ADELFE to define non cooperative situations – necessary ones and optimization ones – opens up a new way toward a living design methodology within which behaviors are assigned to robots (or agents) as design and development progress in terms of designers' requirements (this activity is called *fast prototyping* in the ADELFE process). Of course, this will need to develop a simulation/design platform, as adequate to the cooperative agent model as possible.

Nevertheless, some choices have been taken concerning the affectation of values that can drastically modify the global behavior. By now, ADELFE does not provide any guidance to appropriately instantiate these values; designers must do it by themselves. For instance, the initial weight for markers and the forgetting factor have been adjusted to the time robots spend to cross the entire environment. This might be completely different for a more complex environment with more or less corridors which can dynamically open or close. Some simulations has been done with such environments, and the affected values seem correct unless corridors are too near or frequence of closure is too fast. These values also may be learned during run-time, which is one of our perspectives.

Moreover, from the resource transportation problem, we focused on particular NCS: conflict and uselessness. If robots were equipped with high-level communication capabilities (to exchange data as markers in order to share their experiences), incomprehension and ambiguity may raise. In this case, ADELFE proposes to analyze interaction protocols between agents and identify such situations.

Lastly, the application we chose and the solution we considered are typical examples of "flat" systems within which no *a priori* hierarchy is defined. Self-organization leads the society to an adequate functioning without having specified a static organization; that is due to the homogeneity of the collective. On the contrary, if the collective is heterogeneous (different speeds, different functions, complementary or not), notions of hierarchy and/or priority are relevant. So as to ensure extensionality[7] and irreductibility[8] properties of emergent systems [14], predefining an organization is prohibited; in this case, the function of the system is intentionally defined, and therefore is not adaptive. Consequently, organization is an emergent phenomenon of relations between agents and is not a predefined schema.

7   Conclusion

In this paper, we presented an instantiation of the cooperative agent model proposed by ADELFE in the domain of Collective Robotics. This application helps us highlighting the possibility to iteratively and compositionally design agents' behaviors. Considering the ignorance of the global task and the environment, the self-organizing collective reaches an emergent coherent behavior, which is then more robust to environmental risks (such as traffic jams). Our simulation application tackles a simple problem with a simple environment.

Concerning the cooperative agent model, extending the ADELFE method to development and automatic code generation based on the MDA (*Model Driven Architecture*) paradigm seem to be promising perspective [15]. Actually, by formally specifying the model and by defining transformation rules, proceeding from design models to development instantiations becomes conceivable.

References

1. Capera, D., Georgé, J., Gleizes, M.P., Glize, P.: The AMAS theory for complex problem solving based on self-organizing cooperative agents. In: 1st International Workshop on Theory and Practice of Open Computational Systems (TAPOCS) at IEEE 12th International Workshop on Enabling Technologies: Infrastructure for Collaborative Enterprises (WETICE 2003), IEEE (2003) 383–388

---

[7] This means the function of the system is defined by relations between input and output, but not by an algorithm.

[8] Churchland defines the emergence in terms of the irreductibility of properties assigned to a high-level theory associated to components in a lower-level theory.

2. Georgé, J.P., Gleizes, M.P., Glize, P., Régis, C.: Real-time simulation for flood forecast: an adaptive multi-agent system staff. In Kazakov, D., Kudenko, D., Alonso, E., eds.: Proceedings of the AISB'03 symposium on Adaptive Agents and Multi-Agent Systems(AAMAS'03), University of Wales, Aberystwyth (2003)

3. Picard, G., Gleizes, M.P.: The ADELFE Methodology – Designing Adaptive Cooperative Multi-Agent Systems. In Bergenti, F., Gleizes, M.P., Zambonelli, F., eds.: Methodologies and Software Engineering for Agent Systems, Kluwer (2004)

4. Bernon, C., Camps, V., Gleizes, M.P., Picard, G.: Designing Agents' Behaviours within the Framework of ADELFE Methodology. In: Fourth International Workshop on Engineering Societies in the Agents World (ESAW'03), Imperial College London, UK, 29-31 October. Volume 3071 of Lecture Notes in Artificial Intelligence., Springer-Verlag (2004)

5. Picard, G., Capera, D., Gleizes, M.P., Glize, P.: A Sample Application of ADELFE Focusing on Analysis and Design : The Mechanism Design Problem. In: Fifth International Workshop on Engineering Societies in the Agents World (ESAW'04), 20-22 October 2004, Toulouse, France. (2004)

6. Vaughan, R., Støy, K., Sukhatme, G., Matarić, M.: Blazing a trail: Insect-inspired resource transportation by a robotic team. In: Proceedings of 5th International Symposium on Distributed Robotic Systems. (2000)

7. Bonabeau, E., Dorigo, M., Theraulaz, G.: Swarm Intelligence: From Natural to Artificial Systems. Oxford University Press (1999)

8. Vaughan, R., Støy, K., Sukhatme, G., Matarić, M.: Go ahead make my day: Robot conflict resolution by aggressive competition. In: Proceedings of the 6th International Conference on Simulation of Adaptive Behaviour. (2000)

9. Ferber, J.: Multi-Agent System: An Introduction to Distributed Artificial Intelligence. Harlow: Addison Wesley Longman (1999)

10. Lucidarme, P., Simonin, O., Liéègeois, A.: Implementation and Evaluation of a Satisfaction/Altruism Based Architecture for Multi-Robot Systems. In: Proceedings of the 2002 IEEE International Conference on Robotics and Automation, ICRA 2002, May 11-15, 2002, Washington, DC, USA, IEEE (2002) 1007–1012

11. Topin, X., Fourcassié, V., Gleizes, M.P., Theraulaz, G., Regis, C., Glize, P.: Theories and experiments on emergent behaviour: From natural to artificial systems and back. In: Proceedings of the 3rd European Conference on Cognitive Science (ECCS'99), Certosa di Pontignano, SI, Italy (1999)

12. Picard, G., Gleizes, M.P.: An Agent Architecture to Design Self-Organizing Collectives: Principles and Application. In Kazakov, D., Kudenko, D., Alonso, E., eds.: AISB'02 Symposium on Adaptive Multi-Agent Systems (AAMASII). Volume 2636 of LNAI., Univerity of London, UK, Springer-Verlag (2002) 141–158

13. Müller, J.P.: Emergence of collective behaviour: simulation and social engineering. In: Fourth International Workshop on Engineering Societies in the Agents World (ESAW'03), Imperial College London, UK, 29-31 October. (2004)

14. Ali, S., Zimmer, R., Elstob, C.: The question concerning emergence : Implication for Artificiality. In Dubois, D., ed.: Computing Anticipatory Systems : CASYS'97 - First International Conference. (1997)

15. Soley, R., the OMG Staff Strategy Group: Model driven architecture. White paper Draft 3.2, OMG (2002)

From Self-Organized Systems to Collective Problem Solving

Chevrier Vincent

LORIA UMR 7503,BP 239, F-54506 Vandoeuvre cedex
chevrier@loria.fr

Abstract. The reactive multi-agent approach emphasizes individual simplicity over the collective complexity of the task being performed. However, to apply such an approach to a problem, the components of the multi-agent system have to be designed in such a way that the society be able to fulfill its requirements with a reasonable efficiency. Inspiration from natural self-organized systems is a way to solve this conception issue.

This article illustrates two cases of how natural self-organized systems can be transposed to engineer societies of agents that collectively solve problems. It presents two original self organized models conceived in cooperation with biologists and details how transposition principles have been used to design collective problem solving systems.

1 Introduction

This article concerns the design of multi-agent systems that collectively solve a problem. It focuses on reactive systems made up of simply behaving agents with decentralized control that despite their individual simplicity are able to collectively solve problems whose complexity is beyond the scope of individuals: "'intelligence"' of the system can be envisaged as a collective property.

One of the difficulties in the design of reactive multi-agent systems is to specify simple interactions between agents and between them and their environment so as to make the society be able to fulfill its requirements with a reasonable efficiency. This difficulty is proportional to the distance between the simplicity of individuals and the complexity of the collective property.

Taking inspiration from self-organized phenomena in biology is a way to tackle this engineering problem. This article describes two original models, transposed from collective behavior in biology, to engineer societies of agents that collectively solve problems.

2 Context of the Work

Reactive multi-agent systems [1] are systems made up of simply behaving units with decentralized control. Agents are situated in a dynamic environment through

M.-P. Gleizes, A. Omicini, and F. Zambonelli (Eds.): ESAW 2004, LNAI 3451, pp. 222–230, 2005.

which they interact. They are characterized by limited (possibly no) representation of themselves, of the others and of the environment. Their behaviors are
based on stimulus-response rules. Decision-making is based on limited information about the environment and on limited internal states and does not refer to
explicit deliberation. The individuals do not have an explicit representation of
the collective task to be achieved because of their simplicity. Therefore, the solution of the problem is a consequence of successive interactions between agents
and the environment. In such systems, the regulation of activities can be achieved
by self-organization.

Camazine et al [2] define self-organization as a process in which pattern at the
global level emerges solely from numerous interactions among lower-lever components of the systems. Self-organized mechanisms are robust, decentralized, and
can resist to perturbations. Reactive multi-agent systems can be viewed as artificial self organized ones. Their characteristics enable them to adapt dynamically
their function or structure to changing conditions without external intervention.
This is one of the reasons why their applications are becoming more and more
attractive: from scene animation in movies [1] to optimization problems [3,4]; or
flood forecast [5]. A lot of examples of transposition of natural self-organized
systems for problem solving can be found in [6].

Applying a self-organized approach to solve a given problem requires designing a system as three components: the environment, the agent behaviors and the
dynamics of the whole such that the agent society is able to fulfill its requirements
with a reasonable efficiency. The difficulty is proportional to the distance between
the simplicity of individuals and the complexity of the collective property.

Designing such systems can be achieved by applying some guidelines or
methodologies such as [7,8,1] or using some formal framework [9].

Another approach can be the transposition of natural self-organized systems.
Social models in biology can be a source of inspiration for designing reactive
multi-agent systems. Several collective phenomena exist in nature and knowledge
about the organization of animal societies can be transposed into multi-agent
systems as collective problem solving methods, or at least used as a metaphor
in view of designing these systems.

In this article, we detail how two original self organized models built in cooperation with biologists have been transposed to collective problem solving. The
first is inspired from the collective weaving in social spiders and it has been transposed to region detection in grey scale images; the second models specialization
among a group of rats and it has been transposed to allocation problem.

3   Principles for Transposition

The key idea of transposition is to reuse a collective mechanism that exists in a
biological self organized system. The hypothesis underlying this approach is that

---

[1] MASSIVE: Multiple   Agent   Simulation   System   In   Virtual   Environment,
http://www.massivesoftware.com

the complex collective behavior exhibited by societies of animals is a response to some environmental problem faced by the society.

In our case, a self-organized system that collectively solve a problem is described as:

- An environment that is a representation of the problem (its initial conditions and constraints);
- A collective pattern that is interpreted as a solution of the problem at macro level;
- Individual behaviors at micro level that generates the pattern from the environmental constraints.

Transposition consists of adapting each of these elements found in a biological system to the context of the problem concerned, and in preserving the collective response. Concretely, it needs to encode the problem and relating it to swarm mechanism and to interpret the collective results as an exploitable solution in the problem domain:

- the pattern in problem domain is the same as in natural systems; the dynamics principles that enable it are unchanged,
- the environment is modified to model the problem,
- agents' behavior is adapted to make the link between the environment and the system dynamics
- For efficiency purposes, some new behaviors can be added.

The next sections describe two natural self organized systems and detail how we applied these transposition principles.

4   From Web Weaving to Region Detection

This section presents a collective phenomena in social spiders and its transposition to region detection in gray level images. Details about the simulation model and the problem solving can be found in [10].

4.1   Biological Considerations

Among the thousands of spider species in the world, only about fifteen species can be qualified as social spiders. *Anelosimus eximius* is a species of social spider which can be found in French Guiana. The individuals live together, share the same web and cooperate in various activities such as brood care, web weaving, hunting, ...

Despite their apparent individual simplicity, these spiders are exhibit interesting collective behavior such as web weaving. *A. eximius* are small animals (5 mm) and yet they are able to collectively build silky structures bigger than ten m^3 that always respect architectural properties whatever be the biological environment. Webs are not geometrical but twofold: an horizontal hammock and an aerial network of silk lines.

4.2   Simulation Model

We built a multi-agent model to reproduce the collective behavior of web weaving. It is a reactive model characterized by the absence of social reference and by simple individual behavioral items.

In our proposal, the environment models the natural vegetation and the web being built. It is implemented as a square grid in which each position corresponds to a stake characterized by its height. The web is constituted by the set of silk drag lines whose extremities are fixed on the top of two stakes. The set of agents is composed of spiders. They are always located on the top of a stake and behave according to two independent items:

1. a **movement** item which consists of the spider moving to a reachable stake : one of the 8 adjacent stakes or one linked by (at least) one silk drag line;
2. a **silk fixing** item which consists of the spider dropping a silk drag line on the top of the current stake.

All behavioral items are stochastic: the silk fixing is ruled by a constant probability and the movements are determined by a contextual probability distribution which depends on the silk attraction factor.

Interactions are mediated by the silk drag lines. As spiders move, they construct silky structures in the environment which offer new paths for their movements. Spiders are attracted by silk drag lines and are likely to follow a drag line instead of moving to an adjacent stake. By this way, past actions put traces in the environment which in turn favor some actions over others. This kind of coordination is called stigmergy[11].

The simulation of this activity starts with an environment empty of silk and consists, during a fixed number of cycles, of making the spiders execute successively their two behavioral items. These simulations show that the silk attraction factor plays a key role in the building: when it is too low, the silk is fixed everywhere in the available space, when it is about average, a collective web is built; and when its is too high, spiders are trapped in their own web and separate webs are built.

4.3   Transposed Model

The problem we chose was of extracting various regions from an image. Segmenting an image A consists of providing a partition of pixels (a set of regions) that share some properties: mainly they must be a connected set of pixels of homogeneous radiometric characteristics, in our case the gray level; their intersection has to be empty.

This problem shows some similarities to collective weaving. It requires an exploration of a space that has to be restricted to a subset of its elements (the pixels of the region). Furthermore, such an application enables visual assessment.

Initially, the *environment* corresponds to an image. Basically, all spiders are put in it and are in charge of detecting one region. The agents will explore the image and lay down drag lines on some pixels: those that are interesting.

Silk fixing is then a way to ensure pixel selection. Each agent is described by the same behavior and provided with parameters, which characterize the region it has to detect. Finally, the environment contains collective webs that will be interpreted to deduce regions by considering the pixels on which the web is fixed. The environment corresponds to a gray level image and is represented by a two dimensions array whose elements are the pixels of the image, the gray level correspond to height of stakes. Silk drag lines are put between pixels.

Agents are characterized by three items executed sequentially:

1. the movement item that is the same as in the simulation model;
2. the silk fixing item is now contextual: the probability to fix the silk is proportional to the distance between the gray level of the pixel and the gray level the spider has to detect
3. otherwise the 'Return to web' item that makes the spider to return to the web according to constant probability.

The last item is a new one. It is needed to ensure the spider does not build a web on pixels that share the same gray level but that are not necessarily connected and do not correspond to a region. This item restricts the exploration to pixels in the neighborhood of the already selected ones.

The interaction is still based on stigmergy as it was in the simulation model and therefore the dynamics of the system is the same as in simulation.

By gathering all the pixels an agent has woven on, we obtain a region; that is, pixels are put together without a consideration of the number of times the agent has woven on them. By applying a threshold on the number of fixed drag lines, we can restrict the pixels that belong to a region.

4.4   Comments

All the ingredients for detecting various regions are available in our approach if the required parameters are well assessed. It is also possible to detect simultaneously several regions by gathering agents with the same initial parameters into groups. However, a drawback has to be solved in order to produce a real application: parameters have to be empirically adjusted and we have to determine the number of agents and their initial position.

5   From Specialization to Task Allocation

This part presents a reactive model that enables the reproduction of the specialization that is observed in groups of rats confronted by an increasing difficulty to reach food. Details of the simulation model and especially its adaptive properties can be found in [12].

5.1   Biological Considerations

The self-organized phenomenon in biology, modeled in this section, is social differentiation in a group of rats in a diving-for-food situation. This situation is a complex social task in which, for a group of 6 rats, the food accessibility is made difficult by progressive immersion in water of the only path of access to the food source (the feeder). This experimental schedule leads to the emergence of a specialization in the group of rats, in two stable profiles: supplier and non-carrier rat. The non-carrier (a) animals never dive, but get food only by stealing it from the suppliers by fighting for it. The supplier (b) rats dive, bring the food back to the cage and cannot defend the food they carried. So, putting groups of rats in a situation in which they have an increasing difficulty to reach food, leads to the emergence of a social structure.

5.2   Simulation Model: Hamelin

We propose a reactive model to reproduce this phenomenon in which agents don't have cognitive abilities (even if rats do have).

In this model, the environment corresponds to the feeder and the water-submerged path.

All rats are reactive agents characterized by 4 internal states and 3 behavioral items. The states are:

- The strength of the agent s, which stands for its ability to win when it is involved in a fight.
- Its anxiety (or fear) for the water θ corresponding to its reluctance to dive into water.
- Its hunger h which embodies the need for food and constitutes the motivation for the agent.
- The possessed amount of food $Food$ implemented as the size of the owned pellet.

The behavior of the agent is a combination of items: to dive, to attack (and fight) and to eat. Each of them is stochastically triggered or carried out. The associated probability is computed according to the internal state of the rat and biological observations.

The dive action is modeled as a response threshold [13]. Fight is modeled as a dominance relationship [14]. We reused these existing models and coupled them. When the action is effectively performed a reinforcement alters the internal state of the agents allowing them to learn and modify their behaviors according to their past actions.

This model prove to be sufficient to reproduce the collective phenomenon and to exhibit adaptive properties both at collective and individual levels.

5.3   Transposed Model

The general framework to transpose the Hamelin model consists of a dynamic task allocation problem among machines, connected together in a network. Initially the tasks are available on a central server. The machines can acquire the data by accessing directly the server or by 'attacking' each other. As some policies are put on the server in order to avoid crashes, some agents can easily access the server while others not so easily(and the more an agent can connect, the easier it is for it to access).

We use this toy example to assess the transposition principles we expressed in case of the Hamelin model; and in that context proposed a first transposed model. The expected pattern is a specialization of agents according to their access mode to the server.

The *environment* corresponds to the server and the network between machines. Environment is characterized by such features as the maximum number of connections, the data size, etc.

The machines are the *agents* of the system. Their internal states are transposed as follow:

- The strength has the same meaning as in the simulation model.
- The anxiety characterizes the difficulty to connect to the server.
- The hunger corresponds to the available space to store data.
- The amount of food represents the data stored.

The transposition of behavioral items was made as follow. Diving corresponds to accessing directly the data on the server, fighting is unchanged and is ruled by the same principles as in simulation. Eating is now associated to the processing of the data.

The *dynamics* of the system is, as in the simulation model, based on the coupling of the diving and fighting items.

We ran experiments with this transposed model and the results are encouraging. They show that specialization appears in the set of machines and that there is a gain in processing time when using the specialization model with respect to a system with no specialization.

However, they are obtained on specific instances of problem and we need more experiments to have a better assessment of the transposed model, especially, by applying the model to a wider range of problem instances.

6   Concluding Remarks

This article described how self-organized models in biology can be transposed to engineer societies of agents that collectively solve problems.

It focused on two original self organized models established in cooperation with biologists and detailed how transposition principles have been instantiated in those cases.

The first model concerned the web weaving activity of social spiders. This model extends the repertoire of biologically inspired systems by providing a new collective mechanism of stigmergy based on silk. The main difference with existing mechanisms is that there is the possibility in the spider model to integrate non-local information in local processing. The second model deals with social differentiation in group of rats. It proposes a reactive model with no social cognition nor global stimulus that produces a social structure.

This article also pointed out that the development and analysis of these transposed system requires experiments[15, 16] to find the relevant value of parameters that enable efficient solving of the problem. This is the reason why our current direction of work is the development of a platform for the analysis of artificial self-organized systems[17].

Acknowledgment

The author would like to acknowledge Christine Bourjot for her valuable comments on this text.

Part of the work presented here was partially funded by the Région Lorraine in the Pôle de Recherche Scientifique et Technologique "Intelligence Logicielle".

References

1. Parunak, H.V.D.: Go to the ant. Engineering Principles from Natural Agent Systems. Annals of Operations Research **5** (1997) 69–101
2. Camazine, S., Deneubourg, J.L., Franks, N., Sneyd, J., Theraulaz, G., Bonabeau, E.: Self-Organization in Biological Systems. Princeton University Press. (2001)
3. Bonabeau, E., Dorigo, M., Theraulaz, G.: Swarm Intelligence. Oxford University Press. (1999)
4. Dury, A., Le Ber, F., Chevrier, V.: A reactive approach for solving constraint satisfaction problems. In: Proceedings of the 5th International Workshop on Intelligent Agents V, Agent Theories, Architectures, and Languages, LNAI 1555, Springer-Verlag (1999) 397–412
5. Georgé, J.P., Gleizes, M.P., Glize, P., Regis, C.: Real-time simulation for flood forecast: an adaptive multi-agent system S. In: Proceedings of the AISB'03 symposium on Adaptive Agents and Multi-Agent Systems, University of Wales, Aberystwyth, 7-11 April. (2003)
6. Di Marzo Serugendo, G., Foukia, N., Hassas, S., Karageorgos, A., Mostéfaoui, S.K., Rana, O.F., Ulieru, M., Valckenaers, P., van Aart, C.: Self-organization: paradigms and applications. In: Engineering Self-Organising Systems: Nature-Inspired Approaches to Software Engineering LNAI 2977, Springer-Verlag (2004) 1 – 19
7. Bernon, C., Camps, V., Gleizes, M.P., Picard, G.: Designing agents behaviours within the framework of ADELFE methodology. In: Proceedings of Engineering Societies in the Agents World, ESAW 03, LNAI 3071, Springer Verlag (2004) 311 – 32
8. Muller, J.P.: Emergence of collective behavior and problem solving. In: Proceedings of Engineering Societies in the Agents World, ESAW 03, LNAI 3071., Springer Verlag (2004) 1 – 21
9. Kazadi, S., Chung, M., Lee, B., Cho, R.: On the dynamics of puck clustering systems. Robotics and Autonomous Systems **46(1)** (2004) 1–27
10. Bourjot, C., Chevrier, V., Thomas, V.: A new swarm mechanism based on social spiders colonies : from web weaving to region detection. Web Intelligence and Agent Systems : An International Journal - WIAS **1** (2003) 47–64

11. Grassé, P.P.: La reconstruction du nid et les coordinations interindividuelles chez bellicositermes natalensis et cubitermes sp., la théorie de la stigmergie : essais d'interprétation du comportement des termites constructeurs. Ins. Soc. **6** (1959) 41–84
12. Thomas, V., Bourjot, C., Chevrier, V., Desor, D.: Hamelin: A model for collective adaptation based on internal stimuli. In: From animals to animats 8 - Eighth International Conference on the Simulation of Adaptive Behaviour - SAB'04, Los Angeles, USA. (2004) 425–434
13. Theraulaz, G., Bonabeau, E., Deneubourg, J.L.: Response threshold reinforcement and division of labour in insect societies. Proc. Roy. Soc. London B 265 (1998) 327–332
14. Hemelrijk, C.K.: Dominance interactions, spatial dynamics and emergent reciprocity in a virtual world. In: Proceedings of the fourth international conference on simulation of adaptive behavior. (1996) 545–552
15. Edmonds, B.: Using the experimental method to produce reliable self-organised systems. In: Proceedings of the 2nd International Workshop on Engineering Self-Organising Applications (ESOA 2004) at 3rd AAMAS, New York. (2004)
16. Edmonds, B., Bryson, J.: The insufficiency of formal design methods the necessity of an experimental approach for the understanding and control of complex mas. In: Proceedings of the 3rd Internation Joint Conference on Autonomous Agents and Multi Agent Systems (AAMAS'04), New York, ACM (2004) 936–943
17. Bourjot, C., Chevrier, V.: A platform for the analysis of artificial self-organized systems. In: Proceedings of Advances in Intelligent Systems - Theory and Applications AISTA 2004. Luxembourg. (2004)

A Sample Application of ADELFE
Focusing on Analysis and Design
The Mechanical Synthesis Problem

Davy Capera, Gauthier Picard, Marie-Pierre Gleizes,
and Pierre Glize

IRIT, Université Paul Sabatier,
F-31062 Toulouse Cedex, France
{picard, capera, gleizes, glize}@irit.fr
http://www.irit.fr/SMAC

Abstract. This paper aims at explaining how to follow an agent-oriented process to develop a multi-agent mechanism design system. ADELFE
methodology is devoted to adaptive multi-agent systems in which adaptation is enabled by cooperative self-organization. Two main works are
emphasized. First, the analysis leads to the agent identification by studying the interactions both between the system and its environment and
within the system itself. Second, the different modules of the agents and
their cooperative attitude are modeled during the design phase. Such an
approach is promising, but raises some difficulties considering the notion
of cooperation, which is discussed before concluding.

1 Introduction

In spite of the ever increasing number of developed agent-oriented applications,
Multi-Agent Systems have still not manage to break through to the industrial
side. This lack of acknowledgment may have two main reasons. First, to transmit
any technology to industrial level, academics must provide guidelines, formalisms
and tools to manipulate their technologies. MAS community has done a large
effort in this methodological domain. DESIRE [1] or GAIA [2] are examples of
early agent-oriented methodologies embedded in industrial projects that provide
rich formalisms. Moreover, for a few years, a real work has been made in nor-
malizing agent-oriented concepts, as in the AUML community within the OMG
[3]. Some methodologies, such as ADELFE[1] [4] has been enriched by pedagogical tutorials –significant examples of how to develop an application with a given
method– and tools to enlarge the multi-agent developers community, in the same
way than MESSAGE/INGENIAS [5] or agentTool [6]. The second reason may
be the lack of real applications for everyday industrial use. MAS community has

---

[1] ADELFE a French RNTL-funded project which partners are ARTAL Technologies
and TNI-Valiosys from industry and IRIT and L3I from academia.

M.-P. Gleizes, A. Omicini, and F. Zambonelli (Eds.): ESAW 2004, LNAI 3451, pp. 231–244, 2005.

to exhibit proofs of the agent technology efficiency and to tackle unsolved or mis-solved problems. For instance, the time table (or scheduling) problem has not been really solved by agent-technology, even if some works seem promising [7]. But real comparisons to already used technology, such as CSP-based or evolutionary solvers, has not yet exhibited agents' relevance. In this article, as an example of this kind of application, we will expound a problem which has been proposed by the aeronautics industry: the mechanism design.

Mechanism design consists in assembling mechanical components such as links (rigid bodies, bars) and joints (hinges, cams, etc.), in order to build a mechanical system which performs a specific function such as following a precise trajectory. Our objective is to develop an automated tool – based on the adaptive multi-agent systems paradigm – which is able to synthesize a mechanism from a given set of goals and constraints through a self-assembling process. ADELFE method is devoted to develop applications in which components cooperatively self-organise to reach an adequate and adapted functionnality, and thus ADELFE is relevant to tackle the mechanical synthesis problem. Currently, there is no software, used by industrial mechanism designers, that includes any tool to support the synthesis phase of the mechanism design. Nevertheless, some researches were done in this way by [8], using a multi-expert system based on agent principle, or [9] which is based on an abstract representation of the kinematic structures.

With the aim of illustrating the use of the ADELFE methodology to a problem of mechanical synthesis, the article is structured as follows. Section 2 expounds the ADELFE methodology and its foundations. Sections 3 and 4 explain the application of the analysis and design phases, i.e. how to fill in the different modules of the agents. Finally, after a brief discussion in section 6, the paper is concluded with some perspectives.

2   ADELFE Overview

ADELFE enables the development of software with emergent functionality and consists in a notation based on UML/AUML, a design method, a platform made up of a graphical design tool [10] and a library of components that can be used to make the application development easier.

2.1   Process, Notations and Tools

The objective of ADELFE is to cover all the phases of a classical software design from the requirements to the deployment. ADELFE process is an extension of the RUP (Rational Unified Process) [4] and adds some specific steps to design adaptive systems. Only the requirements, analysis and design require modifications in order to be tailored to AMAS and are presented in the next paragraphs. ADELFE focuses on some aspects not already considered by existing methodologies such as complex environment, dynamics or software adaptation led by self-organization during which models are specified using UML/AUML notations [3]. OpenTool software, released by TNI-Valiosys, has been modified to fit with these notations and Adaptive Multi-Agent Systems (AMAS) requirements. Likewise, the process is supported by an interactive tool with the aim of easing following the process by monitoring the advancement, the produced models and documents, and by providing a guideline example. These tools are freely available at `www.irit.fr/ADELFE`.

2.2   Theoretical Foundations

The Adaptive Multi-Agent System (AMAS) theory has been used in several projects and applications. It aims at defining adaptive multi-agent systems in which self-organization is led by local cooperation. In such systems, adaptation is viewed as a three-level concept. At the higher level, the system has to compute an adequate coherent function as a reaction to the dynamisms of its environment. To obtain a new function that fits better with the environment, the system has to change its internal organization at the medium level. The organization of the MAS is represented by links between the agents. These links can be for instance workflow links, belief links or more simply communication links. Organizational changes are consequences of local link changes between agents. Therefore, at the lower level, agents must know how to change their links with their acquaintances to produce a new organization, and then a new coherent function, which induces the need of a local –i.e. not explicitly informed of the global function– criterion to decide when changes are necessary. The AMAS theory proposes to use the cooperation criterion as the engine of self-organization. Cooperation is defined in three points corresponding to the "perceive - decide - act" agents' life-cycle [11]:

(c_1) All perceived signals must be understood without ambiguity
(c_2) The received information is useful for the agent's reasoning
(c_3) Reasoning leads to useful actions toward other agents

Consequently, an agent must change its links when it detects it does not fit with this criterion. We then use a proscriptive definition of cooperation ($\neg c_1 \lor \neg c_2 \lor \neg c_3$) called non cooperative situations (or NCS). If an agent is in a NCS, it acts to try to act to come back to a cooperative situation (to be as cooperative as possible). This approach can be viewed as an exception oriented specification, where the program functionality is principally defined by "what it must not do" instead of "what it must do" in classical programming. This framework enables to prove the functional adequacy theorem [11]: *"For any functionally adequate system in a given environment, there is a system having a cooperative internal medium which realizes an equivalent function"*. It has an important methodological impact : to design a system, designers only have to ensure agents' behaviors are cooperative to ensure the system provides an adequate function. It also raises some problems : "How can we design agents to obtain coherent societies?" The ADELFE methodology aims at providing an answer to these design difficulties.

3 Analysis

The analysis work aims at abstracting the application domain into classes start-ing from the requirements. In an agent-oriented process, it should also lead to the identification of the agent classes by analyzing the interaction models.

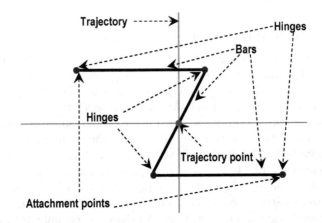

Fig. 1. An example of a 4-bars mechanism

3.1 Domain Analysis

As we are working collaboratively with partners coming from aeronautical indus-try (European project SYNAMEC[2]), our software – named Mechanical Synthesis Solver or MSS – focuses on solving design problems for "X-bars" mechanisms. This kind of mechanisms contains only three types of mechanical components: rigid bodies, joints (rotoidal or prismatic) and attachment points. Usually, the goal of the mechanism consists in following a given trajectory, in avoiding obsta-cles and in staying contained in a given envelope. Mechanisms devoted to control plane wings ailerons or outer flaps of nozzle fit with this "X-bars" mechanisms pattern. The figure 1 shows a "4-bars" mechanism made up by four rotoidal joints (hinges), three rigid bodies (bars) and two attachments points to the en-velope – which is not drawn here[3]. The actuation is a rotation of the upper left hinge which cyclically performs a top-down wipe while the "trajectory point" roughly fits with the vertical trajectory all along. In section 2.2, we claimed that the system adaptation is triggered by interactions occurring between the system and its environment. Obviously, the motion computation of mechanisms is not a trivial task and so we will use an external tool MECANO to compute this

---

[2] SYNAMEC is a Growth European project involving Samtech (Belgium), ALA (Italy), Cranfield University (England), INTEC (Argentina), Paul Sabatier Univer-sity (France), SABCA (Belgium), SNECMA (France).

[3] The envelope on which the attachment points are fixed is topologically viewed as the fourth bar

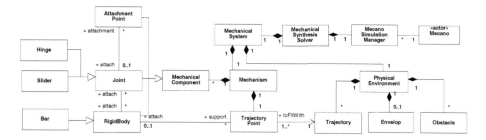

Fig. 2. Preliminary class diagram of the MSS domain

simulation of the system activity. Thus, the MSS learns a relevant mechanism by using a loop composed of the following phases:

1. The simulation engine computes the motion of the current mechanism.
2. Data related to the new mechanism state are sent to the mechanical components in order to update their state.
3. In compliance with the AMAS theory, MSS performs optimization by solving NCS detected by the agents, which leads to a new mechanism.

The interface with the simulator is performed through files which describe, in input, characteristics of the mechanism, the environment and the commands related to the desired motion (the "actuation function"). Moreover this interface allows to recover the new mechanism characteristics after MECANO has computed the motion. The domain description is represented in a preliminary class diagram shown in figure 2.

3.2 AMAS Adequacy

The next activity of ADELFE analysis is related to the AMAS theory. With through eleven questions, an ADELFE tool provides a measure of the AMAS adequacy degree. That tool answers two main questions : Is the use of an adaptive multi-agent system useful to tackle the problem ? Are there any parties of the system which need to be broken up into adaptive multi-agent systems ?

The main criterion that leads to use an AMAS for the mechanism design problem, is the complexity: there is a huge number of mechanisms to check. Moreover, this search space is discontinuous: minor topological modifications can lead to drastic modification of the global behavior. The fact that the system is open (some components are added to the mechanism during the process) and dynamical (the user can interact with the system to drive the process) increases the complexity. Finally, mechanisms are made up by several, and potentially very numerous, more simple entities, which match with multi-agent system paradigm.

3.3 Agent Identification

Agent identification relevance depends on the nature of the problem to tackle. When considering systems with which humans strongly interact, designers nat-

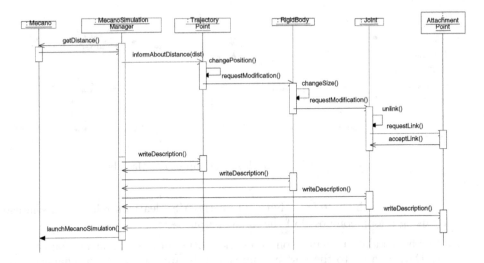

Fig. 3. A sample MSS sequence diagram

urally identify agents as representative of human actors. Therefore, methodologies which are specific to this kind of problems do not address this issue. In the analysis workflow of GAIA [2], the agents are already identified and the methodology does not provide anything to realize this identification. But, when considering simulation-based solving systems, such as MSS, agent identification is not so clear.

As a function of the theoretical paradigms used, methodologies propose several ways to identify agents. In TROPOS the agents are found inside the set of actors, but it results from the analysis of the predefined goals and soft-goals [12]. In AAII, the elaboration and refinement of the agent model and the interaction model help the designer to define agents [13]. The agent definition, which is given in MESSAGE [14] and in ADELFE, defines the features that will be ascribed to the entities that the developer will choose to consider as agents. Moreover, ADELFE proposes to analyze preliminary interaction models to identify high-risk entities in terms of cooperation or cognition.

Figure 3 shows a typical information flow from the MECANO application to each part of a mechanism (and the other way round). Considering ADELFE, agent identification focuses on the analysis of active objects. From the MECANO result file, the MecanoSimulationManager gets the distance between the Trajectory and the TrajectoryPoint. So, if this distance is different from zero, the position of the TrajectoryPoint has to be changed to get closer to the Trajectory. Either, the TrajectoryPoint changes its position by itself, or this modification is performed by the RigidBoby which it is attached to, as in this example. In the same way, a RigidBody modification could be obtained by changing its shape, its position or by delegating the problem to its neighbors –Joint in the example. Therefore, in a general way, this kind of problem can be solved either by changing properties of the given component or by propagating the problem. But, sometimes the problem could not be solved thanks to these modifications, and so the topology of the mechanism has to be changed. In our example, the link between the RigidBody and the Joint is broken and a new link with a compatible component (AttachmentPoint for instance) has to be created. Finally, the mechanical components inform the manager of their positions as input for the next MECANO computation.

By using AMAS terminology, TrajectoryPoint can be in a NCS –called incompetence– when it does not fit with the trajectory. In the same manner, a RigidBody or AttachmentPoint are useless if not attached to joints, and vice versa. In addition, these MechanicalComponent classes and the TrajectoryPoint have to manage their acquaintances not to flood the system by information exchange, and have to be able to add or remove agents from their acquaintance data base. These criteria are sufficient to identify these classes as being cooperative agent classes. To sum up, the identified agent classes are: MechanicalComponent and all its sub-classes, and TrajectoryPoint (see figures 2 and 4). To encapsulate common properties, a top-level generic MechanicalAgent class from which the two previous classes inherit is defined.

4   Agent Design

Generally, in object-oriented methodologies, the design works lead to a precise definition of classes in terms of fields, methods, and also results in the model of the dynamic behaviors of these classes by using sequence diagrams and state-machines. In ADELFE, these two aspects – static and dynamic – are met by filling the different modules of the agents (including their cooperative attitude) and by modeling their interaction languages with AUML protocols.

4.1   Agents' Modules

ADELFE proposes a generic cooperative agent model [15]. This model decomposes agent's cognitive functions into six modules. The main mechanical agents' modules are shown in figure 4, in *bold face* : characteristics, perceptions, actions, skills, aptitudes, representations and cooperation.

The Characteristic module which manages the intrinsic properties of agents. These mainly are the points (named "noeuds" or nodes in MECANO) which describe the mechanical components (the two extremities of a bar, the two attach points of a hinge, etc.). Each characteristic can be updated either by the agent itself or consequently to a specific message reception from MECANO (after a simulation step).

The Interaction module is the interface between the agent and its environment. This module is made up of two submodules: the Action module and the Perception module. The Action module contains the actions available for the agent and manages the messages sending (sendMessage), i.e. the outputs. Figure 4 shows agents always have actions related to their characteristics (linkAttach1, linkAttach2, unlinkAttach1 or unlinkAttach2) and other specific actions (changePosition in Bar and TrajectoryPoint).The Perception module mainly manages the re-

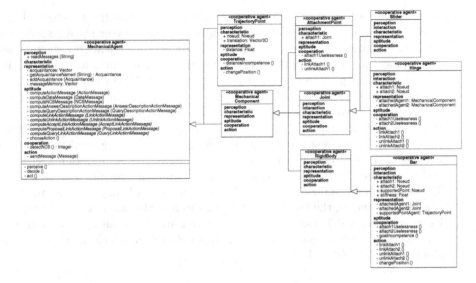

Fig. 4. The agent class diagram for MSS

ceived messages (a mechanical agent only perceives its environment through messages by using readMessage method), i.e. the inputs.

The Representation module manages information about the agent's environment (social or physical) or itself. It contains the acquaintances of the agent, i.e. information about the other agents of the system. For each known agent, the representation module contains its type, its name, etc. This knowledge base is dynamically updated during the agent lifetime (addAcquaintance). MechanicalAgent can also store previously received messages into a messageMemory. Moreover agents can have information on themselves in terms of their type – for example a Bar and Hinge owns information about agents they are connected to – or specific data such as the distance to the trajectory for the TrajectoryPoint.

The Cooperation module contains the list of the NCS (see section 2.2). Each NCS is described by a conditional trigger and by the list of actions that the agent can use to solve the problem. This module is described in the section 4.2.

The Aptitude module manages messages processing according to the message type and action selection. For instance every MechanicalAgent can ask its description to another agent and answer to such a query. Therefore, it must have aptitudes to process these kind of messages (computeQueryDescriptionActionMessage and computeAnswerDescriptionActionMessage). Moreover, since MechanicalAgents has to self-assembly, they must be able to process messages about link or unlink actions (computeLinkActionMessage, computeUnlinkActionMessage, computeQueryLinkActionMessage, etc.). These abstract methods must be implemented in every MechanicalAgent's subclass. The chooseAction method selects the actions to do at a given time considering the current state of knowledge (perception, messages, representation and triggered NCS).

The Skill module is not used for MechanicalAgents because they don't perform their "function" themselves (it is simulated by MECANO) and then they can't have any knowledge about their real activity – MECANO computation is a black-box from the agents' point of view.

4.2   Agent's Cooperative Attitude

The Cooperation module contains the local cooperation rules that lead agents' self-organization. Ideally, every agent knows when it is no more cooperative and then knows what to do to come back to a cooperative state. This is the main design challenge of AMAS: find all the NCS. In the MSS application, two main NCS have been identified:

uselessness: when an agent does not have all its partners. For example, a Bar or a Hinge or a AttachmentPoint is useless if one of its attachment points is not connected to another MechanicalComponent. To solve this NCS, agents must find a partner by negotiating for example as seen in section 4.3.

incompetence: when an agent does not reach its goal. For example, a TrajectoryPoint agent is incompetent if its distance to the trajectory is different from zero. This situation has already been detected during the agent identification as being a criterion to "agentify" the TrajectoryPoint class. The relevant action that agents must perform in such situations is to change their position to get closer to their goal for example.

Every agent owns a method called detectNCS which applies cooperation rules and put the solving actions in an "action-to-do" list that will be used by the Aptitude module when it performs chooseAction.

4.3   Agents' Interactions

ADELFE proposes to model agent interactions by specifying AUML protocols [3]. These protocols enable to describe agents' interaction languages (the meth-

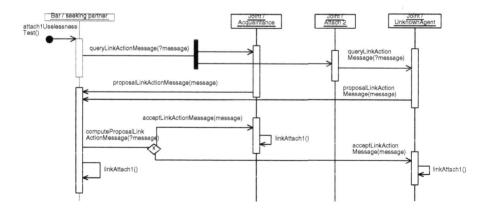

Fig. 5. A sample protocol diagram for MSS

ods they need to communicate) and resolution negotiation algorithm. For example, the figure 5 shows the resolution protocol for a Bar agent to solve a uselessness NCS. Here, the Bar sends a query to two Joints it knows: the one which is already linked to (Attach2 role) and another it may have encountered before (Acquaintance role). This last one directly answers positively. On the other hand, Attach2 cannot answer positively because it is already linked. Therefore, it delegates and informs another agent it knows about the situation (UnknownAgent role). This last one answers positively too. Now, the Bar must analyze the proposals and decide which agent will be connected to the free attachment. This decision making process is labeled by the computeProposalLinkActionMessage method on the XOR node. In terms of the results of this decision, the Bar may send acceptance to its preferred partner and then perform a link action.

5   Some Results for Dimensional Adjustment

A prototype of the modeled system has been implemented for "X-bars" mechanism problems, and especially to study the dimensional adjustment. These experiments focus on the resolution actions related to distanceIncompetence and goalIncompetence NCS.

5.1   Reactive Algorithm

Firstly, a very reactive algorithm has been tested. The Bar's NCS resolution action is directly induced by the stiffness value it perceives – the Bar applies a

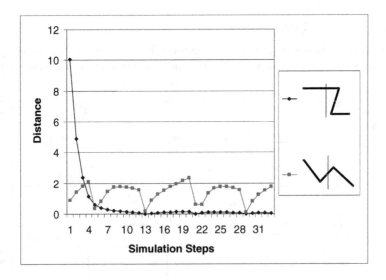

Fig. 6. Results for two different 4-bars mechanisms with a reactive resolution algorithm

translation vector to each of its ends – that leads to a modification of its position and/or length. In the same manner, the TrajectoryPoint computes a translation for its position.

Figure 6 shows the results for two different 4-bar simulations with initial mechanisms whose dimensions are faulty. Distance between the trajectory point and the trajectory quickly decreases for the first example. Simulation results in a well-sized mechanism as shown in figure 1. Nevertheless, the distance is not exactly null because the only solution is not a straight line (as specified by the user) but a very thin 8-shaped cycle. On the other hand, the reactive algorithm fails to find a solution for the second example. In fact, this algorithm cannot find solutions that requires the mechanism to reach and cross a singular position in the search space (a straight-line-shaped mechanism for example).

5.2   Learning-Based Algorithms

To address this problem, a second kind of algorithms has been tested by adding learning capabilities to agents. Each agent learns the modification it has to perform by reasoning on the intensity of the NCS it perceives (based on reinforcement learning principles). A new problem occurs with the Bar when it changes its ends, because MECANO has to re-assembly the mechanism, which disturbs the agents' learning (agents cannot rightly judge the impact of their actions). To address this second problem, a solution is to remove physical resolution actions to the Bars, i.e. they can only send messages and propagate their NCS to other agents (Hinges). Nevertheless, this solution is equivalent to algorithms based on cost functions, and therefore implies the same problems of crossing local maxima or singular points.

5.3   Further Works

Previous algorithms could be used by designers to optimize dimensions of a given roughly well-designed mechanism. But, our system aims at autonomously designing the best possible mechanism by self-assembly of elementary components (i.e. self-organization of MechanicalAgents). Therefore, the system must be able to find the best dimensioning for a given topology, independently of the initial state, which is not the case of previously proposed algorithms. The idea is now to explore other local criteria to lead dimensional adjustments, such as length balance of bars connected to the same joint, minimization of dimensions and motion lock avoidance.

6   Discussion

AMAS theory proposes an interesting approach to develop adaptive system by designing cooperative agents. The main outcome of this kind of theory is to support the design of artificial systems with a theoretical background whereas to "mimic" natural systems. In a near future, the key of artificial system design will be to understand mechanisms which implement complex systems and relations between micro and macro behaviors.

Nevertheless, the notion of cooperation raises some methodological problems. Firstly, AMAS theory ensures the multi-agent system will produce an adequate function if all the agents composing it are cooperative. It means that designers must exhaustively list all the possible local non cooperative situation. Currently, ADELFE only proposes an analysis by NCS type, state by state, for each agent. But during this analysis there is no mean to ensure the exhaustiveness of NCS enumeration - only hints and guidance. Moreover, cooperation notion remains vague and strongly depends on the granularity of agents. Secondly, if we suppose NCS as being exhaustively found, what are the actions to perform to solve them? Once again this problem is strongly linked to the notion of cooperation and many algorithms might be used. For example, several algorithms have been tested for actions related to incompetence NCS: reactive algorithms, learning-based algorithms, cooperative memory-based algorithms. In this last solution, each agent stores errors (size and direction) it perceives into a cooperative memory module (which is recursively defined as an AMAS). Then, each error is represented by a cooperative agent which acts according to NCS rules. For example, if two errors are similar, the smallest one disappears, since it is a concurrent situation. At the agent's decision phase, this module computes the most cooperative action to decrease the size of errors –the main idea is to decrease the worse error avoiding creating a new worse one.

To tackle these problems, two paths could be explored: theoretical or/and experimental. By developing theories on adaptive multi-agent systems, we could find new properties on cooperation. Yet, the AMAS theory employs cooperation notion as a generic behavior of an entity which has to be instantiated for a given application. Therefore, discovery of new NCS types cannot result from demonstrations, but only from observation and generalization. Considering a more experimental angle of attack seems more relevant. Future works should focus on more interactive methodologies, as the *Living Design* concept does [16]. This approach proposes to shift agent design to more living phases (test, deployment and maintenance) compared to classic object-oriented design processes. Designing agents becomes a more interactive activity during which designers equip running agents with their modules, in real time. It requires defining minimal behavior and norms on agent concepts. FIPA does a lot of work in this direction. In addition, ADELFE project will now focus on such problematics thanks to the MDA paradigm, by defining more detailed agent models.

7   Conclusion

In this article, the ADELFE methodology has been applied to a mechanical synthesis problem. The two main phases, analysis and design, led to a self-organizing multi-agent model where each mechanical component is "agentified". Self-organization of the collective is a way to reach an adequate structure using agents' cooperative attitude.

Nevertheless, the notion of cooperative attitude raises some problems such as exhaustiveness of the cooperation rules for each agent and the choice of the most cooperative action at a given time to reach a more cooperative state. This implies to study different heuristics and algorithms to tackle as close as possible the notion of cooperation as defined in the AMAS theory. Thus, two main future work directions are opened. First, by formalizing agent and multi-agent models or refining their meta-models, some new properties may be discovered, such as the relevance of a local cooperation measure. Second, experience is the main way to succeed in finding cooperation rules. The concept of Living Design may be an real solution to interactively define agents' models and cooperative attitude.

Finally, a prototype called Mechanical Synthesis Solver (MSS) has been developed and shows promising results on dimensional adjustments [17]. The next step of these experiments is to use self-organization to modify the topology of mechanisms by adding, removing and spatially re-organizing agents.

References

1. Brazier, F., Jonker, C., Treur, J.: Compositional Design and Reuse of a Generic Agent Model. International Journal of Cooperative Information Systems **9** (2000)
2. Wooldridge, M., Jennings, N., Kinny, D.: A Methodology for Agent-Oriented Analysis and Design. In Oren Etzioni and Jörg P. Müller and Jeffrey M. Bradshaw, ed.: Proceedings of the 3rd International Conference on Autonomous Agents (Agents 99), ACM Press (1999)
3. Odell, J., Parunak, H., Bauer, B.: Extending UML for Agents. In: Proceedings of the Agent Oriented Information Systems (AOIS) Workshop at the 17th National Conference on Artificial Intelligence (AAAI). (2000)
4. Picard, G., Gleizes, M.P.: The ADELFE Methodology – Designing Adaptive Cooperative Multi-Agent Systems (Chapter 8). In Bergenti, F. and Gleizes, M-P. and Zambonelli, F., ed.: Methodologies and Software Engineering for Agent Systems, Kluwer Publishing (2004)
5. Gomez Sanz, J., Fuentes, R.: Agent Oriented System Engineering with INGENIAS. In: Fourth Iberoamerican Workshop on Multi-Agent Systems, Iberagents'02. (2002)
6. DeLoach, S., Wood, M.: Developing Multiagent Systems with agentTool. In Castelfranchi, C. and Lesperance, Y., ed.: Intelligent Agents VII. AgentTheories Architectures and Languages, 7th International Workshop (ATAL 2000), Springer-Verlag (LNCS 1986) (2001)
7. Bernon, C., Gleizes, M.P., Peyruqueou, S., Picard, G.: ADELFE: a Methodology for Adaptive Multi-Agent Systems Engineering. In Petta, P. and Tolksdorf, R. and Zambonelli, F., ed.: Third International Workshop on Engineering Societies in the Agents World (ESAW-2002), Springer-Verlag (LNAI 2577) (2002)
8. Campbell, M., Cagan, J., Kotovsky, K.: Agent-based Synthesis of electro-mechanical design configurations. In: Proceedings of DETC98 1998 ASME Design Engineering Technical Conferences. (1998)
9. Tsai, L.W.: Mechanism Design: Enumeration of kinematic structures according to function. CRC Press (2001)
10. Bernon, C., Camps, V., Gleizes, M.P., Picard, G.: Tools for Self-Organizing Applications Engineering. In: First International Workshop on Engineering Self-Organizing Applications (ESOA) at AAMAS'03, Melbourne, Australia (2003)

11. Capera, D., George, J., Gleizes, M.P., Glize, P.: The AMAS theory for complex problem solving based on self-organizing cooperative agents. In: 1st International workshop on Theory and Practice of Open Computational Systems (TAPOCS) at IEEE 12th International Workshop on Enabling Technologies: Infrastructure for Collaborative Enterprises (WETICE 2003), IEEE Computer Society (2003) 383–388

12. Castro, J., Kolp, M., Mylopoulos, J.: A Requirements-driven Development Methodology. In Dittrich, K., Geppert, A., Norrie, M., eds.: Proceedings of the 13th International Conference on Advanced Information Systems Engineering (CAiSE'01), Springer-Verlag (LNCS 2068) (2001) 108–123

13. Kinny, D., Georgeff, M., Rao, A.: A methodology and modelling technique for systems of BDI agents. In de Velde, W.V., Perram, J.W., eds.: Agents Breaking Away: Proceedings of the Seventh European Workshop on Modelling Autonomous Agents in a MultiAgent World, Springer-Verlag (LNAI 1038) (1996) 51–71

14. Caire, G., Coulier, W., Garijo, F., Gomez, J., Pavon, J., Leal, F., Chainho, P., Kearney, P., Stark, J., Evans, R., Massonet, P.: Agent Oriented Analysis Using Message/UML. In Wooldridge, M., Wei, G., Ciancarini, P., eds.: Agent-Oriented Software Engineering II, Second International Workshop, AOSE 2001, Springer-Verlag (LNCS 2222) (2001) 119–135

15. Bernon, C., Camps, V., Gleizes, M.P., Picard, G.: Designing Agents' Behaviors within the Framework of ADELFE Methodology. In: Fourth International Workshop on Engineering Societies in the Agents World (ESAW-2003), Imperial College London, UK (2003)

16. George, J.P., Picard, G., Gleizes, M.P., Glize, P.: Living Design for Open Computational Systems. In: International Workshop Theory And Practice of Open Computational Systems (TAPOCS) at 12th IEEE International Workshop on Enabling Technologies: Infrastructure for Collaborative Enterprises (WETICE'03), Linz, Austria, IEEE Computer Society (2003)

17. Capera, D., Gleizes, M.P., Glize, P.: Mechanism Type Synthesis based on Self-Assembling Agents. Journal on Applied Artificial Intelligence **18** (To appear in 2004)

SONIA: A Methodology for Natural Agent Development

Fernando Alonso, Sonia Frutos, Loïc Martínez, and César Montes

Facultad de Informática, Universidad Politécnica de Madrid,
28660 Boadilla del Monte (Madrid), Spain
{falonso, sfrutos, loic, cmontes}@fi.upm.es

Abstract. *Agent-Oriented Software Engineering* has emerged as a powerful engineering discipline that can deal with the complexity of today's software systems (primarily in distributed and open environments) better than other more traditional approaches. However, AOSE does not provide a software development process that naturally leads, if the problem so requires, to an agent architecture. Current agent development methodologies have two separate drawbacks. One is that development processes tend to target an agent organization, which is not necessarily always the best structure, as of the requirements definition stage. The other is that the identification and design of agents are complex, and designer experience plays an essential role in their definition. In this paper, we present the SONIA methodology (Set of mOdels for a Natural Identification of Agents) in an attempt to solve these problems. Based on a generic problem-independent analysis and a bottom-up agent identification process, SONIA naturally outputs an agent-based system.

1 Introduction

Agent-Oriented Software Engineering (AOSE), based on the agent paradigm, has materialized as a powerful technology for developing complex software systems, and it is well suited for tackling the complexity of today's software systems [1]. Having emerged, like so many other disciplines, from Artificial Intelligence, it is now a melting pot of many different computing sciences areas (Artificial Intelligence, Software Engineering, Robotics, and Distributed Computing).

The AOSE concept includes the development of *autonomous software agents* (autonomous elements, with reactive and proactive social ability, trying to accomplish their own task [2]), *multi-agent systems* (MAS) (a set of autonomous agents that interact with each other, each representing an independent focus of system control [3]), and *agent societies* (where the social role of the agents and social laws delimit agent operation [4]).

Agents, MAS and agent societies are now well enough known for researchers and companies to be attracted by the prospects of large-scale agent engineering. The interest they are showing is actually the logical consequence of the successes achieved in this direction, resembling the sequence of events that already took place in other development engineering disciplines (like objects, for example) [5].

M.-P. Gleizes, A. Omicini, and F. Zambonelli (Eds.): ESAW 2004, LNAI 3451, pp. 245–260, 2005.
© Springer-Verlag Berlin Heidelberg 2005

In this paper, we describe the SONIA methodology, an approach for naturally producing a MAS from the system requirements. In section 2, we explain what problems AOSE faces. Section 3 contains an analysis of current agent development methodologies. Section 4 describes the structure of the proposed SONIA methodology and its application to the ALBOR project. Finally, section 5 states the conclusions on the natural development of agents.

2 Problems of AOSE

AOSE is obviously not a panacea, as its use is not always justified. There are problems that an agent approach cannot solve, and others where the outlay and development time required by such an approach would be too costly to be acceptable for companies. We have identified a set of topics to be taken into account when applying AOSE to real problems [6]:

- *Reach agreement on agent theory.* This new paradigm will not be able to expand unless the agent model is standardized with respect to what characteristics define an agent, what types of architecture are available for agents, what agent organizations are possible, what types of interactions there are between agents, etc. Just as UML (Unified Modeling Language) [7] was established to model objects, a modeling language for agents needs to be agreed upon (perhaps AUML [8]).
- *Provide mechanisms for deciding whether the problem should be dealt with using a MAS.* Even if it is initially justified to conceive a multi-agent solution for a given problem, a MAS could turn out to be no good in the end, because, for example, no agents can be identified or there are no interactions between the identified agents.
- *Train development team members in the field of agents and MAS.* A team of developers is not usually familiar with agents and MAS these days, which means that they will have to be trained beforehand in this field if they are to be receptive to such projects and to prevent delays in project development.
- *Provide special-purpose programming languages and development tools.* Although the last few years have seen new languages for programming agent behavior take root, general-purpose languages like Java and C++, etc., are widely used. On the other hand, there are fewer development tools for representing agent structure, and they focus mainly on a particular agent architecture.
- *Use methodologies suited to the development processes.* For organizations to adopt MAS development, the right methodology needs to be provided to guide the team of developers towards the achievement of objectives, without this requiring in-depth training in this field. A critical stage in the development of a MAS is the selection of the methodology to be followed. A good methodology should provide the models for defining the elements of the multi-agent environment (agents, objects and interactions) and the design guidelines for identifying these elements, their components and the relationships between them.

As regards the question of methodology, a wide variety of *methodological proposals* have emerged for AOSE development [9][10][11][12]. Although they have all played an important role in establishing this field, they do not provide suitable mechanisms for formulating a *natural* process for developing a MAS system or an agent society from system requirements. That is, the gradual discovery and identification of concepts, relationships, tasks, knowledge, behaviors, objects, agents, MAS and agent societies from the problem statement. Additionally, a good methodology should not force a given architecture (object-oriented, agent-oriented, etc.) upon developers from the beginning. It is the system specifications analysis that should point developers towards the best suited architecture for solving the problem.

Based on research and development efforts in the field of AOSE, we think that an agent-oriented development methodology should have the following features [6]:

- *It should not condition the use of the agent paradigm right from analysis.* It is too risky to decide whether the system is to be designed using a multi-agent architecture in the analysis or conceptualization phase, as the problem is not fully specified at this early stage of development. It is not until the design phase that enough is known about the problem specifications and architecture to make this decision.
- *It should naturally lead to the conclusion of whether or not it is feasible to develop the system as a MAS.* At present, it is the developer who has to decide, based on his or her expertise, whether or not to use a MAS to solve the problem. Because of its high cost, this is a tricky decision that cannot be made using heuristics. Note that, depending on the application domain, design and implementation using a multi-agent architecture may have a high development cost (time, money and resources), apart from calling for experienced personnel. On the other hand, the modularity of multi-agent systems may improve development costs.
- *It should systematically identify the components of a MAS.* Current methodologies leave too much to the designer with respect, for example, to agent identification. Designer experience is therefore vital for producing a quality MAS.

  Component-driven bottom-up agent identification is the most objective criterion, as it depends exclusively on the problem and eases the systematization and automation of the identification process. On the other hand, the role (or actor)-driven criterion is more subjective, as roles or actors depend on the analyst/designer who identifies them.
- *If the problem specifications call for an agent society, it should naturally lead to this organizational model.* The development of a software system using a reductionist, constructivist or agent society architecture should be derived from the problem specifications, which will lead to the best suited architecture. Current agent-oriented methodologies focus on the development of the actual agent architecture (internal agent level) and/or its interactions with other MAS agents (external agent level), but very few cover the concept of social organization.
- *It should produce reusable agents, should be easy to apply and not require excessive knowledge of agent technology.* The concept of reuse has been one of the biggest contributions to software development. The provision of libraries has furthered procedure-, object-, or component-oriented engineering. For this advance to take place in AOSE, agent components (interaction protocols, etc.) need to be reusable and easy to use. Current agent-oriented design methodologies and methods do not account for reusable systems and call for high proficiency in MAS

technology for use. As MAS technology is related to many disciplines (artificial intelligence, psychology, sociology, economics, etc.), intensive knowledge of agent technology is required. This relegates the design of these systems to universities, research centers and companies with the latest technology.

The specific characteristics of MAS and MAS development-related problems indicate that agent-based problem solving cannot be dealt with intuitively. It calls for a methodological process that naturally leads to the use of agents in problem solving.

3   Analysis of Current Agent Development Methodologies

On account of the advance in agent technology over the last ten years, several methodologies have emerged to drive MAS development [9][10][11][12]. These methodologies are classed according to the discipline on which they are based (Fig. 1):

- *Agent Technology-Based Approaches*: they focus on social level abstractions, like the agent, group or organization.
- *Object Orientation-Based Approaches*: they are characterized by extending object-oriented techniques to include the notion of agency.
- *Knowledge Engineering-Based Approaches*: they are characterized by emphasizing the identification, acquisition and modeling of knowledge used by the agent components.

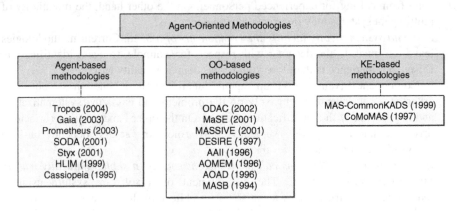

Fig. 1. Agent-Oriented Methodologies

3.1   Agent Technology-Based Methodologies

Agent Technology-Based Methodologies focus on social level abstractions, like the agent, group or organization.

The most representative methodologies are: Tropos [13], Gaia [14], Prometheus [15], SODA [16], Styx [17], HLIM [18] and Cassiopeia [19]. Table 1 describes the most significant methodological aspects of agent technology-based methodologies for our analysis.

Table 1. Agent Technology-Based Methodologies

agent paradigm selection	specification or analysis phase (all)	design phase (none)
agent identification process	role-driven top-down (all)	component-driven bottom-up (none)
MAS aspects	intra- & inter-agent (Tropos, Gaia, Prometheus, Styx, HLIM)	social structure (SODA, Cassiopeia)
environment analysis	environment (SODA)	objects (Tropos, Prometheus, Styx, SODA)

Although this methodological line is gaining in importance in agent development, the methodologies suffer from some limitations on key points:

- These methodologies propose the use of the agent paradigm as of the specification (Prometheus, HLIM, Cassiopeia) or analysis (Tropos, Gaia, SODA, Styx) phases. The choice of a multi-agent system should be a *design* decision. Therefore, a good agent-oriented methodology should not conduct a specific agent-oriented analysis. None of the methodologies account for the use of a generic analysis model that can be used to evaluate whether or not a multi-agent approach is suitable.
- All of the methodologies identify agents from social roles (Gaia, SODA, Styx, HLIM, Cassiopeia) or actors (Tropos, Prometheus) following a top-down identification process and none from their components.
- Three aspects need to be dealt with to develop a MAS: intra-agent structure, inter-agent structure and social structure. Most of the methodologies cover the intra-agent and inter-agent aspects (Tropos, Gaia, Prometheus, Styx, HLIM), but only SODA and Cassiopeia account for social structure.
- The analysis of the environment is a key point. SODA is the only methodology to analyze the environment, its entities and their interactions.

3.2 Object Orientation-Based Methodologies

Object Orientation-Based Methodologies are characterized by extending object-oriented techniques [20] to include the notion of agency.

The most representative methodologies are: ODAC [21], MaSE [22], MASSIVE [23], DESIRE [24], AAII [25], AOMEM[26], AOAD[27] and MASB[28]. Table 2 lists which of the examined methodological features object orientation-based methodologies have.

Table 2. Object Orientation-Based Methodologies

agent paradigm selection	specification or analysis phase (ODAC, AOAD)	design phase (MaSE, MASSIVE, DESIRE, AAII, AOMEM, MASB)
agent identification process	role-driven top-down (ODAC, MaSE. MASSIVE, AAII, AOMEM, AOAD, MASB)	component-driven bottom-up (DESIRE)
MAS aspects	intra- & inter-agent (ODAC, MASB, DESIRE, AAII, AOMEM, AOAD, MASB)	social structure (MASSIVE, AOAD)
environment analysis	environment (MASSIVE)	objects (ODAC, MASB)

From the viewpoint of correct agent orientation, this methodological line is beset by the following problems. It does not account for the use of a generic analysis model. Some methodologies (ODAC and AOAD) identify agents during analysis. Only the DESIRE methodology implements a proper component-driven bottom-up agent identification process. Almost all the methodologies (ODAC, MASB, DESIRE, AAII, AOMEM, AOAD and MASB) cover the intra-agent and inter-agent aspects, but only MASSIVE and AOAD cover the social structure. Finally, with the exception of MASSIVE, none of the methodologies takes into account the environment features.

These methodologies treat agents like complex objects, which is wrong, because agents have a higher level of abstraction than objects. They also fail to properly capture the autonomous behavior of agents, interactions between agents, and organizational structures [17].

3.3 Knowledge Engineering-Based Methodologies

Knowledge Engineering-Based Methodologies are characterized by emphasizing the identification, acquisition and modeling of knowledge used by the agent components.

The most representative methodologies originate from the CommonKADS methodology [29] are MASCommonKADS [30] and CoMoMAS [31]. Table 3 lists the features of these methodologies for our analysis.

Table 3. Knowledge Engineering-Based Methodologies

agent paradigm selection	specification or analysis phase (MAS-CommonKADS)	design phase (CoMoMAS)
agent identification process	role-driven top-down (MAS-CommonKADS)	component-driven bottom-up (CoMoMAS)
MAS aspects	intra- & inter-agent (all)	social structure (none)
Environment analysis	environment (none)	objects (none)

These methodologies also present some problems. Like the other approaches described earlier, these methodologies do not account for the use of a generic analysis model. MAS-CommonKADS identifies agents during analysis, following a role-driven top-down process (identifying actors). Both of them account for the intra-agent and inter-agent aspects, but do not cover social issues or analysis of the environment.

3.4 Analysis of Current Agent Development Methodologies

The methodological approach based directly on agent technology is perhaps better than the other two, because it is based on the intrinsic concept of agent and agent organization in a MAS. It basically falls down on the point that it confines problem analysis to the agent paradigm, whereas this paradigm may turn out to be unsuitable if agent technology is not a good option for dealing with the problem in question.

Briefly, we believe that a good AOSE methodology is one that defines an architecture-independent *generic analysis model* and a *design model* that can systematically identify agents following a component-driven bottom-up agent identification process, can identify the intra-agent, inter-agent and social structure of the system, can analyze the environment and can identify environment objects.

4 SONIA Methodology

The SONIA (Set of mOdels for a Natural Identification of Agents) methodology [6] allows the generation of a multi-agent architecture to solve a problem (whose conceptualization is not conditioned by the agent paradigm) according to a *Multi-Agent Design Model* that systemizes and automates the activities of identifying the MAS components.

The phases and stages of which the SONIA methodology is composed are listed below, along with the models generated in each stage (Fig. 2):

- *Conceptualization:* The problem is analyzed on the basis of the problem statement using an analysis model that does not condition the design paradigm. The result is an initial *Structural Model*, which describes the overall structure of the domain and an initial *Task Model*, which describes how to solve problems occurring in the domain.
- *Extended Analysis*: The above models are refined and expanded to include the features of the environment and the external system entities, producing the following models: an *Environment Model*, which defines the external system entities and system interactions with these entities; a *Structural Model*, which includes domain knowledge structures of the external system entities that interact with the system; and a *Task Model*, which adds the functionalities required for interaction with the external system entities.

  The Conceptualization and Extended Analysis stages form the MAS analysis phase.
- *Synthesis*: This stage is aimed at improving the identification of agents from their components. For this purpose, the elements of the Structural and Task Models are grouped depending on concepts that are characteristic of agents such as knowledge, behaviors and responsibilities.

  This stage provides a smooth transition from analysis to design, outputting: a *Knowledge Model*, which identifies the knowledge components inherent to the problem by grouping concepts and associations from Structural Model; a *Behavior Model*, produced by grouping tasks, subtasks and methods from the Task Model; and a *Responsibility Model*, output by establishing the relationships between knowledge components and behaviors.
- *Architectural Design*: In this stage, we decide whether or not the system will be designed following a multiagent architecture. If a MAS is designed, the entities of the architecture are also defined.

  The generated models are: an *Agent Model*, which identifies and defines what elements should be designed as autonomous agents; an *Object Model*, which identifies and defines what passive elements there are in the environment; and an

Interaction Model, which identifies and defines the relationships among agents and between agents and objects.

The stages of Synthesis and Architectural Design are what make up the design phase.

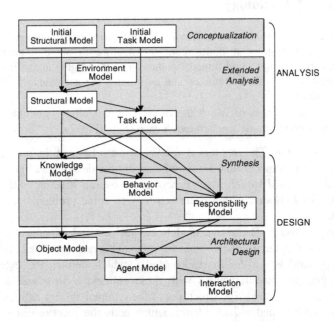

Fig. 2. Phases of the SONIA methodology

Although the methodological process is top-down, this methodology follows a bottom-up process to build the MAS architecture. Instead of identifying the MAS entities and then the components of these entities, the methodology starts by identifying the atomic elements (concepts, associations, tasks, etc.) output by system analysis, which are then grouped into more complex elements (components), from which the agents and objects of the MAS architecture will be able to be identified. This makes the generated system highly extensible and facilitates agent and component extension, modification and reuse.

In the following, the phases and stages of the SONIA methodology and their application to the development of the ALBOR project (Barrier-Free Computer Access) are briefly described [32][33].

ALBOR was conceived as an Internet-based intelligent system designed to provide guidance on the evaluation of disabled people's computer access skills and on the choice of the best suited assistive technologies.

Each system session is divided into four stages:

1. *User identification*: user personal particulars and other information are collected in order to start the session.

2. *Session preparation*: the user is informed about the goals of the questionnaire, how the session will be performed and whether any preliminary training is necessary.
3. *Survey taking*: the user is asked a series of questions, which will be depend on responses to questions already answered and will be confined to the questions strictly necessary for the evaluation of the person in question.
4. *Result evaluation*: an evaluation report with several recommendations for the user to decide which is best suited for her/him is sent to the user.

4.1 Analysis

The elicited requirements are analyzed using the Set Theory Based Conceptual Model (SETCM) [33][34], an analysis method that was defined to achieve several goals. First, the method is design independent: it uses terminology other than design languages to give a real understanding of the problem under analysis. Second, SETCM is able to analyze problems of different kinds, ranging from the simpler, algorithmic problems to more complex and knowledge-based problems. Third, the method has a solid formal foundation, thanks to which it can unambiguously represent the results of the analysis. Fourth, SETCM includes a comprehensive and easy-to-understand textual notation, which is a deterrent to the use of mathematical notations. Finally, the method includes a graphical notation, which eases the understanding of large models.

SETCM is design independent and capable of analyzing complex problems thanks to the fact that the SETCM modeling elements were carefully chosen and defined. These elements were selected from the elements commonly used in other approaches, eluding design-specific terms and incorporating new elements where necessary. Some of these elements are concepts, associations, attributes, classifications, tasks and task-methods. The elements were defined using Set Theory vocabulary, which is the basis of mathematics. For instance, an association is a subset of the Cartesian product of the elements involved. The SETCM elements are grouped into two components: the *Structural Model*, which represents the structure of a domain (elements and relationships between them) and the states that can occur within this domain, and the *Task Model*, representing domain problem solving.

To achieve the goal of establishing a formal foundation, all the modeling primitives were formalized using the main elements of Cantor's naïve set theory, while defining a rigid modeling structure that eludes the contradictions of this theory. Thus, SETCM has a formal modeling core (with more than 700 formalized symbols). This core contains a large set of formal primitives that can be added to in the future by defining and formalizing new elements based on existing components.

The last two goals (textual and graphical notations) are concerned with resolving pragmatic issues. The textual notation represents all the SETCM modeling primitives, is a substitute for the use of mathematics and is highly readable. The graphical notation is based on UML using stereotypes and eases the understanding of large quantities of information, reduces the apparent complexity of the analytical models and is more expressive than the textual notation [34].

SETCM has been applied to develop real systems, which were finally designed using a variety of paradigms (structured, object-oriented, knowledge-based) and even a combination of paradigms.

As mentioned earlier, the Initial Structural Model and the Initial Task Model of SONIA are built using SETCM. These models are refined and expanded to capture the system Environment and External Entities, successively producing:

- An *Environment Model*, which defines the system external entities and their interactions with the system.
- A *Structural Model*, which includes structures from the knowledge domain of the external entities that interact with the system.
- A *Task Model*, which adds the functionalities required to interact with the system external entities defined in the Environment Model.

4.2 Design of the Multi-agent Architecture

The Analysis phase is followed by the Multi-Agent Architecture Design, which is divided into two stages: Synthesis and Architectural Design.

The *Synthesis* stage allows the component-driven identification of agents (bottom-up process) in the Multi-Agent Architecture Design stage. The elements of the Structural Model and Task Model are grouped depending on characteristics of agents, such as knowledge, behaviors and responsibilities, outputting the following models:

- A *Knowledge Model*, which identifies the knowledge components by grouping Structural Model concepts and associations. These groupings are identified because the internal cohesion of their members is high, coupling with other groupings is low and they are used to perform tasks of the same behaviors. The knowledge components will be used internally or shared by the agents.

  The groupings resulting from the first version of the model only check for high cohesion and low coupling among their members. The final version will be built when the responsibilities between knowledge components and behaviors (Responsibility Model) are established and will also check that the members of the groupings are used to do the same tasks.
- A *Behavior Model*, produced by grouping Task Model tasks, subtasks and methods. The behaviors will be part of the agents. These groupings are identified because their tasks and subtasks depend on each other through their methods and they use the same knowledge components in problem solving.

  The groupings from the first version of the model only check for the dependence of some tasks on others through task methods. The final version, which is built when the responsibilities between knowledge components and behaviors (Responsibility Model) are established, will also check that they use the same knowledge in problem solving.
- A *Responsibility Model*, output by relating knowledge components to behaviors. The purpose of this model is to be able to identify agents and environment objects.

  A key activity during the design of this model is to refine the Knowledge and Behavior Models to meet all the conditions.

The *Architectural Design* stage focuses on the definition of the architectural components by means of the following models: Agent Model, Object Model and Interaction Model.

Not until the Agent Model is built is a decision made as to whether the architecture can be implemented by means of agents or a different paradigm needs to be used. This choice is chiefly based on whether or not agents can be identified. For an entity to be able to considered as an autonomous agent, it should have a behavior and the right knowledge components to perform the tasks of this behavior, have at least one defined goal and one utility, and perceive and act in the environment.

If no agents can be identified, another design paradigm will have to be chosen. One possible alternative would be an object-oriented design, reusing objects and interactions identified in the multi-agent architecture design stage. Another possibility would be to design the system as a knowledge-based system, reusing the knowledge components, behaviors and responsibilities output in the synthesis stage.

The Architectural Design models are:

- An *Agent Model*, which identifies and defines, from the Responsibility, Knowledge and Behavior Models, what entities should be designed as autonomous agents. An agent is identified because it is an environment-sensitive entity (it perceives and acts in the environment) that has knowledge to bring into play its behaviors in pursuit of goals and is activated when its utilities are required.

  Therefore, *knowledge* is groupings of concepts and associations that the agent uses to reason and *behaviors* are groupings of tasks that allow the agent to develop the function for which it was conceived. The result of executing a behavior can affect the environment objects or its internal knowledge.

  Goals are objectives pursued by the agent. The agent will execute behaviors to achieve its goals. *Utilities* are triggers that activate the agent. The agent will assess the execution of some of its behaviors if their utilities are met. Goals and utilities are logical conditions on the state of the environment objects or on the state of their internal knowledge.

  Sensors listen to the environment objects and notify the agent every time a change takes place in the objects they are listening in on. This notification can cause some of the agent's utilities or goals to be met. *Actuators* modify environment objects, and the agent will use the respective actuator every time it needs to modify an environment object during behavior execution.

- An *Object Model*, which identifies and defines, from the Responsibility, Knowledge and Behavior Models, what passive elements are part of the environment. These objects are knowledge components identified during the synthesis phase. The main feature of an object is that the knowledge of this object is responsible for more than one behavior or, in other words, is shared by several behaviors. Access to objects will be divided by *levels*, and the knowledge components that are accessed by the same behavior tasks will be grouped at the same level.

- An *Interaction Model*, which identifies and defines what relationships there are in the system among agents and between agents and objects.

  Agent-agent relations occur when both agents interact to take any particular action. This interaction takes place according to interaction protocols based on *speech act theory* [35]. In the case of a reductionist MAS system (designed by one and the same person), the interaction protocol is designed at the same time as the actual agent. In the case of a constructivist MAS system (designed by different people), the interaction protocols are located in a library and are accessed by the agents at interaction time. *Agent-object relations* occur when an agent accesses an object level, either through a sensor or an actuator.

This architecture accounts for the two communication types: *asynchronous communication*, using environment objects to subscribe to events of interest to the agent; and *synchronous communication*, through protocols contained in the Interaction Model.

4.3 Design of the ALBOR System

Fig. 3 shows how the Analysis, Synthesis and Architecture Models are built. For simplicity's sake, it shows only the concepts and associations that are the source of the "Questionnaires" knowledge component, and tasks and methods that are the source of the "TakeSurvey" behavior.

The concepts and associations gathered in the Analysis phase were synthesized as knowledge components using a technique based on Kelly's constructs [36], and the tasks and methods as behaviors using heuristics applied to task decomposition and task dependencies. These techniques, used to output the knowledge components and behaviors, assure highly coherent and low-coupled groupings. Then the responsibilities between knowledge components and behaviors were established from the relationships of concept/association used in task/subtask. These responsibilities lead to changes in the Knowledge and Behavior Models. The models are modified according to knowledge and behavior grouping/division rules based on the cardinalities of the relationships of concept/association used in task/subtask. The Knowledge, Behavior and Responsibility Models are the final result of the synthesis.

It is not until the Agent Model is built that a decision is made as to whether the architecture can be implemented by means of agents or a different paradigm needs to be used. This choice is chiefly based on whether or not agents can be identified. For an entity to be able to be considered as an autonomous agent, it should have a behavior and the right knowledge components to perform the tasks of this behavior, have at least one defined goal and one utility, and perceive and act in the environment.

To complete the multi-agent architecture design phase, the environment agents and objects were identified. The objects were identified from the Responsibility Model, and the knowledge shared by several behaviors was chosen as environment objects. Following this criterion, we identified the "Users", "External" and "Media" objects. Agents were also identified from responsibilities. Again, agents should have a behavior, knowledge components, goals and utilities, and sensors and actors. For example, the responsibility between "Questionnaires" knowledge and "TakeSurvey" behavior produces "Survey-Taker". The Agent, Object and Interaction Models are the final result of the architecture design stage.

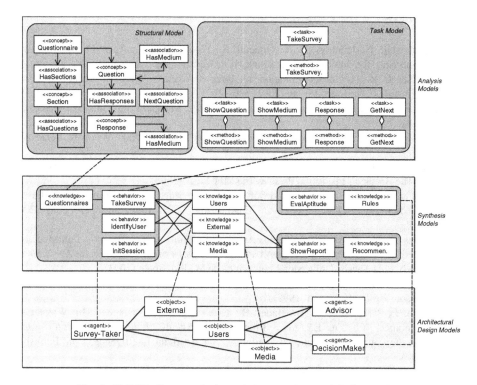

Fig. 3. ALBOR: From analysis models to architectural design models

5 Conclusions

AOSE is unquestionably a very good technique for solving complex problems, especially in distributed, open and heterogeneous environments. For this technology to be routinely used in companies like object-oriented approaches are, there is a need for mechanisms suited for deciding whether or not the problem should be solved using agents. Also the identification and design of agents should be a natural and straightforward process that does not require a lot of expertise so that there is no obstacle to its application by developers. Although they have made a big contribution to improving AOSE, current agent development methodologies do not satisfactorily solve the above-mentioned problems.

In this paper, we have pointed out some features that an agent-oriented development methodology should have and detailed which of these features are missing from the most important methodologies used within the agent paradigm. Also, we have presented an overview of the SONIA methodology, illustrated by the ALBOR case study, which includes these features and naturally leads from requirements elicitation to MAS and agent-based development.

References

1. Zambonelli, F., Jennings, N. R., Omicini, A., Wooldridge, M.: Agent-Oriented Software Engineering for Internet Applications. In: Omicini, A., Zambonelli, F., Klusch, M., Tolksdorf, R. (eds.): Coordination of Internet Agents: "Models, Technologies and Applications". Springer-Verlag (2001) 326-346
2. Huhns, M., Singh, M. P. (eds.): Readings in Agents. Morgan Kaufmann, San Mateo, CA. (1998)
3. Wooldridge, M.: An Introduction to MultiAgent Systems. John Wiley & Sons, LTD (2002)
4. Epstein, J. M., Axtell, R. L.: Growing Artificial Societies: Social Science from the Bottom Up. The Brooking Institution Press & The MIT Press (1996)
5. Lind, J.: Issues in Agent-Oriented Software Engineering. In: Ciancarini, P., Wooldridge, M. (eds.): Agent-Oriented Software Engineering, LNAI 1957. Springer-Verlag (2001) 45-58
6. Frutos, S.: Modelo de Diseño de una Arquitectura Multi-Agente Basado en un Modelo de Sociedad de Agentes (*Multi-Agent Architecture Design Model based on an Agent Society Model*). PhD Thesis. Universidad Politécnica de Madrid, Spain (2003)
7. Booch, G., Rumbaugh, J., Jacobson, I.: The Unified Modeling Language User Guide. Addison-Wesley Longman (1999)
8. Odell, J., Parunak, H. V. D., Bauer, B.: Extending UML for Agents. In: Wagner, G., Lesperance, Y., Yu, E. (eds.): Proc. of the Agent-Oriented Information Systems Workshop at the 17th National Conference on Artificial Intelligence. ICue Publishing (2000)
9. Weiss, G.: Agent Orientation in Software Engineering. Knowledge Engineering Review, Vol. 16(4) (2002) 349-373
10. Wooldridge, M., Ciancarini, P.: Agent-Oriented Software Engineering: The State of the Art. In: Ciancarini, P., Wooldridge, M. (eds.): Agent-Oriented Software Engineering, LNAI 1957. Springer-Verlag, Berlin (2001) 1-28
11. Tveit, A.: A Survey of Agent-Oriented Software Engineering. First NTNU CSGSC (2001)
12. Iglesias, C.A., Garijo, M., González, J.C.: A Survey of Agent-Oriented Methodologies. In: Müller, J.P., Singh, M. P., Rao, A. (eds.): Intelligent Agents V (ATAL'98), LNAI 1555. Springer-Verlag, Berlin (1999) 317-330
13. Bresciani, P., Giorgini, P., Giunchiglia, F., Mylopoulos, J.: Tropos: An Agent Oriented Software Development Methodology. Int. Journal of Autonomous Agent and MultiAgent System, Vol. 8(3) (2004) 203-236
14. Zambonelli, F., Jennings, N. R., Wooldridge, M.: Developing Multiagent Systems: The Gaia Methodology. ACM Transactions on Software Engineering and Methodology, Vol. 12(3) (2003) 317-370
15. Padgham, L., Winikoff, M.: Prometheus: A Methodology for Developing Intelligent Agents. In: Giunchiglia, F., Odell, J., Weiss, G. (eds.): Agent-Oriented Software Engineering III, LNCS 2585. Springer-Verlag. Berlin (2003) 174-185
16. Omicini, A.: SODA: Societies and Infrastructures in the Analysis and Design of Agent-Based Systems. In: Ciancarini, P., Wooldridge, M. (eds.): Agent-Oriented Software Engineering, LNAI 1957. Springer-Verlag. Berlin (2001) 185-194
17. Bush, G., Cranefield, S., Purvis, M.; The Styx Agent Methodology. The Information Science Discussion Paper Series, Number 2001/02. University of Otago. New Zealand (2001)

18. Elammari, M., Lalonde, W.: An Agent-Oriented Methodology: High-Level and Intermediate Models. Proc. of the First Bi-Conference. Workshop on Agent-Oriented Information Systems (AOIS'99). Heidelberg, Germany (1999)

19. Collinot, A., Carle, P., Zeghal, K.: Cassiopeia: A Method for Designing Computational Organizations. Proc. of the First Int. Workshop on Decentralized Intelligent Multi-Agent Systems. Krakow, Poland (1995) 124-131

20. Jacobson, I., Booch, G., Rumbaugh, J.: The Unified Software Development Process. Addison Wesley Longman. Reading, MA (1999)

21. Gervais, M.: ODAC: An Agent-Oriented Methodology Based on ODP. Journal of Autonomous Agents and Multi-Agent Systems, Vol. **7**(3) (2002) 199-228

22. Wood, M. F., DeLoach, S. A.: An Overview of the Multiagent Systems Engineering Methodology. In: Ciancarini, P., Wooldridge, M. (eds.): Agent-Oriented Software Engineering, LNAI 1957. Springer-Verlag, Berlin (2001) 207-222

23. Lind, J.: Iterative Software Engineering for Multiagent Systems: The MASSIVE method, LNCS- 1994. Springer-Verlag (2001)

24. Brazier, F. M. T., Dunin-Keplicz, B., Jennings, N., Treur, J.: Desire: Modeling Multi-Agent Systems in a Compositional Formal Framework. Int. Journal of Cooperative Information Systems, Vol. 6. Special Issue on Formal Methods in Cooperative Information Systems: Multiagent Systems (1997)

25. Kinny, D., Georgeff, M., Rao, A.: A Methodology and Modeling Technique for Systems of BDI Agents. In: van de Velde, W., Perram, J. W. (eds.): Agents Breaking Away (MAAMAW'96), LNAI 1038. Springer-Verlag, Berlin (1996) 56-71

26. Kendall, E. A., Malkoun, M. T., Jiang, C. H.: A Methodology for Developing Agent Based Systems. In: Zhang, C., Lukose, D. (eds.): Distributed Artificial Intelligence - Architecture and Modeling, LNAI 1087. Springer-Verlag, Germany (1996) 85-99

27. Burmeister, B.: Models and Methodology for Agent-Oriented Analysis and Design. In: Fischer, K. (ed.): Working Notes of the KI'96 Workshop on Agent-Oriented Programming and Distributed Systems, Saarbrücken, Germany (1996)

28. Moulin, B., Cloutier, L.: Collaborative Work Based on Multi-Agent Architectures: A Methodological Perspective. In: Aminzadeh, F., Jamshidi, M. (eds.): Soft Computing: Fuzzy Logic, Neural Networks and Distributed Artificial Intelligence. Prentice-Hall, N.J., USA (1994) 261-296

29. Schreiber, G., Akkermans, H., Anjewierden, A., de Hoog, R., Shadbolt, N., Van de Velde, W., Wielinga, B.: Knowledge Engineering and Management. The CommonKADS Methodology. The MIT Press. Cambridge, MA (1999)

30. Iglesias, C.A., Garijo, M., González, J.C., Velasco, J. R.: Analysis and Design of Multiagent Systems using MAS-CommonKADS. In: Singh, M. P., Rao A. S., Wooldridge, M. (eds.): Intelligent Agents IV: Agent Theories, Architectures, and Languages (ATAL97), LNAI 1365. Springer-Verlag, Berlin (1999) 313-326

31. Glaser, N.: The CoMoMAS Methodology and Environment for Multi-Agent System Development. In: Zhang, C., Lukose, D. (eds.): Multi-Agent Systems - Methodologies and Applications, LNAI 1286. Springer-Verlag, Berlin (1997) 1-16

32. Alonso, F., Barreiro, J. M., Frutos, S., Montes, C.: Multi-Agent Framework for Intelligent Questionnaire on the Web. Proc. of the Third World Multiconference on Systemics, Cybernetics and Informatics (SCI-99) and the Fifth Int. Conference on Information Systems Analysis and Synthesis (ISAS'99), Vol. III. Orlando, USA (1999) 8-15

33. Alonso, F., Frutos, S., Fuertes, J. L., Martínez, L. A., Montes, C.: ALBOR. An Internet-Based Advisory KBS with a Multi-Agent Architecture. Int. Conference on Advances in Infrastructure for Electronic Business, Science, And Education on the Internet (SSGRR 2001), L'Aquila, Italy (2001) 1-6
34. Martínez, L.A.: Método para el Analysis Independiente de Problemas (*Method for Independent Problem Analysis*). PhD Thesis. Universidad Politécnica de Madrid. Spain (2003)
35. Austin, J.L.: How to Do Things with Words. Harvard University Press. Cambridge, MA (1962)
36. Kelly, G. A.: The Psychology of Personal Constructs. Norton (1995)

Deployment of Distributed Multi-agent Systems

Lars Braubach[1], Alexander Pokahr[1], Dirk Bade[1],
Karl-Heinz Krempels[2], and Winfried Lamersdorf[1]

[1] University of Hamburg, Dept. of Computer Science,
Distributed and Information Systems,
Vogt-Klln-Str. 30, 22527 Hamburg, Germany
{braubach, pokahr, lamersd}@informatik.uni-hamburg.de
[2] University of Aachen, Dept. of Computer Science, Informatik IV,
Ahornstr. 55, 52074 Aachen, Germany
krempels@informatik.rwth-aachen.de

Abstract. The agent metaphor has shown its usefulness for modelling as well as implementing complex and dynamic applications. Although a number of agent applications has been successfully realised and used, it must be stated that the distribution of commercial off-the-shelf applications is very scarce. For this discontenting situation, at least two reasons can be identified. On the one hand, the development of agent-based applications is difficult suffering from insufficient standards and tools and on the other hand deployment issues are little researched and supported. In this paper, several deployment-related topics are discussed and a vision for the deployment of distributed multi-agent systems is conceived. From the vision, requirements for launching and configuring agent applications are derived. According to these requirements, a platform independent reference model of the proposed deployment infrastructure is presented. The reference model provides the basis for the development of our AS-CML (Agent Society Configuration Manager and Launcher) tool, which is currently implemented for the JADE and Jadex multi-agent platforms.

1 Introduction

Multi-agent systems (MAS) are composed of autonomous, interacting, more or less intelligent entities. The agent metaphor has proven to be a promising choice for building complex and adaptive software applications, because it addresses key issues for making complexity manageable already at a conceptual level [1]. Furthermore, agent technology can be seen as a natural successor of the object-oriented paradigm and enriches the world of passive objects with the notion of autonomous actors. Therefore, one would suppose agent applications to be in widespread use in academic as well as in industrial projects. The contrary is the case. Even though many agent applications are developed in various domains [2], most of them are specialised solutions that are deployed in at most one setting. The question arises: Why are agent applications not yet widely distributed?

One reason for this is that the development of MAS is inherently difficult and error prone, because of several intricate issues. First, the development process for

M.-P. Gleizes, A. Omicini, and F. Zambonelli (Eds.): ESAW 2004, LNAI 3451, pp. 261–276, 2005.

building agent applications is in most cases ad-hoc and not based on a generally accepted methodology, like for example the well-known Unified Process for UML [3] in the object-oriented world. For agent systems, no such common ground exists due to different agent architectures and missing standards. In consequence, a methodology has to be chosen independently for each project among several alternatives. This choice is crucial for the project's success and is constrained by domain and implementation aspects [4]. In addition, whatever methodology is selected, the tool support is always relatively poor and does not cover all phases of the development process.

Besides the methodology, the development of agent-based applications is difficult, because the software is distributed and dynamic in nature and demands various new skills and a new way of thinking from the developers. E.g. an object-oriented software engineer cannot easily change to the agent paradigm without considering ontology descriptions and studying the abstract speech-act based agent communication. Additionally, intelligent agents often use mentalistic notions or employ rule-based approaches.

Another important reason for the scarce distribution of commercial off-the-shelf agent applications is that there is currently no support for the deployment of agent applications. In areas such as distributed object systems, systematical guidelines and mechanisms for all activities concerned with deployment issues have been developed. These guidelines ensure that a properly developed distributed application can be packaged into a reusable, maintainable, and configurable piece of software. However, although multi-agent systems composed of autonomous proactively (inter-)acting entities differ considerably from distributed object systems, the issue of appropriate deployment techniques for MAS is not yet very much researched.

The vision of this paper is to specify agent applications at a high-level using constraints to declare what system properties need to be fulfilled for the application to work properly. E.g. one could demand certain services and agent roles to be available, whereby the deployment environment has the task to interpret and supervise these constraints and has to start agent instances accordingly. As a first step towards this high-level deployment for MAS we propose a reference model for the launching of distributed multi-agent applications that are specified by declaring which and how many agent instances shall be instantiated in what order. As part of the reference model a generic meta-model for the specification of agent applications is described, which consists of one layer for the definition of agent types and another one for the ordered composition of agent instances belonging to a certain application scenario. To underline the applicability of the proposed model a prototype implementation is presented.

The rest of the paper is structured as follows. The next section presents some background on deployment in general and deployment of agents in particular. We use our vision to derive requirements for deployment of distributed multi-agent systems in section 3. To meet these requirements, in section 4 a reference model is presented, and it is explained in section 5 how the reference model is implemented in our Agent Society Configuration Manager and Launcher tool (ASCML). The last section summarises the paper, gives some conclusions, and outlines areas for future work.

2   Background

The Object Management Group (OMG) defines deployment as "the processes between acquisition of software and execution of software". In [5] a general deployment process for distributed systems is specified, which consists of five phases. In the installation step the software is acquired and stored in a local repository that not necessarily needs to be the program's execution location. Next, the software can be functionally configured in the sense that application specific properties are set to certain values. This may result in several different application configurations. Thereafter a deployment plan taking into account the target environments and the software requirements is developed. With the help of this deployment plan, the code placement can be done in the preparation phase. Finally, the application can be launched, which demands the starting and runtime configuration of software at the planned nodes in the target environment.

For agent-based applications, this process is more dynamic and flexible, because the application constituting elements are autonomous agents instead of passive components. Nevertheless, the above-mentioned activities are important for MAS as well and will be discussed with respect to their peculiarities in the following. Concerning the installation step, two distinct kinds of software have to be available. On the one hand, the agent infrastructure, which is responsible for offering the basic agent services like messaging, white and yellow pages service needs to be acquired. For this purpose, normally agent platforms are used. On the other hand, the application specific agent software needs to be accessible, whereby for certain types of applications it may be sufficient to load portions of agent code dynamically. The functional configuration of MAS can be done by adjusting the available agent start-parameters and by fine-tuning the number of agents to be started. E.g. the number of service agents could be used to tune the application's scalability for small and large enterprises accordingly. The planning and preparation steps for MAS involve the decisions about the placement of infrastructure and application code on the environment nodes. Therefore, considerations about possibly mobile agents and dynamic code retrieval have to be taken into account; e.g. movements of agents may require platforms to be installed on network nodes, where no agents are initially running.

The launching of MAS differs to a great extent from starting a component-based application. Component-based applications have a hierarchical structure and are usually launched using a single starting point, which creates the necessary subcomponents. On the contrary, agent-based applications consist of a bundle of autonomous actors that are self-dependent after birth. Hence, to define configurations of agent applications notions conceptually more abstract than single agents are necessary. Minimum for the description of an agent application at a concrete level is that agent instances and dependencies between these instances can be expressed. Nevertheless, specifications that are more abstract are desirable and could support a higher degree of robustness and maintainability.

In [6] several agent platforms are compared with respect to their support for the analysis, design, implementation, and deployment phase. In correspondence to our actual research, it turns out that only very few platforms address issues of deployment at all. Positive exceptions can be found within Agent Academy [7], AgentBuilder [8], ZEUS [9], AgentFactory [10] and BlueJADE [11]. To our knowledge only the Agent Academy and the somewhat outdated AgentBuilder frameworks offer tool support for the specification and launching of agent applications. Both platforms allow the simple designation of parameterised agent instances from formerly defined agent types. These agent instances will be started altogether, when the so defined agent application is launched. ZEUS and Agent-Factory utilise tools for the generation of human readable starting scripts that contain a list of ordered commands for instantiating and starting agents. In contrast to the aforementioned tools, BlueJADE is an attempt to integrate an agent framework into an application server treating the platform as manageable service. Hence, it shifts the responsibility of agent management to the application server, which allows starting and stopping individual agents as well as platforms. The conceptual problems of specifying agent applications are not addressed.

One obvious drawback of all solutions found, consists in the missing possibility to define any kinds of dependencies that may constrain the order of agents to start. Additionally, the agent application meta-models are specified only implicitly, rendering the creation of a cross-platform launching tool almost impossible. With respect to our vision it has to be stated that currently available solutions carry out the definition of agent applications merely at the concrete level, what makes it difficult having flexible and scalable applications. By utilising a more abstract approach, agents could be started in response to certain application and environmental demands. This more abstract way of an agent application is also related to organisational approaches [12, 13]. These aim to structure MAS with respect to the organisational settings found in the addressed problem domain. Hence, the motivation for structuring agents is different but the concepts have some similarities and probably will allow a consolidation of both directions.

Directly related to the starting of agent applications is the dynamic application reconfiguration, which either could be done automatically by the configuration environment, or could be done manually by some administration authority. An abstract application specification could be a promising starting point for dynamic configuration mechanisms as well, because application constraints could be supervised and used to trigger reconfiguration actions.

Until now, the extent to which dynamic reconfiguration is supported by agent platforms, is mostly reduced to the allocation of agents to network nodes to cope with varying network loads. E.g. the RECoMa [14] reconfiguration manager of the RETSINA [15] framework was developed to launch agents, reallocate them to other computers, and monitor their runtime states. Some aspects of more advanced configuration mechanisms for agent-based applications have been covered by a preliminary and now deprecated FIPA specification [16], which underlined the importance of agent dependency specifications, life cycle management, and monitoring mechanisms. The idea of the FIPA Agent Configuration Management work group was to introduce configuration domains in which a designated management agent is responsible for monitoring this domain.

Due to the fact that there are only few agent applications in the market, it is not astonishing that the development of configuration concepts and tools has not gained much interest until to date. Widening the horizon of considered configuration targets from agent-based to distributed component-based applications, it is interesting that agent-based approaches for configuring *component-based* applications can be found. E.g. in [17] a hierarchical agent-based infrastructure for monitoring and configuring distributed applications is proposed.

3   Requirements

Having presented the current state of the art with respect to deployment of multi-agent systems, a lack of concepts, standards, and tools can be identified, in particular for *launching* and dynamic *reconfiguration* of complex agent-based applications. These two aspects of deployment are essential to achieve the vision of specifying agent applications at a high level. In the following, we will discuss the desirable features with respect to the launching of preconfigured multi-agent systems and investigate what is needed to achieve dynamic reconfiguration of agent-based applications.

Before going into details about launching of agent applications, we have to clarify some terms used in the following. Configurations of component-based applications can be defined at two levels: Component level configurations and application level configurations [18]. For agent-based systems, the agent level and the application level can be distinguished. Considering a single agent, a distinction can be made between the static implementation parts and the running processes. When we need to highlight this distinction, we refer to the former as *agent type* and to the latter as *agent instance*. This distinction can also be made at the application level. We use the term *society type* to refer to the static properties of a multi-agent application. A *society type* in our terms is a composition of agent types, supplemented with some (e.g. interaction) constraints. A *society instance* refers to the instantiation of a society, and is composed of single agent instances and concrete dependencies between those instances. The model should be recursive to allow societies to be part of larger societies on the type as well as on the instance level.

3.1   Basic Management Services

To support the launching of distributed multi-agent applications several basic services can be identified. First of all, services are needed for starting and stopping agent and society instances. For invoking these services, at least the following information has to be supplied. The start of an agent instance should be based on a given agent type definition which has to contain a reference to the agent implementation (e.g. a Java class) and should declare the parameters that can be supplied to an agent of this type. To instantiate an agent, its type definition, the name for the agent instance (according to FIPA) and the assigned values for the parameters have to be supplied. To stop an agent instance only the agent identifier has to be known.

A society instance definition should contain all additional information required to instantiate a multi-agent application based on a society type definition. Therefore, a society instance definition has to contain the concrete agent instances with names and parameter assignments, as well as any dependencies that have to be respected when launching the application. This allows starting a complete society by just referring to the instance definition. To be able to identify a running application, a unique name should be given to each started society. It has to be assured that the agent instances belonging to a society are known, so that a society instance can also be stopped as a whole.

In order to launch *distributed* applications these basic services should be available remotely, therefore issues of security and accounting have to be considered [19]. In addition, it is desirable that only minimal requirements are necessary for the manual configuration of network nodes, which could be achieved by code distribution and a service that allows remotely starting new agent platforms.

The basic services additionally require a launch process management that has to make sure, that the correct agents, societies, and platforms are launched at the correct nodes at the correct times. One can imagine several ways to specify this. At the concrete level, it is possible to directly define the dependencies between agent instances of a society instance. The launch process management can then determine the launch order based on a topological sort of the dependency graph.

Constraints that are more abstract such as dependencies to specific services or roles can be employed to define application characteristics already at the type level (i.e. in agent type or society type definitions). In addition, application specific constraints and network load characteristics can be used to determine the allocation of agent instances to the available network nodes.

3.2   Monitoring and Reconfiguration

Once an application has been launched, the monitoring and reconfiguration of the running societies and agent instances should be supported. On the one hand, an administrator might want to observe a running application and manually add or remove agent instances or reallocate mobile agents to new network nodes. On the other hand a monitoring service should take care of the constraints and dependencies specified in the type and instance definitions and perform appropriate actions when the constraints get violated, e.g. by starting additional service agents to assure a given response time. By detecting failures and relaunching of agents, as well as detecting agents which are no longer needed by any application, the monitoring service can increase the robustness of agent applications. The exact mechanisms available to the monitoring service to alter a running system have to be customized carefully for each application to reflect the varying degree of autonomy for each agent.

To support monitoring and reconfiguration of agents and applications it is necessary to provide the responsible monitoring entities with relevant state information about the monitored entities and vice versa to be able to communicate back reconfiguration commands to the relevant agents. In addition, the reconfiguration of a larger application often requires a coordinated set of reconfigurations against the individual agents that constitute the system. Furthermore, reconfigurations need to assure that the system is in a consistent state after the reconfiguration has been performed [17, 18]. These issues are beyond the scope of this paper and will not be further elaborated.

4   Deployment Reference Model

In the following, we describe our approach towards realising the vision of distributed deployment of multi-agent applications. The approach is based on the idea of specialised service agents that are responsible for launching and managing agents and societies on their platform. These service agents are called ASCML (Agent Society Configuration Manager and Launcher). Fig. 1 depicts the deployment reference model. On each agent platform, at least one ASCML agent will be available to manage the societies on that platform. ASCML agents may respond to remote requests, e.g. from other ASCMLs, in order to start (subordinated) society instances remotely. In the reference model, each society instance will be managed by exactly one ASCML. A society instance is a virtual concept only known to the ASCML agent that started it and has no representation on the agent platform. Therefore, societies may easily span across several platforms, having one root ASCML responsible for the whole society instance and local ASCMLs responsible for different subparts. Agent instances (e.g. generic agents such as a yellow page service) may belong to several society instances at once, and therefore - knowingly or not - may be under control of several ASCML agents.

The reference model is able to capture most of the requirements of the last section. The ASCML agent provides the basic management services for starting and

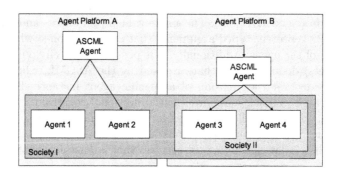

Fig. 1. Deployment reference model

stopping agent and society instances, and is also responsible for launch-process-management as well as monitoring and dynamic reconfiguration. This *external* approach is considered advantageous compared to an *internal* approach where configuration management is built into the single entities [18]. The ASCML is a self-contained component with a standardised interface. Porting the ASCML to different FIPA-compliant agent platforms should be straightforward, making the reference model well suited to achieve deployment capabilities in heterogeneous environments. The reference model does not directly support starting and stopping of remote agent platforms, as an ASCML and a running agent platform have to be present at each network node. To meet this requirement some kind of bootstrapping component would be necessary, which is out of the scope of this paper.

Launching, as well as the planned monitoring and reconfiguration services are based on specifications of agents and societies. To facilitate reusability of specifications a society instance is not defined in one large file, but in two different types of files describing an agent application at different levels. Agent type specifications define self-contained agents at the single-agent level. Society specifications define multi-agent applications by referencing the specifications of included agents and society instances. Both specifications follow an XML schema definition[3] as described in the next two sections.

While we are currently creating the specification files manually, we envisage that graphical user interfaces will be used to compose and configure larger agent applications. Additionally, tools can be developed to crosscheck created specifications for consistency. Once the specifications have been created, the deployment engineer has to take care, that each ASCML agent has access to the specification files for those agents and societies that it has to start on its platform.

4.1   Agent Type Specification

Fig. 2 depicts the structure of an agent type specification. An ASCML agent will read the agent type specification e.g. when it is requested to instantiate an agent of that type. The agent element captures important properties of an agent such as the agent's implementation class and the type, which identifies the required agent platform (e.g. JADE [20]). The single-valued parameters and multi-valued parameter sets represent typed arguments that can be supplied when creating a new instance of the agent. Additionally, it is possible to specify one or more (for parameter sets) default values that are used by the ASCML, when no explicit value is provided for the creation of a specific agent instance. Both kinds of parameters can be further elaborated with additional constraint elements, used for restricting the set of allowed values for the parameter. Furthermore, FIPA-compliant service and agent descriptions [21] can be included in the agent type definition. These allow specifying the services that an instance of this agent type can provide when it is instantiated.

---

[3] available at http://jadex.sourceforge.net/schemas/

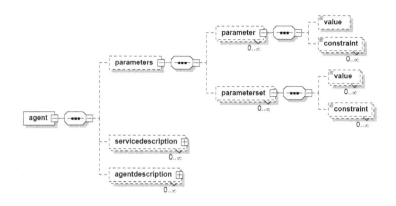

Fig. 2. The agent meta-model

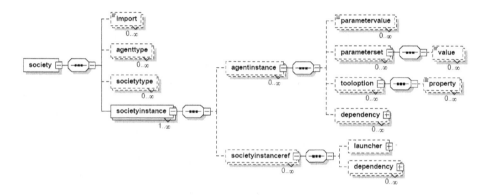

Fig. 3. The agent society meta-model

4.2   Society Type Specification

A society type (see Fig. 3) defines a multi-agent application at the type level. The society contains a declaration part in which all agent types and enclosed subsocieties have to be defined. This declaration part is not necessary from the technical point of view, but it enhances the readability of the application specifications and facilitates model checking by making explicit the available element types. The contained society instances represent different application configurations, whereby each society has to provide at least one default society instance. This society instance will be selected for instantiation when the society needs to be launched without further information available.

A society instance consists of concrete agent instances and subsociety instances that need to be created when the society is started. For the specification of agent instances, at least the mandatory parameter values have to be supplied. Additionally, platform dependant tool options can be specified in a generic way. They can be used to activate tools and e.g. can be utilized to facilitate the debugging process by using agent observation tools such as the Sniffer agent in JADE. Dependency elements are used to establish an implicit ordering of the entities to be started.

In addition to the agents to be created, a society can contain an arbitrary number of subsocieties that can contain further subsocieties as well. This allows a recursive application definition and facilitates the creation of distributed MAS. Each referenced subsociety instance refers to a concrete society instance, which itself belongs to a declared society specification. For the purpose of starting a remote society, a so-called launcher identifier can be declared. This identifier designates the remote ASCML agent responsible for starting the corresponding remote society. In analogy to agent instances, dependencies can be specified for subsocieties as well.

4.3   Dependencies

Dependencies are used to express relationships between elements at the instance level. If one element declares itself dependent from another element this means that the declaring element cannot be started until the referenced element is available. In our model five different types of dependencies can be distinguished: *agent type*, *agent instance*, *society type*, *society instance* and *service dependencies*. An agent type dependency can be used to wait for an arbitrary number of agents of a specified type to be running, while an agent instance dependency exactly refers to a designated agent, identified by its unique name. Both kinds of dependencies also exist for the society element, which means that it is possible to wait for a specified number of societies with a certain type as well as for directly known societies. The last kind of dependency is the most abstract one and allows defining indirect relationships between elements, because the element depends on a service (following FIPA) to be available.

All kinds of dependencies can either be marked active or passive denoting if the ASCML has the duty to actively engage in action when the dependency does not hold. If a dependency is declared *active* the ASCML will try to start missing entities, whereby the mechanism for deciding what instance need to be launched depends on the type of dependency and its parameterisation. In case of a *passive* dependency, the ASCML will wait until the dependency condition holds (e.g. retesting the condition from time to time).

4.4   Example

The following example further explains the meta-model presented in the prior subsections. It relies on a slightly modified version of the *JADE Party* example application provided with the JADE-distribution. In this scenario, guests are invited to a party by an organizer and spread a rumour until it is known by all guests and the party ends (cf. JADE Party Java docs). Hence, the JADE Party consists of two different types of agents, a *Host*- and a *Guest*-agent that make up the basis for the corresponding society type. By defining different settings, e.g. specifying the number of guests taking part in the party, different society instances may be set up.

```
1 <agent name="Guest" package="examples.party" class="GuestAgent" type="JADE"/>

1 <agent name="Host" package="examples.party" class="HostAgent" type="JADE">
2    <parameters>
3        <parameter name="guestsToWaitFor" type="Integer" optional="false"/>
4    </parameters>
5 </agent>
```

Fig. 4. Guest- and Host-agent type definitions

With the agent type definition all required information for starting an agent of this type is specified (see Fig. 4). The definition of both agent types contains the name, which is used in connection with the package declaration to uniquely identify a model within the ASCML's scope. The class-attribute reflects the agent's implementation class, which is instantiated at the agent's start-up and the type-attribute serves as the agent-platform type identifier (e.g. JADE) and is evaluated by the ASCML to choose among the set of platform-dependent managing-services for starting and stopping agents. Additionally, for the Host agent type one parameter for the number of party guests is specified, in this case obliging the Host not to start the party before at least the specified number of guests has arrived. The parameter is non-optional meaning that a concrete value has to be specified by an agent instance of this type.

Besides the definition of the agent types, an additional definition of the society type, together with a set of society instances is needed (see Fig. 5). It contains

```
01 <society name="BirthdaySociety" package="examples.party">
02
03    [import and declaration of used agenttypes and referenced societies are omitted]
04
05    <societyinstances default="SmallParty">
06
07        <societyinstance name="SmallParty">
08            <agentinstances>
09                <agentinstance name="Birthday Child" type="Host">
10                    <parametervalue name="guestsToWaitFor"> 10 </parametervalue>
11                </agentinstance>
12            </agentinstances>
13            <societyinstanceref name="Guests" societytype="BirthdaySociety" societyinstance="SmallGuestpool">
14                <dependency active="false">
15                    <agenttype name="Host" quantity="1"/>
16                </dependency>
17                <launcher name="ASCML@remotecomputername:5000/JADE">
18                    <address> http://192.168.0.170:5010/acc </address>
19                </launcher>
20            </societyinstanceref>
21        </societyinstance>
22
23        <societyinstance name="SmallGuestpool">
24            <agentinstances>
25                <agentinstance name="Guest No._%N" type="Guest" quantity="10" />
26            </agentinstances>
27        </societyinstance>
28
29    </societyinstances>
30
31 </society>
```

Fig. 5. Definition of the JADE Party-society type

the definition of the *SmallParty* society instance (lines 7-21), which represents the main application and a helper society instance called *SmallGuestpool* (lines 23-27).

One agent instance, named "Birthday Child", is contained within the Small-Party. This instance relies on the agent type Host, indicated by the attribute type (line 9), and therefore has to supply a value for the guestsToWaitFor-parameter (cf. agent type definition). Besides the agent instance also the subsociety *Guests* (line 13-20) is defined as reference to the SmallGuestpool society instance. To make sure the guests do not join the party before the host is ready, a dependency is specified (lines 14-16) forcing the ASCML to first wait for the dependency before going on starting the referenced society instance. Once the dependency is satisfied, the ASCML may try to start the subsociety by sending a request to the launcher (lines 17-19). The launcher, identified by its FIPA-conform name and a set of addresses, has to be an ASCML-agent as well. Assuming this ASCML also has access to the given society instance, it may now start the agent instances contained within the society instance.

The subsociety SmallGuestPool consists of a collection of guests, which are agents of the same type (line 25). For convenience, not every individual agent has to be provided with its own definition. It is sufficient to specify the number of agents contained within the collection by using the quantity-attribute and a naming scheme for enumerating the agent instances.

5   Prototype Realization

The deployment reference model is the basis for the currently developed ASCML prototype. The reference model as described above is platform independent, therefore allowing agent applications not only to be spread across different hosts but also to be composed of agents developed for different platforms. The launcher tool currently exists in two (slightly different) versions, developed for the JADE [20] and Jadex [22, 23] platforms.

5.1   Architecture

The ASCML is subdivided into three co-operating subsystems: the launcher, the repository, and the GUI. To enable subsystems being individually exchanged, modified or enhanced the connection between these components is lightweight based on interfaces and event mechanisms. In the following each of the subsystems is described in more detail and their role within the ASCML's architecture (as depicted in Fig. 6) is highlighted.

The repository-subsystem provides facilities to manage all necessary data used within the ASCML such as agent- and society models, properties and project-management data. The repository is used as an abstract shared data structure and may be accessed by all other subsystems. Furthermore, it is responsible for loading and saving model-objects from and to different data sources, like XML-files or databases. Changes made to the data contained within the repository are acquainted by events to all registered listeners.

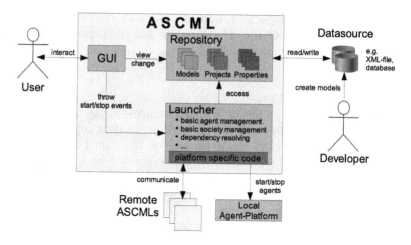

Fig. 6. The ASCML architecture

The GUI-subsystem facilitates the interaction between the user and the underlying subsystems. It provides dialogs to view and change data contained within the repository and allows the user to interact with the launcher to perform actions such as starting and stopping of agent and society instances.

The launcher-subsystem realises the interface between the ASCML and the underlying agent-platform. It is responsible for the basic agent- and society management, which includes starting and stopping of agent instances, delegation of action-requests to remote ASCMLs and resolving dependencies defined by soci-

Fig. 7. The ASCML tool screenshot

eties. It encapsulates the logic for communicating with the local agent-platform as well as with remote ASCMLs. Therefore parts of the launcher are platform-dependent, but may easily be exchanged to support different agent-platforms.

5.2   Example Usage

The graphical user interface of our ASCML implementation is depicted in figure 7. On the left hand side, one can see the specification repository tree with some known agent and society types, whereas on the right hand side details of the selected tree element are shown. In this example, the society type called BirthdaySociety and a couple of tool agents are available. In the BirthdaySociety, two different instances (SmallGuestpool and SmallParty) are predefined as ready to run application configurations. In the depicted scenario, two tool agents (sniffer and introspector) already have been started. On the right hand side some details of the SmallGuestpool such as the contained agent instances are presented.

6   Conclusion and Outlook

In this paper, we have argued that deployment techniques are important for the wide-spread and industrial adoption of multi-agent system technology. We have investigated the general requirements and the extent to which existing deployment techniques can be adapted to support the launching and configuration of distributed multi-agent systems.

To address the arising issues we have proposed a reference model that specifies the general launching and configuration infrastructure. The reference model is based on the notions of agents and societies as constituting entities. For the reference model a FIPA-compliant service interface has been designed, which allows (parts of) applications to be started on different hosts and possibly on different platforms. A prototype of the deployment tool (ASCML) has been implemented for the JADE and Jadex frameworks.

Future extensions will be done on two levels. On the conceptual level we will further investigate, which elements and relationships are necessary for the specification of abstract multi-agent applications according to our vision of scalable and adaptive systems. For this purpose, we need to extend our definition of agent societies incorporating more advanced concepts such as roles and constraints, taking into account existing organisational models. The usage of roles promises e.g. to capture the relationships between agents at a more abstract level enabling dependencies to be specified between roles and not only at the agent instance level. The introduction of application constraints will not only leverage the abstraction level of the application specification, but also can be seen as a starting point for dynamic application reconfiguration. This is because the configuration environment could use these constraints to ensure certain properties of the application and engage in appropriate actions whenever this becomes necessary.

On the tool level, the ASCML will be extended to live up to its name by introducing user interfaces for the easy construction of agent-based applications. This will further improve the tool's usability and additionally can be exploited to reduce the number of application specification mistakes. Monitoring capabilities (e.g. observing the lifecycle state of agents) will be added to the tool to facilitate automatic reconfiguration of running applications.

Acknowledgements

This work is partially funded by the DFG German priority research programme SPP 1083: *Intelligent Agents in Real-World Business Applications.*

References

1. Jennings, N.R.: An agent-based approach for building complex software systems. Communications of the ACM **44** (2001) 35–41
2. Jennings, N.R., Wooldridge, M.J.: Agent Technology - Foundations, Applications and Markets. Springer Verlag (1998)
3. Arlow, J., Neustadt, I.: UML and the Unified Process: Practical Object-Oriented Analysis and Design. Addison-Wesley (2002)
4. Sudeikat, J., Braubach, L., Pokahr, A., Lamersdorf, W.: Evaluation of Agent-Oriented Software Methodologies – Examination of the Gap Between Modeling and Platform. In: Proc. of the 5th Int. Workshop on Agent-Oriented Software Engineering (AOSE-2004). (2004)
5. (OMG), O.M.G.: Deployment and Configuration of Component-based Distributed Applications Specification. (2003) http://www.omg.org/.
6. Ricordel, P., Demazeau, Y.: From analysis to deployment: A multi-agent platform survey. In: Engineering Societies in the Agents World, Springer-Verlag (2000) 93–105
7. Mitkas, P.A., Kehagias, D., Symeonidis, A.L., Athanasiadis, I.N.: A framework for constructing multi-agent applications and training intelligent agents. In: Proc. of the 4th Int. Workshop on Agent-Oriented Software Engineering (AOSE-2003). (2003) 96–109
8. Systems, R.: AgentBuilder User's Guide. (2000) http://www.agentbuilder.com/.
9. Nwana, H., Ndumu, D., Lee, L., Collis, J.: ZEUS: a toolkit and approach for building distributed multi-agent systems. In: Proc. of the 3rd conference on Autonomous Agents, ACM Press (1999) 360–361
10. Collier, R.W.: Agent Factory: A Framework for the Engineering of Agent-Oriented Applications. PhD thesis, University College Dublin (2001)
11. Cowan, D., Griss, M., Burg, B.: BlueJADE - A service for managing software agents. Technical Report HPL-2001-296R1, Hewlett Packard Laboratories (2002)
12. Ferber, J., Gutknecht, O., Michel, F.: From Agents to Organizations: an Organizational View of Multi-Agent Systems. In Giorgini, P., Mller, J., Odell, J., eds.: AOSE. Volume 2935 of Lecture Notes in Computer Science., Springer (2003) 214–230
13. Odell, J.J., Parunak, H.V.D., Fleischer, M.: The role of roles in designing effective agent organizations. In: Software Eng. for Large-Scale MAS, Springer (2003) 27–38

14. Giampapa, J., Juarez-Espinosa, O., Sycara, K.: Configuration Management for Multi-Agent Systems. In: The 5th International Conference on Autonomous Agents (Agents 2001), ACM Press (2001) 230–231
15. Sycara, K., Giampapa, J., Langley, B., Paolucci, M.: The RETSINA MAS, a Case Study. In: Software Engineering for Large-Scale Multi-Agent Systems: Research Issues and Practical Applications. Volume LNCS 2603. Springer-Verlag (2003) 232–250
16. Foundation for Intelligent Physical Agents: FIPA Agent Configuration Management Specification. Document no. FIPA00090 (2001)
17. Castaldi, M., Carzaniga, A., Inverardi, P., Wolf, A.: A Light-weight Infrastructure for Reconfiguring Applications. In Westfechtel, B., van der Hoek, A., eds.: Software Configuration Management, ICSE Workshops SCM 2001 and SCM 2003, Springer (2003)
18. Castaldi, M.: Dynamic Reconfiguration of Component Based Applications. PhD thesis, Department of Computer Science, University of L'Aquila, Italy (2004)
19. Sloman, M.: Management issues for distributed services. In: Proc. of the 2nd Int. Workshop on Services in Distributed and Networked Environments, IEEE (1995) 52–55
20. Bellifemine, F., Rimassa, G., Poggi, A.: JADE – A FIPA-compliant agent framework. In: 4th Int. Conf. on the Practical Applications of Agents and MAS (PAAM-99). (1999)
21. for Intelligent Physical Agents, F.: FIPA Agent Management Specification. Document no. FIPA00023 (2002)
22. Pokahr, A., Braubach, L., Lamersdorf, W.:   Jadex: Implementing a BDI-Infrastructure for JADE Agents. EXP – in search of innovation **3** (2003) 76–85
23. Braubach, L., Pokahr, A., Lamersdorf, W.:   Jadex: A Short Overview.   In: Net.ObjectDays 2004: AgentExpo. (2004) 76–85

Using Stand-in Agents in Partially Accessible Multi-agent Environment

Martin Rehák, Michal Pěchouček, Jan Tožička, and David Šišlák

Department of Cybernetics,
Czech Technical University in Prague,
Technická 2, Prague 6, 166 27 Czech Republic
{rehakm1, pechouc, tozicka}@labe.felk.cvut.cz
sislakd@feld.cvut.cz

Abstract. This contribution defines a metrics and proposes a solution for the problem of agents inaccessibility in multi-agent systems. We define the stand-in pattern for knowledge maintenance and remote presence in distributed agent systems with communication inaccessibility. Our implementation has been designed and tested in the *A*-**globe** agent platform. We also present a set of measurements quantifying agents' inaccessibility in our domain and comparing the usefulness of different solution in the environments with different inaccessibility.

1   Introduction

Nowadays, most agent systems are physically localized in one location or connected by fixed networks. Therefore, the inaccessibility is coped with on the lower parts of the protocol stack. The agents themselves treat the inaccessibility situations as rare, error causes and can not react appropriately in such situations. With the increasing use of physically distributed agent systems in the external environment and the appearance of mobile or static mesh networks [1] for their connection, agent developers will have to solve accessibility or inaccessibility related problems to make their systems more reliable and useful.

Therefore, agents' inaccessibility [2] in a multi-agent community is an uneasy problem of a high practical importance. Agents become inaccessible when they want to communicate but it is not possible. There are several different reasons why an agent may become inaccessible from the other members of the multi-agent community - such as malfunction of the communication links, communication traffic overload, agent leaving the communication infrastructure for accomplishing a specific mission, agent failing to operate, etc.

Consequently, there is a need for an unified and general technology for maintaining social stability/sustainability in multi-agent system with inaccessible agents.

Within the frame of our work we have been comparing the original concept of the **stand-in agents** with the classical relaying approaches. While relaying provides a simple re-direction technology used in computer networks (e.g. it provides only routing of messages in order to implement accessibility between two

M.-P. Gleizes, A. Omicini, and F. Zambonelli (Eds.): ESAW 2004, LNAI 3451, pp. 277–291, 2005.

agents where direct connection is not possible), deployment of stand-in agents represents more advanced concept and suggest a whole set of interesting research problems. Conversely, the stand-in agent is a distant representative of a respective agent – the owner. Stand-in agents are created by their owner and they migrate to different segments of the communication infrastructure that may become inaccessible in the near future. When inaccessibility occurs the stand-in agent acts on the owners behalf.

In this article we will discuss the problem of inaccessibility and suggest specific quantities for measuring inaccessibility. In the section 3 we will discuss possible solutions for inaccessibility. Selected approaches will be then compared in section 4, together with validation of applicability of theoretical concepts presented in the section 2.

2   Measuring Inaccessibility

Systematically we distinguish between several classes of inaccessibility. Inaccessibility can be caused e.g. by unreliability of the communication infrastructure, balancing the cost of the communication, dynamic changes of the communication infrastructure topology, etc.

Quantification of inaccessibility in a multi-agent system is an important problem. In the following we discuss several metrics of inaccessibility that we have been using throughout our research project.

Let us introduce a **measure of inaccessibility**, a quantity denoted as $\overline{\vartheta} \in [0; 1]$. This measure is supposed to be dual to the **measure of accessibility** $- \vartheta \in [0; 1]$, where $\vartheta + \overline{\vartheta} = 1$. We will want ϑ to be 1 in order to denote complete accessibility and ϑ to be 0 in order to denote complete inaccessibility. In the following text we will mostly describe the agents' accessibility while the inaccessibility is its complement.

We will use the random graph theory [3] in order to describe some general properties of communication inaccessibility in multi-agent systems. Random graph theory has been recently successfully used for theoretical studies of complex networks [4]. Let us represent the multi-agent community as a graph. The agents are represented by nodes and available communication links – connections where the information exchange is possible – by edges. Unlike in the general case of agents inaccessibility, the random graphs theory works with an assumption that all edges are present with the same probability p. In our domain, this probability is represented by **link accessibility**: $p = \vartheta$.

The ϑ link accessibility can be determined in two ways. Firstly as time accessibility ϑ_t:

$$\vartheta_t = \frac{t_{\mathrm{acc}}}{t_{\mathrm{inacc}} + t_{\mathrm{acc}}}, \tag{1}$$

where t_{acc} denotes the amount of time when communication is possible while t_{inacc} denotes time when agents are disconnected.

Similarly, we may measure accessibility as a function of sent communication messages (communication accessibility ϑ_m):

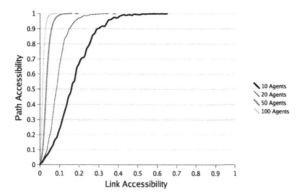

Fig. 1. The dependency of probability of existence path between two agents and link accessibility. This graph is the same for the link accessibility with or without the symmetry

$$\vartheta_m = \frac{|m| - |m_{\text{fail}}|}{|m|},\qquad(2)$$

where $|m|$ denotes the total number of messages sent and $|m_{\text{fail}}|$ the number of messages that failed to be delivered. The accessibility measure ϑ_t is symmetrical between entities A and B

$$\vartheta_t(A, B) = \vartheta_t(B, A),\qquad(3)$$

while the accessibility measure ϑ_m is not necessarily symmetrical.

In the following we will discuss ϑ_t while most conclusions apply equally to ϑ_m.

We have been investigating primarily the domain of mobile ad-hoc networking among computational units constantly changing their physical location. In this domain, ϑ_t accessibility depends on the environment agent positions only, while ϑ^m accessibility depends also on other factors, like communication link load or limited social knowledge of the agents.

We have determined the probability of existence path between two agents - **path accessibility** - depending on link accessibility in simple mathematical simulation. The result is shown in Figure 1. Classical result of the random graph theory is that there exists a critical probability at which large cluster appears. In our domain, we assume that there is a **critical accessibility** – ϑ^c such that below ϑ^c the agent community is composed of several isolated groups but above ϑ^c most of agents become mutually path-accessible (using relay agents). The ϑ^c value is represented by the quick growth in the Figure 1. This observation is similar to a percolation transition known in the field of mathematics and statistical mechanics [5]. In the field of multi-agent systems, it means that the relay agents are more efficient than isolated stand-in agents for link accessibility bigger than ϑ^c. Our testing scenario, presented in section 4 and implemented using actual multi-agent system based on $\mathcal{A}$-**globe** [6] allows to set up and verify properties of both cases.

Table 1. Different cases of accessibility as described by random graph theory

$\vartheta_t n < 1$	The network is typically composed of isolated trees. The diameter is equal to the diameter of trees.
$\vartheta_t n > 1$	A large cluster is formed. The diameter is equal to the largest cluster diameter and if $\vartheta_t n > 3.5$ it is proportional to $\frac{\ln(n)}{\ln(\vartheta_t n)}$.
$\vartheta_t n > \ln(n)$	The graph is probably totally connected and the diameter is very close to $\frac{\ln(n)}{\ln(\vartheta_t n)}$.

Second relevant result of random graph theory is the average length l^* of path between any two vertices and the diameter l^d of a graph (i.e. maximal distance between any two nodes). It holds [4]:

$$l^* \sim l^d = \frac{\ln(n)}{\ln(\vartheta_t n)},$$

where n is number of agents.

In our domain, the length of the path says how many relays has to be used in order to convey a message between the agents A and B. And as a result of random graph theory, the maximal number of relays necessary is not much greater then the number of relays in average case.

Table 1 summarizes several results of random graph theory important for our study of inaccessibility.

These properties are well observable also in our domain (see section 4.2).

3   Solving Inaccessibility

We are now going to analyze existing methods coping with inaccessibility. Two main approaches can be distinguished between them: building **remote awareness** or **remote presence**.

When an agent builds remote awareness, allows the remote agents to update their social knowledge with relevant information about itself and to let them operate using this information. This process may be implemented using either pull or push information retrieval operations. Typical examples are acquaintance models described in section 3.3, matchmaking middle agents (3.2) or synchronization and search in peer-to-peer networks [7].

When an agent builds a remote presence, it does so in order to operate **actively** in the remote location. As a collateral effect of this action, the agent may also build a remote awareness - as in the stand-in case, but this does not necessarily apply when we use middle agents. Examples of this approach are relaying (3.1), stand-ins (3.4) or broker middle agents (3.2).

3.1   Relay Agents and Adaptive Networks

First, and perhaps the most classical solution to the inaccessibility problem are relay agents (or low-level entities), responsible for setting up a transmission path through other elements when the direct contact between parties is impossible. Such protocols are currently widely implemented for routing in various types of networks, like TCP/IP [8] or on lower levels [1]. However, this solution is efficient only if the network is in a "reasonably connected" state (see third row of Table 1 and Figure 1). Besides this limitation, that can be clearly distinguished in the results of our experiments, there are several other factors limiting the use of relayed connection. These factors are for example reduced battery life due to the fact that all the messages must be transmitted several times, or network maintenance overhead, especially in case of mobile networks. Another factor limiting the use of relaying in agent systems is the dynamic nature of their topology if the agent platforms are based on moving entities. In this case, relaying cost increases as the link maintenance and path-finding in dynamic environment is a non-trivial process.

3.2   Middle Agents

Middle agent is a term that can cover a whole range of different facilitators in a multi-agent system. In an overview article [9], authors list different types of middle agents - **Matchmakers** and **Brokers** (Facilitators). Matchmakers may provide remote awareness by notifying interested agents about the presence of service providers, while the brokers can act as intermediaries and pass actual service requests between two mutually inaccessible parties. Even if this solution may perform very well in many situations, it may be unusable if middle agents are difficult to find, unreliable, or can not be trusted with private preferences of different parties. Stand-in agents described later are intended to close this gap.

3.3   Social Knowledge and Acquaintance Models

Social knowledge represent necessary and optional information which an agent needs for its efficient operation in the multi-agent community. The social knowledge is mainly used for reduction of communication, provides self-interested agents with a competitive advantage and allows agents to reason about the others in environments with partial accessibility.

The acquaintance model is a very specific knowledge structure containing agent's social knowledge. This knowledge structure is in a fact a computational model of agents' mutual awareness. It does not need to be precise and up-to-date. Agents may use different methods and techniques for maintenance and exploitation of the acquaintance model. There have been various acquaintance models studied and developed in the multi-agent community, eg. *tri-base acquaintance model* [10] and *twin-base acquaintance model* [11]. In principle, each acquaintance model is split into two parts: **self-knowledge** containing information about an agent itself and **social-knowledge** containing knowledge about other members of the multi-agent system.

While the former part of the model is maintained by the **social knowledge provider** (an owner), the latter is maintained by the **social knowledge requestor** (a client).

Social knowledge can be used for making operation of the multi-agent system more efficient. The acquaintance model is an important source of information that would have to be repeatedly communicated otherwise. Social knowledge and acquaintance models can be also used in the situations of agents' short term inaccessibility. However, the acquaintance models provides rather *'shallow'* knowledge, that does not represent a complicated dynamics of agent's decision making, future course of intentions, resource allocation or negotiation preferences. This type of information is needed for inter-agent coordination in situation with longer-term inaccessibility.

3.4   Stand-in Agent

An alternative option is to integrate the agent self-knowledge into a mobile computational entity that is constructed and maintained by the social knowledge provider. We will refer to this computational entity as a **stand-in agent**. The stand-in agent resides either on the same host where the social knowledge requestor operates or in the permanently accessible location. While using stand-in, the social knowledge requestor does not create an acquaintance model of its own. Instead of communicating with the provider or middle agent, it interacts with the stand-in agent. Therefore, the client agent is relieved from the relatively complex task of building and keeping up-to-date detailed acquaintance model and both provider and requestor may benefit from the full-fledged remote presence. Factoring the acquaintance model out of the each requestor agent internal memory allows it to be shared between all locally accessible agents, further minimizing the traffic and computational resources necessary for model maintenance.

In our implementation the community of stand-in agents operates in two phases: **stand-in swarming, information propagation** and **social knowledge synchronization**.

During the swarming phase, stand-ins propagate through the system to reach the locations that may become inaccessible in the future. First, existing stand-in agent or knowledge provider determines set of currently accessible locations using broadcast-like mechanism of underlying communication infrastructure. It analyzes the locations and decides which entities are interesting for further stand-in agent deployment, either because of the presence of knowledge requestor agent or because it considers the location to be interesting for future spread. Then, it may decide to create and deploy its clones on one or more of these accessible locations. After its creation, each deployed stand-in agent chooses the type of functionality it will provide in its location and repeats the evaluate/deploy process. The swarming propagation strategy is a crucial element of agent system tuning, as we must find a delicate balance between information spread efficiency and resources consumed by stand-ins.

Information propagation between members of the stand-in community is also a challenging process to tune, because the information flows not only from the knowledge provider towards the stand-in community, but also from the stand-in community towards knowledge provider, or even within the isolated parts of the stand-in community.

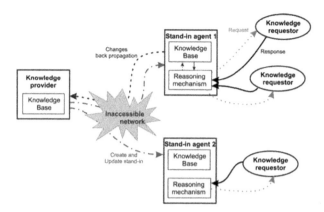

Fig. 2. The concept of the stand-in agent

When a member of the stand-in community receives an update of the shared knowledge, or updates this knowledge after having acted on behalf of knowledge provider, it must determine if the information update is valuable enough to be propagated to other members of the community and eventually to the knowledge provider itself. It determines the list of currently accessible stand-ins in the community to which it will send the updated knowledge set or relevant subset and keeps the updated information ready for future synchronization with currently inaccessible stand-ins.

In our current implementation, we do present two limit approaches to information synchronization. In the first configuration, we consider the cost of communication to be important and the stand-ins therefore synchronize their knowledge only when they encounter. When they receive an information update, they don't propagate it to other accessible members of the community.

Our second approach is based on an assumption that communication is cheap and that all updates are worth to be propagated to all accessible members of the community. In this approach, any stand-in that updates the information or receives more recent version sends this update to all accessible members of the community. When two stand-ins become accessible, they exchange their information and join it into the shared common version, as ensured by domain-specific joining algorithm. This policy ensures an optimum information quality on domain elements, but must be optimized for domains with big number of locations and represented agents, for example using existing results from peer-to-peer networks research domain [7].

The most important added value of stand-in agent is not in providing remote awareness, but in providing rich and proactive remote presence by acting on behalf of knowledge provider. However, as in any system working on the shared data, synchronization problems arise in the agent community when the stand-ins accept commitments in place of knowledge provider. Situation is further complicated by the fact that no reasonable locking protocol may be implemented between the components that are inaccessible in a given moment. Until now, we have not explicitly addressed the synchronization problem. Its solution may use e.g. sophisticated multi-level negotiation protocols, the concept of structured (rich) commitments or advanced methods of synchronization between locally accessible agents.

The concept stand-in agents are currently advantageous in the two very specific situations:

- in the **very dynamic environment**, with relatively low path accessibility (this can be e.g. in situations where a low number of unmanned vehicles are collaboratively inspecting large areas), or
- in the **non-trusted environment** with at least some communication inaccessibility (in these cases the agent do not want to provide sensitive knowledge for sharing while off-line).

In our current work, we are analyzing and optimizing the collaboration patterns of the stand-in community to make the approach scalable.

3.5   Towards Optimization of the Stand-in Approach

The measurements presented in the next section (4) provide us with the **limits** of performance of various inaccessibility solutions depending on the accessibility of the environment. They show that the use of stand-ins (see 3.4) or other remote awareness and presence technologies allows the multi-agent system to operate in highly inaccessible environments. Currently, we are answering many crucial practical questions concerning the efficient stand-in use.

All these questions are related to the scalability of the approach - until now, we have considered the processing power and bandwidth as either cheap and unlimited or very expensive. With the use of stand-ins in larger domains, these basic assumptions are not valid anymore and consequent issues must be addressed.

The first problem is stand-in deployment. In the large domains featuring significant number of nodes, the complete flooding with stand-ins and their deployment in each container would mean that the stand-ins would outnumber all other agents by a large factor, making their use prohibitive. This would not only consume the memory and processing power of the nodes, but it would also increase the bandwidth necessary for information synchronization and action coordination in the system.

Therefore, we must optimize both the stand-in deployment and information synchronization using domain independent methods. We will try to maintain the system performance close to the theoretical limit established in the experiments (sect. 4.2), while minimizing the number of stand-ins and synchronization messages. On the other hand, this optimization shall not decrease system robustness in respect to the failures - it shall adapt rapidly to the changing situation and keep the information up-to-date under most circumstances.

In our current research, we have pre-selected two approaches to system optimization. The pre-selection criteria were very simple ones - efficiency, robustness to the failure of elements and stability in the rapidly changing environment of mobile ad-hoc networks. The first model is inspired by biology, the second one by micro-economy.

Social dominance and altruism models [12, 13] were successfully used to partition the group of agents into those who work for the good of the community and the others who profit from the altruism of the first group. Interestingly, observations during the experiments with rats in the laboratory environment confirm that such approach actually *maximizes* the survival rate for the members of the community and is stable with respect to changes in the groups of observed rats - both properties being of particular interest to us.

During the experiments with rats, it was determined that a sufficient number of individuals behaves in an altruistic manner. They bring the food and share it with the others, who only consume. Surprisingly, when the group is split, half of the previous altruists change their behavior and become passive, while half of the group that was previously lazy becomes altruistic. This behavior is formalized by a simple mathematical model presented in [12].

I our approach, the stand-ins will be split between altruists and "lazy" individuals. Altruists will form a backbone of the community, as they will pass the information to other altruists and adjacent lazy stand-ins. While the configuration of the community changes, we expect the stand-ins to adopt the new social role and maintain the functionality of the community. The main problem to solve is the actual modification of the model and automatic adaptation to various types of environments with diverse accessibility and mobility characteristics.

Simulated micro-payments model. In this model, stand-ins answer the information updates with a micro-payment, indicating the usefulness of the received information. As the agents subtract the virtual price attributed to the sending of the synchronization message from the received payment, the network shall optimize itself if the agents value the information most upon the first reception and decrease the payment for the updates that are already known. To optimize the number of agents, the approach is similar. Agents who don't generate sufficient gain from representing the owner agent or from relaying the updates to the others in the community terminate themselves.

The main challenge in this approach is in fine-tuning the mechanism - optimizing the virtual costs and payments and determining the probabilities which will be applied to sending unsolicited updates or re-creation of already self-destroyed stand-ins by adjacent stand-ins - both parameters are essential for community re-adaptation in changing environment. All the mentioned parameters will be hardly constant - they will undoubtedly vary in function of the accessibility characteristics, defined in section 2.

We are also analyzing the methods how to enhance these essentially emergent models with a global vision - in a way similar to the adaptive adaptation (or meta-adaptation) as proposed for example by Bedau and Packard [14]. Both emergent (bottom-up) and meta-reasoning approaches are analyzed for this task.

Using the stand-ins as a part of the system brings another interesting aspect. As the owner gives more power to the stand-ins, it increases the likelihood of identifying the optimum partner for the operation. On the other hand, as the parts of the stand-in community may get isolated, an issue of concurrence must be solved. This problem is very similar to adjustable autonomy in human-agent relationship, as studied by Sierhuis et al. [15].

4   Experiments

In this section, we will describe a set of accessibility experiments with a multi-agent simulation. The goal of the experiments was to validate the relevance of the theory presented in the first part (Section 2) of this contribution on a real multi-agent system and to determine the boundaries of applicability of the solutions to the inaccessibility problem presented in the second part (Section 3). First we will investigate and analyze inaccessibility in our scenario and after this we will study how inaccessibility affects performance of our system. Three techniques for coping with inaccessibility will be analyzed.

In our measurements, we will validate if the classical random-graph model presented in Section 2 is appropriate for our case, or if we need to apply more realistic network modelling techniques [16]. Then, we will measure the influence the inaccessibility has to the solution of the model domain and the efficiency of three possible approaches dealing with the problem.

4.1   Testing Scenario

For our measurements, we have prepared a simulation featuring a logistics problem in collaborative environment, where the humanitarian aid must be delivered to the zone ravaged by a disaster. In the domain, we will deploy three main types of entities: 5 aid sources, called **ports**, where the material comes in; 5 aid sinks, called **villages**, where it is consumed and 7 **transports** carrying the aid between ports and villages. Each transport has its predefined route that does not change during the simulation. Aid requests in the villages are generated by predefined script to ensure uniformity between simulation runs. They must be transmitted to the ports to ensure that the proper material is loaded on the transport going to the village. The way these requests are transmitted depends on the inaccessibility solution that is currently applied. We suppose that the physical communication links between the entities are limited-range radios, therefore the link exists if the distance is smaller then parameter ϱ. This parameter varies between different scenario runs to model different possible configurations, from complete link accessibility to only local (same position) accessibility Test domain is shown in Fig. 3.

In total, 33 results are presented, with 11 different communication ranges and 3 different approaches solving the inaccessibility problem:

- relaying transmissions by relay agents (3.1) – loading of the goods on a transport is possible only if a communication path exists between the destination village and the port in the moment when port-based entities negotiate the cargo to load,

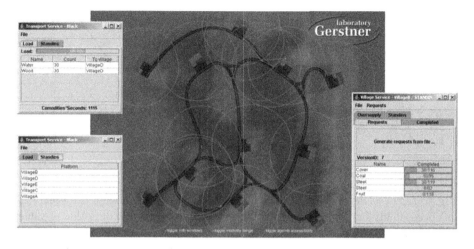

Fig. 3. Test domain used for the experiments contains 5 ports, 5 villages and 7 transports. Circles represent the accessibility ranges, while the lines the actual accessibility and ongoing communication between nodes

- stand-in agents that only carry the information with no sharing in the stand-in community (see section 3.4),
- community stand-in agents, sharing the information updates with other members of the stand-in agent community (see also section 3.4).

To guarantee the uniformity of results, we have used the same negotiation protocols and work-flow for the interaction between the acting agents and their environment. Both the requests in villages and goods in ports are generated from unique pseudorandom sequence used for all measurements. The only aspect that differentiates the scenarios is the mode of information transmission between requesting villages and goods providers in the ports.

4.2   Measuring Accessibility

On Figure 4, we can identify three major states of the community from the accessibility point of view, as defined in section 2. At first, before the communication radius reaches 60, static community members are isolated and information is not transmitted (see first row of Table 1), but only carried by moving entities. In this state, path accessibility is not significantly different from link accessibility. Therefore, probability of relaying is almost negligible.

Then, with increasing communication radius, larger connected components do start to appear, covering several static and mobile entities and allowing the use of relaying over these portions of the graph. This phase appears around the percolation threshold, that can be observed above radius of 80, corresponding with link accessibility of 0.2. This state is characterized by important variability of connected components. Due to the dynamic nature of our system, these components are relatively short-lived, resulting in a high variability of the system,

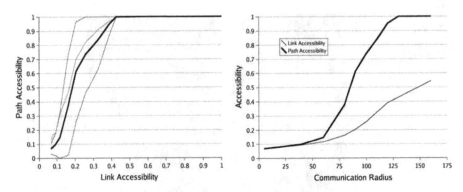

Fig. 4. *Left:* The dependency of probability of existence path between two agents and link accessibility in our test scenario. The dot lines show average deviation of values. The gray thin line shows theoretical value for random graph with 10 nodes (see Fig. 1). *Right:* The dependency of link and path accessibility on communication radius

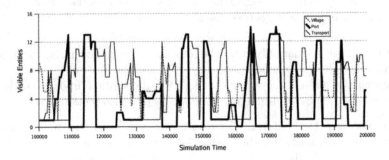

Fig. 5. Number of visible entities for different types of entities in our scenario, for communication radius of 80, near percolation threshold

as we can see on Figure 5. Path accessibility in the community may be described by relation (see second row of Table 1).

In the last state, when communication radius is above 120 and link accessibility reaches 0.4, the entities become almost completely connected. This state of the community is described by relation (see third row of Table 1). System properties does not change when we further increase the radius and link accessibility.

The dynamic nature of our network near percolation threshold is clearly visible on the following graph (Figure 5), where we present the number of locations visible from one randomly chosen entity of each location type over a period of time. As we are near the percolation threshold, in the state described by second row of Table 1, we can observe the appearance of relatively large, but short lived, accessible components.

In the Figure 5, we may also note that the transport is accessible from significantly more locations than static elements. As this holds for all transports in

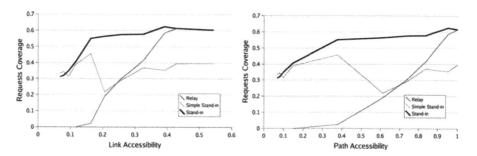

Fig. 6. The average requests coverage of three presented inaccessibility solutions and different accessibility settings

our scenario, a parallel with scale-free networks [16] arises. In these networks, a small number of nodes called hubs has significantly more connections with others than the rest, while in the random networks most nodes have the same number of adjacent edges. In this respect, transport platforms with stand-ins on them serve as hubs of our system, spreading the information as they roam through the map. In our future experiments, we will examine this possibility and test the hypothesis on a larger agent community.

4.3   Comparing the Solutions

After having determined the extent of inaccessibility in our system, we will study the effects inaccessibility has on the system performance. The system performance is given by a number of goods successfully delivered to villages. Zero value means complete failure, when no goods were transported, while 1 implies that all orders were completed.

On the following graph (see Figure 6), we can observe the relationship between path accessibility and overall system performance for each of three solutions. Here we present the average requests coverage for different solution of inaccessibility. Results do follow the accessibility state partitioning from the previous paragraph. We can see that relay agents start to be reasonably useful when the link accessibility reaches 0.2, in the middle of the transition phase, well corresponding to the percolation threshold. Performance of isolated, non communicating stand-in remains constant. This is easy to understand, as these agents communicate only locally. They present an optimal solution for disconnected networks, as they require only a small number of messages to function.

On the other hand, performance of interacting community of stand-ins is more than a mere supremum of both previous methods. This is allowed by the dynamic nature of the system, where the stand-ins on mobile entities carry the up-to-date information through the system and spread it in small local communities, but relatively often. Thanks to this approach, the efficiency of system with these stand-ins approaches the optimum level with path accessibility of 0.4, instead of 0.9 for relay agents.

5   Conclusions and Future Work

In our experiments, we have proved that the theory describing the behavior of random graphs can serve as a basis for formalization and measure of the inaccessibility within multi-agent systems. In the future, we will extend our experiments to verify the hypothesis that the scale-free approach can be used to precise description of our system around percolation threshold. Moreover, we have provided several solutions, including new concept of stand-in agent, for inaccessibility and experimentally determined their boundaries of applicability.

As we have illustrated above, stand-in agents provide more than a viable alternative to message relaying in environments with low link accessibility or high cost of communication. They allow efficient coordination and collaboration in communities with low and transient accessibility and they match the performance of relaying in connected communities. However, the implementation of the stand-in agents for a given domain is not trivial and its use in larger communities of agents requires some additional tuning of two principal methods they use – swarming of the stand-in agents and knowledge distribution/synchronization. Currently implemented version of stand-ins is appropriate for environments with low and moderate accessibility, due to the fact the number of messages used for knowledge updates grows rapidly with increasing accessibility and the size of the domain. To extend its operational use for environments with the accessibility beyond the "transition phase", stand-ins shall be aware of the typical information flows in their neighborhood and better target their information updates, as mentioned in section 3.5.

Given the plummeting prices of hardware and many emerging low cost platforms designed specifically to be embedded with the environment to provide the measurements [17], we will often face the situations when the communication ability will be a limiting factor of such systems, due to the limited battery power and constraints on their emitters. In such cases, the sole cost of communication would prohibit the use of advanced negotiation or auctioning techniques between the agents residing on different nodes of the system. Stand-ins, created by all interested agents and deployed on an agreed node that provides sufficient computational resources and where the negotiation takes place, can be a solution to this problem too.

Acknowledgement

The research described in this chapter has been supported in parts by the EOARD/AFRL projects number FA8655-04-1-3044, FA-8655-02-M-4057 and ONR grant N00014-03-1-0292.

References

1. Woo, A., Tong, T., Culler, D.: Taming the underlying challenges of reliable multi-hop routing in sensor networks. In: Proceedings of the first international conference on Embedded networked sensor systems, ACM Press (2003) 14–27

2. Pĕchouček, M., Dobíšek, M., Lažanský, J., Mařík, V.: Inaccessibility in multi-agent systems. In: Proceedings of International Conference on Intelligent Agent Technology. (2003) 182–188
3. Bollobas, B.: Random Graphs. 2nd edn. Cambridge University Press (2001)
4. Albert, R., Barabási, A.L.: Statistical mechanics of complex networks. Rev. Mod. Phys. **74** (2002) 47–97
5. Grimmett, G.: Percolation. Springer-Verlag, New York (1989)
6. A-Globe: A-Globe Agent Platform. `http://agents.felk.cvut.cz/aglobe` (2004)
7. Elias Leontiadis, Vassilios V. Dimakopoulos, E.P.: Cache updates in a peer-to-peer network of mobile agents. In: Proceedings of the Fourth IEEE International Conference on Peer-to-Peer Computing, IEEE Computer Society (2004) 10–17
8. Stallings, W.: Data and computer communications (5th ed.). Prentice-Hall, Inc. (1997)
9. Sycara, K.: Multi-agent infrastructure, agent discovery , middle agents for web services and interoperation. In: Mutli-agents systems and applications, Springer-Verlag New York, Inc. (2001) 17–49
10. Pĕchouček, M., Mařík, V., Štěpánková, O.: Role of acquaintance models in agent-based production planning systems. In Klusch, M., Kerschberg, L., eds.: Cooperative Infromation Agents IV - LNAI No. 1860, Heidelberg, Springer Verlag (2000) 179–190
11. Cao, W., Bian, C.G., Hartvigsen, G.: Achieving efficient cooperation in a multi-agent system: The twin-base modeling. In Kandzia, P., Klusch, M., eds.: Cooperative Information Agents. Number 1202 in LNAI, Springer-Verlag, Heidelberg (1997) 210–221
12. Thomas, V., Bourjot, C., Chevrier, V., Desor, D.: Hamelin : A model for collective adaptation based on internal stimuli. In Schaal, S., Ijspeert, A., Billard, A., Vijayakumar, S., Hallam, J., Meyer, J.A., eds.: From animal to animats 8 - Eighth International Conference on the Simulation of Adaptive Behaviour 2004 - SAB'04, Los Angeles, USA. (2004) 425–434
13. Simonin, O., Ferber, J.: Modeling self satisfaction and altruism to handle action selection and reactive cooperation. In: Proceedings Supplement SAB 2000, The Sixth International Conference on the Simulation of Adaptative Behavior, From Animals to Animats 6, Paris, France (2000) 314–323
14. Bedau, M.A., Packard, N.H.: Evolution of evolvability via adaptation of mutation rates. Biosystems **69** (2003) 143–162
15. Sierhuis, M., Bradshaw, J., Acquisiti, A., van Hoof, R., R., J., Uszok, A.: Human-agent teamworks and adjustable autonomy in practice. In: Proceedings of the 7th International Symposium on Artificial Intelligence, Robotics and Automation in Space: i-SAIRAS - NARA, Japan (2003)
16. Barabi, A.L., Albert, R.: Emergence of scaling in random networks. Science **286** (1999) 509–512
17. Estrin, D., Culler, D., Pister, K., Sukhatme, G.: Connecting the physical world with pervasive networks. IEEE Pervasive Computing **1** (2002) 59–69

Controlled Experimentation with Agents — Models and Implementations

Mathias Röhl and Adelinde M. Uhrmacher

University of Rostock,
Department of Computer Science and Electrical Engineering,
Albert-Einstein-Str. 21, 18059 Rostock, Germany
{mroehl, lin}@informatik.uni-rostock.de

Abstract. The deployment of multi-agent systems demands for justified confidence into their functioning, both with respect to correctness of behaviour and with respect to timeliness thereof. Depending on the stage of the development process different mechanisms and abstractions are needed to facilitate the evaluation of interacting agents. We propose a modelling and simulation framework based on a discrete-event formalism for supporting the development process of multi-agent systems; from specification to implementation. The framework allows for the incremental refinement of agents and experimental set-ups while providing rigorous observation facilities. The benefit of using discrete-event modelling and simulation techniques for evaluating agents is illustrated using a simple example based on the *Contract Net Protocol*.

1 Introduction

Approaches for developing agents have matured to a broad spectrum of methods. Design methodologies support the development of agents by an agent-oriented development process [1] or by providing modelling languages enriched with agent concepts [2]. Formal analysis of agents based on logics are particularly aimed at rational agents and pruned for reasoning about changing beliefs [3]. Other approaches suggest to develop communities of agents by defining social norms and regulations [4]. In contrast to static techniques, testing activities are dynamic analysis methods that require the execution of software. Testing concentrates on the validation of an implementation against a specification and thereby complements software design and static analysis.

Developing agents is of an intrinsically experimental and exploratory nature: "the development of any agent system — however trivial — is essentially a process of experimentation" [5]. Surprisingly, only little work has been done so far on developing methods for testing agents [6]. Current methodologies and tools for MAS concentrate on supporting the design and implementation of agents, leaving a gap between specifications and implementations [7].

For exploiting the potential of MAS formal design methodologies and methods for observing and evaluating emergent behaviour have to be brought together

M.-P. Gleizes, A. Omicini, and F. Zambonelli (Eds.): ESAW 2004, LNAI 3451, pp. 292–304, 2005.

by a rigorous experimental approach allowing for consistent observation of MAS [8]. Pursuing a simulation-based approach rooted in general systems theory, our work is addressing this deficiency.

2   Experimentation with Multi-Agent Systems

To construct agents essentially means to develop software that is able to successfully accomplish specified tasks in a certain environment [9]. Consequently, validation of agent behaviour has to take into account the conditions under which the agent is intended to work correctly, i.e., testing has to treat agents as systems that frequently interact with their environment. The usage of a virtual environment in contrast to the real environment typically reduces costs and efforts and allows to test a system's behaviour in "rare event situations". Virtual environments are easier to observe and to control, and probe effects are easier to manage. "For software engineers, virtual environments offer a powerful means of integration and systems testing" [10]. Environment models can be used to generate the different test cases dynamically during simulation, including specific interaction patterns and time constraints [11]. As testing cannot show the absence of faults but only their presence [12], the validity of the environmental models will be crucial, independently whether abstract models of agents are experimentally evaluated [13], single agent modules are embedded for testing [14], or entire agent systems are plugged into the virtual environment [15].

Simulation is an experiment performed on a model and "a model M of a system S and an experiment E is anything to which E can be applied in order to answer questions about S" [16]. This definition of model emphasises that a model is not developed for a system "per se", but always for a combination of a system to be analysed and questions to be asked. According to this definition, multiple objectives require multiple models. The concept of *experimental frame* has been introduced to model experimental assumptions and system's requirements explicitly [17]. Developing an experimental frame for testing agents requires a modelling formalism that is sufficiently expressive to model complex dynamic environments for agents and that is able to express different kinds of timing requirements.

2.1   Discrete-Event Modelling and Simulation

DEVS (Discrete EVent System specification) is one of the formal approaches to discrete event modelling and simulation stemming from general systems theory [18]. It provides a powerful basis for modelling test settings by being able to encode many other modelling formalisms like *statecharts* and *petri nets* [19]. For example, Giambiasi et al. made concrete use of this capability by transforming *timed input/output automata* specifications into a DEVS simulation model for validating a control system [20].

DEVS distinguishes between atomic and coupled models. An atomic model is described by a state set, a set of input ports, a set of output ports, an internal and external transition function, an output function, and a time advance function (cf. Definition 1). The internal transition function dictates state transitions due to internal events, the time of which is determined by the time advance function. At an internal event, the model produces output. The external transition function is triggered by inputs.

Definition 1. *An atomic* DEVS *model is a structure* $\langle X, Y, S, s_0, \delta_{int}, \delta_{ext}, \lambda, ta \rangle$, *where*

- $X = \{(i,v) | i \in InPorts, v \in X_i\}$ *is the set of input ports and values*
- $Y = \{(o,v) | o \in OutPorts, v \in Y_o\}$ *is the set of output ports and values*
- S *is the set of sequential states*
- s_0 *is the initial state*
- $\delta_{int} : S \to S$ *is the internal transition function*
- $\delta_{ext} : Q \times X \to S$ *is the external transition function, with*
  $Q = \{(s,e) : s \in S, 0 \le e \le ta(s)\}$ *the set of total states*
- $\lambda : S \to Y$ *is the output function*
- $ta : S \to \mathbb{R}^{\ge 0} \cup \{\infty\}$ *is the time advance function [21]*

Coupled DEVS models support the hierarchical, modular construction of models. The interface of a coupled model equals that of an atomic model. It is described by a set of component models, which may be atomic or coupled, and by the couplings that exist among the components, and between the components and its own input and output ports. Coupled DEVS models do not add to the expressiveness of the formalisms, as atomic and coupled DEVS models have shown to be bisimilar. Nevertheless, coupled models enable the structuring of large models into smaller ones and they are the means for modular, hierarchical modelling. For the definition of syntax of coupled models and the definition of semantics of DEVS models the reader is referred to [21].

In simulation, we distinguish between physical time, simulation time, and wall clock time. Whereas simulation time and physical time are connected by a semantic relation, i.e. one tick in simulation time refers to a fixed quantum in physical time, wall clock time is not necessarily related to either of both. Execution is normally done in an unpaced mode, which means, that simulation time jumps as fast as possible from one event to the next, neglecting the simulation time (and thus the represented physical time) that lies inbetween [22]. Figure 1 shows part of an execution of two DEVS models. While the wall clock time continuously progresses throughout the simulation, simulation time increases at distinct time points according to scheduled events. The production of output by *Model1*, the reception of the according input by *Model2*, the internal transition of *Model1*, and the determination of next internal event times are all realised at the same simulation time t_i^{sim}. In the depicted case the value of the next simulation time would be calculated by $t_{i+1}^{sim} = t_i^{sim} + min(ta(s_1), ta(s_2))$.

2.2   Modelling and Simulation of Multi-Agent Systems

The agent metaphor promotes the design of systems as consisting of entities which concurrently act and interact, and whose configuration and environment

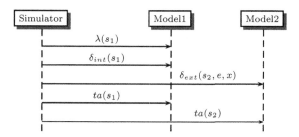

Fig. 1. Execution Fragment of two DEVS Models

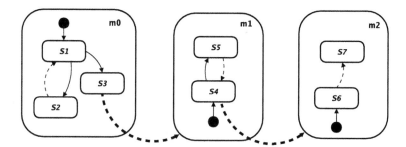

Fig. 2. State transitions versus model transitions

is frequently changing. Variable structure models are a prerequisite to specify and analyse such systems adequately.

To support the modelling and simulation of agents that dynamically adapt their interaction, composition, and behaviour pattern the formalism DYNDEVS was developed [23], which adds reflection to the DEVS formalism. An atomic model in DYNDEVS is defined as a set of model incarnations $\mathcal{M}(m_0)$ that inherit state set, transition functions, output, and time advance function from DEVS atomic models. The reflectivity is introduced by the model transition function ρ_α which maps states of incarnations into a set of model incarnations.

$$\rho_\alpha : S \to \mathcal{M}(m_0) \tag{1}$$

Thereby, sequences of models are produced (cf. Figure 2), starting with the initial model incarnation m_0. By switching to another incarnation, a model can change its own state and its behavior pattern, i.e. its transition, output, and time advance function, during simulation.

As the coupled model holds the information about composition and interaction between components, a change of composition or interaction, even though induced by atomic models, takes effect at the level of coupled models. Therefore, coupled DYNDEVS models were introduced, that are the means for modelling adaptable system structures. For a more detailed discussion of the formalism and the definition of semantics of DYNDEVS models, see [23].

2.3   External Processes

To test planning and commitment strategies of agents [24], DYNDEVS models have been equipped with peripheral ports (XP, YP), which are now used to support the interaction of atomic models with external processes in general.

The classical ports of DEVS models collect and offer events that are produced by models. In addition, the peripheral ports allow DYNDEVS-models to communicate with processes that are external to the simulation. Thereby, the simulation system does not interact with external agents as one black box, but each single model can function as an interface to external processes. The model functions were extended to handle input and output from respectively to external processes:

$$\delta_{int} : S \times XP \to S \times YP \tag{2}$$

$$\delta_{ext} : Q \times X \times XP \to S \times YP \tag{3}$$

$$\lambda : S \times XP \to Y \tag{4}$$

The state transition functions and the λ-function of the interface model describe how incoming data is transformed into data that can be used within the simulation. The functions δ_{int} and δ_{ext} are furthermore responsible for the transformation of simulation data into data usable by the externally running software.

The role of the ta-function is typically to model the pro-activeness of an entity, as it triggers internal events by the flow of time. In the case of externally running software, "pro-activeness" from the point of view of the simulation is triggered by incoming data. The simulation system uses the time model function tm to translate the resource consumption of the externally running software into simulation time:

$$tm : \mathbb{R}^{\geq 0} \to \mathbb{R}^{\geq 0} \tag{5}$$

External processes are invoked by the simulation system and the information put into the peripheral output ports is forwarded to them. After the external computation has finished, the results of these invocations arrive at the peripheral input ports of the according model at a simulation time which is determined by the time model. The time model might be constant for abstracting from actual resource consumption of external processes.

3   An Example — Evaluating Collaborative Agents

Depending on the actual phase in developing agents specifications , single modules, or entire agents might be tested. In the following we will illustrate how simulation can be used to facilitate controlled experimentation within virtual environments during different phases of the development. A simple, however extensible experimental set-up, shall help to answer the question: How well are certain models or implementations of collaborative agents suited for solving a global task?

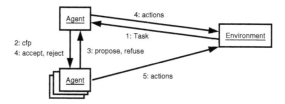

Fig. 3. Cooperation via the contract net protocol

The example comprises multiple agents with individual bounded capabilities. Tasks appear frequently in the environment. Only one of the agents is notified. To solve a task agents use deliberation to select appropriate action sequences. If the agent notices that he is not capable of performing all necessary actions by himself he may use the *Contract Net Protocol* [25] for getting help. To initiate coordination he launches a call for proposals (*cfp*) into the network of agents. Receivers of a *cfp* respond either with a *proposal* or by *refusing* the call. The initiator of the *cfp* may either *reject* or *accept* a proposal. Depending on the current task each agent may be the initiator or a participant of a contract.

For reasons of simplicity we make several assumptions. All agents are benevolent. (Sub)tasks committed to are really solvable by the responsible agent. Tasks are decomposable into a set of sub-tasks with no causal inter-relationships. Only one level of delegation is sufficient for solving the task. At each time point only one task is launched into the network of agents. However, due to the time needed for solving tasks the agents might be confronted with different tasks at a time.

Engineering agents for such a scenario will at least require to i) formalise the requirements for the agents, ii) design a prototype and evaluate it, and iii) implement the agent and test the implementation against the requirements. These development phases can be naturally supported by modelling and simulation based on DYNDEVS. We will illustrate this, by starting to construct an experimental frame that formalises the conditions under which the agents are expected to work.

The next step will be to model a prototype agent for the above scenario. First everything will be modelled within the simulation system. Arriving at a point, where the modelled network of agents works as it is supposed to do we can start to successively replace parts of models by implementations that shall be tested. This is illustrated by providing an implementation for the most critical functional part of the agent model: the deliberative one. Subsequently, time models can be used for the execution of tests.

3.1   Specification of the Experimental Frame

Our first step is to model an experimental set-up according to the informal description above. At the level of experimental frame the network of agents is treated as a black box, which interact via two communication channels with the task environment. This abstraction is directly supported by the modelling formalism by means of a coupled model.

The *Environment* model defines the conditions under which agents are required to work correctly. It is modelled as an atomic model responsible for generating new tasks every 10 time units and evaluating actions of the agents. The group of agents failed if after 10 time units not all actions necessary for solving the tasks were received. Example 1 shows the according model definition. The actual calculation whether the set of received actions suffices takes place within the function *evaluate()*, which is referenced by the model definition.

Example 1. The *Environment* is defined as an atomic DYNDEVS model, where

- $InPorts = \{$"fromAgents"$\}$, with $X_{fromAgents} = Actions$
- $OutPorts = \{$"toAgents"$\}$, with $Y_{toAgents} = Tasks$
- $S = \{2^{Actions} \times Tasks\}$
- $s_0 = (\emptyset, t)$, with $t \in Tasks$
- $\delta_{ext}(s, e, x, xp) =$

  ```
  Object input = x.getPortValue("fromAgents");
  if (input instanceof Action)
      s.executedActions.add(input);
  ```

- $\delta_{int}(s, xp) =$

  ```
  evaluate(s.curTask, s.executedActions);
  s.curTask = new Task();
  ```

- $\lambda(s, xp) =$

  ```
  send("toAgents", s.curTask);
  ```

- $ta(s) =$

  ```
  return 10.0;
  ```

- $XP = \emptyset$, $YP = \emptyset$, $tm(s) = 0$
- $\mathcal{M}(m_0) = \{m_0\}$, $\rho_\alpha(s) = m_0$

For the environment model no variable structures and no peripheral ports are needed. An intuitive, statechart-like representation of the dynamics of the environment is given within Figure 4. The dashed arrows represent internal transitions and the solid lines denote external transitions.

Please note, that model functions of atomic DEVS and DYNDEVS models can be arbitrary functions. Within the simulation system JAMES [23] these functions can be specified by using the Java programming language.

3.2   The Network of Agents

Having formalised the experimental frame for our agent(s), the next step is to model the network of agents. The collaboration diagram of the contract net protocol 3 can be easily mapped to a coupled model. Figure 5 shows the components of the network and the couplings between them. The *Network* model is responsible for the routing of messages between the agents. For our example a very simple network model suffices that delivers messages with randomised delays.

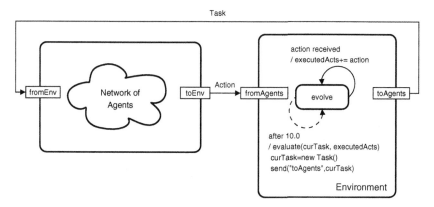

Fig. 4. Experimental Frame for Evaluating a Group of Problem Solving Agents

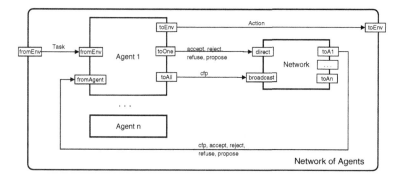

Fig. 5. The network of agents refined according to the contract net protocol

3.3 Modelling an Agent

Now we are ready for modelling a prototypical agent. Example 2 shows part of the definition for a sample agent.

Example 2. Part of the agent's definition:

- $S = \{Phases \times 2^{Actions} \times \{true, false\}\}$, where
  $Phases = \{\text{"idle"}, \text{"deliberate"}, \text{"wait4Proposals"}, \dots\}$
- $\delta_{ext}(s, e, x, xp) =$

```
Object input = x.getPortValue("fromEnv");
if(s.phase.equals("idle") && (input instanceof Task)) {
  s.phase="deliberate";
  s.actions = Planner.plan(s.availableActions, input);
  s.able = true;
}
...
```

- $ta(s) =$

```
if(s.phase.equals("deliberate"))
  return 3.0;
...
```

- $\lambda(s, xp) =$

```
if(s.phase.equals("deliberate")) {
  if(s.able) output("toEnv", s.actions);
  else output("toAll", new CFP());
}
...
```

- $\delta_{int}(s, xp) =$

```
if(s.phase.equals("deliberate")) {
  if(s.able) s.phase="idle";
  else s.phase="wait4proposals";
}
...
```

- $XP = \emptyset,\ YP = \emptyset,\ tm(s) = 0$

By default the agent waits for tasks appearing in his environment (phase *idle*). In phase *deliberate* the agent tries to generate a plan for successfully accomplishing the announced task. The set of actions which he is not able to execute are interpreted as sub-tasks that he may delegate to other agents. Consequently, he launches a call for proposal for these sub-tasks to other agents. In phase *wait4proposals* the initiator of a *cfp* waits for proposals. Agents receiving a *cfp* turn themselves to deliberation for deciding how to achieve sub-tasks and whether the *cfp* can be accepted or must be rejected.

The agents dynamically generate plans for solving a task. We omit the entire definition of the agent model and concentrate on a critical part, namely the deliberation. In the definition of example 2 the task decomposition is done by simply calling a *plan* method that implements a planner prototypically. Due to the fixed *ta*-value, resources consumed for task selection are abstracted to a constant amount of time, i.e. the agent will always finish the deliberation after 3.0 units of simulation time.

Using such prototypical models the coordination mechanism of the agents can be evaluated and whether the set of actions the network of agents comes up with is sufficient for solving the task offered by the environment or not.

Many extension of this simple scenario can be imagined. E.g. if an agent is busy solving one task and receives another call for proposal it might decide to clone itself and to launch the new agent into the network, hoping that free capacities for calculation are somewhere available in the network. Depending on the degree of specialisation of agents this strategy might improve the performance of the multi-agent system.

3.4   From Models to Implementations

When models have matured and parts of the agent become implemented, the focus of analysis moves from models to implementations. Having constructed a logically valid model, which means that the agents really succeed in the experimental frame, the timing behaviour can move into the focus of interest.

Critical parts of the agents are no longer mere models but implemented software and thereby external to the simulation. If the implementation does not possess an own clock, a synchronous interaction of simulation and the external software will prove beneficial, as it gives the simulation system full control over the experiment.

Suppose the development group responsible for implementing the deliberation comes up with a run-time optimised *Planner* implementation. The implementation should now be used instead of the prototype within the transition functions. Example 3 shows how the agent model communicates with the external planner.

Example 3. Using peripheral ports to communicate with an external planner:

- $XP = \{(i, v) | ep \in ExtInPorts \land v \in XP_i\}$, where $ExtInPorts = \{\text{"fromP"}\}$ and $XP_{fromP} = Actions$
- $YP = \{(o, v) | op \in ExtOutPorts \land v \in YP_o\}$, where $ExtOutPorts = \{\text{"toP"}\}$ and $YP_{toP} = Tasks$
- $\delta_{ext}(s, e, x, xp) =$

```
Object input = x.getPortValue("fromEnv");
if(s.phase.equals("idle") && (input instanceof Task)) {
    s.phase="deliberate";
    Object[] params = {s.availableActions, input};
    outputExt("toP", new YPMsg("Planer", "plan", params));
}
...
```

- $ta(s) =$

```
if(s.phase.equals("deliberate"))
    return Double.POSITIVE_INFINITY;
...
```

- $\lambda(s, xp) =$

```
if(s.phase.equals("deliberate")) {
    s.actions = xp.actions;
    s.able = xp.able;
    if(s.able) output("toEnv", s.actions);
        else output("toAll", new CFP());
}
...
```

Java reflection will be used to instantiate the Planner and invoke its *plan()*-method with the task received from the environment and the set of possible

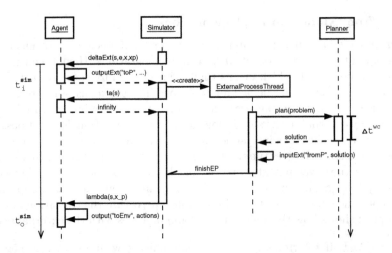

Fig. 6. Synchronous interaction with an externally running Planner instance

actions. Now, not only the correctness of the generated plan is evaluated but the execution performance as well.

The simulation system and software interact in a synchronous manner. The peripheral input ports are filled by the simulator with data from the external software at a time determined by the time model, e.g., $t_o^{sim} = t_i^{sim} + tm(\Delta t^{wc})$ (cf. Figure 6).

Using the time model different types of temporal abstraction can be realised between wall clock time, consumed resources on the one hand and simulation time on the other hand. Most often the consumed wall clock time is used as a resource, as it is easily accessible. However, its usage endangers the repeatability of simulation runs and implicitly introduces uncertainties due to hardware configuration and current work load. To avoid this type of uncertainties other approaches for defining time models exist, that require more efforts and depend on the type of implementation, the language used, or the underlying operating system. For some planning systems the number of expanded nodes might be a suitable measure for the consumed resources, some languages facilitate the overloading of operators [26], and sometimes a performance counter on top of the operation system may be used [27].

4   Discussion and Future Work

DYNDEVS provides a general framework for discrete event simulation and is firmly rooted in systems theory. Models are defined as time-triggered, composite, and reflective automata. The operational semantic is clearly defined by abstract simulators. Extended by peripheral ports that allow to specify how models interact with external processes DYNDEVS supports the re-use and successive refinement of experimental settings from specification to implementation.

Based on the formalism DYNDEVS the simulation system JAMES has been implemented [23]. Due to its variable structure facilities it is cut tailored for the modelling and simulation of open dynamic systems. The flexibility of the simulation system has been and is being put to test in such diverse areas as cell biology [28], testing of mobile agents [29], and testing of software aimed at running on mobile robots [30]. Furthermore, JAMES has been applied to analyse economic and demographic dynamics in pre-modern European towns in the aftermath of mortality crises [31].

To illustrate basic principles in moving from models to implementations we presented an abstract MAS scenario comprising an experimental frame which launches tasks into a network of agents. In spite of the simplicity of the scenario, an effective and timely accomplishment of tasks cannot be foretold by a static analysis. The sample scenario assigns work load, efficiency of single agents, and effort required for accomplishing sub-tasks arbitrarily. Therefore, future work will be directed towards applying the presented framework to a concrete agent application, e.g., for evaluating the efficiency of data querying in P2P networks.

References

1. Castro, J., Kolp, M., Mylopoulos, J.: Towards requirements-driven information systems engineering: the Tropos project. Information Systems **27** (2002) 365–389
2. Odell, J., Parunak, H.V.D., Fleischer, M., Breuckner, S.: Agent UML: A formalism for specifying multiagent software systems. In Giunchiglia, F., Odell, J., Weiss, G., eds.: Agent-Oriented Software Engineering III. Volume 2585 of Lecture Notes in Computer Science. Springer (2003) 16–31
3. van der Hoek, W., Wooldrige, M.: Towards a logic of rational agency. Journal of Autonomous Agents and Multi-Agent Systems **11** (2003) 133–157
4. Ryan, M., Schobbens, P.Y.: Agents and roles: Refinement in alternating-time temporal logic. In Meyer, J., Tambe, M., eds.: Intelligent Agents VIII: Agent Theories, Architectures, and Languages. Volume 2333 of Lecture Notes in Artificial Intelligence. Springer-Verlag (2002) 100–114
5. Wooldridge, M., Jennings, N.R.: Pitfalls of agent-oriented development. In: Proceedings of the 2nd International Conference on Autonomous Agents. (1998) 385–391
6. Dam, K.H., Winikoff, M.: Comparing agent-oriented methodologies. In: Proceedings of the Fifth International Bi-Conference Workshop on Agent-Oriented Information Systems, Melbourne (2003)
7. Hilaire, V., Koukam, A., Gruer, P., Müller, J.P.: Formal specification and prototyping of multi-agent systems. In: ESAW 2000. Volume 1972 of Lecture Notes in Artificial Intelligence. Springer Verlag (2000) 114–127
8. Moro, G., Viroli, M.: On observing and constraining active systems. In: ESAW 2000. Volume 1972 of Lecture Notes in Artificial Intelligence. Springer Verlag (2000) 34–51
9. Wooldridge, M.: The computational complexity of agent design problems. In: Proceedings of the Fourth International Conference of Multi-Agent Systems (ICMAS-2000), Boston (2000) 341–348
10. Lutz, R.: Software engineering for safety: A roadmap. In Finkelstein, A., ed.: ICSE - Future of SE Track, ACM Press (2000) 213–224

11. Schütz, W.: The testability of distributed real-time systems. Kluwer Academic Publishers, Boston / Dordrecht / London (1993)
12. Myers, G.J.: The Art of Software Testing. John Wiley & Sons, Inc. (1979)
13. Wolpert, D.H., Lawson, J.W.: Designing agent collectives for systems with markovian dynamics. In: AAMAS 2002: Autonomous Agents and Multi-Agent Systems. (2002)
14. Montgomery, T.A., Durfee, E.H.: Using MICE to Study Intelligent Dynamic Coordination. In: Second International Conference on Tools for Artificial Intelligence, Washington, DC, Institute of Electrical and Electronics Engineers (1990) 438–444
15. Pollack, M.E.: Planning in Dynamic Environments: The DIPART System. In Tate, A., ed.: Advanced Planning Technology. AAAI (1996)
16. Minsky, M.: Models, minds, machines. In: Proc. IFIP Congress. (1965) 45–49
17. Zeigler, B.P.: Multifacetted Modelling and Discrete Event Simulation. Academic Press, London (1984)
18. Zeigler, B.P.: Theory of Modelling and Simulation. John Wiley, New York (1976)
19. Vangheluwe, H.: DEVS as a common denominator for multi-formalism hybrid system modeling. In: Proceedings of the IEEE International Symposium on Computer Aided Control System Design, Anchorage, Alaska (2000) 129–134
20. Giambiasi, N., Paillet, J.L., Châne, F.: From timed automata to DEVS models. In Chick, S., Sánchez, P., Ferrin, D., Morrice, D., eds.: Proceedings of the 2003 Winter Simulation Conference, New Orleans, USA (2003) 923–931
21. Zeigler, B.P., Praehofer, H., Kim, T.G.: Theory of Modeling and Simulation. 2nd edn. Academic Press, London (2000)
22. Fujimoto, R.M.: Parallel and Distributed Simulation Systems. John Wiley and Sons (2000)
23. Uhrmacher, A.M.: Dynamic Structures in Modeling and Simulation - a Reflective Approach. ACM Transactions on Modeling and Simulation 11 (2001) 206–232
24. Schattenberg, B., Uhrmacher, A.M.: Planning agents in James. Proceedings of the IEEE 89 (2001) 158–173
25. FIPA: FIPA Contract Net Interaction Protocol Specification. http://www.fipa.org/specs/fipa00029 (2002)
26. Anderson, S.D.: Simulation of multiple time-pressured agents. In: Proc. of the Wintersimulation Conference, WSC'97, Atlanta (1997)
27. Browne, S., Dongarra, J., Garner, N., Ho, G.S., Mucci, P.: A portable programming interface for performance evaluation on modern processors. The International Journal of High Performance Computing Applications 14 (2000) 189–204
28. Degenring, D., Röhl, M., Uhrmacher, A.M.: Discrete event, multi-level simulation of metabolite channeling. BioSystems 75 (2004) 29–41
29. Uhrmacher, A.M., Röhl, M., Kullick, B.: The role of reflection in simulating and testing agents: An exploration based on the simulation system james. Applied Artificial Intelligence 16 (2002) 795–811
30. Himmelspach, J., Röhl, M., Uhrmacher, A.: Simulation for Testing Software Agents – An Exploration Based on James. In Chick, S., Sánchez, P., Ferrin, D., Morrice, D., eds.: Proceedings of the 2003 Winter Simulation Conference, New Orleans, USA (2003) 799–807
31. Ewert, U.C., Röhl, M., Uhrmacher, A.M.: What good are deliberative interventions in large scale disasters? Exploring the consequences of crisis managment in pre-modern towns with agent-oriented simulation. In: Agent Based Computational Demography. Physica Verlag (Springer) (2003)

Techniques for Analysis and Calibration of Multi-agent Simulations

Manuel Fehler, Franziska Klügl, and Frank Puppe

Lehrstuhl für Künstliche Intelligenz und Angewandte Informatik,
Institut für Informatik, Universität Würzburg, Am Hubland, 97074 Würzburg
{fehler, kluegl, puppe}@ki.informatik.uni-wuerzburg.de

Abstract In this paper we present analysis and calibration techniques that exploit knowledge about a multi agent society in order to calibrate the system parameters of a corresponding society simulation model. The techniques address typical problems of multi agent simulation calibration like the vast amount of parameters that need to be calibrated, the complex parameter dependencies due to interactions between the simulated agents and the generally enormous computational cost of running a multi agent simulation.

1 Motivation

Multi-Agent Simulation forms a useful tool for understanding and designing societies. As in standard simulation, existing, planned or hypothetic systems are mapped to models. Multi-agent simulation is special as agents and societies in the original are explicitly represented in the model with their autonomy, individual goals, etc. This form of micro simulation provides several advantages not only compared to macro models, but also to other individual- or process based paradigms for simulation, like object-oriented simulation, cellular automatons, queuing or petri networks [1].

However, there are some drawbacks. The most important one is due to the micro-macro link that is often hardly explicitly treatable. Independent of the particular aim of simulating – e.g. for explanation or prediction – the modeler wants to produce a simulated system which's behavior satisfies a global or partial goal or condition, e.g. the global goal of optimal nectar influx or specific coalition structures that are observable from the global view. However, the model is designed bottom up from the agents perspective based on some (hypothetic) individual goals or behavior. Its basic structure mostly forms no problem as the entity of observation is the entity of modeling: the individual agent. But the particular parameter setting used for the concrete simulation, is not found easily. In multi-agent simulation the set of parameters is clearly more extensive than in other, more restricted forms of modeling. Thus, this problem of parameter calibration has to be tackled carefully and thoroughly. Often some parameter can be set based on empirical findings, but the others have to be estimated in a

M.-P. Gleizes, A. Omicini, and F. Zambonelli (Eds.): ESAW 2004, LNAI 3451, pp. 305–321, 2005.

reasonable way. As parameters on the local level of a simulated multi-agent system have to be set in a way that a certain global goal is reached, we may call this problem a society calibration problem to denote its multi-level characteristic.

The rest of the paper is organized as follows: In the next section we will present these concepts in more detail. Instead of proposing a try-and error calibration scheme we show how this problem can be solved as a black box optimization problem in section 3. The main part of the paper tries to use knowledge about the original system and the general requirements onto the model to suggest different approaches for white box optimization. The paper ends with a short discussion and presentation of further work.

2   Society Calibration Problem and Its Solutions

Calibration is an important step in every process concerning the development of simulation models – independent from the actual modeling paradigm used. Model parameters, like birthrate, agent movement speed, or local goal adaptation have to be set in a way that a structurally correct model produces a valid outcome. This problem is particularly hard for multi-agent simulations, due to the multi-level characteristics that have to be met, the dynamic and flexible interaction behavior and often practically unforeseeable feedback loops. Multi-agent models are often highly sensible to parameter changes, especially when agent-class level parameters are changed and a huge number of agents is concerned. Although this problem is present in every multi-agent system design, not only for simulated environments, it is not explicitly tackled in any agent-oriented software design method proposed. Extensive test and simulation phases are responsible not only for identifying problematic parameter settings, but also for identifying structural deficits [2, 3].

The simple try and simulate step is quite unsatisfying as it is quite ineffective. A good alternative seems to be to tackle calibration as an optimization problem – which was already proposed for standard simulation techniques [4]. Parameter settings form the input values, simulation outcome the fitness values to be fed into a optimization algorithm. This is tackled in the following sections.

3   Black Box Optimization Solutions

Standard society calibration techniques treat a society simulation model as a black box, which computes a function that cannot be written down explicitly [5]. In general black box calibration methods try to obtain and use an approximate relationship between input and output variables of the simulation for determining the "optimal" input setting. Some popular black box calibration approaches are gradient based search methods, stochastic approximation methods, sample path optimization, response surface optimization and heuristic search methods [6]. An advantage of the black box approach is that it is not important for the calibration procedure what kind of simulation has to be calibrated.

This advantage is also a big drawback. Since no knowledge about the internal structure and the parameter dependencies of the simulation model is used, the search spaces that have to be searched by the calibration algorithms are often so big that they cannot be searched thoroughly in a limited amount of time. The disadvantage is aggravated by the fact that specially running a multi-agent simulation is very computationally expensive which limits the number of simulation runs that can be made in a limited amount of time. Extra knowledge can only be applied to black box calibration via constraints on the input parameters. An example of black box calibration for MAS is the evolutionary programming integrated into the SADDE methodology for MAS design by Sierra et. al. [7].

4   White Box Calibration

In white box simulation calibration we explicitly use model knowledge to enhance the calibration process. That way structural properties of the simulation model and knowledge about dependencies between the parameters that are to be calibrated can be exploited in order to reduce the configuration search space and the complexity of parameter dependencies and to decrease the computational cost of parameter configuration evaluation.

4.1   Example Used to Illustrate the White Box Calibration Approach

The white box society calibration concepts will be illustrated by applying them to an exemplary multi agent simulation model of a honey bee society in which we simulate the foraging and the brood attending behavior of honey bees. A bee hive is situated in the center of an environment with different food sources. Inside the bee hive we simulate the brood area of the bees in which bee larvae are fostered. The simulated brood area consists of a single comb. The cells of this comb contain bee brood that needs to be fed. The brood is attended by bees specialized on feeding brood. The nectar that is needed to feed the brood is harvested by specialized foraging bees that leave the bee hive to find nectar patches that are scattered in the environment around the bee hive, collect nectar from discovered patches and transport the nectar to the hive. The nectar patches have variable qualities and distances from the hive. Since the flight of foraging bees is an energy consuming process, the bees need to find patches that are close to the bee hive and that offer a maximum nectar quality in order to harvest a maximum amount of nectar in a limited amount of time. The only way to find a nectar patch is to fly around randomly or to use information about a patch discovered by other bees. Bees share information about patches by dancing after returning from a successful foraging flight. These dances encode quality and position of the corresponding patch. By dancing bees can recruit other bees to collect from the same patch. Bees that are already collecting from a certain patch can forget that patch in order to find a better one.

The honey bee MASim described contains a large amount of parameters that need to be calibrated. The most interesting ones include thresholds for feeding the brood, parameters that direct the search for hungry brood and bee agent parameters that guarantee maximum nectar gain, e.g. parameters that define when a bee agent should search for new patches, when a bee agent should forget its current patch in order to find a better one or when a bee agent should dance for the patch it is collecting from in order to recruit another bee, etc.

5   Starting Points for White Box Calibration

In this section we introduce several techniques that can help to decrease the complexity of parameter relationships in a MASim, which may lead to smaller search spaces for the calibration process and can decrease the computational complexity of single simulation runs needed for the calibration process. For each technique we give certain requirements that need to be met by a simulation model to which we want to apply the technique. In general each technique can be applied to any multi-agent simulation that meets these requirements. Thus, the techniques are also suited for adaptive and open MASims. In adaptive MASims we can use the techniques to calibrate the parameters that control the adaption mechanism. In open MASims the calibration of the parameters of the environment is especially important. They define the behavioral constraints for all agents which enter the system.

5.1   General Model Decomposition

In general model decomposition is a method to break the MASim model into smaller submodels that can be treated as individual models by the calibration process. Using smaller models can result in reduced parameter search spaces and decreased computational complexity for each of these models. This can result in faster convergence to the optimal parameter configuration for each of the individual submodels. The hope in doing this is to be able to combine the optimally calibrated submodels to a nearly optimally calibrated full model, by having to calibrate only those model parameters that link the individual submodels. This is also possible if the parameter calibration of one submodel depends on the parameter configuration of another submodel. In that case an ordered calibration of the submodels can lead to the desired calibration of the combined model. However, if the parameter configurations of two submodels have a too strong influences on each other, individual calibration can result in useless configurations for the combined model. There are several reasonable dimensions for decomposition.

5.2   Functional Decomposition

Independent Macro Model Parts as Functional Units: Certain parts of a MASim model may be mostly independent from the rest of the model.

Example: The honey bee MASim can be decomposed into a brood attendance submodel and an foraging submodel, only linked via the collected nectar that is fed to the brood. If we simply assume that the foraging bee agents collect enough nectar for the brood to be fed the models are independent and can be calibrated separately.

Possible Gain: Less environmental computation and less agent updates for each of the submodels.

Individual Agents as Functional Units: Society MASims are inherently modular simulations due to the fact that individual agents are simulated. This offers the possibility to calibrate the individual agents separately.

Requirements: Calibrating the individual agents separately is often not possible since the interaction between the agents leads to strong dependencies between their parameters. However certain parts of the agents' behavior may be independent from the rest of the system parameters we have to calibrate.

Example: For a given environment the patch search process by random flight of an individual bee agent is independent from the rest of the simulated society and world.

Possible Gain: Simulation and parameter calibration of only one agent at a time required.

Groups of Agents as Functional Units: In society MASims groups of agents often work together to solve some problem. If a group and each agent that is part of the group are mostly independent from the rest of the system parameters, the problem solving process of such a group can be calibrated separately from the rest of the system.

Example: The group of foraging bees and the group of brood attending bees are independent from each other and can be calibrated separately.

Speedup: Possible Gain: Less agent updates and reduced dimension of parameter configuration search space. No calibration of internal group behavior.

Environment as a Functional Unit: A MASim consists of two main parts: the environment and the multi agent system. Often the environment describes the problem setting for the simulated MAS. Without a valid environmental model the parameters of the MAS cannot be calibrated correctly. In general the environment may consist of more than agents, e.g. the physics of the simulated world. In such cases and especially with a complex environment, the environment can and have to be calibrated separately before the rest of the MASim.

Example: We extend the brood attendance submodel of the honey bee example in such a way that the brood not only needs to be fed but it needs to be kept warm as well. To simulate the warming of the brood we need a model of heat dispersion in the brood nest. Heat dispersion between cells of the brood comb is independent from any agent interaction. The parameter for heat dispersion between cells can be calibrated without having to simulate any agents.

Possible Gain: Static agent-environment relationships calibrated using help variables representing agent actions.

5.3   Decomposition Based on Goal Oriented Top-Down MAS-Design

In many agent-oriented software engineering methods the design of a MAS happens in a Top-Down fashion, i.e. the global problem that is to be solved by the MAS is decomposed into a subproblem hierarchy [8]. Roles are identified for solving the subproblems and agents are designed to fill into the identified roles. If the multi agent society model can be decomposed in a similar way, this can be exploited for the reduction of parameter configuration search spaces in the society calibration process as well.

Requirements: In order to calibrate subproblems from the subproblem hierarchy of a simulated MAS the subproblems need to be nearly independent from each other.

Another requirement for calibration along a goal hierarchy is that we need to be able to link the calibrated subproblems together in order to find a calibration for the overall model. This may require additional calibration of parameters that influence how separate subproblem solutions are combined in the full simulation.

Example: We decompose the foraging submodel of the honey bee example. The global goal of the foraging bee agents is to collect a maximum amount of nectar during a certain time interval. To achieve this goal the agents need to find patches with optimal nectar gain and share information about discovered patches in order to enable other agents to collect from good patches without having to find them on their own. Figure 1 visualizes an exemplary subproblem hierarchy.

Requirements: To overcome dependencies on resources and problem solving features of other agents we can build simplified models in which simplified resources and features are supplied by the simulation system. This is only possible if the parameters to be calibrated can be clearly separated into parameters in-

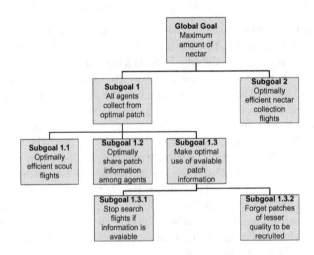

Fig. 1. An exemplary subproblem hierarchy

fluencing actual problem solving and parameters influencing resource and help acquisition.

Example: To switch efficiently between different patches the parameter that defines when a bee agent ought to forget its patch needs to be calibrated. Since a bee can profit from information about already discovered patches only if it is recruited by other agents the parameter influencing when a bee recruits others for its patch needs to be calibrated as well. If we simply supply patch information artificially to a bee agent that needs to decide if it is reasonable to forget its patch we do not need to calibrate the recruitment parameter. We simply need to calibrate the way available patch information is handled by a forgetting bee agent (also see section 5.6).

Possible Gain: Reduction of the parameter space for each submodel and shorter simulation runs due to reduced internal simulation times.

5.4   Decomposition Based on Behavioral Agent Models

Another way of decomposing the parameter configuration search space is to classify parameters into categories based on the possible different agent behaviors. In general there will be two types of parameters: parameters that influence what type of behavior the agent adopts and parameters that influence the outcome of a specific agent behavior. Once the parameters are categorized each category can be associated with a goal, like optimal behavior adoption or optimal action performance for a certain behavior. If these goals can be measured by evaluation functions the parameters of each category can be calibrated separately which reduces the configuration parameter search space.

Requirements: For each parameter it has to be possible to clearly associate it with one category. If a parameter influences the choice of a behavior and outcome of a behavior as well, these two categories cannot be calibrated separately. Finally we need to be able to decide for each category about an evaluation function for that category.

Example: Figure 2 shows a visualization of the behavior of an agent performing some abstract task. First the agent is inactive. Then some threshold triggers the agent's willingness to accomplish a task. He moves out to find a task. There are several different tasks the agent could solve. Every task is associated with a threshold that triggers the agent's willingness to solve the task. During task accomplishment certain environmental influences or the occurrence of another task with higher activation values can make the agent switch tasks or simply stop task accomplishment.

In this example each threshold is defined by an own parameter. The global goal is to accomplish a maximum amount of tasks in a limited amount of time. To calibrate the parameters we check whether tasks are found, how many of the found tasks were selected for accomplishment and how many tasks were accomplished at all. If we find that no tasks were accomplished, we check whether the parameters for the selection mechanism need to be adjusted. If no tasks were found to be selected, we need to calibrate parameters for the search mechanism and so on.

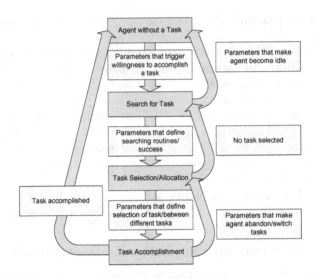

Fig. 2. An exemplary behavioral model

Possible Gain: Simplification of the parameter search space structure.

5.5   Decomposition Based on Temporal Phases

It may be possible to identify mostly independent time phases during a MASim run. These time phases can be on different hierarchical levels, e.g. the goal of the whole simulated MAS can change over time or the problem solving process of single agents can be decomposed into different phases.

Example: An example in which temporal decomposition can be applied would be a MASim with a day/night cycle. If the simulated society shows different and independent behavior during day and night time, the parameters relevant for MASim behavior at each of these phases can be calibrated separately.

Possible Gain: Restriction of the parameter search space dimension to only those parameters which are required during each phase. Furthermore simulating the individual situations may require less internal simulation time for each submodel.

5.6   Abstractions and Metamodels

Abstraction of a MASim model is a convenient way to reduce the computational cost of a MASim and the complexity of the parameter configuration search space that needs to be searched in order to find the optimal calibration for the MASim. Although an abstracted society model may not be able to answer the question we want to tackle with the full multi agent society simulation, the information gained from simulating the abstract model may be used to reduce the parameter configuration search space in a more detailed model.

Abstraction by Aggregation. Abstraction by aggregation reduces model complexity by aggregating micro parts of the model into valid macro model representations. The following MAS properties can be exploited for abstraction by aggregation:

- **Aggregation of functional groups:** Functional groups of agents that have already been calibrated can be abstracted and be replaced by macro agents with the same behavior as the groups.
  Possible Gain: Less agent updates. No calibration of internal group parameters.
- **Abstraction at model scale:** Society MASim models can be represented at different scales without loosing validity. A model is referred to as being of lower scale than another if the society consists of fewer agents and a possibly smaller environment is used, but the same simulation results are achieved. Simulation of MASim models of lower scale is often computationally less expensive since fewer agents need to be updated each turn. MASim components that can be scaled are numbers of agents or resources of the same type or the measures of the MASim environment. In order to scale the model we need to know the scaling relationship between the different system components that we want to scale. We need to know if a bisection of the number of agents requires a bisection of the size of the environment in order to remain a valid model or if the relationship may be exponential.
  Example: If X foraging bee agents can harvest a environment of size Y, fewer bee agents can harvest a smaller environment as efficiently if the proportion of patches stays the same.
  Possible Gain: Reduction of computational complexity for reduced model.
- **Abstraction of deterministic agent actions and inactive agents:** MASims can consist of highly stochastic processes. However certain deterministic aspects may be found, like deterministic agent actions with outcomes that can be computed directly. If there is no further system interaction, the agents or components can be removed from the system and returned at appropriate time with the results of their actions. A special case of such deterministic agents are agents that do essentially nothing. Updating these agents is completely redundant and can be omitted.
  Example: Once a bee agent has learned of the position of a new patch it flies there and returns with the amount of nectar that is defined by the quality of the patch and the energy loss from flying to the patch. We can remove the agent and save the relevant information, i.e. amount of nectar and patch that was harvested, in a hashtable. Each simulation step the system checks the hashtable whether a foraging bee agent returns to the hive. The outcome of the collection flight is then added to the simulation. A simple counter can be used to keep track of inactive agents waiting in the hive.
  Possible Gain: The described technique is a form of implementation optimization to speed up the computation of a single simulation run. Besides the computational gain such model optimization techniques often makes editing editing and changing the model after calibration impossible. For this rea-

son all model implementation techniques, like code optimization, should be handled with great care.

– **Abstracting simulation modules as metamodels and probability distributions:** The modularity inherent in MASims can be exploited to learn functions (e.g. neural networks [9]) that exhibit the same input/output behavior as the original modules or, if an appropriate stochastic distribution can be found, that represents the distribution of certain input variable values supplied by some agents during a simulation, the input variables and possibly the agents can be replaced by a pseudo-random number generator with the desired distribution. In this manner internal processes of agents or other system modules, whose interiors have already been optimized, can be computed directly from a learned function, an appropriate lookup table or a probability distribution. A drawback of learning a function or distribution is that it requires additional simulation runs which can diminish the gain from using the function afterwards.

Example: The only connection between the inside and the outside world of the bee hive is the harvested nectar needed to feed the bee brood agents. Once the nectar harvesting process is calibrated it may be possible to learn a function that represents the foraging submodel. This function have to return the amount of nectar that is returned to the hive at each point in time during a simulation. Another possibility would be to replace the submodel by a pseudo-random number generator with the learned distribution of nectar income.

Abstraction by Reducing Heterogeneity. Abstraction techniques that reduce heterogeneity try to create simulation models that are simpler in terms of parameter complexity relationships by replacing heterogenic MASim modules by simpler homogeneous variants.

Requirements: The simplified models must still be valid representations of the original model. It is much more difficult to justify the validity of a model with reduced heterogeneity than to justify the validity of an aggregated model.

Example: In order to calibrate the foraging submodel of the honey bee MASim we reduce the heterogeneity of the patch environment. The randomly distributed patches with random quality of are replaced by only two patches, one with better and one with lesser quality. The MASim model can then be calibrated in such a way that the bee agents choose optimally between these two patches. However it is not sure if the calibration of the simplified model can help for the calibration of the original model.

Possible Gain: Reduction of the parameter configuration search space structure and therefore faster convergence of an applied black box search method.

Abstraction by Reducing Systems of Mass Agents for Easier Model analysis. In simulations of societies of masses of agents of the same type, e.g. ant or bee societies [10, 11], the global problem of the simulated MAS is solved by solving identical smaller problems very often. The individual agents solve small parts of the global problem. The combination of these small solutions results in a solution for the full problem. In this case the settings for all agents of the same type can be found by analyzing an individual agent and calibrating the parameters influencing the agent in such a way that the solution of the small problem solved by that agent is optimized.

Example: We want to find a relation between parameters influencing when bee agents should dance for a patch and when bee agents should forget a patch in order to find a better one. The global goal of the foraging collecting a maximum amount of nectar is achieved by a massive amount of identical foraging bee agents. Each of these agents solves its individual problem of collecting a maximum amount of nectar. If we analyze a MAS of a single foraging bee agent, we can draw conclusions when the agent should forget a patch. A patch should be forgotten if there is a chance of finding a better patch. The patch offering maximum nectar gain should never be forgotten. Since a foraging agent needs to collect nectar in a limited amount of time the probability of forgetting a patch should be linearly lower with increasing patch quality. This analysis of the decisions of a single bee agent leads to the following relationships:

$$p_{forget}\left(ThisPatch\right) = 1 - \frac{QualityOfThisPatch}{QualityOfOptimalPatch}$$

Now we analyze a system of two bee agents. The question we want to answer is when a bee agent should dance for its patch in order to recruit the other agent. An agent collecting from a patch with maximum quality should definitely recruit the other agent. An agent collecting from patches with less quality should recruit the other if there is a significant chance that the recruited agent did not collect from patch with better quality than that of the patch in question before. The probability of dancing for a patch with better quality should be higher than for a patch with lesser quality. This results in an equation similar the equation above.

By analyzing a reduced system of one and two foraging bee agents we identified constraints for the dancing and forgetting probabilities of patches that would possibly have been overlooked while dealing with larger numbers of agents.

Possible Gain: Reduction of computational complexity of the submodel. Easier analysis of the resulting model. Substitution of model parameters by identified model relationships.

6   Sketch of a White Box Calibration Method

In this section we give an outline of a method that can be used to apply the described techniques. A calibration process always needs some means to evaluate the validity of structural properties or some model parameter configuration. For this reason we start the calibration of each (sub) model by stating the simulation question, i.e. what defines if the society model is valid? From this question we derive the goal function that will be used to evaluate model realism. As the problem setting, e.g. the non agent environment, constraints the calibration of the rest of the society model, we start model parameter tuning by adjusting the problem setting for the model, i.e. static model relationships that define how the input parameters for dynamic variables need to be tuned. After that we try to decompose the model into submodels in a hierarchical way. A promising order for model decomposition is first to try to decompose the model into several temporal phases and situations. Next we try to decompose each of the resulting submodels further into spatial submodels. These steps may be repeated recursively. Next we try to apply task based decomposition and behavior based decomposition. Finally the creation of reduced and simplified submodels is advisable in order to analyze internal model relationships. For each of the submodels a goal function and critical situations need to be identified. By calibrating the submodels only during those critical situations the time needed for a single simulation run can be reduced. The final step of the calibration process is merging the submodels, i.e. propagation of calibration results to higher levels of the decomposition hierarchy. This may require further calibration of parameters linking the submodels, e.g. threshold parameters describing an agent adaption process via switching between different behaviors.

7   Application Example

In this section we give a coherent calibration description of the honey bee multi agent simulation model used for illustrating the techniques presented in this paper. The simulation model consists of two main parts. An inside world, i.e. the bee hive, and an outside world, which is the environment around the hive with flower patches for nectar collection. As described before the main goal of all bee activity is to keep the bee state alive. To achieve this the bees perform two main activities. The first is to try to collect enough nectar to allow the bees to perform all energy consuming actions necessary for hive survival. The second is to compensate any bee life losses by "creating" as many new bees as possible. The bee queen lays new eggs in the brood nest. Then worker bees which are specialized on fostering brood care for the newly born bees. They do this by making sure that the brood is always fed up and comfortably warm. In our micro model we focus on simulating these two main bee hive activities. A more detailed general description of the model is given in section 4.1.

The goal of applying the proposed calibration techniques is to create easier to handle auxiliary models which allow to focus on calibrating those parameter relationships that cannot be dealt with separately. To do so we use the proposed decomposition and abstraction techniques to strip the preliminary models of all details irrelevant for the current model parameter calibration problem.

7.1   Macro Level Model Decomposition

We start model decomposition on an abstract level. The first step is to specify the global simulation question and derive the corresponding goal function from it. The simulation question is: "What valid local behavior of the honey bees guarantees the survival of the bee state?". The corresponding goal function describes that we want to minimize the number of dead brood while being as energy efficient as possible, i.e. maximizing the amount of collected nectar and minimizing the amount of required energy for fostering the brood. The world inside the bee hive and the outside world are linked by the collected nectar and the hatching new foraging bees. Bee brood fostering is responsible for compensating bee life losses and nectar collection guarantees that bee brood can be successfully fostered. As a result all model parameters of model parts inside the bee hive are in some way linked to all parameters of model parts on the outside world.

However if we simply assume that "enough" nectar is foraged and "enough" new brood is successfully fostered the simulation model can be decomposed into an inside and an outside world. The term "enough" either needs to be specified by a domain expert or is modeled by posing optimality constraints on the two sub models. On the one hand we require that a maximum possible amount of nectar is foraged in a limited amount of time and given a certain constant number of bees. On the other hand we require that a maximum number of brood is successfully fostered given a certain constant number of bees and consuming a minimum amount of energy. The application of these constraints is valid as we may assume that evolution created a very energy efficient bee behavior. In the consequence we only have to deal with two smaller independent simulation models in the further course of the calibration process.

7.2   Auxiliary Foraging Model

In this section we describe the calibration process for the bee foraging sub model.

Goal Oriented Model Decomposition. The first step is to state the new simulation question for this sub model and to derive the corresponding goal function from it. The foraging sub model is valid, if the bee agents collect a maximum amount of nectar in a limited amount of time. The second part of the goal function is important because the bee agents can always collect infinite amounts of nectar in infinite time. Although this is not part of their local knowledge the foraging bees work together solving several sub problems, like searching or information sharing, in order to reach the goal of maximum nectar income. Because of this we can apply goal oriented decomposition to simplify calibration using auxiliary models. Figure 1 shows the goal oriented decomposition for the foraging model. To collect a maximum amount of nectar the bee agents need to collect from a patch which is optimal in terms of net energy gain, i.e. patch gain less required flying energy. Additionally, each individual collection flight needs to be optimally efficient. To enable each bee agent to collect from an optimal patch the bee agents need to search for patches, communicate the quality of discovered patches to other bees and finally reason about the received patch information.

Sub Model 1: Patch Searching Behavior. The first sub goal that has to be reached is to find a patch with optimal net energy gain as quickly as possible. Here we need to design valid agent movement and supply model parameters for valid flying speeds and energy consumption. An additional model parameter concerning searching behavior is a "stop searching" probability value. This value defines when a bee agent should return to the hive before it finds a patch. The optimal value for this model parameter is strongly related to the amount of available patch information in the bee hive and has to be calibrated later. What remains is to calibrate when a bee agent should start a search flight. The value of the corresponding model parameter is also closely linked to the rest of the simulation model, e.g. the amount of available information in the hive. For this reason this model parameter has to be calibrated later. However its value does not influence the actual search behavior which can be tested and validated using a model with only a single bee agent.

Sub Model 2: Information Sharing Behavior. When a bee agent returns from a nectar collection flight it can share information about the position and quality of its patch to recruit other bee agents. In order to collect a maximum amount of nectar in a limited amount of time all bee agents should always collect from the patch with best known quality. However, as the bee agents have only limited time for nectar collection the agents have to collect from suboptimal patches too. The quality of the best patch currently "known" to the hive is available to all bee agents when they return to the hive. This is because the bee agents can observe the quality of the nectar available in the hive. As described in section 5.6 a simple model analysis leads to a linear relationship defining information sharing. The shorter the simulation runtime the more important it is to collect from suboptimal patches.

Sub Model 3: Reasoning About Shared Information. Up to now the bee agents can search for patches and share patch information with other bees. The next step is to calibrate bee agent reasoning behavior for available patch information, i.e. when a bee agent should abandon its current collection patch to be recruited for a better patch. In this case a similar strategy as the one described in the last section applies. A bee should abandon its current patch if the nectar quality available in the bee hive suggests that recruitment for a patch with better quality is possible.

Calibrating Interdependent Model Parameters. The last step of calibrating the foraging sub model is to tune interdependent parameters, namely the model parameter that defines when unsuccessful search flights should be stopped and the parameter that defines when an inactive bee agent should begin a new search flight instead of waiting for recruitment by a another foraging bee agent. The value for the parameter defining when to start search flights depends on the available information about patches. If no bee agent shares information then better patches need to be searched, otherwise bee agents should rather use available information than go in their own search flights. As a result we model the "start search" parameter as a probability for commencing a search flight if no information has been shared with the bee agent. The model parameter value defining when to stop an unsuccessful search flight is modeled as a fixed probability. Actually, the parameter value depends on the amount of available information in the bee hive, but this amount is not known to a bee agent while searching. The decomposition and analysis process up to know allowed us to define certain model parameters without actually having to use black box calibration methods. Only these last two parameters will be calibrated using a global search method.

Applying Implementation Optimization. Before we actually use black box optimization we apply implementation optimization to the foraging micro model as described in section 5.6. We do this to increase the number of model parameter configurations that can be evaluated in a limited amount of time. Inactive agents waiting in the bee hive are represented as a simple counter and bee agents on deterministic collection flights are simply treated in a event-based fashion, i.e. by adding the results of their collection flights to the simulation at the correct time.

7.3   Auxiliary Brood Fostering Model

In this section we describe the calibration process of the inside bee hive sub model. Once again the first step is to state the relevant simulation question: "How do the bees guarantee the survival of as much brood as possible, while being as energy efficient as possible?". A corresponding goal function would measure the number of dead brood in a given amount of time and the amount of energy required. As described before the brood needs to be kept warm and fed up. As the tasks of keeping the brood warm and feeding the brood are independent this allows us to decompose the model.

Auxiliary Heating Model. The simulation question for this sub model is: "What local bee agent behavior is responsible for keeping the hive cells at a constant temperature while requiring a minimum amount of heating energy?". The defining factors for the nest temperature are bee agents heating single cells and temperature dispersion between nest cells. Consequently the heating model can be decomposed into two parts. An environmental model describing realistic heat dispersion between nest cells and a behavioral agent model describing heating behavior optimized in respect to constant nest temperature and energy efficiency. It is clear that the environmental model constraints the behavioral one and has to be calibrated first. The calibration of the heat influence parameters between cells is performed using measurement data from a real bee hive.

The next step is to calibrate the behavioral heating model. This model can be further decomposed based on the different agent behaviors that occur. On the one hand we calibrate behavior that leads to a bee agents decision to heat a certain cell, and on the other hand we have to calibrate what "group" behavior, i.e. agent heating temperatures and heating agent distributions across cells of the nest, leads to an optimally energy efficient warming of the brood nest. We begin with an abstracted model. The bee agents are represented by static heat sources distributed across the nest cells heating at a certain temperature. With this model we analyze what numbers of heating agents and what agent distributions are required to keep the brood nest warm while requiring a minimum amount of heating energy. We are not concerned with how such distributions come to be, but with what distributions are good. Creating a certain bee agent distribution is part of the next calibration stage in which we use the results from the distribution model to model and calibrate bee movement behavior and heating thresholds in such a way that we get as close to the optimal distribution as possible. Of course, the individual bees have no actual local knowledge about what heating distributions are good. The "optimal" heating distribution only serves as a guideline for the further model calibration. As can be seen we are no longer concerned with keeping the brood alive now, which is the goal in the full micro model. Instead our goal is to simply keep the brood nest at a desired temperature. This has the advantage that we do not have to design a temperature damage model for the bee brood in order to measure heating success, which would have been an infeasible task as no valid data is available for his.

Auxiliary Feeding Model. The feeding sub model can be modeled and calibrated similarly to the heating model. The feeding bee agents move around the brood nest randomly and check each brood cell they pass. If the brood is hungry the agents feed the brood. The required state of brood hunger for feeding is modeled using a feeding threshold which is being tuned to be able to feed a number of brood agent with as few fostering agents as possible.

7.4   Combining the Auxiliary Models

This is the final step of the calibration process. We have created valid simulation models of bee foraging and bee brood fostering. To combine these models we link them by modeling death of foraging bees, by replacing them by hatching brood and by using the foraged nectar as an energy supply. The two calibrated sub models constraint these population control parameters. We can simply calibrate them now using black box calibration.

8   Discussion and Further Work

In this paper we argued that black box society calibration methods are problematic due to the high complexity of society MASims in terms of complexity of model parameter relationships and computational costs for simulating the MASim model. We favor a white box approach to the calibration of MAS society simulations instead, that exploits the structural modularity that is inherent to MASims. In the previous sections we described decomposition and abstraction methods that can help to reduce the computational complexity of a MASim and to decrease the complexity of parameter relationships in the MASim model, which results in smaller parameter configuration spaces that have to be searched in order to find an optimal parameter configuration. The described techniques need to be applied with great care. For each submodel a problem setting needs to be identified that allows to transfer the calibration results from lower to higher model decomposition levels. Implementation optimization can lead to computationally faster models but will possibly hinder structural changes to the model after this optimization has been applied. Therefore, to use white box optimization techniques for MASims as efficiently as possible a method for the application of these techniques needs to be defined as it was sketched in Section 6. In this paper we systematically described building blocks for a calibration methodology. The next step is to sort them into a calibration methodology and integrate them into the MASim design methodology by Oechslein [12]. The methodology can then be supported by technical means like parallel calibration of independent sub models and automatic transfer of calibration results between related calibration sub models.

Acknowledgement

The work described in this paper was supported by DFG under SFB 554(D3/4) "Emergent Behavior in Superorganisms"

References

1. Klügl, F., Oechslein, C., Puppe, F., Dornhaus, A.: Multi-Agent Modelling in Comparison to Standard Modelling. AIS'2002 Artificial Intelligence, Simulation and Planning in High Autonomy Systems (2002) 105–110
2. Davidsson, P., Johansson, S.J., Persson, J.A., Wernstedt, F.: Agent-based Approaches and Classical Optimization Techniques for Dynamic Distributed Resource Allocation: A preliminary study. In: AAMAS'03 workshop on Representations and Approaches for Time-Critical Decentralized Resource/Role/Task Allocation, Melbourne, Australia (2003)
3. Himmelspach, J., Röhl, M., Uhrmacher, A.M.: Simulation for testing software agents - an exploration based on james. In Chick, S., Sanchez, P.J., Ferrin, D., Morrice, D.J., eds.: Proceedings of the Winter Simulation Conference 2003. (2003)
4. Andradottir: A Review of Simulation Optimization Techniques. In: Proceedings of the Winter Simulation Conference 1998. (1998)
5. Fu, M.C.: Optimization for Simulation: Theory vs. Practice (Feature Article). INFORMS Journal on Computing, Vol.14, No.3 (2002) 192–215
6. Azadivar, F.: Simulation Optimization Methodologies. In: Proceedings of the Winter Simulation Conference 1999. (1999)
7. Sierra, C., Sabater, J., Agust-Cullell, J., Garcia, P.: Evolutionary programming in SADDE. In: AAMAS 2002. (2003) 1270–1271
8. Wooldridge, Jennings, Kinny: The Gaia Methodology for Agent-Oriented Analysis and Design. Autonomous Agents and Multi-Agent Systems, 3 (2000) 285–312
9. Panayiotou, Cassandras, Gong: Model Abstraction for Discrete Event Systems Using Neural Networks and Sensitivity Information. In: Proceedings of the Winter Simulation Conference 2000. (2000)
10. Gordon, D.M.: The organization of work in social insect colonies. Nature (1996) 121–124
11. Pasteels, J.M., Deneubourg, J.L., Goss, S. In: Self-organization mechanisms in ant societies (1) trail recruitment to newly discovered food sources. (1987) 155–176
12. Oechslein, C.: A Process Model with Integrated Specification- and Implementation Language for Multi-Agent Simulation. Note: In German. Shaker Verlag GmbH (2004)

Stable Multi-agent Systems

Andrea Bracciali[1], Paolo Mancarella[1], Kostas Stathis[2,1],
and Francesca Toni[3,1]

[1] Dipartimento di Informatica, Università di Pisa
{braccia, paolo}@di.unipi.it
[2] Department of Computing, City University London
kostas@soi.city.ac.uk
[3] Department of Computing, Imperial College London
ft@doc.ic.ac.uk

Abstract. We present an abstract declarative semantics for multi-agent
systems based on the idea of *stable set*, and argue that it can be suitably employed to describe, and to some extent verify, the dynamics of
complex systems of autonomous and heterogeneous interacting agents.
We view agents as black-boxes, whose semantics is abstractly understood
as an input-output transformation from the agents' observations about
their environment, to the actions they perform. Stable sets (of actions)
characterise multi-agent systems able to reach an equilibrium point. Our
semantics via stable sets takes into account the possibility that agents
may fail. We illustrate how stability can characterise multi-agent systems
by means of examples. We also draw considerations about how stable sets
can be effectively approximated.

1 Introduction

The increasing complexity of software development calls for enhanced methods
supporting the design, development and verification phases in the life-cycle of
applications. Such methods are required to be formal, possibly supported by
automated tools, and at an architectural level. Indeed, coding is no longer the
main activity in building applications, but rather the emphasis is on the definition of the components which constitute an application and their relationships
within an overall architecture. This approach requires models and verification
tools, which are neither applicable, nor needed, when developing code. Moreover, the advent of a network-centric model of computation fosters the development of applications based on interacting components that may be *autonomous*,
i.e. independent computational units with their own goals, possibly belonging
to different domains, and *heterogeneous*, e.g. following different programming
paradigm.

Many of the models and techniques developed within the field of Multi-agent
systems (MAS) appear to be successfully applicable in the aforementioned context. Indeed, MAS feature architectures of autonomous and heterogeneous "intelligent components," which interact with one another in the environment where

M.-P. Gleizes, A. Omicini, and F. Zambonelli (Eds.): ESAW 2004, LNAI 3451, pp. 322–334, 2005.

they are situated. There are competing models for agent programming (such as BDI[1], AgentSpeak(L)[2], 3APL[3], IMPACT[4], KGP[5], to cite but a few), and MAS design methodologies (such as Gaia [6] and Prometheus [7]), as well as paradigms to describe and reason about the way in which they can interact and coordinate their tasks, possibly in cooperative or competitive ways (such as LAILA [8]). Moreover, a lot of research in MAS has been traditionally influenced by other disciplines, like economics, ecology, psychology, which have contributed to better understand the "organisational" aspects of such systems.

Taking into consideration the amount of different agent programming models proposed, we aim at developing a high-level description framework, which, by reasoning at an abstract semantical level, allows us to formally model the evolution of a MAS, by abstracting away from the peculiarities of a specific agent programming model, paradigm, or methodology. In this paper we show how our abstract approach, originally introduced in [9], can be adapted to the study of MAS, as well as distributed applications in general, where agents/components interact in order to fulfill their own goals, but may fail under certain conditions.

We view agents as "black-boxes", whose "semantics" is expressed as an input-output transformation describing the behaviour of agents in their environment. Given the *environment* of the agent, which may contain the "observable behaviour" of the other agents in the MAS, and an *initial plan* (i.e. a set of actions the agent intends to execute in order to accomplish its goals), the semantics of an agent determines (i) its *observable behaviour*, as an output set of actions from the pool of actions that the agent can perform, and (ii) its *mental state*, which is private and thus inaccessible to other agents. This consists of a representation of the knowledge of the agent, which may include its goal, plans, constraints, etc. In addition, the mental state of an agent and its beliefs about the environment in which it is situated may report a failure condition, for instance when the agent is not able to plan for its goal with respect to a dynamically changing and possibly partially accessible environment. The framework we propose is intended to be instantiated for any concrete agent architecture/theory that can be abstracted away in terms of the aforementioned "semantics".

Building on top of the above agent semantics, we define a notion of *stability* on the set of all actions performed by all agents in the system, and we characterise "good" MASs, as those reaching, by means of the "coordinated contribution" of their agents, an equilibrium point, where, intuitively speaking, no agent needs to further operate within the system and accepts the currently reached state. A set of actions (by the different agents) is *stable* if, assuming that an "oracle" could feed each of the agents with all the actions in the set performed by the other agents (and all events happening in the world), then each agent would do exactly what is in the set, namely their observable behaviour would be exactly what the set envisages. This notion of stability is reminiscent of that of Nash equilibrium state in economics game-theory [10], where players accept a sort of "optimal compromise", and has been also inspired by the notion of stable model semantics for non-monotonic logic [11], according to which a model for a non-monotonic knowledge base exists if a "coherent compromise" between positive and negative knowledge can be reached (the detailed comparison with these works is out of the scope of this paper).

For the purpose of verification, in [9] we have shown how this kind of approach can be used to formalise properties, like individual success of agents and overall success, robustness and world-dependence of a MAS. Moreover, we have also shown how, in a specific case of "well-behaved" logic-based agents, stable sets can be constructively approximated (by adapting well known semantic approximation techniques of Computational Logic, viz. the T_P bottom-up operator [12]).

Here, we extend the approach of [9] by considering the possibility that agents may fail at some stage, a possibility which appears relevant from the viewpoint of engineering complex systems. An agent is in a failure state when it is not able to "properly" operate within its environment. The new approach is illustrated by examples in the context of the well-known Blocks World, chosen as a simple and paradigmatic scenario for the interaction of planning agents. Specifically for this context, an agent may fail when its planned course of actions would lead to a violation of some physical law, like the impossibility for two different blocks to be in the same position. This situation, which may be temporary, is represented by the agent semantics as a failure mental state ($\perp$) and an empty set of actions in response of the current environment and plan. It is worth noting that the agent metaphor we use in the rest of the paper, could be recast in terms of more generic *components* and adapted to different verification scenarios.

We first define the agent semantics and the notion of stable set, showing an example of successful cooperation for agents in a MAS, which corresponds to the existence of a stable set, and an example of failure, for which a stable set does not exists. Then we discuss how stable sets can be approximated by temporarily suspending failing agents, until they are able to reconcile their mental states with the current environment, and letting the successful ones operate. If all the agents are in a failure state we say that the MAS is *compromised*. Few simple examples show cases in which this way of operating may or may not lead to the construction of stable sets, according to which the MAS can evolve. To illustrate the generality of the approach in a simple way, we have abstracted away from modeling the details of time evolution and interleaving of actions. Finally, a brief comparison with similar approaches and some concluding remarks are reported.

2   Single Agent Abstract Semantics

The semantics of single agents is defined in an input-output style, by abstracting away from the agents' internals and, in particular, independently of any programming paradigm. We also refer informally to goals, plans and knowledge of agents, as well as failure and success of agents.

The input for an agent semantics consists of *(i1)* a representation of the world in which the agent is situated (referred to as its *environment*), which may encompass events occurred in the world and actions performed by other agents in the system, and *(i2)* an *initial plan*, namely a set of actions, that the agent has decided to execute in order to fulfill its goals. The output consists of *(o1)* the information that the agent is able to derive, (referred to as the *knowledge* or *mental state* of the agent), possibly encompassing both its goals and a representation of the world that it has observed, and *(o2)* the set of *actions* that the agent decides to perform as a consequence of its inputs (typically, this set includes the actions of the original plan).

Moreover, each agent is equipped with a notion of *failure*, represented as $\perp$. This is used to represent any circumstance in which the agent is not able to cope with the environment, e.g. it is not able to devise any plan, or its observations are not coherent with some of its constraints. A failed agent is required not to commit to the execution of any action. For the sake of simplicity, we do not explicitly deal with the representation of time, but we assume that actions are distinguished by their execution time (i.e. the same action executed at different instants will be represented by different items in $A(i)$) and executed in the "proper" order.

We indicate agents with $1, 2, \ldots i, \ldots n$, and with $A(i)$ and $O(i)$ the set of actions and observations of agent i, respectively. Given a set $\Delta \subseteq \cup_i (A(i) \cup O(i))$, $\Delta(j) = \Delta \cap A(j)$ is the set of actions in Δ pertaining to agent j.

Definition 1. *Given an agent i, its* input-output semantics *is indicated as*

$$\mathcal{S}^i(\Delta_{in}, \Delta_0) = < M, \Delta_{out} >,$$

where $\Delta_{in} \subseteq O(i)$ and $\Delta_0 \subseteq A(i)$ are the observations and initial plan of the agent, respectively, Δ_{out} is the set of actions of the agent, and M is the mental state of the agent, such that either 1) $M = \perp$ and $\Delta_{out} = \emptyset$, and the agent is failed, or 2) $M \neq \perp$ and $\Delta_0 \subseteq \Delta_{out} \subseteq A(i)$, and the agent is successful.

The mental state M, that can be logically understood as a *model* for the agent, is typically *private* to the agent itself, while the set of output actions Δ_{out} is the *public* side of the agent, observable by all the other agents in the system. The initial plan Δ_0 of the agent can be thought of as being determined by the agent itself, whereas the observations Δ_{in} might be about other agents. Notice that, given Δ_{in} and Δ_0, $\mathcal{S}^i(\Delta_{in}, \Delta_0)$ might not be unique (namely $\mathcal{S}^i$ may not be a function), since in general agents may exhibit non-deterministic behaviours. However, in all the examples in this paper, the agent semantics will always be uniquely determined. The following example illustrates Definition 1.

Example 1. In the well-known Blocks World, blocks are piled in stacks, with the usual constraints that a block can be moved only if it is on top of a stack, two blocks can not be in the same place, etc. Since our framework abstracts away from the specific paradigms used to build agents, we adopt an informal, self-explaining, language to describe the mental states and actions of the agents, while the world is represented in pictorial form. We also assume that actions are performed in sequence, abstracting away from any formal representation of temporal ordering. Consider the situation in the figure, with blocks $1, 2$ and 3 on stack A, and an agent i with the initial plan of moving block 2 to stack C, represented as $\Delta_0 = \{2toC\}$. This plan is unfeasible since the planned action $2toC$ violates a law of the physical world (that one cannot move a block which is not clear). Let $\mathcal{W}$ be an appropriate representation of this situation. Then:

(a) The agent may be able to extend its plan, e.g. by first moving block 1 to B. Hence, we will have $\mathcal{S}^i(\mathcal{W}, \{2toC\}) = <M, \{1toB, 2toC\}>$, where M is any appropriate mental state. In this case, the agent is successful.

(b) On the other hand, the agent may not be able to suitably revise Δ_0 to render it feasible, and it may end up in what we consider a failure state, whereby the planned action $2toC$ violates some internal constraint of the agent intended to enforce coherence with the physical world. In this case, $\mathcal{S}^i(\mathcal{W}, \{2toC\}) = <\perp, \emptyset>$, and the agent is failed.

3   MAS Declarative Semantics and Stability

We consider a *multi-agent system* (MAS) as a collection of n agents, $n \geq 2$, situated in a world $\mathcal{W}$. The semantics of the MAS is given in terms of the semantics of the agents that constitute it. We indicate with $\mathcal{W}^i$ the set of observations that agent i is able to draw from $\mathcal{W}$, namely $\mathcal{W}^i = \mathcal{W} \cap O(i)$. In the following we will use the shorthand $<X>_{\mathcal{Y}}$ for the tuple $<X^{i_1}, \ldots, X^{i_k}>$, with $\mathcal{Y} = \{i_1, \ldots, i_k\} \subseteq \{1, .., n\}$. Given $<X>_{\mathcal{Y}}$, X^i is the i-th element of the tuple. The semantics of a MAS can then be defined on top of the single-agent semantics, as follows.

Definition 2. *A multi-agent system* $\mathcal{MAS} = <\mathcal{A}, \mathcal{W}>$ *consists of a set of agents* $\mathcal{A} = \{1, \ldots, n\}$, $n \geq 2$, *and a world* $\mathcal{W}$. *Given the tuple* $<\Delta_{in} \cup \mathcal{W}, \Delta_0>_{\mathcal{A}}$ *of observations and initial plans for each agent, the semantics of* $\mathcal{MAS}$ *is*

$$< M, \Delta_{out} >_{\mathcal{A}},$$

where, for all $i \in \mathcal{A}$, $\mathcal{S}^i(\Delta_{in}^i \cup \mathcal{W}^i, \Delta_0^i) = <M^i, \Delta_{out}^i>$. *A multi-agent system is compromised if, for all* $i \in \mathcal{A}$, $M^i = \perp$.

In a compromised MAS, all the agents are failed. However an autonomously changing environment might allow some of the agents to recover from failure. The input observations of the agents, Δ_{in}^i, refer to events in the world as well as actions by other agents. It is legitimate to characterise these observations so that each agent is aware of what all the others are doing within the system. This can be done by recursively defining the input observations of each single agent as depending on the output actions of all the other agents and those performed by the agent itself. The existence of a solution of such recursive definition of the semantics represents a stability condition of the system. Indeed, all the agents have agreed in a coordinated manner on a course of actions. Such stability condition can be defined as follows.

Definition 3. *A multi-agent system* $\mathcal{MAS} = <\mathcal{A}, \mathcal{W}>$ *is* stable *if there exists* $\Delta = \bigcup_{i \in \mathcal{A}} \Delta_{out}^i$, *such that, for each* $i \in \mathcal{A}$,

$$\mathcal{S}^i(\Delta^{-i} \cup \mathcal{W}^i, \Delta_0^i) = <M^i, \Delta_{out}^i>$$

where $\Delta^{-i} = \bigcup_{\substack{j \in \mathcal{A} \\ j \neq i}} \Delta(j)$. *The set* Δ *is called a* stable set *for* $\mathcal{MAS}$.

Notice that Δ^{-i} is the set of all actions performed by all the agents except agent i. By the previous definition, the sets $\Delta_{out}^1, \ldots, \Delta_{out}^n$ are a solution for the set of mutually recursive equations

$$\mathcal{S}^1(\Delta^{-1} \cup \mathcal{W}^1, \Delta_0^1) = <M^1, \Delta_{out}^1>$$
$$\vdots$$
$$\mathcal{S}^n(\Delta^{-n} \cup \mathcal{W}^n, \Delta_0^n) = <M^n, \Delta_{out}^n>$$

where each Δ^{-i} occurring on the left-hand side of the $i - th$ equation is defined in terms of the Δ_{out}^j sets, occurring in all the other equations. Intuitively, a set of actions (by the different agents) is stable if, assuming that an "oracle" could feed each of the agents with all the actions in the set performed by the other agents (and all events happening in the world), then each agent would do exactly what is in the set, namely their observable behaviour would be exactly what the set envisages. Note that stability could consists in an infinite course of actions (e.g. when agents "steadily" keep on repeating their behaviour) and that stability does not imply the success of all the agents, indeed a failed agent might be part of a stable MAS. The following example illustrates a stable MAS.

Example 2. Consider again the Blocks World situation of Example 1, with the difference that now we have two agents operating according to the picture below.

Agent 1 is responsible to move odd-numbered blocks in the stack B, while agent 2 is responsible to put even-numbered blocks in the stack C. Let us suppose that the agents have initially the goals $mvToB$ and $mvToC$, respectively. Trivially, the set:

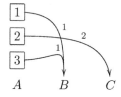

$$\Delta = \{1toB_1, 2toC_2, 3toB_1\}$$

where each action is indexed according to its executor, is a stable set for the system. Indeed, being $\mathcal{W}$ an appropriate representation of the world

$$\mathcal{S}^1(\{2toC_2\} \cup \mathcal{W}^1, \{1toB_1, 3toB_1\}) = <M^1, \{1toB_1, 3toB_1\}>$$
$$\mathcal{S}^2(\{1toB_1, 3toB_1\} \cup \mathcal{W}^2, \{2toC_2\}) = <M^2, \{2toC_2\}>$$

where $M^1 \models mvToB$ and $M^2 \models mvToC$ (i.e. goals are satisfied). The previous equations can be read as "If agent 1 observes that agent 2 is moving block 2 to C, then it will move blocks 1 and 3 to B, while if agent 2 observes that blocks 1 and 3 are moved by agent 1, then it will move block 2 to C". Finally, note that we overlook here, as in the rest of the paper, issues concerning the treatment of time and ordering between actions.

The relevance of the existence of stable sets for a MAS is due to their interpretation as viable courses of actions that satisfy all the agents present in the system, given the current state of the world. The next example illustrates a case where the lack of a stable set corresponds to the impossibility for the agents in the system to coordinately accomplish their tasks, without resulting in a failure. Here, failure is due to the violation of a physical law of the world, which occurs as a consequence of the sum of the actions performed by the agents.

Example 3. Let us consider the different situation of the Blocks World illustrated below, where block 1 is on stack A and block 2 is on stack B. It is easy to agree on the fact that, being $\Delta_0^1 = \{1toB_1\}$, and $\Delta_0^2 = \{2toB_2\}$, there is no stable set for the system. Indeed both agents would like to place their block in the same position, ending up in a failure state. Differently from Example 2, where agent 2 resolves its initial failure state by coordinating its behaviour with that of agent 1, the MAS is here compromised.

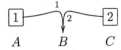

$$
\begin{array}{ccc}
A & B & C
\end{array}
$$

4   Constructing Stable Sets by Means of Successful Agents

In [9] we have shown how stable sets can be constructed for the case of a simple agent programming language based on Abductive Logic Programming. In that context, stable sets can be approximated by exploiting well known bottom-up techniques, traditionally used in Computational Logic. Here, we illustrate how stable set construction can be approached by means of a modification of the same technique, with respect to any agent architecture and language that can be understood abstractly in terms of the defined input-output semantics.

Informally speaking, starting from a current *partial* state of a system, the input for the single agent semantics is extracted, and, if possible, a more defined semantics for the system is returned, taking into consideration the actions executed by the agents according to their semantics and the current inputs. A bit of care is necessary in order to select a (maximal) subset of agents that can successfully operate within the system. This step can be (possibly infinitely) repeated to constructively approximate, if any, a stable set. Suitable assumptions on agent languages may guarantee the convergence of the method, as shown in [9].

The construction of the stable set in Example 2 relies upon agent 2 "waiting" until the state of the world has become consistent with its plans. Recall that failed agents, whose mental state can not deal with the current state of the world, could play a part in future states that the MAS can reach. In a sense, we impose that the set of executed actions at each step represents a stable set for the restricted system of currently successful agents. If the system is compromised, the semantics results in empty sets of actions and all the mental states are $\perp$. The step-wise semantic approximation is defined as follows in terms of the $\mathcal{T}^A$ operator, which maps (tuples of) observations (actions by other agents and events in the world) onto (tuples of) mental states and new observations.

Definition 4 ($\mathcal{T}^{\mathcal{A}}$ operator). *Let $\mathcal{MAS} =< \mathcal{A}, \mathcal{W} >$ be a multi-agent system, and $< \Delta >_{\mathcal{A}}$ be a tuple of sets of actions. The $\mathcal{T}^{\mathcal{A}}$ operator is defined as follows:*

$$
\mathcal{T}^{\mathcal{A}}(< \Delta \cup \mathcal{W} >_{\mathcal{A}}) =
\begin{cases}
< J, \Gamma >_{\mathcal{A}} & \text{if } \mathcal{A}^+ = \mathcal{A} \\
\mathcal{T}^{\mathcal{A}}(< \Delta \cup \mathcal{W} >_{\mathcal{A}^+}) \oplus < \bot, \Delta >_{\mathcal{A}^-} & \text{otherwise}
\end{cases}
$$

where $\mathcal{A} = \mathcal{A}^+ \cup \mathcal{A}^-$ such that

$$\forall k \in \mathcal{A}^+.\ \mathcal{S}^k(\mathcal{W}^k \cup \Delta^{-k}, \Delta^k) = < J^k, \Gamma^k > \neq < \bot, \emptyset >$$

$$\forall k \in \mathcal{A}^-.\ \mathcal{S}^k(\mathcal{W}^k \cup \Delta^{-k}, \Delta^k) = < \bot, \emptyset >$$

and $\oplus$ merges tuples according to the order induced by agent names.

The previous definition can be read as follows. Given the observations $< \Delta >_{\mathcal{A}}$ of the agents and the environment $\mathcal{W}$ (which, for simplicity, we assume to be fixed and unchanging), the MAS is partitioned into:

1. the set $\mathcal{A}^+$ of agents that, taking into consideration the up-to-now plans of the other agents, the world and their own committed actions (at some previous step) $\mathcal{S}^k(\mathcal{W}^k \cup \Delta^{-k}, \Delta^k)$, are *successful* ($J^k \neq \bot$), and
2. the set $\mathcal{A}^-$ of agents that, taking into consideration the up-to-now plans of the other agents, the environment and their own committed actions (at some previous step) $\mathcal{S}^k(\mathcal{W}^k \cup \Delta^{-k}, \Delta^k)$, are *failed* ($J^k = \bot$).

The $\mathcal{T}^{\mathcal{A}}$ operator returns a "more defined" semantics for the overall MAS obtained by recursively seeking ($\mathcal{T}^{\mathcal{A}}(< \Delta \cup \mathcal{W} >_{\mathcal{A}^+})$) whether the restricted set of potentially successful agents $\mathcal{A}^+$ may successfully agree on a set of actions, without taking into consideration the actions of the currently failing agents in $\mathcal{A}^-$. The more defined semantics for the overall MAS is returned as soon as a (sub-)set of "reciprocally" successful agents is found (and in this case their contribution to the system is recombined with the previous one by the idle agents, $\oplus$), or all the agents are failed and the MAS is compromised ($\mathcal{A}^- = \mathcal{A}$).

The world is a parameter of $\mathcal{T}^{\mathcal{A}}$, which is supposed not to change while agents are coordinating themselves, while the mental states are recomputed at each successive application of $\mathcal{T}^{\mathcal{A}}$ for the successful (active) agents. In this way, recomputing at each iteration their mental states, agents are forced to check their consistency against the new situations. The performed actions are recorded in the output of the operator and then used as input at the next application of $\mathcal{T}^{\mathcal{A}}$, and hence, following the idea of stability, notified to all the agents. More precisely,

$$\mathcal{T}^{\mathcal{A}}_{i+1}(< \Delta \cup \mathcal{W} >_{\mathcal{A}}) = \mathcal{T}^{\mathcal{A}}(< \Gamma \cup \mathcal{W} >_{\mathcal{A}}),$$

where $\mathcal{T}^{\mathcal{A}}_i(< \Delta \cup \mathcal{W} >_{\mathcal{A}}) =< J, \Gamma >_{\mathcal{A}}$.

In [9] we have shown that, having chosen a specific agent language based on Abductive Logic Programming, the corresponding $\mathcal{T}^{\mathcal{A}}$ operator enjoys convergence properties to a minimal fix-point, from which a stable set can be extracted.

However, notice that in [9] consistency issues were not taken into account.

Provided that, for a chosen agent language, the $\mathcal{T}^{\mathcal{A}}$ operator of Definition 4 does converge, we can give the following Definition 5, where $\mathcal{T}^{\mathcal{A}}_\infty$ denotes the fix-point of $\mathcal{T}^{\mathcal{A}}$, as a constructive way of approximating, if any, a stable set. This definition is relevant as a basis on which a verification methodology can be developed, according to the idea that the existence of stable sets guarantees the overall good engineering of the system. The study of general conditions for the convergence of $\mathcal{T}^{\mathcal{A}}$ to a stable set is scope for future work. However, we will give an example to show how Definition 5 captures the construction of a stable set for a Blocks World which has a stable set, and another one which shows how Definition 5 correctly fails to produce a stable set in a case where a stable set does not exist.

Definition 5. *Given a multi-agent system* $\mathcal{MAS} =< \{1,\ldots,n\}, \mathcal{W} >$ *and a set of initial plans* $< \Delta_0 >_{\mathcal{A}}$, *the concrete semantics of* $\mathcal{MAS}$ *is defined as*

$$< J, \Delta >_{\mathcal{A}} = \mathcal{T}^{\mathcal{A}}_\infty (< \Delta_0 \cup \mathcal{W} >_{\mathcal{A}}).$$

The next example shows how a stable set can be derived from $< J, \Delta >_{\mathcal{A}}$, the result of the application of $\mathcal{T}^{\mathcal{A}}_\infty$. More precisely, the iteration of the application of $\mathcal{T}^{\mathcal{A}}$ converges to a fix-point after few iterations.

Example 4. The stable set of the MAS in Example 2 can be approximated, and, actually, constructed, by few applications of the $\mathcal{T}^{\mathcal{A}}$ operator. Assuming that the agents have the goals of Example 2, and are not provided with an initial plan, the concrete semantics of the MAS is given by

$$\mathcal{T}^{\mathcal{A}}_\infty (<< \mathcal{W} >, < \mathcal{W} >>).$$

While calculating $\mathcal{T}^{\mathcal{A}}_1(<< \mathcal{W} >, < \mathcal{W} >>)$, the second agent can not find a partial plan, i.e. $\mathcal{S}^2(\mathcal{W}, \emptyset) =< \perp, \emptyset >$, indeed there is nothing it can do at present. Hence $\mathcal{A}^+ = \{1\}$ and $\mathcal{A}^- = \{2\}$:

$$\mathcal{T}^{\mathcal{A}}(<< \mathcal{W} >, < \mathcal{W} >>) = << M_1^1, \{1toB_1\} >, < \perp, \emptyset >> .$$

Analogously, at the next step agent 2 moves block 2 (accomplishing its goal), and agent 1 is suspended ($\mathcal{W}$ is updated with executed actions):

$$\mathcal{T}^{\mathcal{A}}(<< \{1toB_1\} \cup \mathcal{W} >, < \{1toB_1\} \cup \mathcal{W} >>) = << \perp, \emptyset >, < M_1^2, \{2toC_2\} >> .$$

Finally, also agent 1 completes its task $mvToB$ (since $\mathcal{S}^1(\mathcal{W} \cup \{2toC_2\}, \{1toB_1\}) = < M_2^1, \{1toB_1, 3toB_1\} >$):

$$\mathcal{T}^{\mathcal{A}}(<< \{2toC_2, 1toB_1\} \cup \mathcal{W} >, < \{2toC_2, 1toB_1\} \cup \mathcal{W} >>) = \\ << M_2^1, \{1toB_1, 3toB_1\} >, < M_2^2, \{2toC_2\} >> .$$

which is a fix-point of $\mathcal{T}^{\mathcal{A}}$, unless the world changes or agents introduce new plans. The union of the output actions of the agents is the stable set of Example 2.

It is also interesting to verify that a stable set cannot be constructed for the case of Example 3, where two agents are attempting to execute plans that make both the agents not consistent, when executed in the same environment.

Example 5. Let us try to construct a stable set for the Blocks World of Example 3, whose concrete semantics, given the initial plans of the agents, is:

$$\mathcal{T}_\infty^\mathcal{A}(<< \{1toB_1\} \cup \mathcal{W} >, < \{2toB_2\} \cup \mathcal{W} >>).$$

Let us assume that, given the current state of the world, neither agents need to generate further actions in order to accomplish their tasks, and that, without knowing what the other agent is doing, each one can reach a successful mental state encompassing the actions performed in this first step: $\mathcal{S}^1(\mathcal{W}, \{1toB_1\}\}) = < M^1, \{1toB_1\} >$, and $\mathcal{S}^2(\mathcal{W}, \{2toB_2\}) = < M^2, \{2toB_2\} >$. We have that in two steps, the agents, aware of each other's actions, end up in a failure state, and the MAS is compromised:

$$\mathcal{T}^\mathcal{A}(<< \{1toB_1\} \cup \mathcal{W} >, < \{2toB_2\} \cup \mathcal{W} >>) = << M^1, \{1toB_1\} >, < M^2, \{2toB_2\} >> .$$
$$\mathcal{T}^\mathcal{A}(<< \{2toB_2, 1toB_1\} \cup \mathcal{W} >, < \{2toB_2, 1toB_1\} \cup \mathcal{W} >>) = << \bot, \emptyset >, < \bot, \emptyset >> .$$

5   Related Work

The work we present in this paper is close to several approaches, based on Computational Logic, whose aim has been to provide formal models to understand MAS environments, like [13, 14, 15]. While we share with many of these proposals the use of well known logic-based techniques, like bottom-up approximations and the idea itself of stability, the distinguishing aim of our work has been to devise a model for MAS, which, independently of specific agent paradigms, allows us to reason at an abstract and "declarative" level. Moreover, we also aim to define, in agreement with the Computational Logic tradition, an operational counterpart for the declarative settings. This will enable us to support forms of automated verifications.

Modal logic approaches whose aim has been to provide frameworks for proving properties of MAS are also well-documented, for example, see the framework of Lomuscio and Sergot [16] on *deontic interpreted systems*. Earlier work of Wooldridge and Lomuscio [17] define a family of multi-modal logics for reasoning about the information properties of computational agents situated in some environment. We differ from these approaches in the way we understand an environment. Their defininion of an environment is based on a definition often found in distributed systems [18], in that an environment does not contain the other agents. Instead in our approach the environment of an agent contains the state of the world and the other agents, and is closer to [19].

Other formal frameworks exist, for example, Viroli and Omicini in [20] view MAS as the composition of observable systems. These systems are based, like in our framework, on the assumption that the hidden part of an agent manifests itself through interactions with the environment, and on how an agent makes its internal state perceivable in the outside. However, we differentiate ourselves from them by the kind of environment accessibility by agents, i.e. the way agents perceive other agents in terms of their performed actions.

6   Final Remarks

We have illustrated how a semantic characterisation of MAS can be used for checking whether the agents in the system can successfully cooperate, and hence the system can be considered well designed. In particular, in this paper, extending the approach previously introduced in [9], we have addressed the issue of dealing with agents that may temporarily fail, not being "consistent" with the environment in which they operate. We have shown how the notion of stable set, on which the approach is based, can be adapted to deal with this case. Both the semantics and the methodologies adopted are inspired mainly by the field of Computational Logic, but they also appear in other areas, like Economics and Game Theory. We have illustrated the proposed notions by applying them to the simple scenario of Blocks World.

Approaching the modeling of a complex system, like a MAS, at a semantic level allows us to define an abstract framework, which does not depend on the specific, possibly different, agent programming paradigms. However, further (semantical) characterisation of agents would be useful in order to better specify the properties that can be verified by means of the framework, and, also, the computational aspects of such verification. For instance, the choice of a specific agent language in [9] granted some preliminary results about the convergence of the bottom-up approximation of semantics. General conditions for the convergence of $\mathcal{T}^A$, and more general properties of MAS and their stable sets, are scope for future work.

A characterization of time at the agent language level, allowing for a more precise representation of plans as ordered sequence of actions, would add expressiveness to the framework, tightening the relation between agent and system semantics.

The stable set represents an "ideal" course of actions, on which all the agents in the system agree, given the current state of the environment. This notion could be further exploited in order to characterise evolutions of MAS through stability conditions: the system evolves by means of agents aiming to stability, which may be compromised by either a variation in the environment or new plans/actions introduced by some of the agents in the system. Importantly, our declarative approach is provided with a computational counterpart, which seems amenable, under certain assumptions on agent semantics, to support automated verification. This issues, as well as its computational costs (for given classes of agent semantics) is currently under investigation.

Moreover, the relationships between our notion of stability and of that of Nash equilibrium [10], from the field of Economics, are worth being further studied.

Another interesting line of research is the study of the relations between stability and negotiation among agents. Actually, stable sets, when they exist, can be interpreted as a sort of shared agreement between agents. It would be interesting to study how agents can cooperate to the construction of a "preferred" stable set, by coordinating the course of actions they perform. Economics and Game Theory might also be applied.

Finally, we plan to extend our framework in order to incorporate social notions, such as social goals, joint goals amongst agents, social rules, conformance to them, and adoption of multi-agent system's expectations by individual agents. Also, we intend to adopt this extended framework for *KGP* agents, as defined in [5], and study the problem of properties verification in that context.

References

1. Rao, A.S., Georgeff, M.P.: An abstract architecture for rational agents. In: Proceedings of the Third International Conference on Principles of Knowledge Representation and Reasoning (KRR92), Boston, MA (1992)
2. Rao, A.S.: AgentSpeak(L): BDI agents speak out in a logical computable language. In van Hoe, R., ed.: MAAMAW96. Volume 1038 of LNCS., Springer-Verlag (1996) 42–55
3. Hindriks, K.V., de Boer, F.S., van der Hoek, W., Meyer, J.C.: Agent programming in 3APL. Autonomous Agents and Multi-Agent Systems **2(4)** (1999) 357–401
4. Arisha, K.A., Ozcan, F., Ross, R., Subrahmanian, V.S., Eiter, T., Kraus, S.: IMPACT: a Platform for Collaborating Agents. IEEE Intelligent Systems **14** (1999) 64–72
5. Kakas, A., Mancarella, P., Sadri, F., Stathis, K., Toni, F.: The kgp model of agency. In: Proceedings of the 16th European Conference on Artificial Intelligence (ECAI). (2004)
6. Wooldridge, M., Jennings, N.R., Kinny, D.: The gaia methodology for agent-oriented analysis and design. Autonomous Agents and Multi-Agent Systems **3** (2000) 285–312
7. Padgham, L., Winikoff, M.: Prometheus: A methodology for developing intelligent agents. In: Proceedings of the Third International Workshop on AgentOriented Software Engineering at AAMAS 2002, (2002)
8. Ciampolini, A., Lamma, E., Mello, P., Torroni, P.: LAILA: A language for coordinating abductive reasoning among logic agents. Computer Languages **27** (2002) 137–161
9. Bracciali, A., Mancarella, P., Stathis, K., Toni, F.: On modelling declaratively multi-agent systems. In: Proc. of Declarative Agent Languages and Technologies (DALT 2004). LNCS, To appear (2004)
10. Nash, J.: Equilibrium points in n-person games. Proceedings of the National Accademy of Science (1950)
11. Gelfond, M., Lifschitz, V.: The stable model semantics for logic programming. In Kowalski, R., Bowen, K.A., eds.: Proceedings of the 5th International Conference on Logic Programming, MIT Press (1988) 1070–1080
12. Apt, K.R.: Logic programming. In: Handbook of Theoretical Computer Science. Volume B. Elsevier Science Publishers (1990) 493–574
13. Ciampolini, A., Lamma, E., Mello, P., Toni, F., Torroni, P.: Co-operation and competition in *ALIAS*: a logic framework for agents that negotiate. Computational Logic in Multi-Agent Systems. Annals of Mathematics and Artificial Intelligence **37** (2003) 65–91
14. Alferes, J.J., Brogi, A., Leite, J.A., Pereira, L.M.: Computing environment-aware agent behaviours with logic program updates. In Pettorossi, A., ed.: Logic Based Program Synthesis and Transformation, 11th International Workshop, (LOPSTR'01), Selected Papers, Springer-Verlag (2002) 216–232

15. Alferes, J.J., Brogi, A., Leite, J.A., Pereira, L.M.: Evolving logic programs. In Flesca, S., Greco, S., Leone, N., Ianni, G., eds.: Proceedings of the 8th European Conference on Logics in Artificial Intelligence (JELIA'02). Volume 2424 of LNCS, Springer-Verlag (2002) 50–61
16. Lomuscio, A., Sergot, M.: Deontic interpreted systems. In van der Hoek, W., Wooldridge, M., eds.: Studia Logica **75** (Special Issue on The Dynamics of Knowledge). Kluwer Academic Publishers (2003)
17. Wooldridge, M., Lomuscio, A.: A logic of visibility, perception, and knowledge: completeness and correspondence results. Journal of the IGPL **9** (2001)
18. Fagin, R., Halpern, J.Y., Moses, Y., Vardi, M.Y.: Reasoning About Knowledge. MIT Press (1995)
19. Abramsky, S.: Semantics of Interaction. (Technical report) Available at `http://www.dcs.ed.ac.uk/home/samson/coursenotes.ps.gz`.
20. Viroli, M., Omicini, A.: Multi-agent systems as composition of observable systems. In Omicini, A., Viroli, M., eds.: AI*IA/TABOO Joint Workshop - Dagli oggetti agli agenti: tendenze evolutive dei sistemi software" (WOA). (2001)

Welfare Engineering in Practice: On the Variety of Multiagent Resource Allocation Problems

Yann Chevaleyre[1], Ulle Endriss[2], Sylvia Estivie[1],
and Nicolas Maudet[1]

[1] LAMSADE, Université Paris IX-Dauphine,
Paris 75775 Cedex 16 (France)
{chevaley, estivie, maudet}@lamsade.dauphine.fr
[2] Department of Computing, Imperial College London,
180 Queen's Gate, London SW7 2AZ (UK)
ue@doc.ic.ac.uk

Abstract. Many problems studied in the multiagent systems community can be considered instances of an abstract multiagent resource allocation problem. In this problem, which is now better understood theoretically, the goal is to satisfy a criterion of global optimality (formulated in terms of a suitable notion of social welfare), given that the agents sharing a set of resources follow a local rationality criterion reflecting their individual preferences. In this paper, we first show that this simple decentralised resource allocation framework allows us to model a wide variety of applications. These applications thereby benefit from all the theoretical results concerning the framework. We then draw up a list of criteria which can guide the application designer working within the framework and illustrate the relevance of our approach by discussing several applications in view of this list of design criteria.

1 Introduction

In this paper, we further develop the framework of *welfare engineering* [1], which addresses the design of suitable rationality criteria for autonomous software agents participating in negotiations over resources in view of different notions of social welfare, as well as the development of such notions of social welfare themselves. That is, as we shall explain, welfare engineering is complementary to both mechanism design and classical welfare economics.

Several companion papers have studied the theoretical properties of the welfare engineering framework and have, in particular, been concerned with identifying appropriate rationality criteria for a given choice of the notion of social welfare used to assess the quality of negotiation outcomes [2, 3, 1]. The second aspect of welfare engineering, namely the design of suitable notions of social welfare in view of the properties of the application domain, however, has received less attention so far. As we shall illustrate in this paper, the strength of our framework lies in the fact that it is flexible enough to cater for a surprisingly large variety of application domains. All theoretical results concerning this

M.-P. Gleizes, A. Omicini, and F. Zambonelli (Eds.): ESAW 2004, LNAI 3451, pp. 335–347, 2005.

framework thus apply to these applications. The flip-side of the coin is, of course, that in absence of precise guidelines we may soon encounter difficult design issues when trying to translate real applications into our abstract framework. In particular, it leaves the designer with a difficult choice to make when having to decide which social welfare measure is the most appropriate in the context of a given application. The main purpose of this paper is to present a number of criteria (derived from constraints attached to the application domains) that will help the designer in this task, and to illustrate their relevance to several real applications.

The remainder of this paper is organised as follows. Section 2 introduces the general methodology underlying the welfare engineering approach and discusses its relation to classical welfare economics and mechanism design. The basic multiagent resource allocation framework used in this paper is defined in Section 3, which also discusses how to account for additional concepts such as monetary side payments or agent roles. Section 4 introduces the problem of the "designer scope" and Section 5 discusses several concrete applications that can be modelled as multiagent resource allocation problems. A preliminary list of design criteria for applications based on the abstract multiagent resource allocation framework is given in Section 6. These criteria are then discussed in view of the example applications introduced before. Our conclusions are presented in Section 7.

2   Welfare Engineering

As mentioned in the introduction, welfare engineering is closely related to both welfare economics and to mechanism design.

An important issue addressed by *welfare economics* (and specifically by *welfarism*) is the question of how to measure the well-being of society with respect to the welfare of individuals. Technically, an answer to this question can be formalised by defining a *social welfare ordering*, *i.e.* a mapping from a set of individual preference relations or utility functions to a societal preference relation over alternative states of affairs [4]. In the classical literature, the question as to what social welfare ordering is the right one is mostly discussed from a philosophical or ethical point of view [5, 6, 7]. Different answers to this question will typically claim to be rather general in scope (because they are derived from general ethical principles, for instance) and they are, of course, understood to apply to human society. In contrast to this, welfare engineering is concerned with choosing (and possibly designing) tailor-made social welfare orderings that are appropriate for *specific* applications; and the focus is on societies of *artificial* agents. An example is the *elitist* social welfare ordering [1], which favours states in which the most successful agent enjoys a very high utility. This would be considered inappropriate for assessing the welfare of human society, but it may be just the right indicator of success for a distributed computing application in which several software agents are working towards their goals, but the user of the system is only interested in (at least) one of them achieving its goal as quickly as possible. Then, if agents measure their individual welfare in terms of how close they are to achieving their own goal, the elitist social welfare correctly reflects the value of a given state for the user of the system.

Using the terminology of Wolpert and Tumer [8], while understanding the social consequences of agents having certain behaviour profiles constitutes a *forward problem*, the design of such behaviour profiles with the aim of achieving a particular effect at the social level presents us with an *inverse problem*. Mechanism design (referred to as "inverse game theory" by Papadimitriou [9]) is an example for such an inverse problem.

Mechanism design [10, 11] is concerned with the problem of designing suitable rules of interaction between agents such that the outcome of that interaction can be guaranteed to be "optimal", given a suitable criterion for optimality and assuming certain interests on the part of individual agents. A standard example is the design of auction protocols that maximise revenue for the auctioneer and reduce the need for counter-speculation on behalf of the bidders [12]. Often, the notion of optimality can be defined in terms of a social welfare ordering. The interests of individual agents are typically taken to be fixed: agents are assumed to be *rational* in the sense of aiming solely at maximising their personal welfare. In welfare engineering, rather than designing an interaction mechanism for a given notion of social welfare and a given type of agent, we introduce a further variable into the equation by making the *rationality criteria* on the basis of which agents decide on their moves (such as whether or not to accept a proposal) a further object of design. These rationality criteria determine the *behaviour profile* of an agent. For instance, a negotiation system populated by agents that have been designed to accept deals (concerning the exchange of resources) that either benefit themselves or that are inequality-reducing can be shown (under a number of conditions) to converge towards a state that is *Lorenz optimal*, a notion of social optimality combining ideas from both the utilitarian and the egalitarian programme [1, 4].

In summary, a distributed social optimisation problem, such as the problem of finding a socially optimal allocation of resources by means of negotiation, has the following three important parameters:

(*i*) the *social welfare ordering* used to assess the quality of a solution;
(*ii*) the *social interaction mechanism* used by the agents to arrive at a solution;
(*iii*) the *behaviour profiles* of individual agents further restricting their moves within the boundaries given by the interaction mechanism.

Welfare economics provides several off-the-shelf solutions for (*i*), while welfarism is particularly concerned with assessing their respective benefits from a general point of view. Mechanism design is concerned with (*ii*), for a given choice regarding (*i*) and taking (*iii*) as fixed. Welfare engineering addresses all three parameters, but particularly (*i*) and (*iii*): by formulating tailor-made social welfare orderings for specific applications and by designing appropriate agent behaviour profiles (possibly in tandem with a social interaction mechanism).[1]

3   Resource Allocation by Negotiation

Let us consider a society of (at least 2) agents $\mathcal{A}$, and a finite set of discrete (non-divisible) resources $\mathcal{R}$. A resource allocation is a partitioning of the set $\mathcal{R}$ amongst the agents in $\mathcal{A}$. For instance, given an allocation A with $A(i) = \{r_3, r_7\}$, agent i would own resources r_3 and r_7. Given a particular allocation of resources, agents may agree on a (multilateral) *deal* to exchange some of the resources they currently hold. In general, a single deal may involve any number of resources and any number of agents. It transforms an allocation of resources A into a new allocation A'; that is, we can define a deal as a pair $\delta = (A, A')$ of allocations (with $A \neq A'$). To measure their individual welfare, every agent $i \in \mathcal{A}$ is equipped with a *utility function* u_i mapping sets of resources (subsets of $\mathcal{R}$) to rational numbers. We abbreviate $u_i(A) = u_i(A(i))$ for the utility value assigned by agent i to the set of resources it holds for allocation A.

This describes our formal negotiation framework in its most abstract form. As we shall discuss next, this framework allows for many classical concepts to be easily represented.

Monetary Payments. A deal may be coupled with a number of monetary side payments to compensate some of the agents involved for an otherwise disadvantageous deal. Rather than specifying for each pair of agents how much the former is supposed to pay to the latter, we simply say how much money each and every agent either pays out or receives. This can be modelled using a *payment function* p mapping agents in $\mathcal{A}$ to rational numbers. Such a function has to satisfy the side constraint $\sum_{i \in \mathcal{A}} p(i) = 0$, *i.e.* the overall amount of money in the system remains constant. If $p(i) > 0$, then agent i *pays* the amount of $p(i)$, while $p(i) < 0$ means that it *receives* the amount of $-p(i)$. We distinguish *deals with money* and *deals without money*. For the latter, $p(i)$ is required to be 0 for every agent $i \in \mathcal{A}$. Note that for the framework without money, it would be sufficient to model an agent's preferences by means of a (not necessarily strict) total order over alternative bundles of resources.

Limited Money. The model as it is allows the use of arbitrarily high side payments: each agent can give an unlimited amount of money during a deal. This is not realistic, as agents are assumed to be "infinitely rich" [2]. Another, much more realistic, way of handling money is to turn it into a resource. As our model only allows us to use discrete resources, we need to "discretise" money, by choosing the smallest money unit the system will handle (for example a euro), and

---

[1] The idea of working with tailor-made concepts rather than aiming for general solutions is also present in the *automated mechanism design* approach of Conitzer and Sandholm [13].

by creating the corresponding resources. Thus, if we decide to put 1000 euros in the society of agents, we can choose to put 100 resources of 1 euro, and 90 resources of 10 euros each, as if it were bank notes or coins. Thus, in addition to the "normal" resources in $\mathcal{R}$ we create the set of resources

$$R_{mon} = \{r_1{}^1, \ldots, r_{100}^1, r_1{}^{10}, \ldots, r_{90}{}^{10}\}$$

We also have to make sure that these resources have the appropriate value. For each agent i having the resource set R, its individual welfare must be such that:

$$u_i(R) = u_i(R \backslash R_{mon}) \;+\; |R \cap \{r_1{}^1, \ldots, r_{100}^1\}| \;+\; 10 \times |R \cap \{r_1{}^{10}, \ldots, r_{90}{}^{10}\}|$$

Approximating Flows. Using the same idea, it is possible to approximate the representation of continuous resources such as water or energy. For example, if a group of farmers wishes to exploit a river to irrigate their land, the water flow could be divided into 100 resources, each representing one percent of the total.

Roles. In many applications, such as most types of auctions, agents have fixed roles: some agents own resources to begin with and are sellers, while other agents have money and are buyers. This can also be represented in this framework by putting suitable restrictions on the admissibility of deals. For instance, the legality of a deal δ for a buyer i would be modelled as follows:

$$\delta = (A, A') \text{ allowed iff } A(i) \subseteq A'(i)$$

Alternatively, rather than restricting the range of legal deals, we can also model the utility functions of agents in such a way that they will behave as either sellers or buyers. For instance, if one agent values a given resource less than another agent, then the former will have an incentive to sell that resource to the latter.

Protocol Restrictions. We can also express restrictions on the negotiation protocol and the agent communication language used to agree on deals. For instance, if only bilateral negotiation is possible, *i.e.* if any one deal may involve no more than two agents, this can also be modelled by means of suitable restrictions on the admissibility of a deal δ.

4   The Problem of the Designer Scope

As noted by Wurman et al. [14], *"when analyzing any multiagent involving negotiation, we must be very careful to clearly state which elements of the system are under the control of the designer".* These authors distinguish three cases:

- *agent scope* —the designer controls a single agent.
- *mechanism scope* —the designer controls the mechanism, but not the agents that participate in it.
- *system scope* —the designer controls both the mechanism and the agents.

In addition to these cases, we can also envisage mixed situations where the designer may control the mechanism and a subset of the agents of the system. To make things clear, we give some definitions concerning the different roles of the actors in a resource allocation process:

- *proprietor role* —the person who actually owns the application and defines the mechanism. We assume that this role is taken by exactly *one* person.
- *end-user role* —the role taken by people or organisations who will use the application. Each user may own a number of agents.

Note that the roles can be cumulated, that is, the same person can have both the role of the proprietor and that of a user. This could be the case when the proprietor initially owns the resources to be distributed. It is also important to stress that there is, in theory, no requirement for an end-user to own a single agent. In most applications however, it is explicitly forbidden to hold more than one agent. This is a very important problem, considering that it is technically very difficult (or impossible) to design systems that prevent users from adopting this strategy. In *e*-auctions, this problem is known as the *false-name bids* problem [15], and a current trend of research is developing mechanisms that are strategy-proof regarding this issue.

When the proprietor is represented by one or several agents in the system, it can also control and modify their individual utility functions or other aspects of their behaviour profiles.

5   Example Applications

In order to further demonstrate the wide relevance of the abstract resource allocation framework presented in Section 3, we introduce three example applications, which we shall also refer to throughout the next section when we we are going to use these applications to illustrate our design criteria. Amongst these applications, only the last gives the designer a system scope; the others are cases where the designer only has mechanism scope.

E-Auctions. Different kinds of *e*-auctions have been implemented on the Internet, in the context of B2C (business-to-customer), C2C (customer-to-customer), or B2B (business-to-business) applications. Despite a first-sight similarity, C2C *e*-auctions platforms all have different characteristics which make it difficult to offer a single description. We base our discussion on three important C2C *e*-auctions platforms, namely *EmClub*, *EBay*, and *321Enchere*. In these applications, the proprietor does not necessarily hold all the resources initially (the role of the application is just to allow negotiation between users). *E*-auctions platforms have strong constraints on the type of interaction (cf. negotiation protocol). Clearly, there are sellers and buyers in the sense that the former can only sell, and the latter only buy. A famous example of B2B *e*-auctions, possibly involving combinatorial deals, is the spectrum licenses allocation process led by the Federal Communications Commission (FCC) in the United States. This allocation process involves auctioning off thousands of licenses with different geographic coverage and bandwidth. In order to deal with the large number of licences, these auctions were dispatched into several groups. The state (proprietor of the system) initially owns (all) the resources, so it may be represented by an agent in the society. The type of auction used by the FCC is the Simultaneous Multiple Round auction (SMR). This application of course necessitates that we model the roles of seller and buyer, as discussed in the previous section.

Allocation of Satellite Resources. Lemaître et al. [16] describe an earth observation application where users send observation requests to a satellite they have jointly funded. Resources are earth observation images, which are initially held by the virtual proprietor (that is, the coalition of all the users: roles are cumulated). While there is the option to include a proprietor agent in the system (the "satellite agent"), closer inspection of the problem reveals that it may be unnecessary, as we are not concerned with the individual welfare of that agent.

Multiagent Patrolling. To patrol is the act of walking or travelling around an area, at regular intervals, in order to protect or supervise it. This task is by nature a multi-agent task and there are a wide variety of problems that may be formulated as patrolling task. As a concrete example, during the development of an interactive computer game, one may face the problem of coordinating a group of units to patrol a given rough terrain in order to detect the presence of "enemies". The quality of the strategies used for patrolling may be evaluated using different measures. Informally, a good strategy is one that minimises the time lag between two passages to the same place and for all places. In [17], it was shown that in many applications of the patrolling problem, the territory could be represented by a graph. Given such a graph, the patrolling task refers to continuously visiting all the graph nodes so as to minimise the time lag between two visits. The edges may have different associated lengths (weights) corresponding to the real distance between the nodes. Recently [18], the patrolling problem has been formalised as a resource allocation problem. More precisely, each node of the graph to be explored can be represented by a resource, and the utility of each agent represented how well it patrols over the nodes (resources) it owns. In addition, agents can exchange nodes (resources) using a negotiation procedure, in order to maximise their patrolling performance.

6   Criteria for Social Welfare Selection

How do we assess the overall well-being of the society? There exists a large variety of social welfare measures that one can think of. To start with, there are a number of measures that have long been studied in welfare economics. On top of that, one may design new social welfare orderings that may not be appropriate in human societies, but which could be of relevance in artificial ones.

- *Utilitarian* [4, 2] —the utilitarian social welfare of an allocation of resources A is defined as the sum of utilities enjoyed by its members.

- *Nash product* [4] —the Nash product of an allocation of resources A is defined as the product of utilities enjoyed by its members.
- *Egalitarian* [4, 3] —the egalitarian social welfare of an allocation of resources A is defined as the utility enjoyed by the currently weakest agent.
- *Elitist* [1] —the elitist social welfare of an allocation of resources A is defined as the utility enjoyed by the currently happiest agent.
- *Lorenz optimality* [4, 1] —this is a combination of ideas from the utilitarian and the egalitarian approaches.
- *Envy-freeness* [19, 1] —an allocation of resource is envy-free iff there is no agent that would prefer another agent's set of resources over its own.
- *Pareto optimality* [4, 2] —an allocation of resources A is called Pareto optimal iff there is no other allocation that would make at least one of the agents in the society better off without making any of the others worse off.

A key difference between these different social welfare measures lies in the fact that some of them require *interpersonal* comparison of satisfaction levels, while others do not. Utilitarianism and egalitarianism, for instance, only make sense if we have the ability to compare utilities ascribed by different agents to their allocations. Envy-freeness and Pareto optimality, on the other hand, only require that each individual is able to compare its own alternatives.

Our aim is to present a list of criteria that should guide the designer of an application who wants to use the multiagent resource allocation framework, and in particular to support him or her in choosing the appropriate social welfare measure. The list that we are going to put forward is admittedly incomplete, but consists of the criteria we found had the most obvious consequences on the choice of a relevant social welfare measure.

6.1   Type of Proprietor Payment

We start by turning our attention towards an issue of critical importance during the design of a resource allocation system, namely the means by which the proprietor of the application actually gets paid. We envisage different possibilities (not mutually exclusive, as our application examples shall show):

- *Utility-dependent* —this corresponds to cases where users will contribute to the proprietor gain at a level which depends on their own satisfaction, as expressed by their utility functions. Typically that could be done by imposing of a tax on their gains.
- *Transaction-dependent* —the proprietor is payed on the basis of the sequence of transactions. For example, we may have a tax on each transaction (whatever its content), or we may have taxes on the number of resources actually exchanged, and so on. A variant of this case is time-dependence, where only the duration of the negotiation matters, regardless on the actual length (in terms of the number of transactions) of the process.
- *Membership-dependent* —the agents pay a fee when they enter the society in order to negotiate.

Apart from the purely utility-dependent case, it would then be necessary to introduce new global parameters to assess the quality of the negotiation process. In many cases, however, utility functions can be fixed such that they influence the global social welfare. Note that we do not make any assumptions as to how the reward is actually transfered to the proprietor. This can done directly from the users to the proprietor, by means of money transfer for instance. Alternatively, some authority external to the society can interfere and give rewards and penalties. This can be done on the basis of a separate agenda (for instance in the case of public services, you should make sure that everyone has some minimal access to the resources). This authority, however, would in the end base its judgement on one the items listed above.

Example Applications. Each of the C2C *e*-auction applications has specific strategies regarding payment, but they generally use a mixture of transaction-dependent and membership-dependent strategies. *EBay* and *321Enchere* require that sellers pay a fee to enter the auction, and also applies a tax on each deal, which depends on the amount and on the type of object sold. Together with tax, sellers have to pay when they conclude a transaction. In fact, a fourth strategy is also used by these platforms: sellers may have the possibility to pay in order to have options facilitating the deals (advertising, photo, etc.). This is different in the case of the allocation of earth observation images. The fact that users have co-funded the satellite, may be interpreted a partners initially paying some sort of membership fee. Of course, the satellite should also be exploited in the most efficient way, so each user's satisfaction will depend upon its utilities. In the case of the spectrum allocation process led by the FCC, it is clearly a utility-dependent strategy: the (only) seller will collect at the end of the auction process the payments the buyers are committed to pay (which depend on their gains).

Discussion. When the proprietor payment is utility-based, there is a strong incentive to adopt a utilitarian framework. Transaction-dependent payments correspond to very practical cases, for instance situations where we should take into account the cost or the gain induced by a transaction. Membership-dependent payment of the proprietor require a rather different approach. As the gain enjoyed by the proprietor is actually defined at the beginning of an application run, the focus will shift to a different matter, namely making the application attractive for a large number of agents (note that this only makes sense if the application allows for multiple runs, of course). An important ingredient is then to make sure that each agent receives a fair share of the overall gain, *i.e.* in such applications we would typically favour an egalitarian notion of social welfare or we would try to achieve envy-free allocations of resources.

6.2   Application Dynamics During a Run

The next category of criteria that we shall investigate details how the society may evolve over time. It is first important to determine whether (and how) the number of users may vary *during* an application run. We envisage different cases:

- *Fixed* —application users remain unchanged during an application run.
- *Restricted* —the number of users may vary, but only under predefined conditions. These conditions may be of various kinds. First of all, there may be unidirectional restrictions: it is possible that only *new* users are allowed, or symmetrically that users are only allowed to quit the application. On an orthogonal perspective, it is possible that the restriction applies to the whole set of agents (*e.g.* the application must always involve between 10 and 20 simultaneous users), or that agents are permitted to enter the society if they fulfil certain criteria (*e.g.* holding some resources).
- *Unrestricted* —users are allowed to enter and quit the system as they wish.

Similarly, we may also distinguish to what extent the set of resources present in the system may change during an application run.

Example Applications. All C2C *e*-auctions platforms require buyers and sellers to be registered when participating in the auction (they have to create an account). New buyers can enter the auction even if it has already started, bringing along new resources as well. The FCC *e*-auction was open to any eligible company or individual that submitted an application and payment up-front, and that was deemed a qualified bidder by the Commission. To comply with the procedure, each buyer must be uniquely registered, *i.e.* there are no incoming agents.

Discussion. The application dynamics will have a direct impact on the kind of agent society used, and can be related to the well-known classification of agent societies proposed by Davidsson [20]. At first glance, users and resources migration during an application run may look somewhat beyond what our abstract framework can handle. However, although most of the theoretical results on the possibility to negotiate socially optimal allocations reported in previous papers [2, 3, 1] do not directly apply to societies where the number of agents may vary, we do not regard this as a strong limitation. Firstly, we must observe that most of the concepts used still make sense in this extended framework. Under certain restrictions, they may well be used and provide useful results. For instance, if we define utilitarian social welfare in terms of average utility rather than the sum of utilities, this concept can be used in a meaningful manner for societies with varying membership. Secondly, such extensions have been considered to some extent in the welfare economics literature [10] and it seems likely that some results could be transferred to our framework as well.

6.3   Application Dynamics Between Runs

Under the same category, a key concern of the welfare engineer should be to consider whether the application could be run several times, and if so, whether and how the characteristics could be modified between the potential different application runs. It is indeed possible for an application to be run under a fixed policy regarding the number of users, while allowing user or resource migration between different applications runs.

A similar distinction as given above for the application dynamics during a run applies to the application dynamics *between* runs (for both users and resources).

Example Applications. The satellite application can be used several times by the same users. Each negotiation phase starts with a new bundle of images to be allocated. C2C *e*-auctions applications can be run several times, but users may (and actually are likely to) be different. On the other hand, the allocation of spectrum licenses has been run only once.

Discussion. User and resource migration *between* different application runs has quite different consequences. Clearly the proprietor will be motivated to take into account long-term consequences: under the assumption that the proprietor payment is somewhat related to the number of users enjoying the application, it could for instance make sense to design the platform so that the satisfaction of users will motivate them to join the application instead of quitting this one (and possibly joining a concurrent one), hence motivating an egalitarian flavour (even if this may decrease the proprietor's profit for a single run). Also, if the application is expected to be run several times with the same users (as a coalition), it could be important to ensure that envy will not jeopardise the coalition in the long run.

7   Concluding Remarks

In this paper, we have shown that multiagent resource allocation is a powerful paradigm which covers a wide range of applications. Following the ideas of the *welfare engineering* approach, we have also presented a number of criteria an application designer building such an application can use to decide on a suitable social welfare ordering for measuring the quality of a resource allocation.

To conclude, it is interesting to examine whether these applications actually implement the kind of measure hinted at by our discussion of the criteria. *E*-auctions have largely adopted a purely utilitarian approach, even in cases where the possible repetition of application runs with the same users should motivate the introduction of some sort of fair treatment of the users. A few years ago, studying different retailer sites, Guttman and Maes [21] already noticed that *"online auctions are unnecessarily hostile to customers and offer no long-term benefits to merchants"*, even if merchants *"care less about profit on any given interaction and care more about long-term profitability"*. In the specific case of the FCC *e*-auction, which was run only once, we also witness an utilitarian approach, as expected. C2C sites are based on different kinds of payments, and in particular on membership fees. To secure a minimum level of satisfaction of users, they have developed different strategies. One of them is the "reserve price" option: sellers can use it to stimulate bidding on their item, even if they would not sell if the price happens to be lower than their reserve price.

The satellite application requires both a fair treatment of the co-funders, and an efficient use of the satellite. This leads to the adoption of procedures involving notions of social welfare borrowing from both utilitarian and egalitarian principles. In fact, Lemaître et al. [16] propose and experiment with four different procedures to cope with this efficiency/equity tradeoff.

As far as the multiagent patrol application is concerned, the appropriate choice of a social welfare ordering really depends on the target application (video games, Internet applications, etc.). On the one hand, the utilitarian social welfare measures how well the patrolling job is done *on average* and will favour strategies in which the average time lag between two visits is to be minimised. On the other hand, the egalitarian social welfare estimates how bad the worst of the agents does, and will favour patrolling strategies in which all parts of the territory are to be visited equally often.

References

1. Endriss, U., Maudet, N.: Welfare engineering in multiagent systems. In: Engineering Societies in the Agents World IV. LNAI, Springer-Verlag (2004)
2. Endriss, U., Maudet, N., Sadri, F., Toni, F.: On optimal outcomes of negotiations over resources. In: Proceedings of the 2nd International Joint Conference on Autonomous Agents and Multiagent Systems (AAMAS-2003), ACM Press (2003)
3. Endriss, U., Maudet, N., Sadri, F., Toni, F.: Resource allocation in egalitarian agent societies. In: Secondes Journées Francophones sur les Modèles Formels d'Interaction (MFI-2003), Cépaduès-Éditions (2003)
4. Moulin, H.: Axioms of Cooperative Decision Making. Cambridge University Press (1988)
5. Sen, A.K.: Collective Choice and Social Welfare. Holden Day (1970)
6. Rawls, J.: A Theory of Justice. Oxford University Press (1971)
7. Harsanyi, J.C.: Can the maximin principle serve as a basis for morality? American Political Science Review **69** (1975) 594–609
8. Wolpert, D.H., Tumer, K.: An introduction to collective intelligence. Technical Report NASA-ARC-IC-99-63, NASA Ames Research Center (1999)
9. Papadimitriou, C.H.: Algorithms, games, and the Internet. In: Proceedings on 33rd Annual ACM Symposium on Theory of Computing (STOC-2001), ACM (2001)
10. Arrow, K.J., Sen, A.K., Suzumura, K., eds.: Handbook of Social Choice and Welfare. Volume 1. North-Holland (2002)
11. Osborne, M.J., Rubinstein, A.: A Course in Game Theory. MIT Press (1994)
12. Vickrey, W.: Counterspeculation, auctions and competitive sealed tenders. Journal of Finance **16** (1961) 8–37
13. Conitzer, V., Sandholm, T.: Complexity of mechanism design. In: Proceedings of the 18th Annual Conference on Uncertainty in Artificial Intelligence (UAI-2002), Morgan Kaufmann (2002)
14. Wurman, P.R., Wellman, M.P., Walsh, W.E.: Specifying rules for electronic auctions. AI Magazine **23** (2002) 15–23
15. Yokoo, M., Sakurai, Y., Matsubara, S.: The effect of false-name bids in combinatorial auctions: New fraud in Internet auctions. Games and Economic Behaviour **46** (2004) 174–188
16. Lemaître, M., Verfaillie, G., Fargier, H., Lang, J., Bataille, N., Lachiver, J.M.: Equitable allocation of earth observing satellites resources. In: Proceedings of the 5th ONERA-DLR Aerospace Symposium (ODAS'03). (2003)

17. Machado, A., Ramalho, G., Zucker, J.D., Drogoul, A.: Multi-agent patrolling: An empirical analysis of alternative architectures. In: Proceedings of the 3rd International Workshop on Multi-agent Based Simulation (MABS-2002). LNCS, Springer-Verlag (2002)
18. Almeida, A., Ramalho, G., Santana, H., Tedesco, P., Menezes, T., Corruble, V.: Recent advances on multi-agent patrolling. In: Proceedings of the Brazilian Symposium on Artificial Intelligence. (2004)
19. Brams, S.J., Taylor, A.D.: Fair Division: From Cake-cutting to Dispute Resolution. Cambridge University Press (1996)
20. Davidsson, P.: Categories of artificial societies. In: Engineering Societies in the Agents World II. LNAI, Springer-Verlag (2003)
21. Guttman, R.H., Maes, P.: Agent-mediated integrative negotiation for retail electronic commerce. In: Agent Mediated Electronic Commerce. LNCS, Springer-Verlag (1999)

Author Index

Acalovschi, Monica 45
Alonso, Fernando 245

Bade, Dirk 261
Bergeron, Mathieu 152
Boella, Guido 1
Boissier, Olivier 166
Bracciali, Andrea 322
Braubach, Lars 261
Brzeziński, Jacek 191

Calmet, Jacques 33
Capera, Davy 231
Carabelea, Cosmin 166
Castelfranchi, Cristiano 166
Chaib-draa, Brahim 139, 152
Chevaleyre, Yann 335
Cholvy, Laurence 178

Dikenelli, Oguz 74
Dunin-Kęplicz, Barbara 191
Dunin-Kęplicz, Piotr 191

Endriss, Ulle 335
Erdur, Riza Cenk 74
Estivie, Sylvia 335

Fehler, Manuel 305
Flores, Roberto A. 139
Frutos, Sonia 245
Fuentes, Rubén 106

Gómez-Sanz, Jorge J. 106
Garion, Christophe 178
Gleizes, Marie-Pierre 231
Glize, Pierre 231
Gürcan, Önder 74

Hameurlain, Nabil 60
Hammond, Mark 33
Honiden, Shinichi 90

Klügl, Franziska 305
Krempels, Karl-Heinz 261

Lamersdorf, Winfried 261
Letia, Ioan Alfred 45
Lopes Cardoso, Henrique 14
Luck, Michael 119

Mancarella, Paolo 322
Maret, Pierre 33
Martínez, Loïc 245
Maudet, Nicolas 335
Montes, César 245
Munroe, Steve 119

Oliveira, Eugénio 14

Pavón, Juan 106
Pěchouček, Michal 277
Pasquier, Philippe 139, 152
Picard, Gauthier 209, 231
Platon, Eric 90
Pokahr, Alexander 261
Puppe, Frank 305

Rehák, Martin 277
Röhl, Mathias 292

Sabouret, Nicolas 90
Seylan, Inanç 74
Sibertin-Blanc, Christophe 60
Šišlák, David 277
Stathis, Kostas 322

Toni, Francesca 322
Tožička, Jan 277

Uhrmacher, Adelinde M. 292

van der Torre, Leendert 1
Vincent, Chevrier 222

Lecture Notes in Artificial Intelligence (LNAI)

Vol. 3587: P. Perner, A. Imiya (Eds.), Machine Learning and Data Mining in Pattern Recognition. XVII, 695 pages. 2005.

Vol. 3575: S. Wermter, G. Palm, M. Elshaw (Eds.), Biomimetic Neural Learning for Intelligent Robots. IX, 383 pages. 2005.

Vol. 3571: L. Godo (Ed.), Symbolic and Quantitative Approaches to Reasoning with Uncertainty. XVI, 1028 pages. 2005.

Vol. 3559: P. Auer, R. Meir (Eds.), Learning Theory. XI, 692 pages. 2005.

Vol. 3554: A. Dey, B. Kokinov, D. Leake, R. Turner (Eds.), Modeling and Using Context. XIV, 572 pages. 2005.

Vol. 3533: M. Ali, F. Esposito (Eds.), Innovations in Applied Artificial Intelligence. XX, 858 pages. 2005.

Vol. 3528: P.S. Szczepaniak, J. Kacprzyk, A. Niewiadomski (Eds.), Advances in Web Intelligence. XVII, 513 pages. 2005.

Vol. 3518: T.B. Ho, D. Cheung, H. Liu (Eds.), Advances in Knowledge Discovery and Data Mining. XXI, 864 pages. 2005.

Vol. 3508: P. Bresciani, P. Giorgini, B. Henderson-Sellers, G. Low, M. Winikoff (Eds.), Agent-Oriented Information Systems II. X, 227 pages. 2005.

Vol. 3505: V. Gorodetsky, J. Liu, V. A. Skormin (Eds.), Autonomous Intelligent Systems: Agents and Data Mining. XIII, 303 pages. 2005.

Vol. 3501: B. Kégl, G. Lapalme (Eds.), Advances in Artificial Intelligence. XV, 458 pages. 2005.

Vol. 3492: P. Blache, E. Stabler, J. Busquets, R. Moot (Eds.), Logical Aspects of Computational Linguistics. X, 363 pages. 2005.

Vol. 3488: M.-S. Hacid, N.V. Murray, Z.W. Raś, S. Tsumoto (Eds.), Foundations of Intelligent Systems. XIII, 700 pages. 2005.

Vol. 3476: J. Leite, A. Omicini, P. Torroni, P. Yolum (Eds.), Declarative Agent Languages and Technologies II. XII, 289 pages. 2005.

Vol. 3464: S.A. Brueckner, G.D.M. Serugendo, A. Karageorgos, R. Nagpal (Eds.), Engineering Self-Organising Systems. XIII, 299 pages. 2005.

Vol. 3452: F. Baader, A. Voronkov (Eds.), Logic for Programming, Artificial Intelligence, and Reasoning. XI, 562 pages. 2005.

Vol. 3451: M.-P. Gleizes, A. Omicini, F. Zambonelli (Eds.), Engineering Societies in the Agents World V. XIII, 349 pages. 2005.

Vol. 3446: T. Ishida, L. Gasser, H. Nakashima (Eds.), Massively Multi-Agent Systems I. XI, 349 pages. 2005.

Vol. 3445: G. Chollet, A. Esposito, M. Faundez-Zanuy, M. Marinaro (Eds.), Nonlinear Speech Modeling and Applications. XIII, 433 pages. 2005.

Vol. 3438: H. Christiansen, P.R. Skadhauge, J. Villadsen (Eds.), Constraint Solving and Language Processing. VIII, 205 pages. 2005.

Vol. 3430: S. Tsumoto, T. Yamaguchi, M. Numao, H. Motoda (Eds.), Active Mining. XII, 349 pages. 2005.

Vol. 3419: B. Faltings, A. Petcu, F. Fages, F. Rossi (Eds.), Constraint Satisfaction and Constraint Logic Programming. X, 217 pages. 2005.

Vol. 3416: M. Böhlen, J. Gamper, W. Polasek, M.A. Wimmer (Eds.), E-Government: Towards Electronic Democracy. XIII, 311 pages. 2005.

Vol. 3415: P. Davidsson, B. Logan, K. Takadama (Eds.), Multi-Agent and Multi-Agent-Based Simulation. X, 265 pages. 2005.

Vol. 3403: B. Ganter, R. Godin (Eds.), Formal Concept Analysis. XI, 419 pages. 2005.

Vol. 3398: D.-K. Baik (Ed.), Systems Modeling and Simulation: Theory and Applications. XIV, 733 pages. 2005.

Vol. 3397: T.G. Kim (Ed.), Artificial Intelligence and Simulation. XV, 711 pages. 2005.

Vol. 3396: R.M. van Eijk, M.-P. Huget, F. Dignum (Eds.), Agent Communication. X, 261 pages. 2005.

Vol. 3394: D. Kudenko, D. Kazakov, E. Alonso (Eds.), Adaptive Agents and Multi-Agent Systems II. VIII, 313 pages. 2005.

Vol. 3392: D. Seipel, M. Hanus, U. Geske, O. Bartenstein (Eds.), Applications of Declarative Programming and Knowledge Management. X, 309 pages. 2005.

Vol. 3374: D. Weyns, H.V.D. Parunak, F. Michel (Eds.), Environments for Multi-Agent Systems. X, 279 pages. 2005.

Vol. 3371: M.W. Barley, N. Kasabov (Eds.), Intelligent Agents and Multi-Agent Systems. X, 329 pages. 2005.

Vol. 3369: V.R. Benjamins, P. Casanovas, J. Breuker, A. Gangemi (Eds.), Law and the Semantic Web. XII, 249 pages. 2005.

Vol. 3366: I. Rahwan, P. Moraitis, C. Reed (Eds.), Argumentation in Multi-Agent Systems. XII, 263 pages. 2005.

Vol. 3359: G. Grieser, Y. Tanaka (Eds.), Intuitive Human Interfaces for Organizing and Accessing Intellectual Assets. XIV, 257 pages. 2005.

Vol. 3346: R.H. Bordini, M. Dastani, J. Dix, A.E.F. Seghrouchni (Eds.), Programming Multi-Agent Systems. XIV, 249 pages. 2005.

Vol. 3345: Y. Cai (Ed.), Ambient Intelligence for Scientific Discovery. XII, 311 pages. 2005.

Vol. 3343: C. Freksa, M. Knauff, B. Krieg-Brückner, B. Nebel, T. Barkowsky (Eds.), Spatial Cognition IV. XIII, 519 pages. 2005.

Vol. 3339: G.I. Webb, X. Yu (Eds.), AI 2004: Advances in Artificial Intelligence. XXII, 1272 pages. 2004.

Vol. 3336: D. Karagiannis, U. Reimer (Eds.), Practical Aspects of Knowledge Management. X, 523 pages. 2004.

Vol. 3327: Y. Shi, W. Xu, Z. Chen (Eds.), Data Mining and Knowledge Management. XIII, 263 pages. 2005.

Vol. 3315: C. Lemaître, C.A. Reyes, J.A. González (Eds.), Advances in Artificial Intelligence – IBERAMIA 2004. XX, 987 pages. 2004.

Vol. 3303: J.A. López, E. Benfenati, W. Dubitzky (Eds.), Knowledge Exploration in Life Science Informatics. X, 249 pages. 2004.

Vol. 3301: G. Kern-Isberner, W. Rödder, F. Kulmann (Eds.), Conditionals, Information, and Inference. XII, 219 pages. 2005.

Vol. 3276: D. Nardi, M. Riedmiller, C. Sammut, J. Santos-Victor (Eds.), RoboCup 2004: Robot Soccer World Cup VIII. XVIII, 678 pages. 2005.

Vol. 3275: P. Perner (Ed.), Advances in Data Mining. VIII, 173 pages. 2004.

Vol. 3265: R.E. Frederking, K.B. Taylor (Eds.), Machine Translation: From Real Users to Research. XI, 392 pages. 2004.

Vol. 3264: G. Paliouras, Y. Sakakibara (Eds.), Grammatical Inference: Algorithms and Applications. XI, 291 pages. 2004.

Vol. 3259: J. Dix, J. Leite (Eds.), Computational Logic in Multi-Agent Systems. XII, 251 pages. 2004.

Vol. 3257: E. Motta, N.R. Shadbolt, A. Stutt, N. Gibbins (Eds.), Engineering Knowledge in the Age of the Semantic Web. XVII, 517 pages. 2004.

Vol. 3249: B. Buchberger, J.A. Campbell (Eds.), Artificial Intelligence and Symbolic Computation. X, 285 pages. 2004.

Vol. 3248: K.-Y. Su, J. Tsujii, J.-H. Lee, O.Y. Kwong (Eds.), Natural Language Processing – IJCNLP 2004. XVIII, 817 pages. 2005.

Vol. 3245: E. Suzuki, S. Arikawa (Eds.), Discovery Science. XIV, 430 pages. 2004.

Vol. 3244: S. Ben-David, J. Case, A. Maruoka (Eds.), Algorithmic Learning Theory. XIV, 505 pages. 2004.

Vol. 3238: S. Biundo, T. Frühwirth, G. Palm (Eds.), KI 2004: Advances in Artificial Intelligence. XI, 467 pages. 2004.

Vol. 3230: J.L. Vicedo, P. Martínez-Barco, R. Muñoz, M. Saiz Noeda (Eds.), Advances in Natural Language Processing. XII, 488 pages. 2004.

Vol. 3229: J.J. Alferes, J. Leite (Eds.), Logics in Artificial Intelligence. XIV, 744 pages. 2004.

Vol. 3228: M.G. Hinchey, J.L. Rash, W.F. Truszkowski, C.A. Rouff (Eds.), Formal Approaches to Agent-Based Systems. VIII, 290 pages. 2004.

Vol. 3215: M.G.. Negoita, R.J. Howlett, L.C. Jain (Eds.), Knowledge-Based Intelligent Information and Engineering Systems, Part III. LVII, 906 pages. 2004.

Vol. 3214: M.G.. Negoita, R.J. Howlett, L.C. Jain (Eds.), Knowledge-Based Intelligent Information and Engineering Systems, Part II. LVIII, 1302 pages. 2004.

Vol. 3213: M.G.. Negoita, R.J. Howlett, L.C. Jain (Eds.), Knowledge-Based Intelligent Information and Engineering Systems, Part I. LVIII, 1280 pages. 2004.

Vol. 3209: B. Berendt, A. Hotho, D. Mladenic, M. van Someren, M. Spiliopoulou, G. Stumme (Eds.), Web Mining: From Web to Semantic Web. IX, 201 pages. 2004.

Vol. 3206: P. Sojka, I. Kopecek, K. Pala (Eds.), Text, Speech and Dialogue. XIII, 667 pages. 2004.

Vol. 3202: J.-F. Boulicaut, F. Esposito, F. Giannotti, D. Pedreschi (Eds.), Knowledge Discovery in Databases: PKDD 2004. XIX, 560 pages. 2004.

Vol. 3201: J.-F. Boulicaut, F. Esposito, F. Giannotti, D. Pedreschi (Eds.), Machine Learning: ECML 2004. XVIII, 580 pages. 2004.

Vol. 3194: R. Camacho, R. King, A. Srinivasan (Eds.), Inductive Logic Programming. XI, 361 pages. 2004.

Vol. 3192: C. Bussler, D. Fensel (Eds.), Artificial Intelligence: Methodology, Systems, and Applications. XIII, 522 pages. 2004.

Vol. 3191: M. Klusch, S. Ossowski, V. Kashyap, R. Unland (Eds.), Cooperative Information Agents VIII. XI, 303 pages. 2004.

Vol. 3187: G. Lindemann, J. Denzinger, I.J. Timm, R. Unland (Eds.), Multiagent System Technologies. XIII, 341 pages. 2004.

Vol. 3176: O. Bousquet, U. von Luxburg, G. Rätsch (Eds.), Advanced Lectures on Machine Learning. IX, 241 pages. 2004.

Vol. 3171: A.L.C. Bazzan, S. Labidi (Eds.), Advances in Artificial Intelligence – SBIA 2004. XVII, 548 pages. 2004.

Vol. 3159: U. Visser, Intelligent Information Integration for the Semantic Web. XIV, 150 pages. 2004.

Vol. 3157: C. Zhang, H. W. Guesgen, W.K. Yeap (Eds.), PRICAI 2004: Trends in Artificial Intelligence. XX, 1023 pages. 2004.

Vol. 3155: P. Funk, P.A. González Calero (Eds.), Advances in Case-Based Reasoning. XIII, 822 pages. 2004.

Vol. 3139: F. Iida, R. Pfeifer, L. Steels, Y. Kuniyoshi (Eds.), Embodied Artificial Intelligence. IX, 331 pages. 2004.

Vol. 3131: V. Torra, Y. Narukawa (Eds.), Modeling Decisions for Artificial Intelligence. XI, 327 pages. 2004.

Vol. 3127: K.E. Wolff, H.D. Pfeiffer, H.S. Delugach (Eds.), Conceptual Structures at Work. XI, 403 pages. 2004.

Vol. 3123: A. Belz, R. Evans, P. Piwek (Eds.), Natural Language Generation. X, 219 pages. 2004.

Vol. 3120: J. Shawe-Taylor, Y. Singer (Eds.), Learning Theory. X, 648 pages. 2004.

Vol. 3097: D. Basin, M. Rusinowitch (Eds.), Automated Reasoning. XII, 493 pages. 2004.

Vol. 3071: A. Omicini, P. Petta, J. Pitt (Eds.), Engineering Societies in the Agents World. XIII, 409 pages. 2004.

Vol. 3070: L. Rutkowski, J. Siekmann, R. Tadeusiewicz, L.A. Zadeh (Eds.), Artificial Intelligence and Soft Computing - ICAISC 2004. XXV, 1208 pages. 2004.